P9-CMS-814

DISCARD

ALLEGHENY COLLEGE LIBRARY

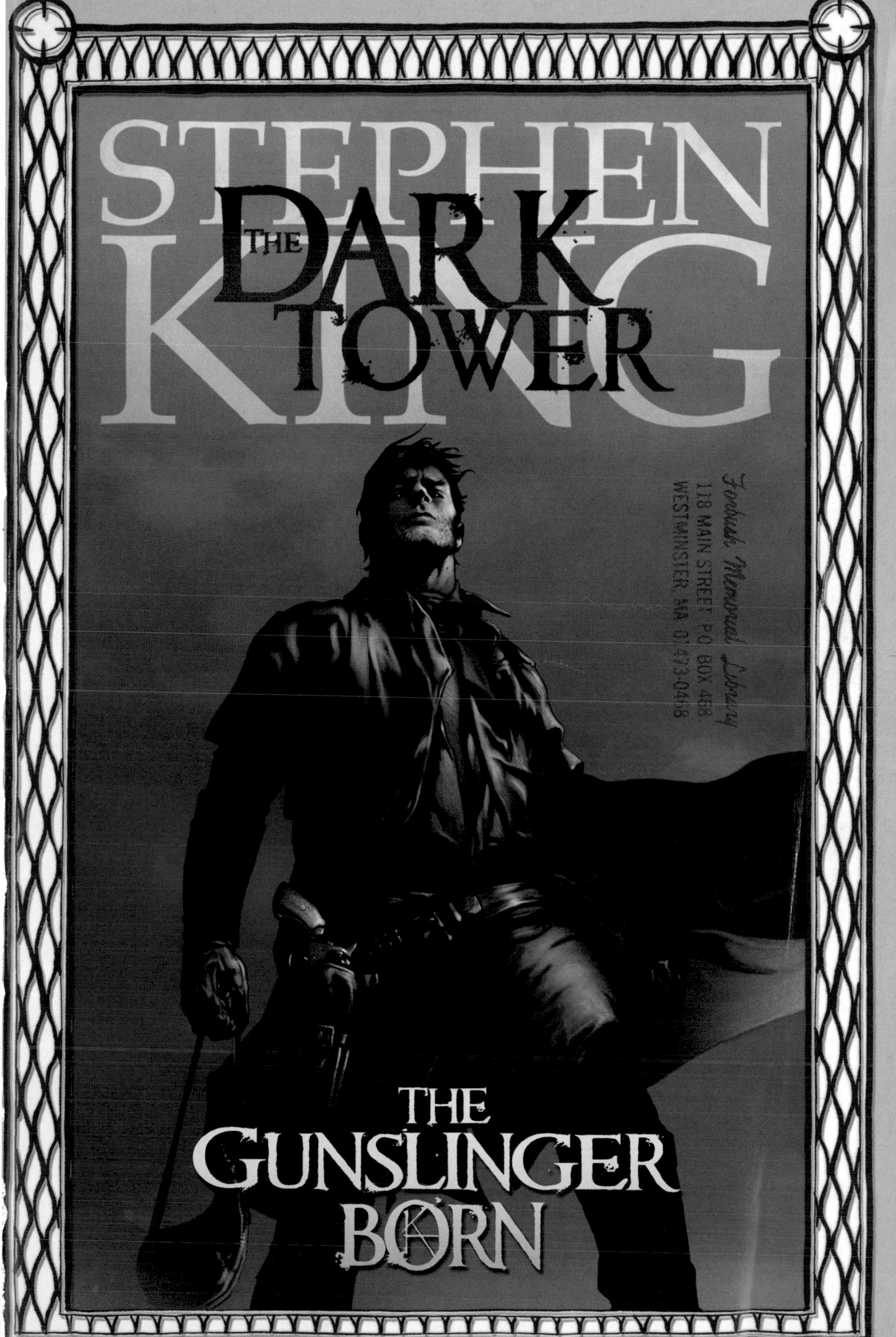
STEPHEN KING
THE DARK TOWER
THE GUNSLINGER BORN

STEPHEN KING

THE DARK TOWER

THE GUNSLINGER BORN

CREATIVE DIRECTOR AND EXECUTIVE DIRECTOR
STEPHEN KING

PLOTTING AND CONSULTATION
ROBIN FURTH

SCRIPT
PETER DAVID

ART
JAE LEE AND RICHARD ISANOVE

LETTERING
CHRIS ELIOPOULOS

ASSOCIATE EDITOR
NICOLE BOOSE

EDITOR
JOHN BARBER

SENIOR EDITOR
RALPH MACCHIO

COLLECTION EDITOR
MARK D. BEAZLEY

ASSISTANT EDITORS
MICHAEL SHORT AND CORY LEVINE

ASSOCIATE EDITOR
JENNIFER GRUNWALD

SENIOR EDITOR, SPECIAL PROJECTS
JEFF YOUNGQUIST

SENIOR VICE PRESIDENT OF SALES
DAVID GABRIEL

VICE PRESIDENT OF DEVELOPMENT
RUWAN JAYATILLEKE

PRODUCTION
JERRY KALINOWSKI

BOOK DESIGNER
PATRICK McGRATH

VICE PRESIDENT OF CREATIVE
TOM MARVELLI

EDITOR IN CHIEF
JOE QUESADA

PUBLISHER
DAN BUCKLEY

SPECIAL THANKS TO CHUCK VERRILL, MARSHA DEFILIPO,
RALPH VICINANZA, JIM NAUSEDAS, JIM McCANN, BRIAN STARK,
RAPHAEL RODRIGUEZ, SALVADOR LARROCA,
JOHN ROMITA JR., CARRIE BEADLE, JEOF VITA, CHRIS ALLO,
JEFF SUTER, RICH GINTER AND JIM CALAFIORE

FOR MORE INFORMATION ON DARK TOWER COMICS, VISIT MARVEL.COM/DARKTOWER.

TO FIND MARVEL COMICS AT A LOCAL COMIC SHOP, CALL 1-888-COMICBOOK.

DARK TOWER: THE GUNSLINGER BORN. Contains material originally published in magazine form as DARK TOWER: THE GUNSLINGER BORN #1-7. First printing 2007. ISBN# 978-0-7851-2144-2. Published by MARVEL PUBLISHING, INC., a subsidiary of MARVEL ENTERTAINMENT, INC. OFFICE OF PUBLICATION: 417 5th Avenue, New York, NY 10016. © 2007 Stephen King. All rights reserved. $24.99 per copy in the U.S. and $29.99 in Canada (GST #R127032852); Canadian Agreement #40668537. All characters featured in this issue and the distinctive names and likenesses thereof, and all related indicia are trademarks of Stephen King. No similarity between any of the names, characters, persons, and/or institutions in this magazine with those of any living or dead person or institution is intended, and any such similarity which may exist is purely coincidental. **Printed in the U.S.A.** ALAN FINE, CEO Marvel Toys & Publishing Divisions and CMO Marvel Entertainment, Inc.; DAVID GABRIEL, Senior VP of Publishing Sales & Circulation; DAVID BOGART, VP of Business Affairs & Editorial Operations; MICHAEL PASCIULLO, VP Merchandising & Communications; JIM BOYLE, VP of Publishing Operations; DAN CARR, Executive Director of Publishing Technology; JUSTIN F. GABRIE, Managing Editor; SUSAN CRESPI, Production Manager; STAN LEE, Chairman Emeritus. For information regarding advertising in Marvel Comics or on Marvel.com, please contact Joe Maimone, Advertising Director, at jmaimone@marvel.com or 212-576-8534.
10 9 8 7 6 5 4 3 2 1

OF MID-WORLD AND MARVEL

This was the great God a'mighty steam shovel that young Stephen King got behind in 1970 when he penned the first volume of this now, much-heralded series of novels. During the intervening three and half decades, King crafted a seven-volume masterpiece that owes allegiance to no single literary genre. It is first and foremost a Great Quest; a gunslinger's journey to reach the fabled Dark Tower at the center of existence before it collapses and chaos reigns. Its themes are legion. Its iconography is unique.

There are elements of everything from heroic fantasy to the spaghetti westerns of Sergio Leone in the Dark Tower books. King was irresistibly drawn back time and again to Roland Deschain's "world that had moved on" as if he were, in fact, narrating the gunslinger's journey from Mid-World to End-World as it was being revealed to him rather than creating the saga from scratch. So real did Roland's universe become that many of King's other works contained allusions to the Dark Tower. And the author, himself, became a character in the latter books.

Then, several years after completing the final volume, Stephen King and his people began negotiating with Marvel Comics to bring this incredibly valuable property here. The result of those highly productive talks was the hugely successful Dark Tower comics which, in their first seven issues, chronicled the early days of Roland Deschain and his ka-tet as they traveled from storied Gilead to the outlying town of Hambry, where Roland met the love of his life, Susan Delgado. It has been my considerable privilege to have edited those issues and watched as the gunslinger's world transitioned from the printed page to this visual medium we call comics.

The hardcover you're holding now is one of which I'm immensely proud. It contains the first, all-important story arc of a larger undertaking, much of it culled from the fourth book in the series: WIZARD AND GLASS. Little about its creation has come easily. There were few guideposts to point us in the right direction. The creators went on instinct and talent—the best guides of all, in the last analysis.

If you've never experienced the Dark Tower, Stephen King's magnificent magnum opus, I envy you. Within these pages you will embark on a singular journey to misty realms of the imagination that will both terrify and enchant you.

Now, let the everyday world quietly slip away. We have a date in the desert—the apotheosis of all deserts—with the mysterious Man in Black. And he hates to be kept waiting.

Enjoy,

Ralph Macchio

Ralph Macchio
2007

STEPHEN KING

THE DARK TOWER

THE GUNSLINGER BORN

CHAPTER ONE

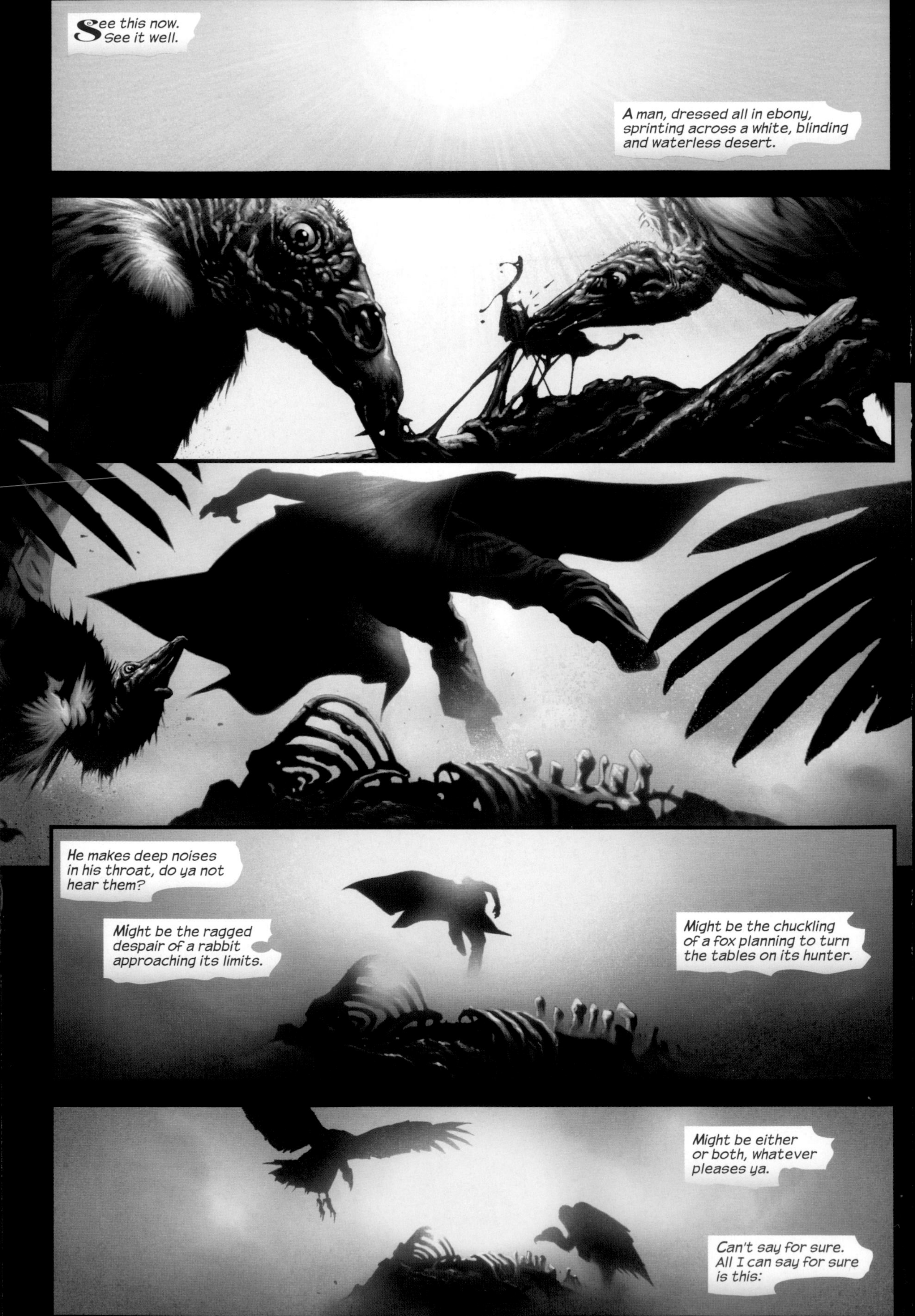
See this now. See it well.
A man, dressed all in ebony, sprinting across a white, blinding and waterless desert.
He makes deep noises in his throat, do ya not hear them?
Might be the ragged despair of a rabbit approaching its limits.
Might be the chuckling of a fox planning to turn the tables on its hunter.
Might be either or both, whatever pleases ya.
Can't say for sure. All I can say for sure is this:

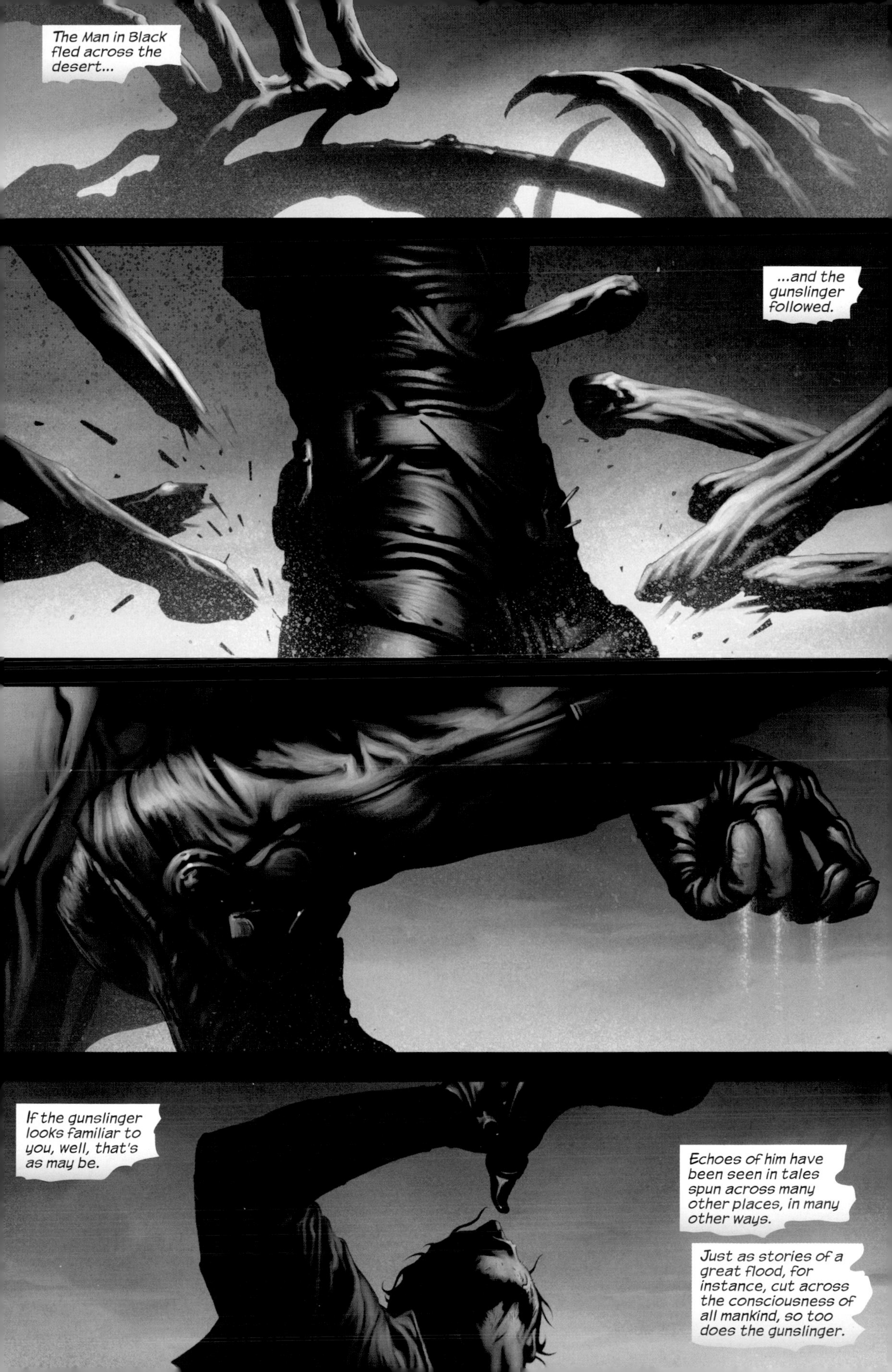
The Man in Black fled across the desert...
...and the gunslinger followed.
If the gunslinger looks familiar to you, well, that's as may be.
Echoes of him have been seen in tales spun across many other places, in many other ways.
Just as stories of a great flood, for instance, cut across the consciousness of all mankind, so too does the gunslinger.

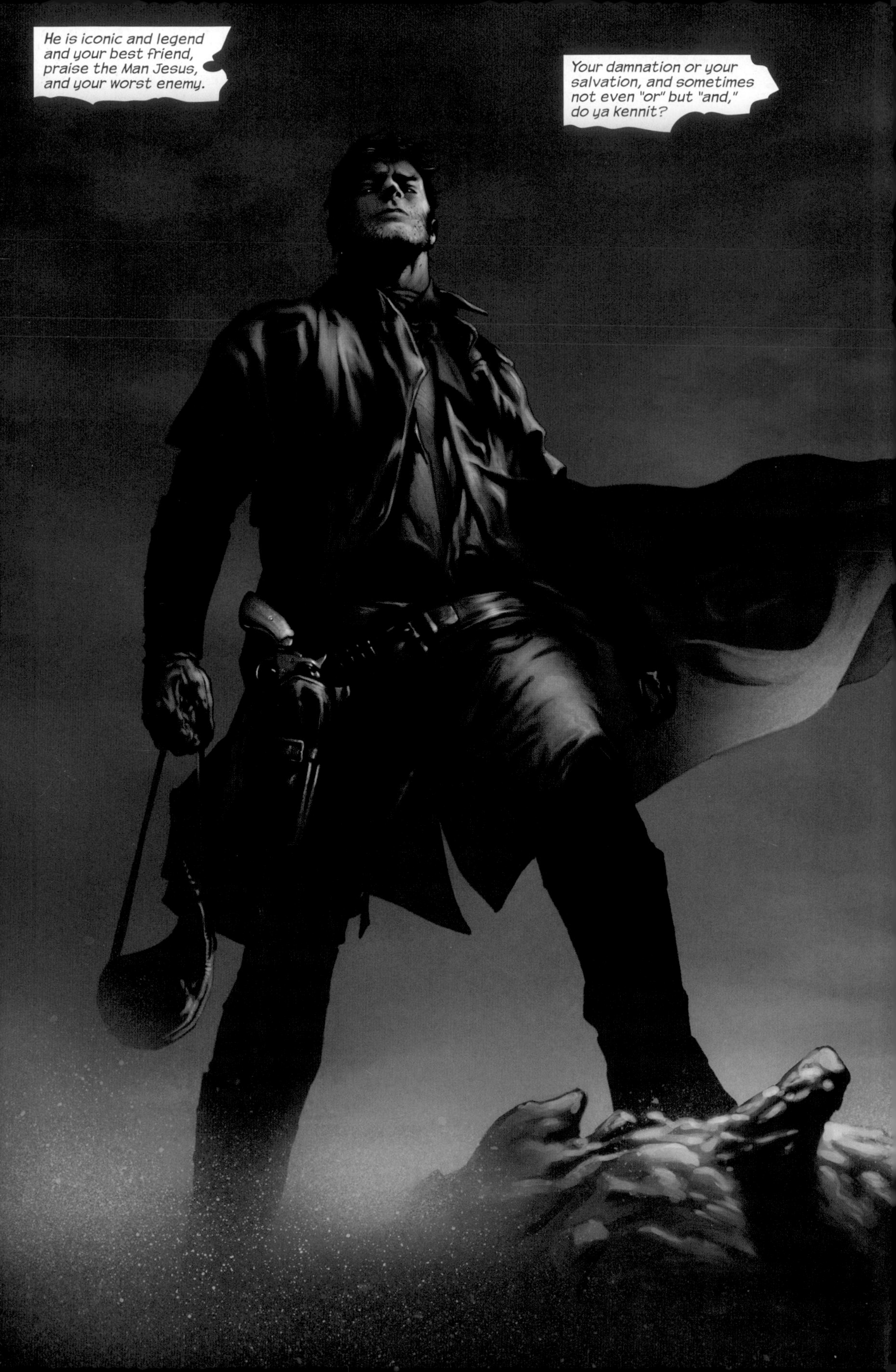
He is iconic and legend and your best friend, praise the Man Jesus, and your worst enemy.
Your damnation or your salvation, and sometimes not even "or" but "and," do ya kennit?

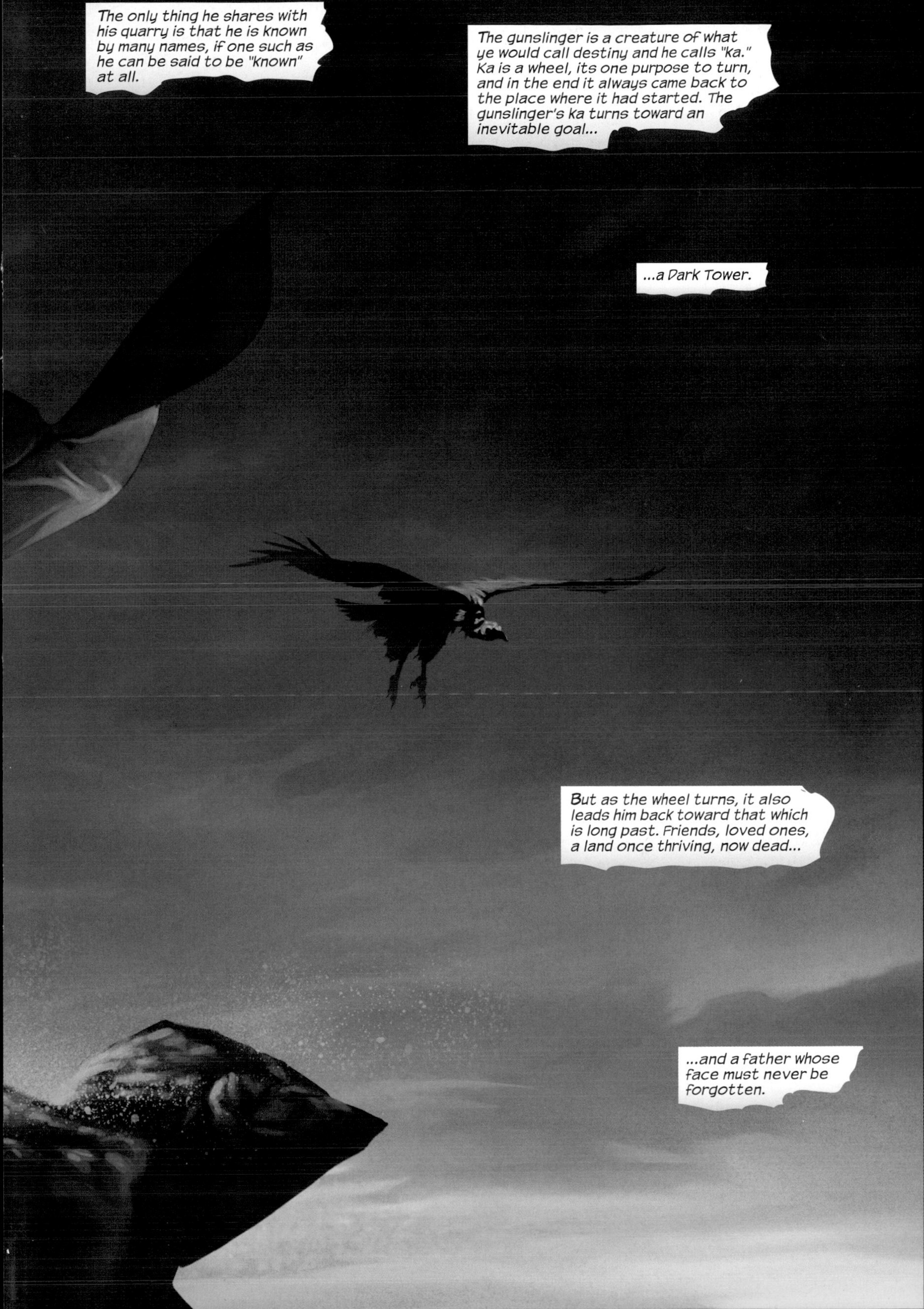
The only thing he shares with his quarry is that he is known by many names, if one such as he can be said to be "known" at all.
The gunslinger is a creature of what ye would call destiny and he calls "ka." Ka is a wheel, its one purpose to turn, and in the end it always came back to the place where it had started. The gunslinger's ka turns toward an inevitable goal...
...a Dark Tower.
But as the wheel turns, it also leads him back toward that which is long past. Friends, loved ones, a land once thriving, now dead...
...and a father whose face must never be forgotten.

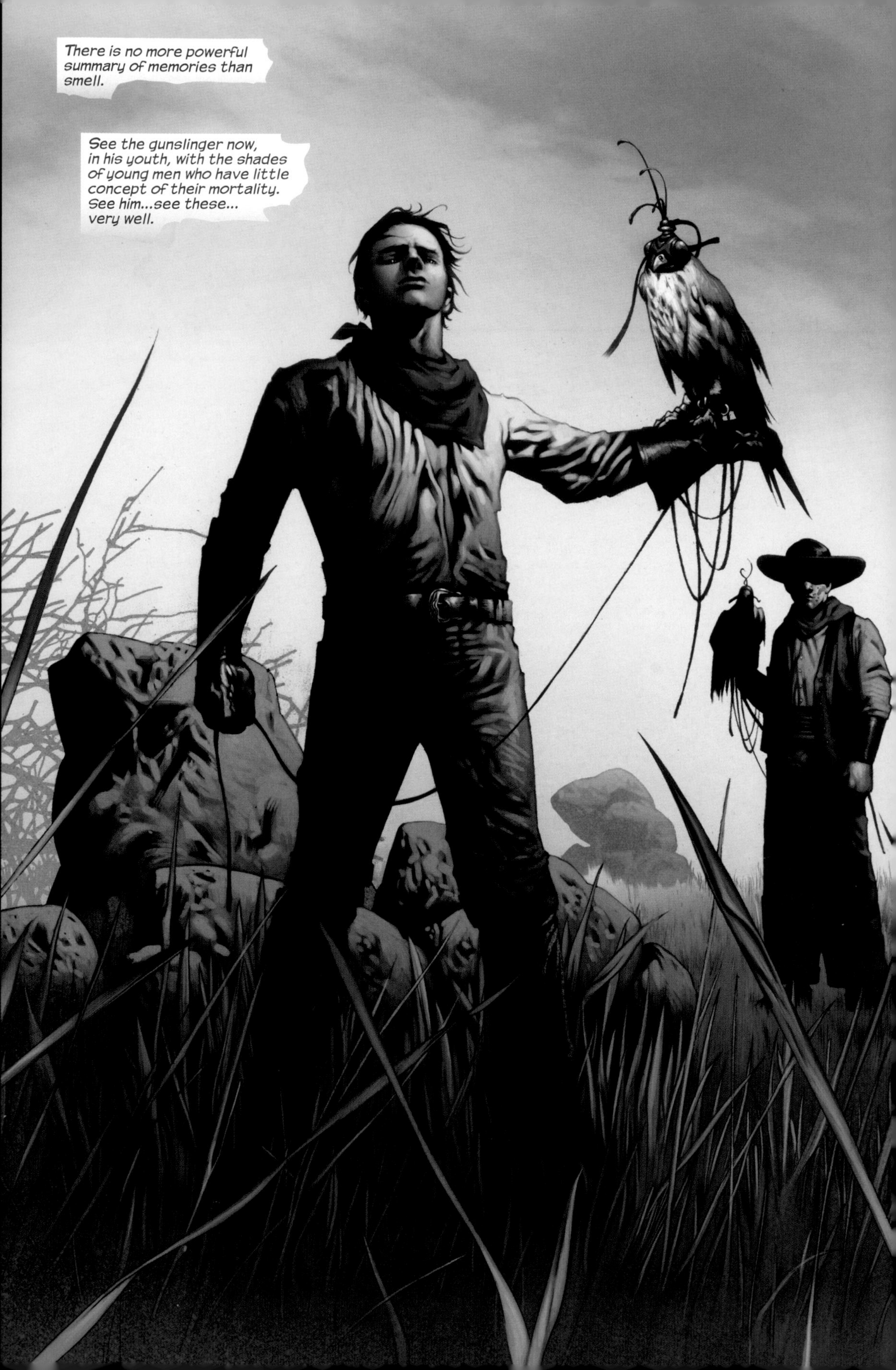
There is no more powerful summary of memories than smell.
See the gunslinger now, in his youth, with the shades of young men who have little concept of their mortality. See him...see these... very well.

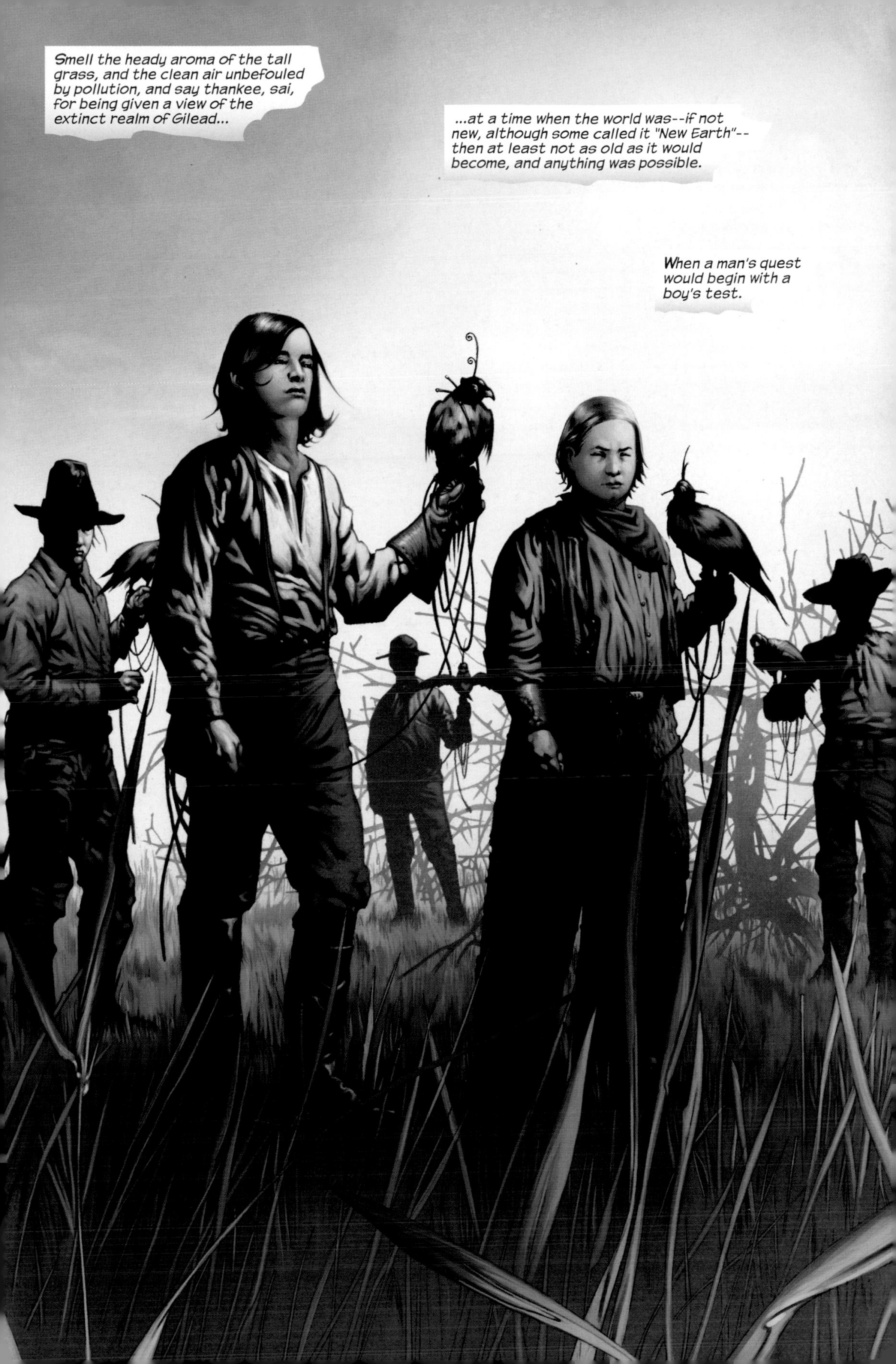
Smell the heady aroma of the tall grass, and the clean air unbefouled by pollution, and say thankee, sai, for being given a view of the extinct realm of Gilead...
...at a time when the world was--if not new, although some called it "New Earth"--then at least not as old as it would become, and anything was possible.
When a man's quest would begin with a boy's test.

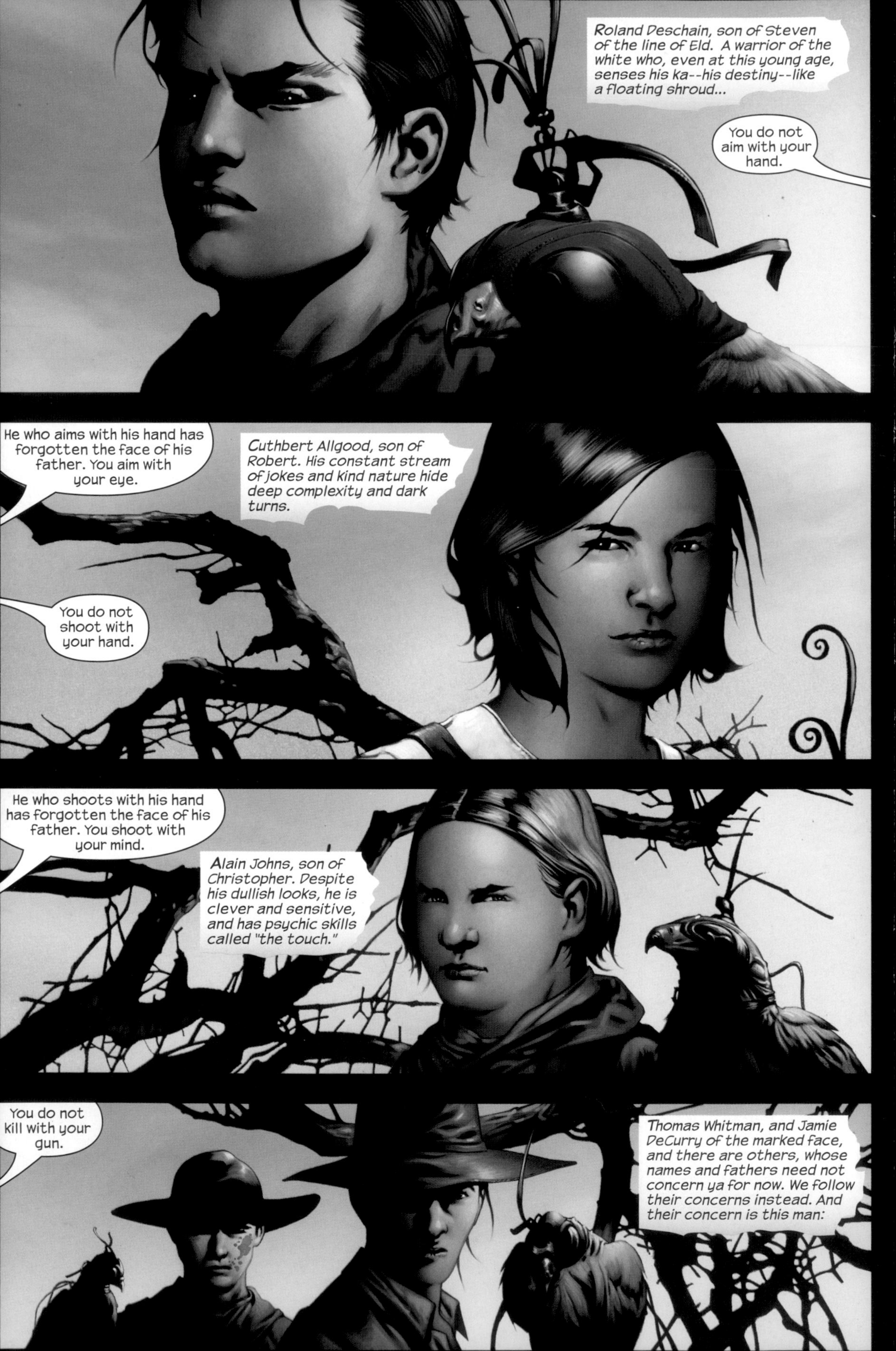
Roland Deschain, son of Steven of the line of Eld. A warrior of the white who, even at this young age, senses his ka--his destiny--like a floating shroud...
You do not aim with your hand.
He who aims with his hand has forgotten the face of his father. You aim with your eye.
Cuthbert Allgood, son of Robert. His constant stream of jokes and kind nature hide deep complexity and dark turns.
You do not shoot with your hand.
He who shoots with his hand has forgotten the face of his father. You shoot with your mind.
Alain Johns, son of Christopher. Despite his dullish looks, he is clever and sensitive, and has psychic skills called "the touch."
You do not kill with your gun.
Thomas Whitman, and Jamie DeCurry of the marked face, and there are others, whose names and fathers need not concern ya for now. We follow their concerns instead. And their concern is this man:

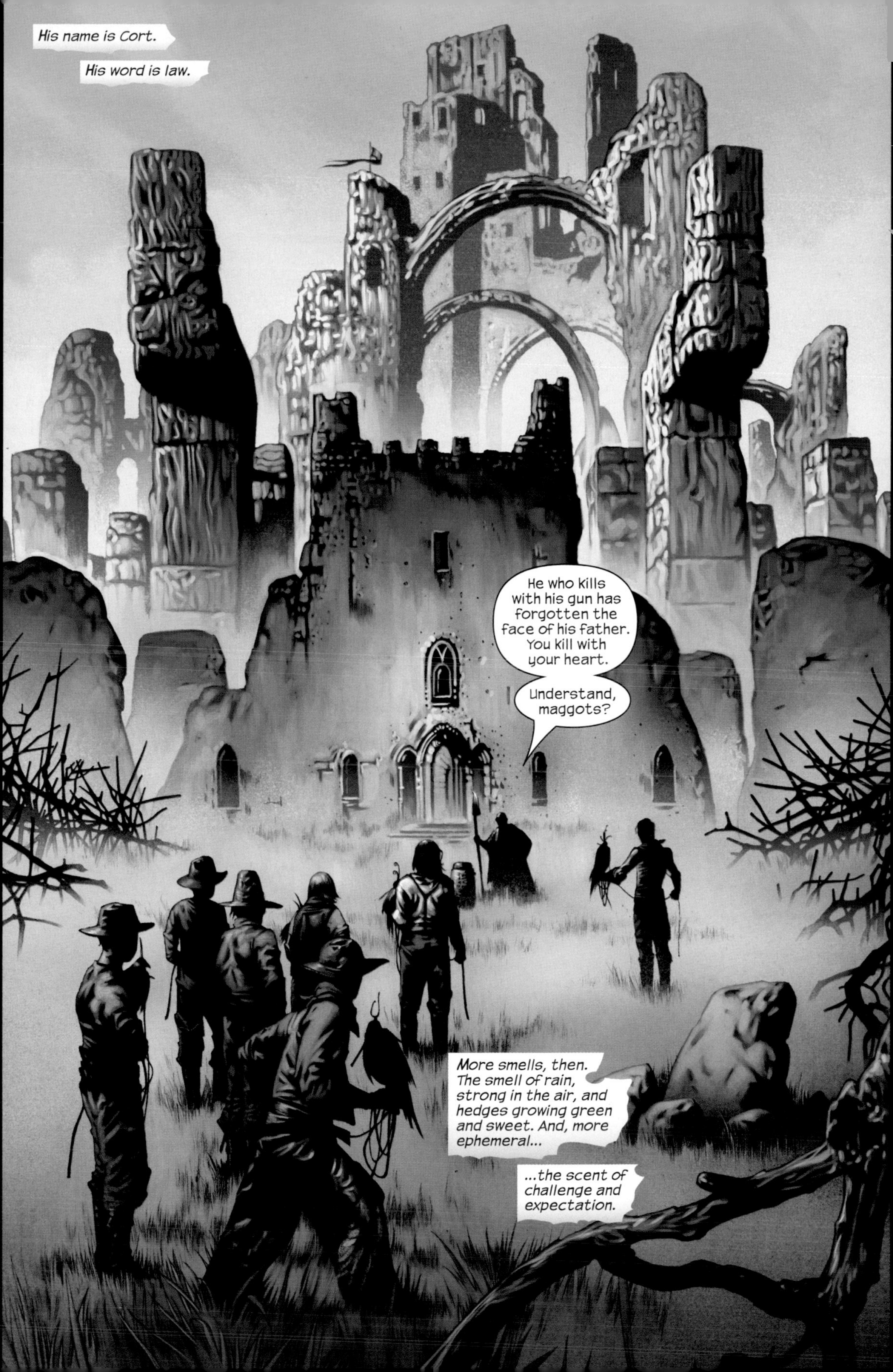
His name is Cort.
His word is law.
He who kills with his gun has forgotten the face of his father. You kill with your heart.
Understand, maggots?
More smells, then. The smell of rain, strong in the air, and hedges growing green and sweet. And, more ephemeral...
...the scent of challenge and expectation.

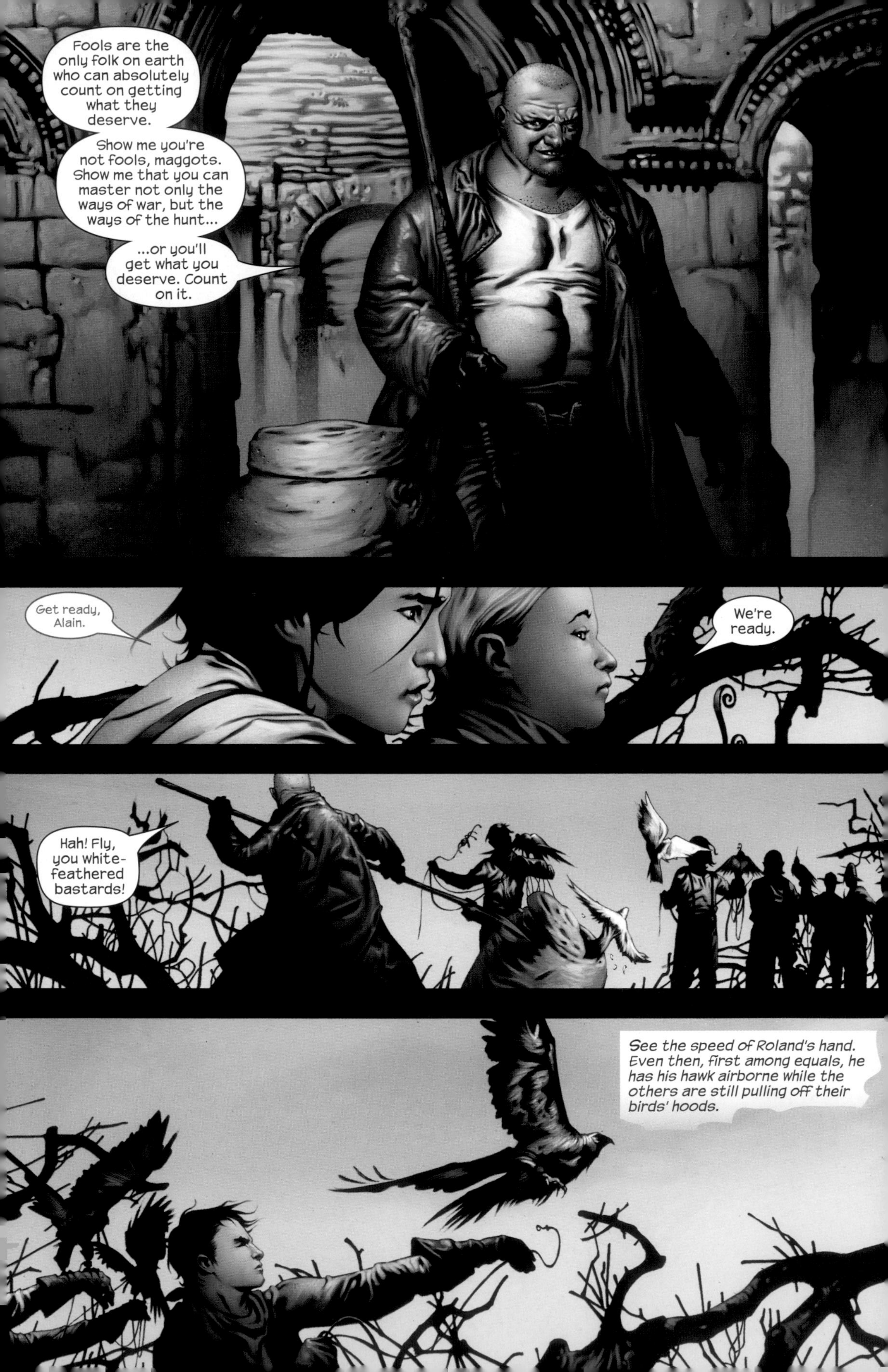
Fools are the only folk on earth who can absolutely count on getting what they deserve.
Show me you're not fools, maggots. Show me that you can master not only the ways of war, but the ways of the hunt...
...or you'll get what you deserve. Count on it.
Get ready, Alain.
We're ready.
Hah! Fly, you white-feathered bastards!
See the speed of Roland's hand. Even then, first among equals, he has his hawk airborne while the others are still pulling off their birds' hoods.

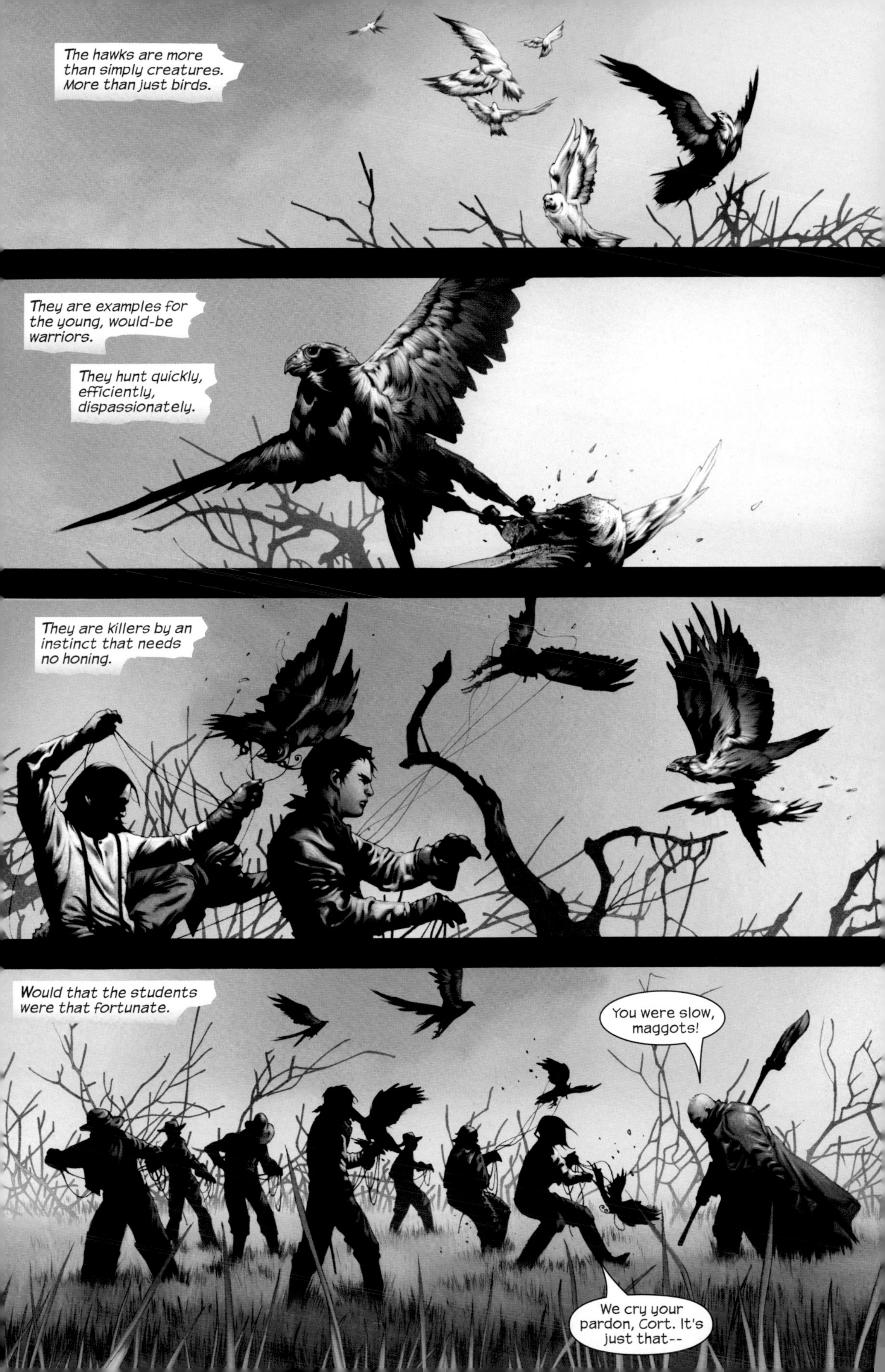
The hawks are more than simply creatures. More than just birds.
They are examples for the young, would-be warriors.
They hunt quickly, efficiently, dispassionately.
They are killers by an instinct that needs no honing.
Would that the students were that fortunate.
You were slow, maggots!
We cry your pardon, Cort. It's just that--

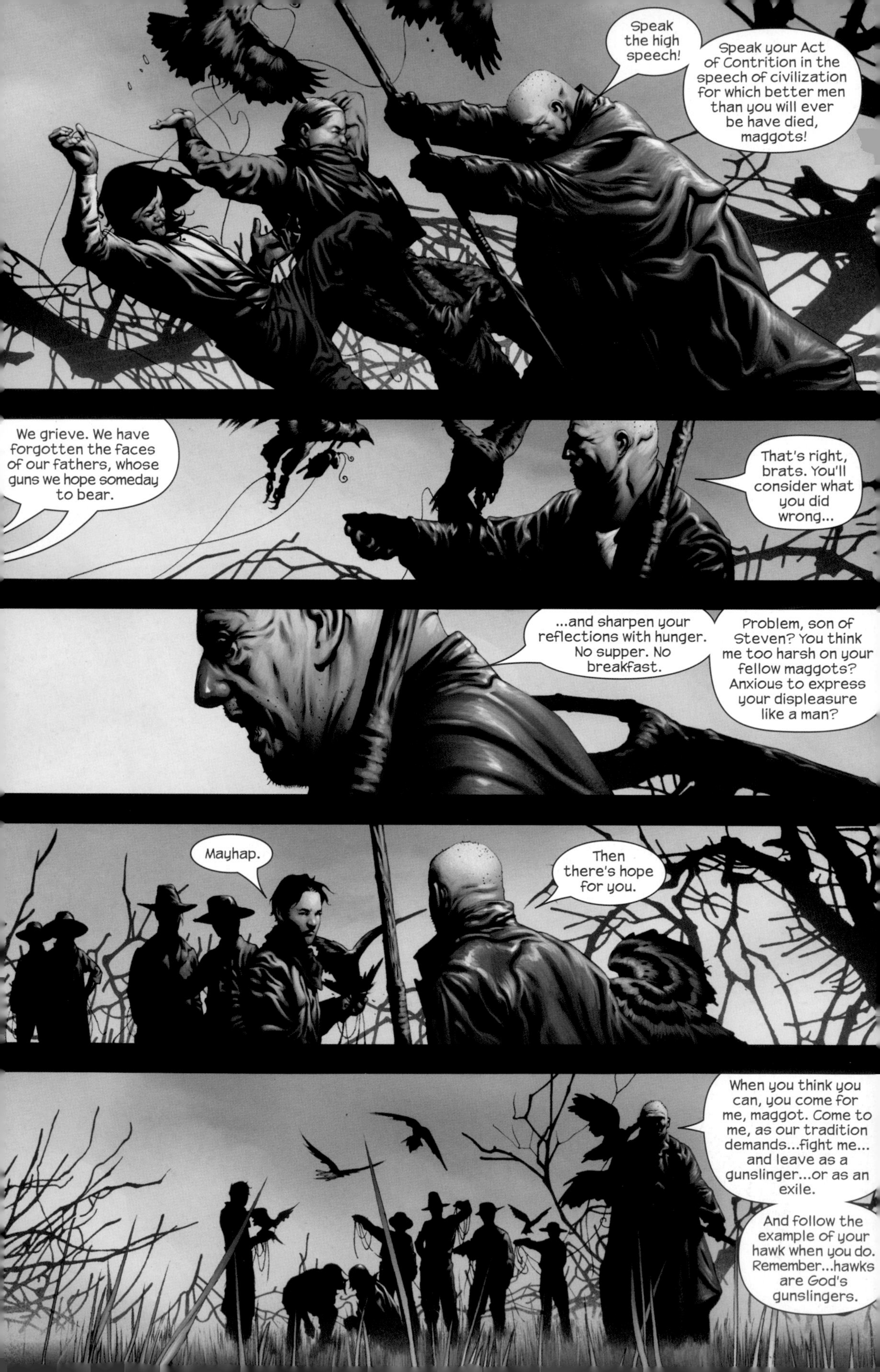
Speak the high speech!
Speak your Act of Contrition in the speech of civilization for which better men than you will ever be have died, maggots!
We grieve. We have forgotten the faces of our fathers, whose guns we hope someday to bear.
That's right, brats. You'll consider what you did wrong...
...and sharpen your reflections with hunger. No supper. No breakfast.
Problem, son of Steven? You think me too harsh on your fellow maggots? Anxious to express your displeasure like a man?
Mayhap.
Then there's hope for you.
When you think you can, you come for me, maggot. Come to me, as our tradition demands...fight me... and leave as a gunslinger...or as an exile.
And follow the example of your hawk when you do. Remember...hawks are God's gunslingers.

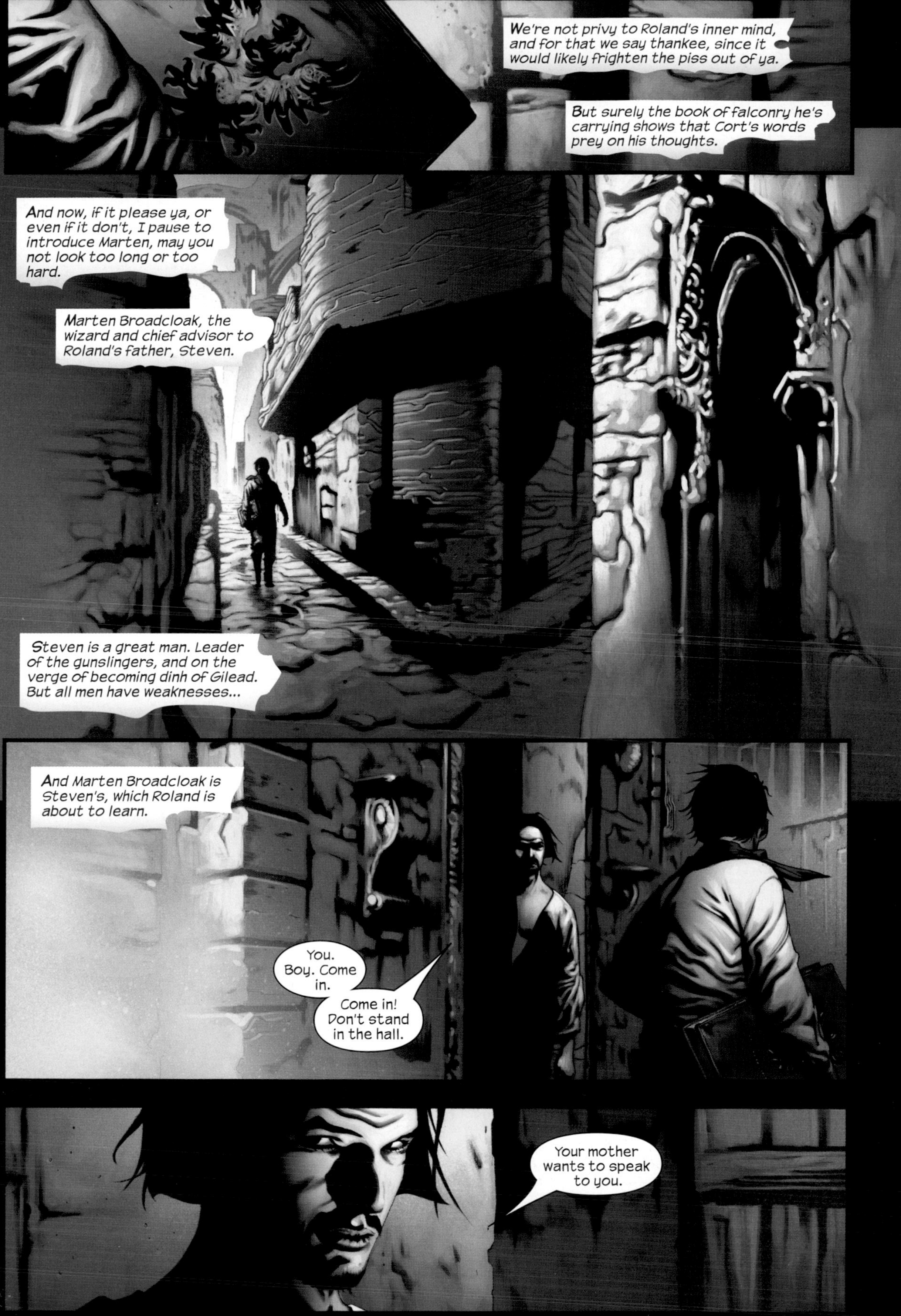
We're not privy to Roland's inner mind, and for that we say thankee, since it would likely frighten the piss out of ya.
But surely the book of falconry he's carrying shows that Cort's words prey on his thoughts.
And now, if it please ya, or even if it don't, I pause to introduce Marten, may you not look too long or too hard.
Marten Broadcloak, the wizard and chief advisor to Roland's father, Steven.
Steven is a great man. Leader of the gunslingers, and on the verge of becoming dinh of Gilead. But all men have weaknesses...
And Marten Broadcloak is Steven's, which Roland is about to learn.
You. Boy. Come in.
Come in! Don't stand in the hall.
Your mother wants to speak to you.

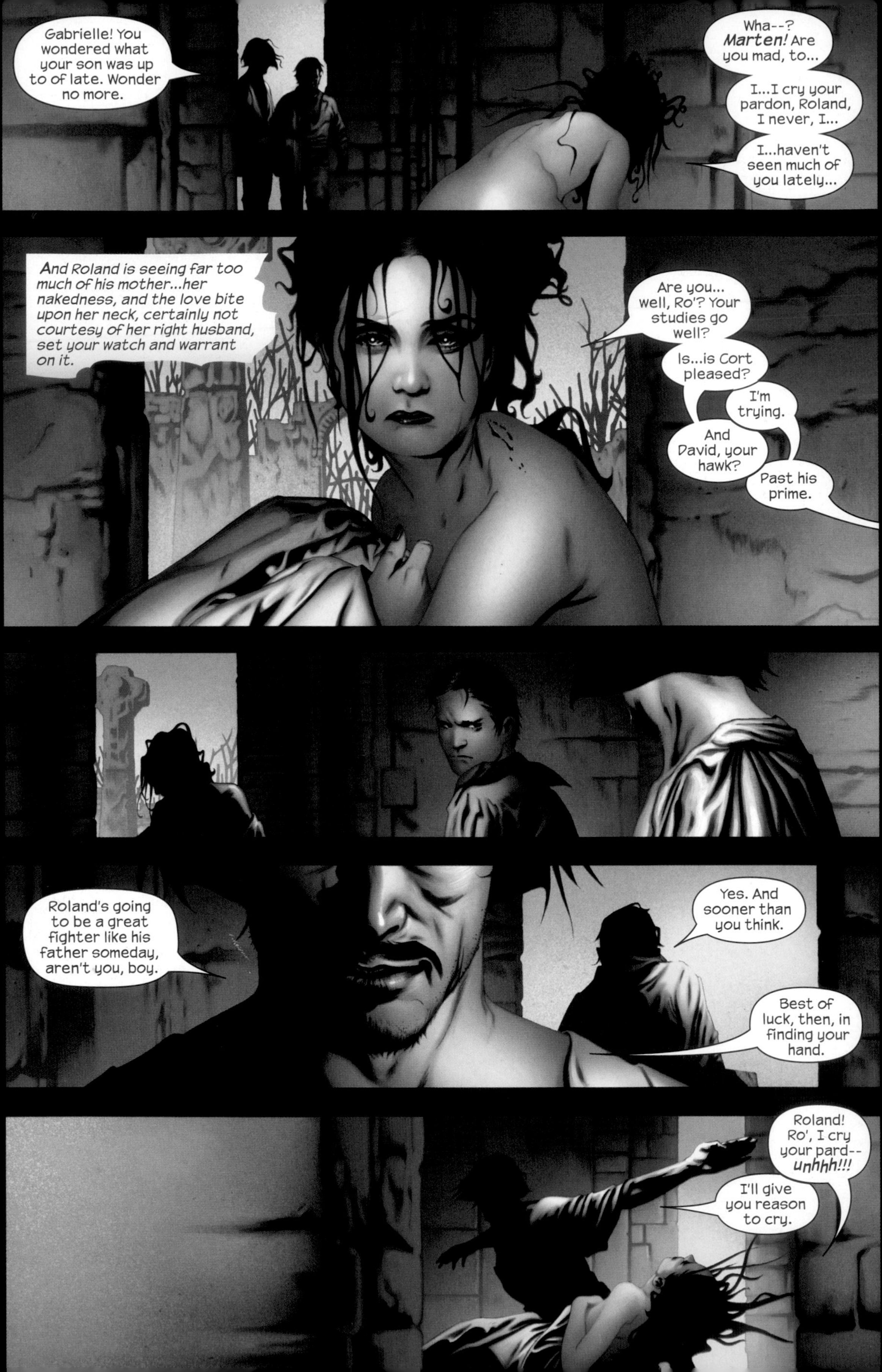
Gabrielle! You wondered what your son was up to of late. Wonder no more.
Wha--? Marten! Are you mad, to...
I...I cry your pardon, Roland, I never, I...
I...haven't seen much of you lately...
And Roland is seeing far too much of his mother...her nakedness, and the love bite upon her neck, certainly not courtesy of her right husband, set your watch and warrant on it.
Are you... well, Ro'? Your studies go well?
Is...is Cort pleased?
I'm trying.
And David, your hawk?
Past his prime.
Roland's going to be a great fighter like his father someday, aren't you, boy.
Yes. And sooner than you think.
Best of luck, then, in finding your hand.
Roland! Ro', I cry your pard-- unhhh!!!
I'll give you reason to cry.

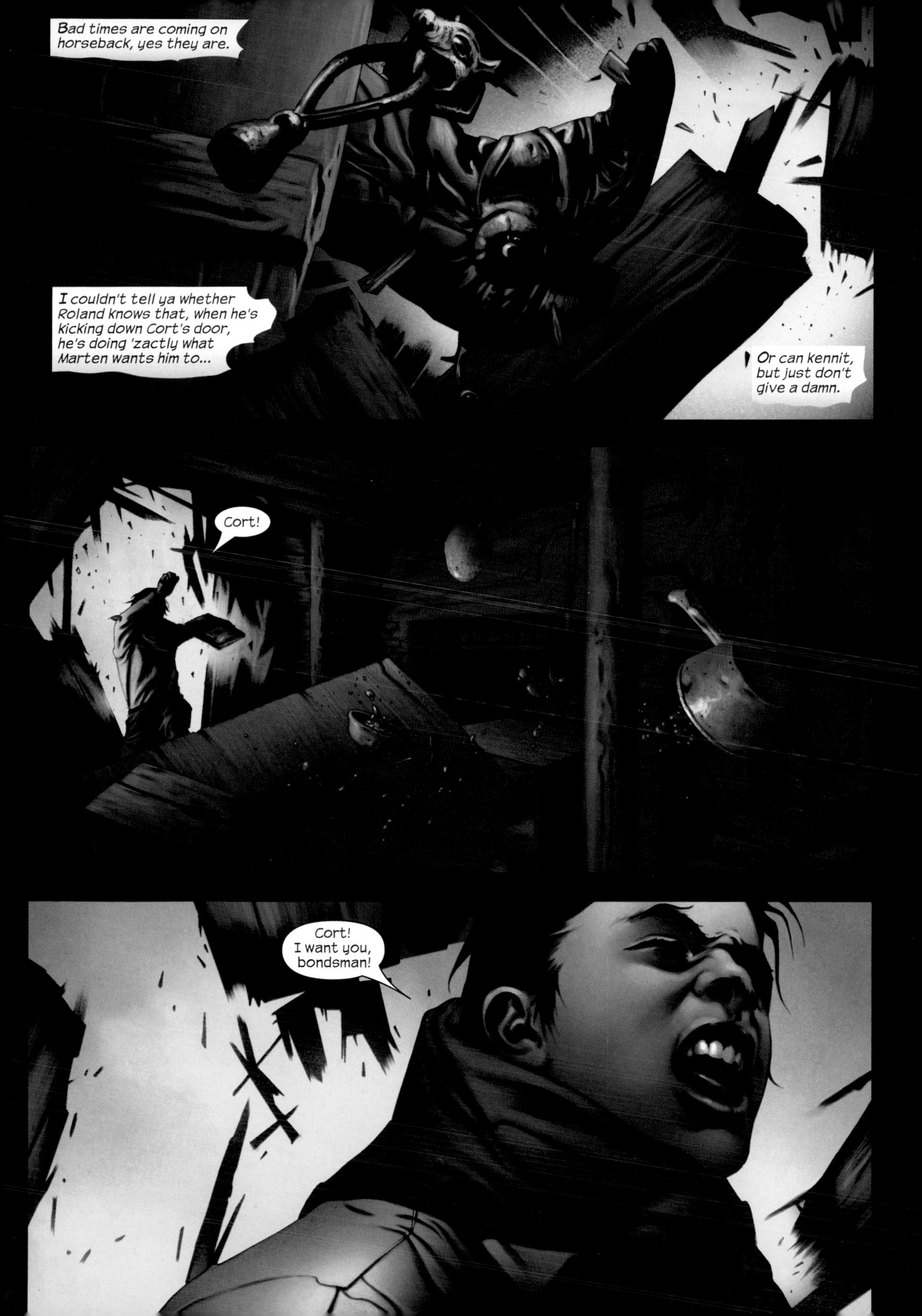

Bad times are coming on horseback, yes they are.
I couldn't tell ya whether Roland knows that, when he's kicking down Cort's door, he's doing 'zactly what Marten wants him to...
Or can kennit, but just don't give a damn.
Cort!
Cort! I want you, bondsman!

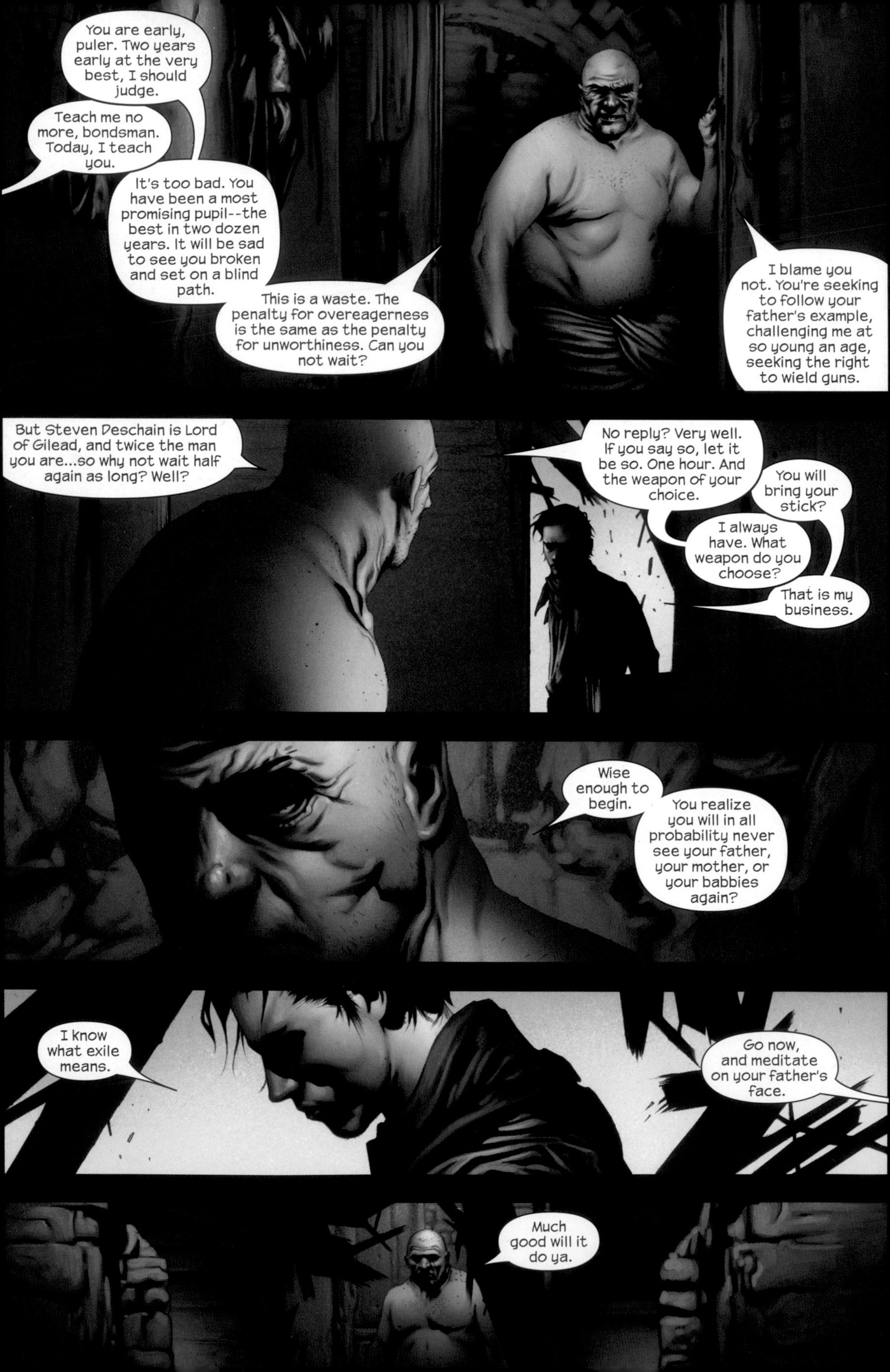
You are early, puler. Two years early at the very best, I should judge.
Teach me no more, bondsman. Today, I teach you.
It's too bad. You have been a most promising pupil--the best in two dozen years. It will be sad to see you broken and set on a blind path.
This is a waste. The penalty for overeagerness is the same as the penalty for unworthiness. Can you not wait?
I blame you not. You're seeking to follow your father's example, challenging me at so young an age, seeking the right to wield guns.
But Steven Deschain is Lord of Gilead, and twice the man you are...so why not wait half again as long? Well?
No reply? Very well. If you say so, let it be so. One hour. And the weapon of your choice.
You will bring your stick?
I always have. What weapon do you choose?
That is my business.
Wise enough to begin.
You realize you will in all probability never see your father, your mother, or your babbies again?
I know what exile means.
Go now, and meditate on your father's face.
Much good will it do ya.

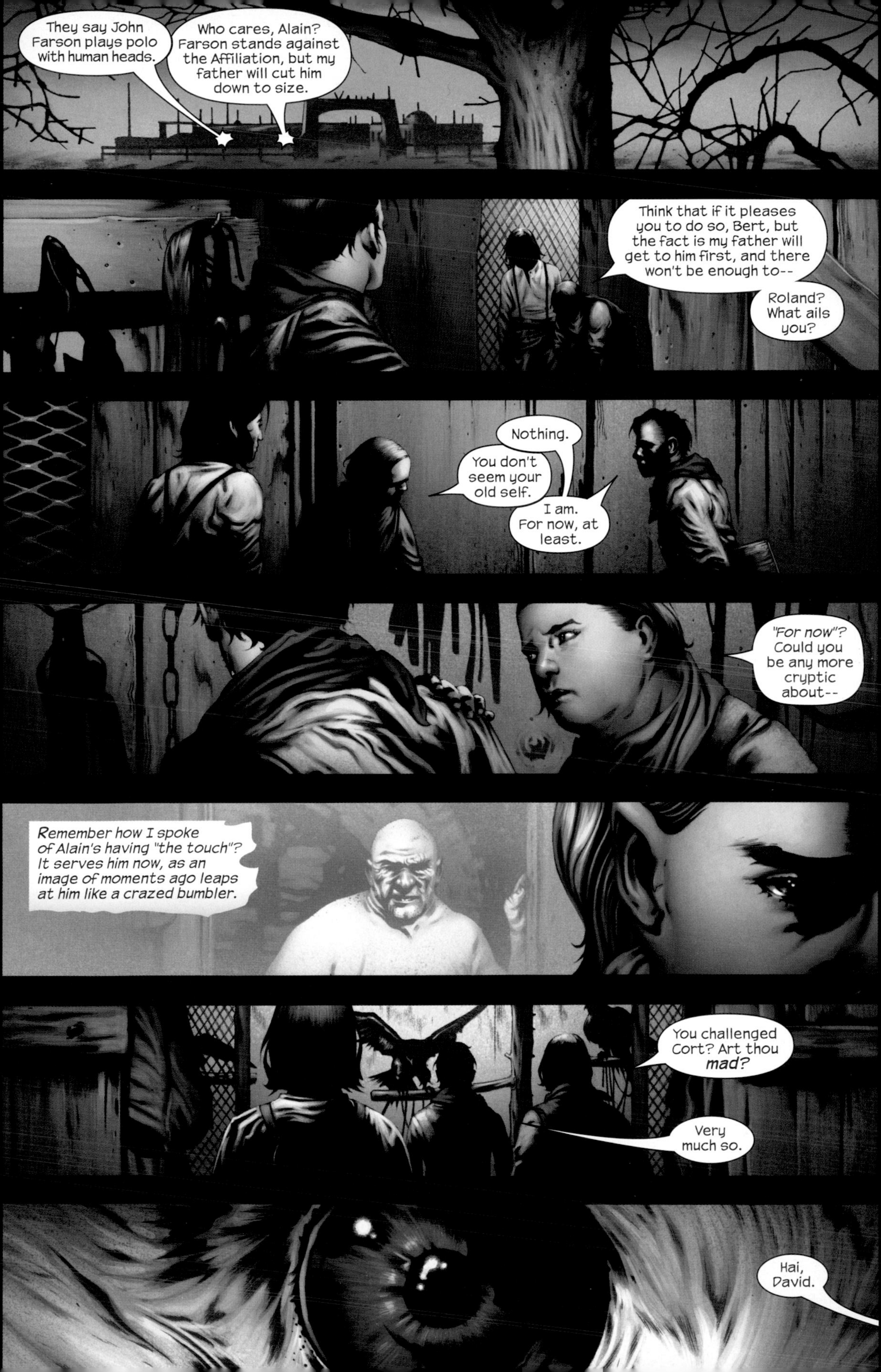

They say John Farson plays polo with human heads.
Who cares, Alain? Farson stands against the Affiliation, but my father will cut him down to size.
Think that if it pleases you to do so, Bert, but the fact is my father will get to him first, and there won't be enough to--
Roland? What ails you?
You don't seem your old self.
Nothing.
I am. For now, at least.
"For now"? Could you be any more cryptic about--
Remember how I spoke of Alain's having "the touch"? It serves him now, as an image of moments ago leaps at him like a crazed bumbler.
You challenged Cort? Art thou *mad?*
Very much so.
Hai, David.

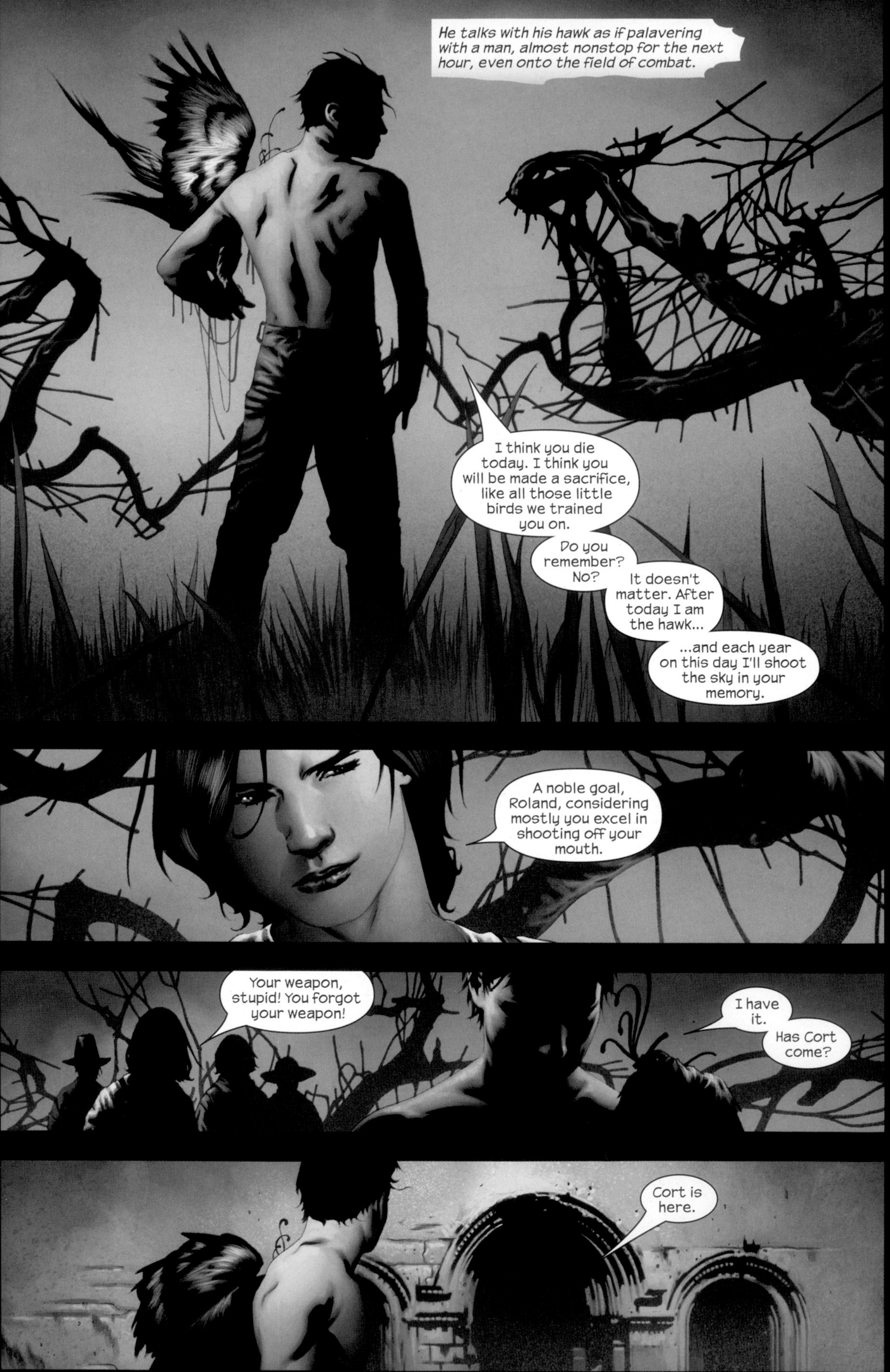
He talks with his hawk as if palavering with a man, almost nonstop for the next hour, even onto the field of combat.
I think you die today. I think you will be made a sacrifice, like all those little birds we trained you on.
Do you remember? No?
It doesn't matter. After today I am the hawk...
...and each year on this day I'll shoot the sky in your memory.
A noble goal, Roland, considering mostly you excel in shooting off your mouth.
Your weapon, stupid! You forgot your weapon!
I have it.
Has Cort come?
Cort is here.

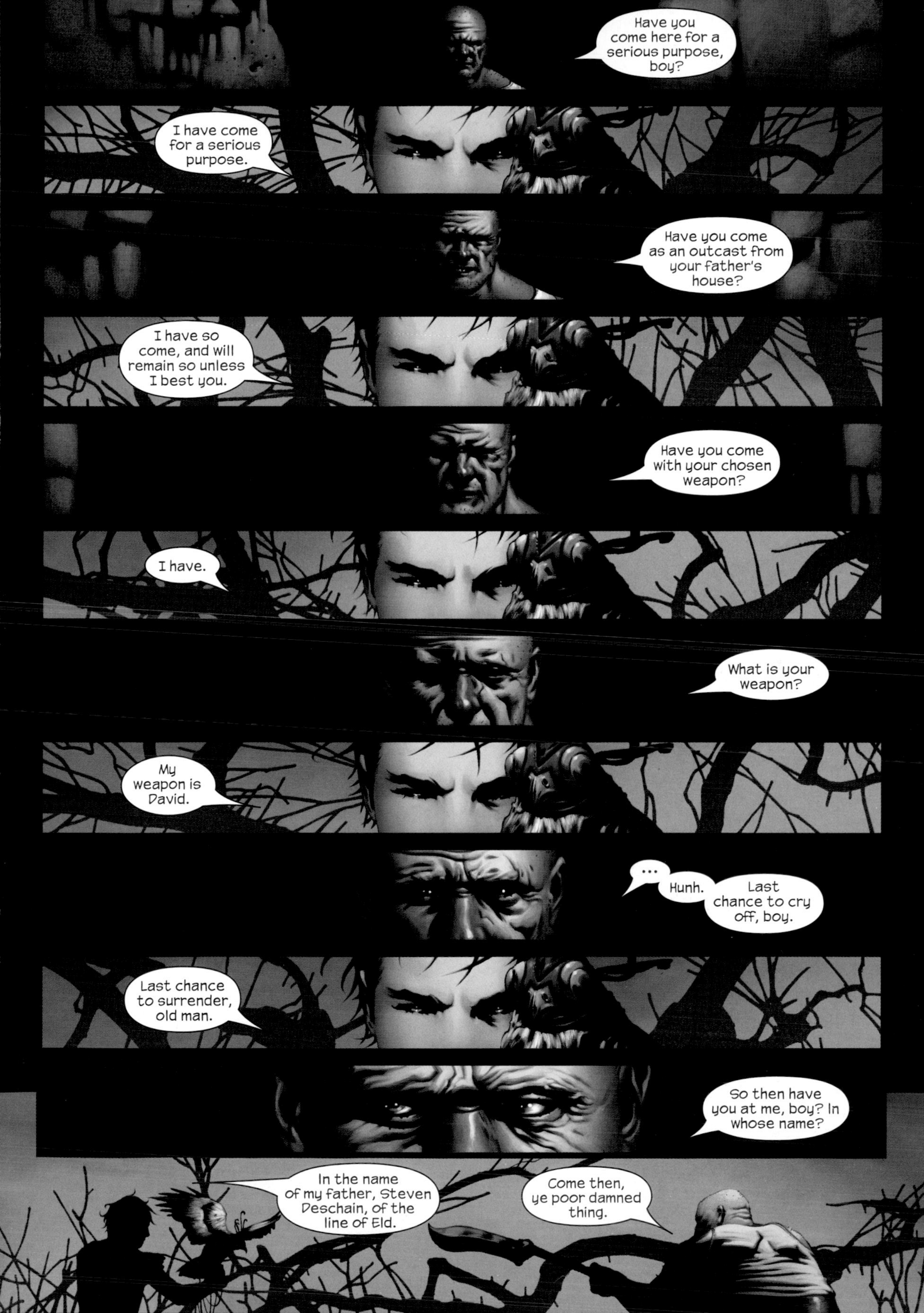
Have you come here for a serious purpose, boy?
I have come for a serious purpose.
Have you come as an outcast from your father's house?
I have so come, and will remain so unless I best you.
Have you come with your chosen weapon?
I have.
What is your weapon?
My weapon is David.
...
Hunh.
Last chance to cry off, boy.
Last chance to surrender, old man.
So then have you at me, boy? In whose name?
In the name of my father, Steven Deschain, of the line of Eld.
Come then, ye poor damned thing.

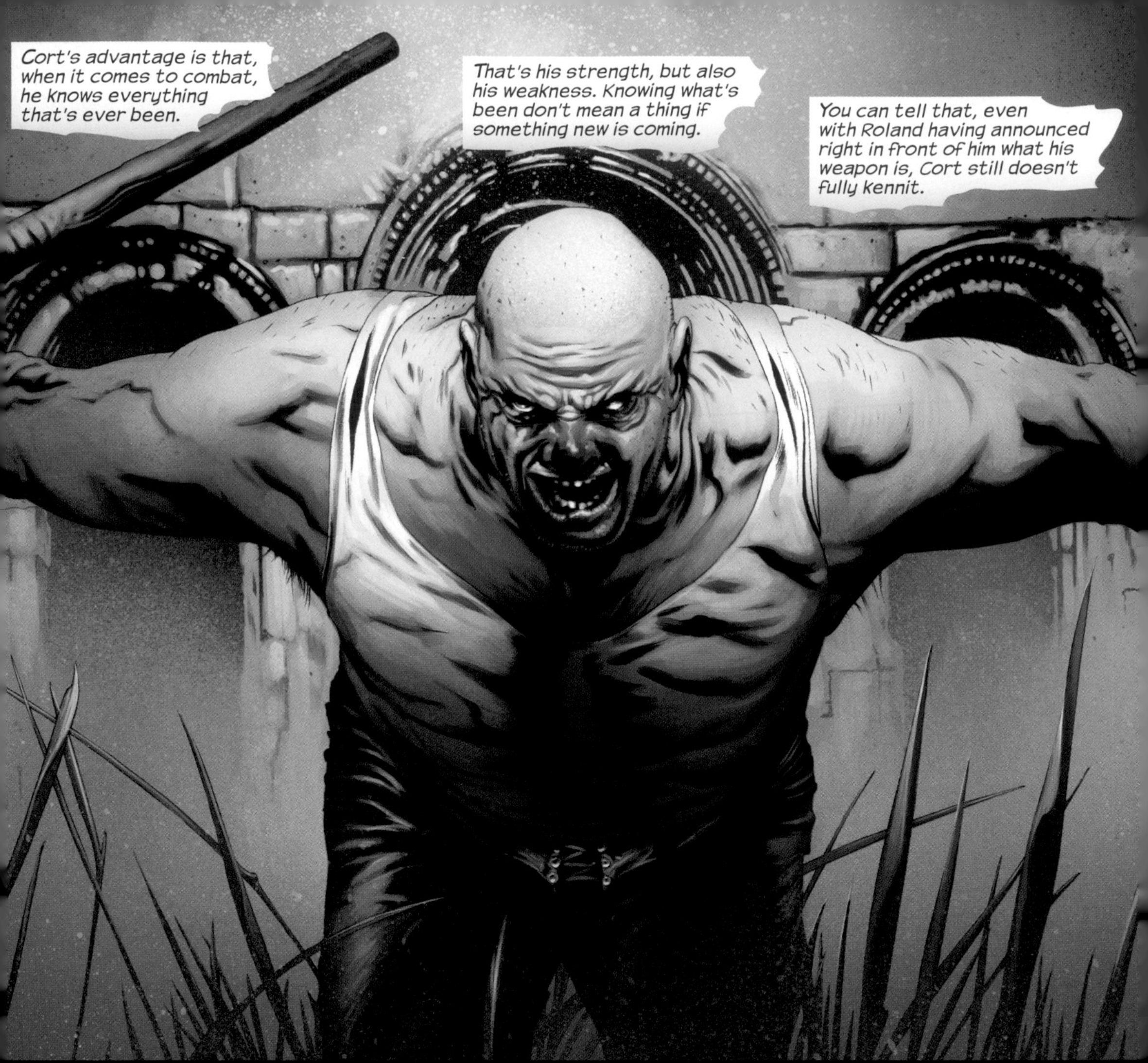
Cort's advantage is that, when it comes to combat, he knows everything that's ever been.
That's his strength, but also his weakness. Knowing what's been don't mean a thing if something new is coming.
You can tell that, even with Roland having announced right in front of him what his weapon is, Cort still doesn't fully kennit.

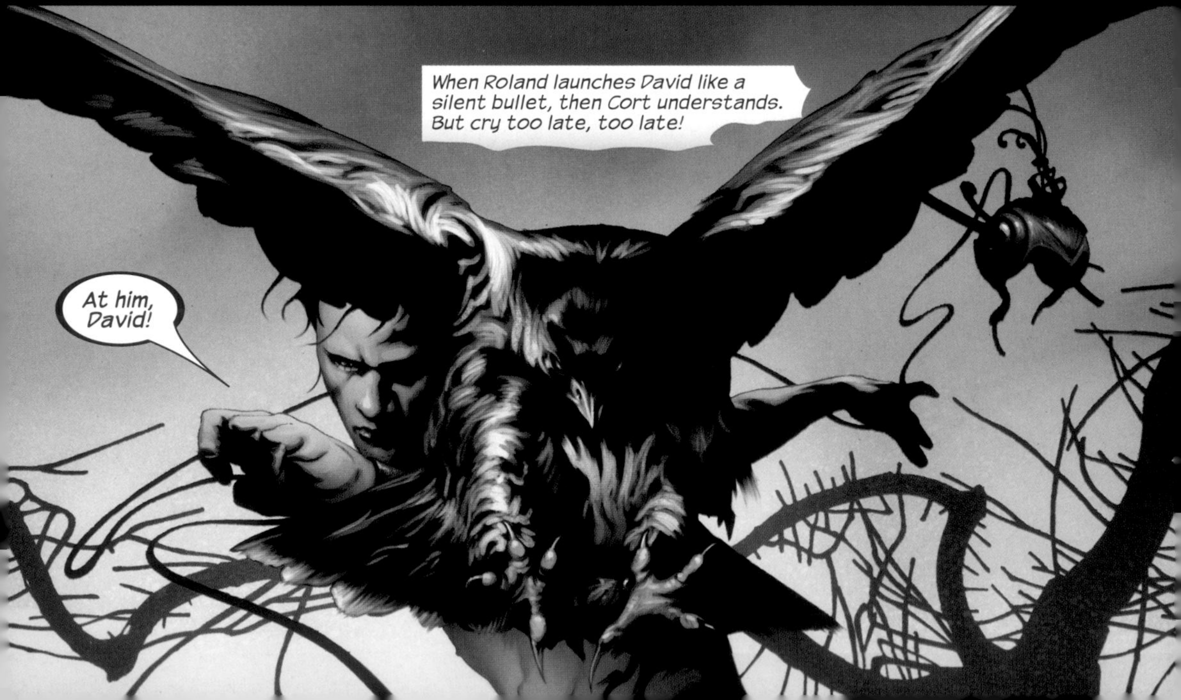
When Roland launches David like a silent bullet, then Cort understands. But cry too late, too late!
At him, David!

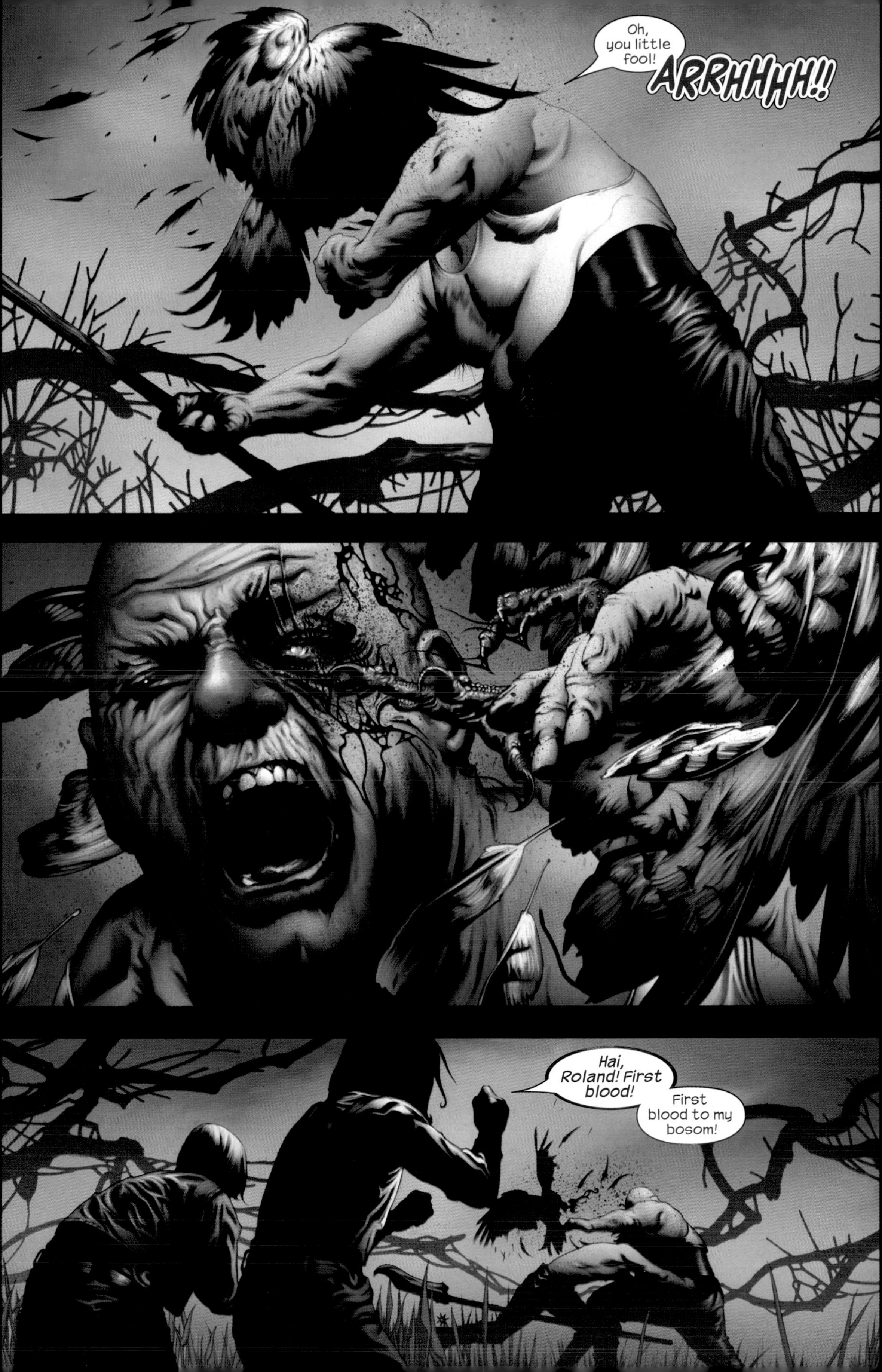
Oh, you little fool!
ARRHHHH!!
Hai, Roland! First blood!
First blood to my bosom!

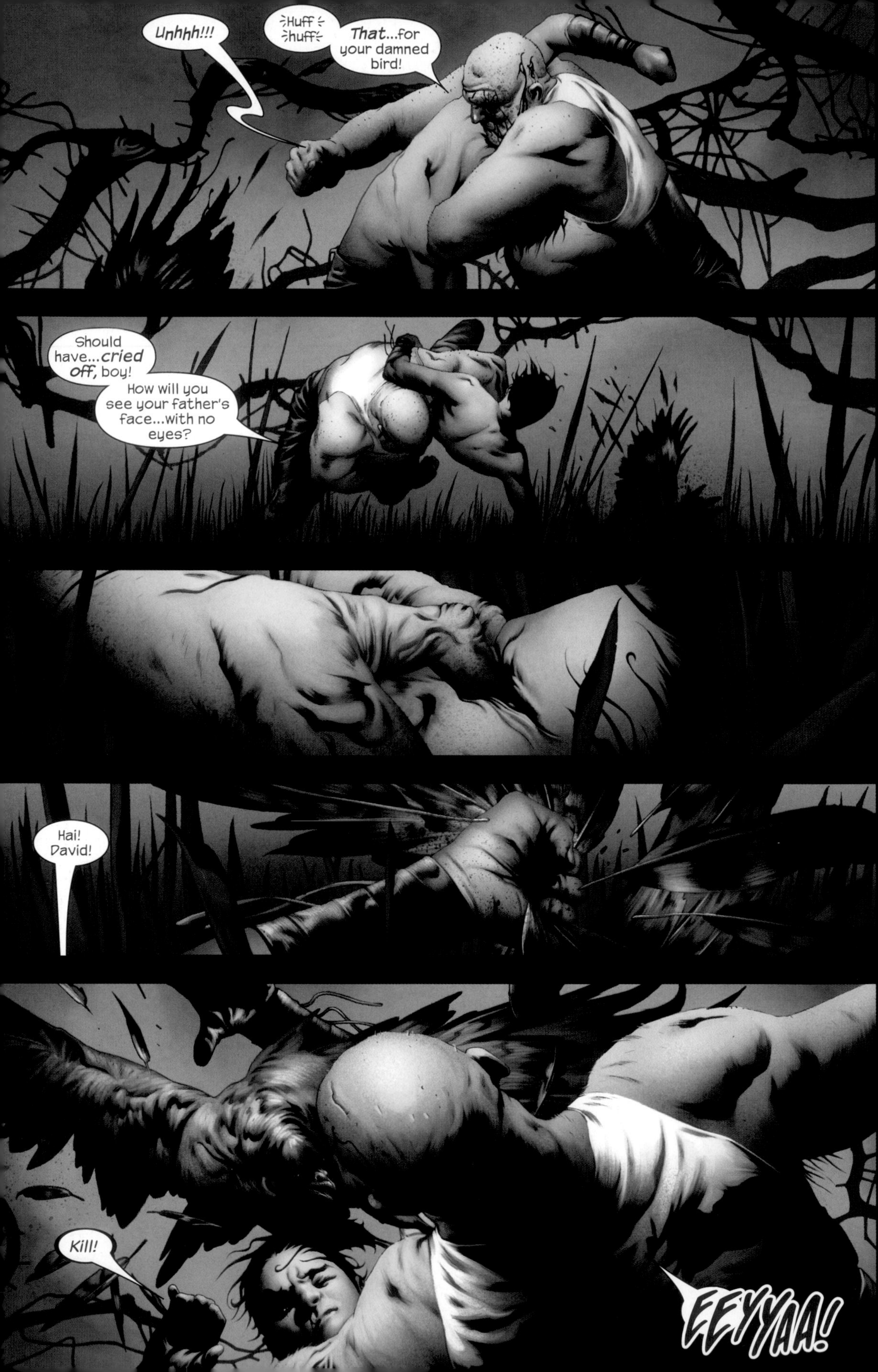
Unhhh!!!
Huff huff
That...for your damned bird!
Should have...cried off, boy!
How will you see your father's face...with no eyes?
Hai! David!
Kill!
EEYYAA!

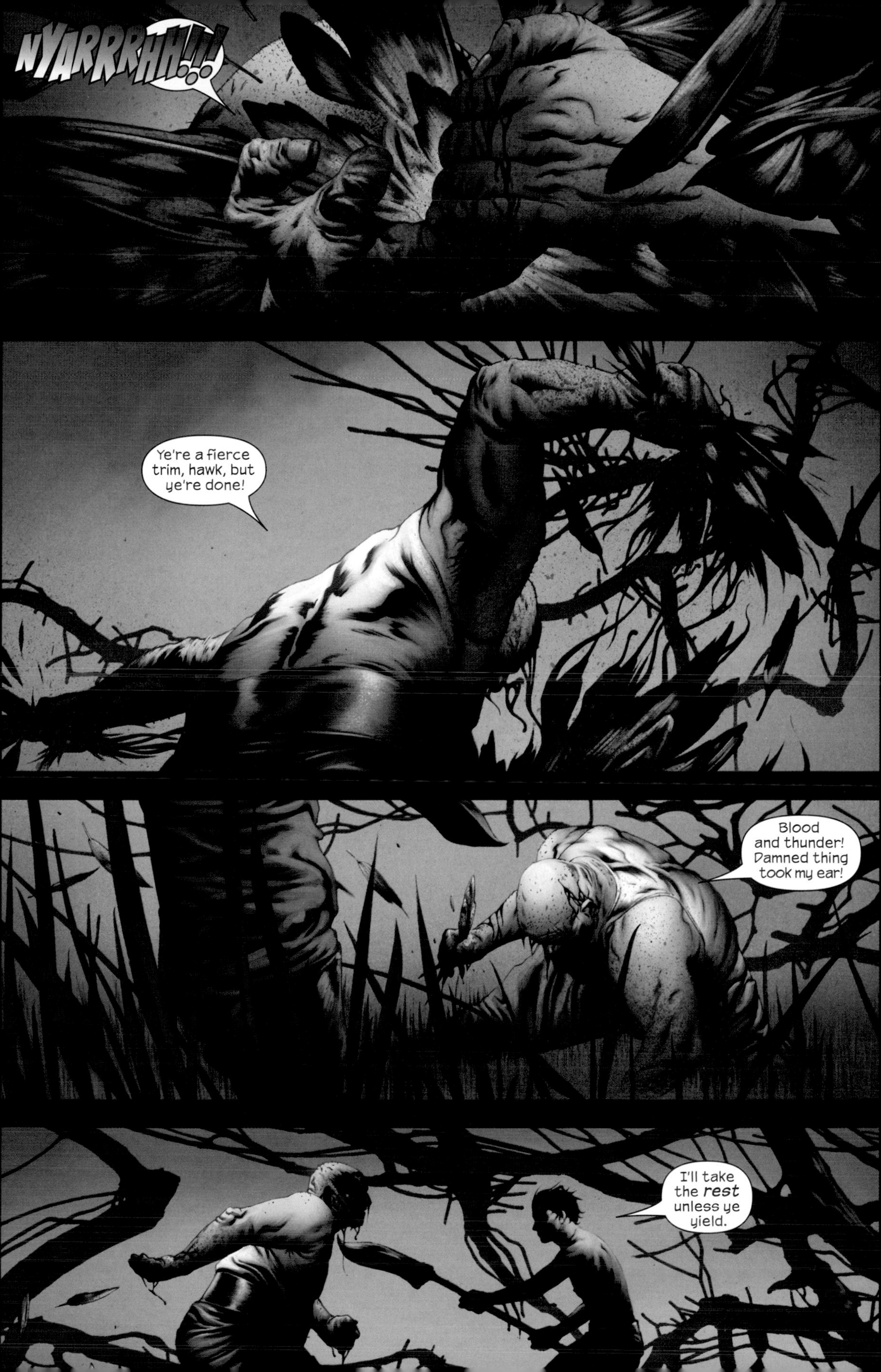
NYARRRHH!!!
Ye're a fierce trim, hawk, but ye're done!
Blood and thunder! Damned thing took my ear!
I'll take the *rest* unless ye yield.

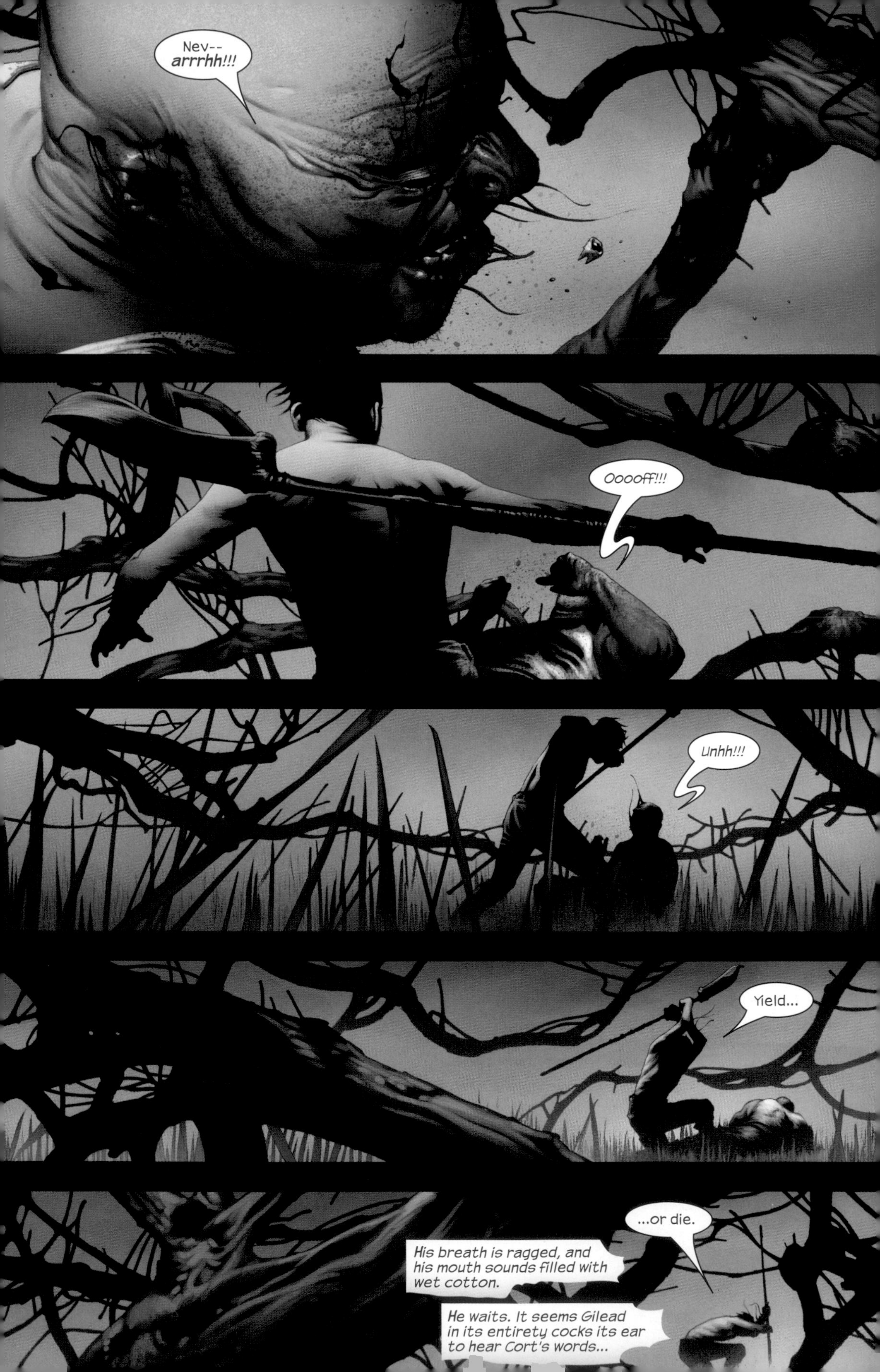
Nev-- arrrhh!!!
Ooooff!!!
Unhh!!!
Yield...
...or die.
His breath is ragged, and his mouth sounds filled with wet cotton.
He waits. It seems Gilead in its entirety cocks its ear to hear Cort's words...

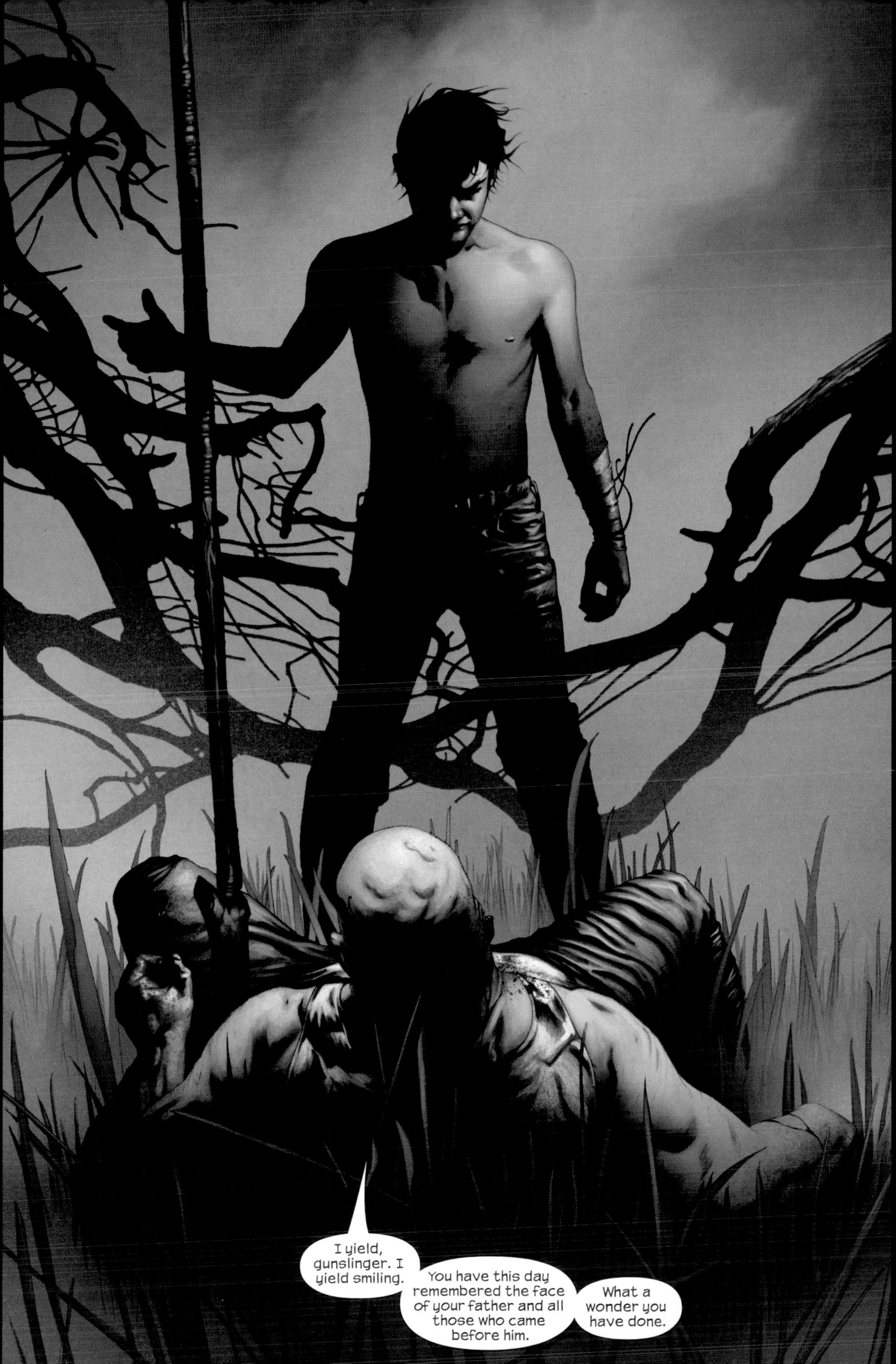
I yield, gunslinger. I yield smiling.
You have this day remembered the face of your father and all those who came before him.
What a wonder you have done.

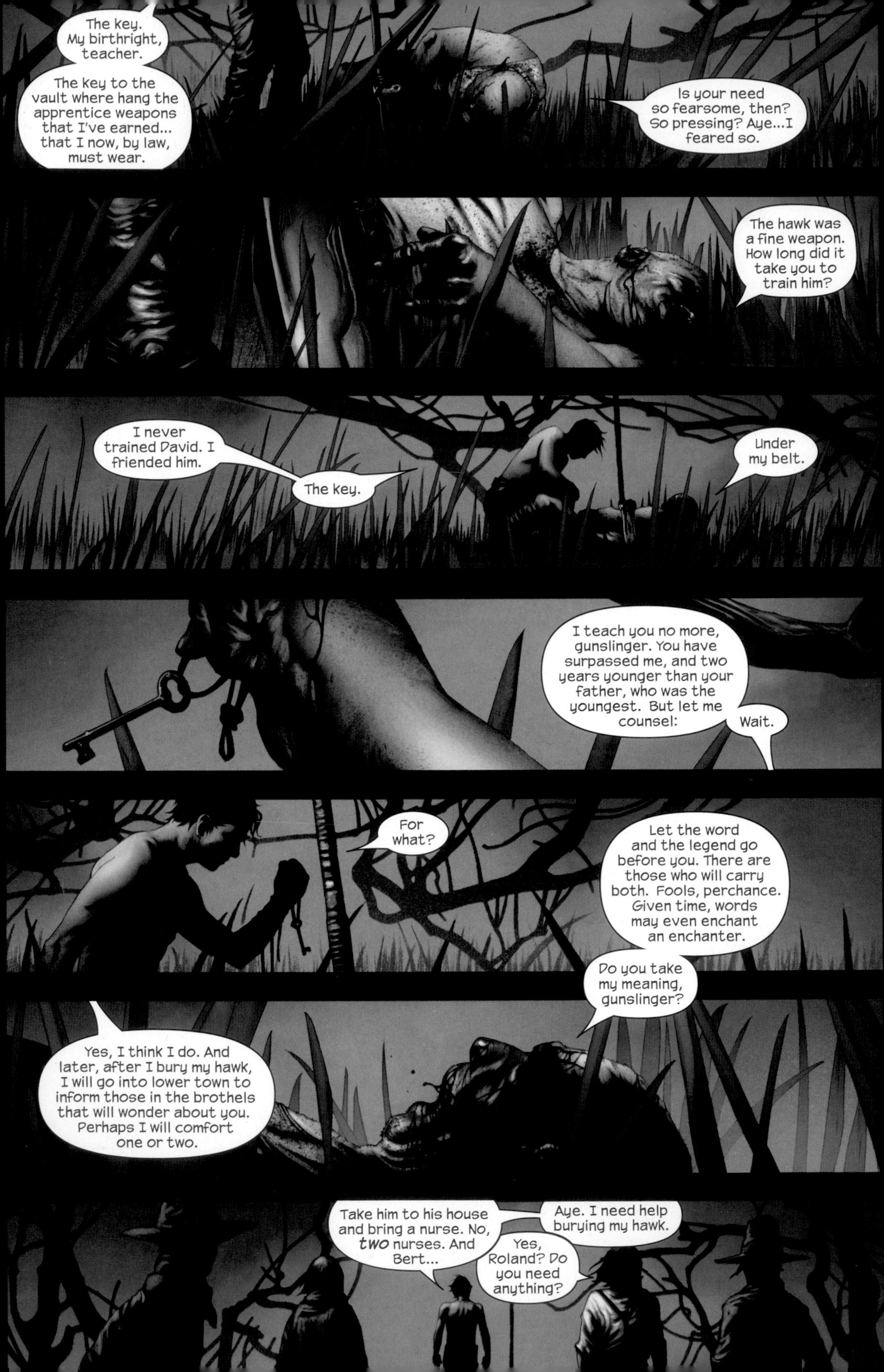
The key. My birthright, teacher.
The key to the vault where hang the apprentice weapons that I've earned... that I now, by law, must wear.
Is your need so fearsome, then? So pressing? Aye...I feared so.
The hawk was a fine weapon. How long did it take you to train him?
I never trained David. I friended him.
The key.
Under my belt.
I teach you no more, gunslinger. You have surpassed me, and two years younger than your father, who was the youngest. But let me counsel:
Wait.
For what?
Let the word and the legend go before you. There are those who will carry both. Fools, perchance. Given time, words may even enchant an enchanter.
Do you take my meaning, gunslinger?
Yes, I think I do. And later, after I bury my hawk, I will go into lower town to inform those in the brothels that will wonder about you. Perhaps I will comfort one or two.
Take him to his house and bring a nurse. No, *two* nurses. And Bert...
Yes, Roland? Do you need anything?
Aye. I need help burying my hawk.

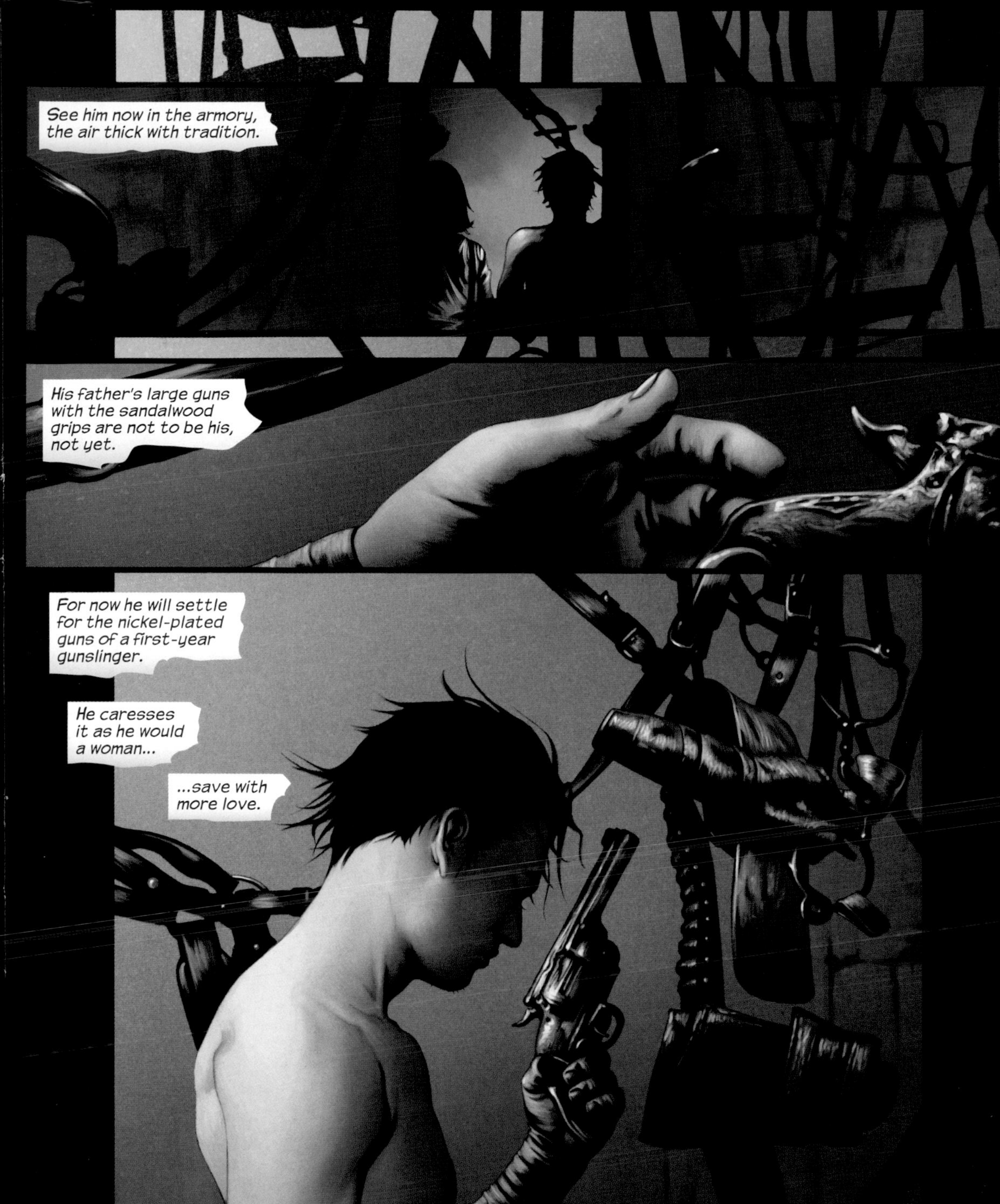
See him now in the armory, the air thick with tradition.
His father's large guns with the sandalwood grips are not to be his, not yet.
For now he will settle for the nickel-plated guns of a first-year gunslinger.
He caresses it as he would a woman...
...save with more love.

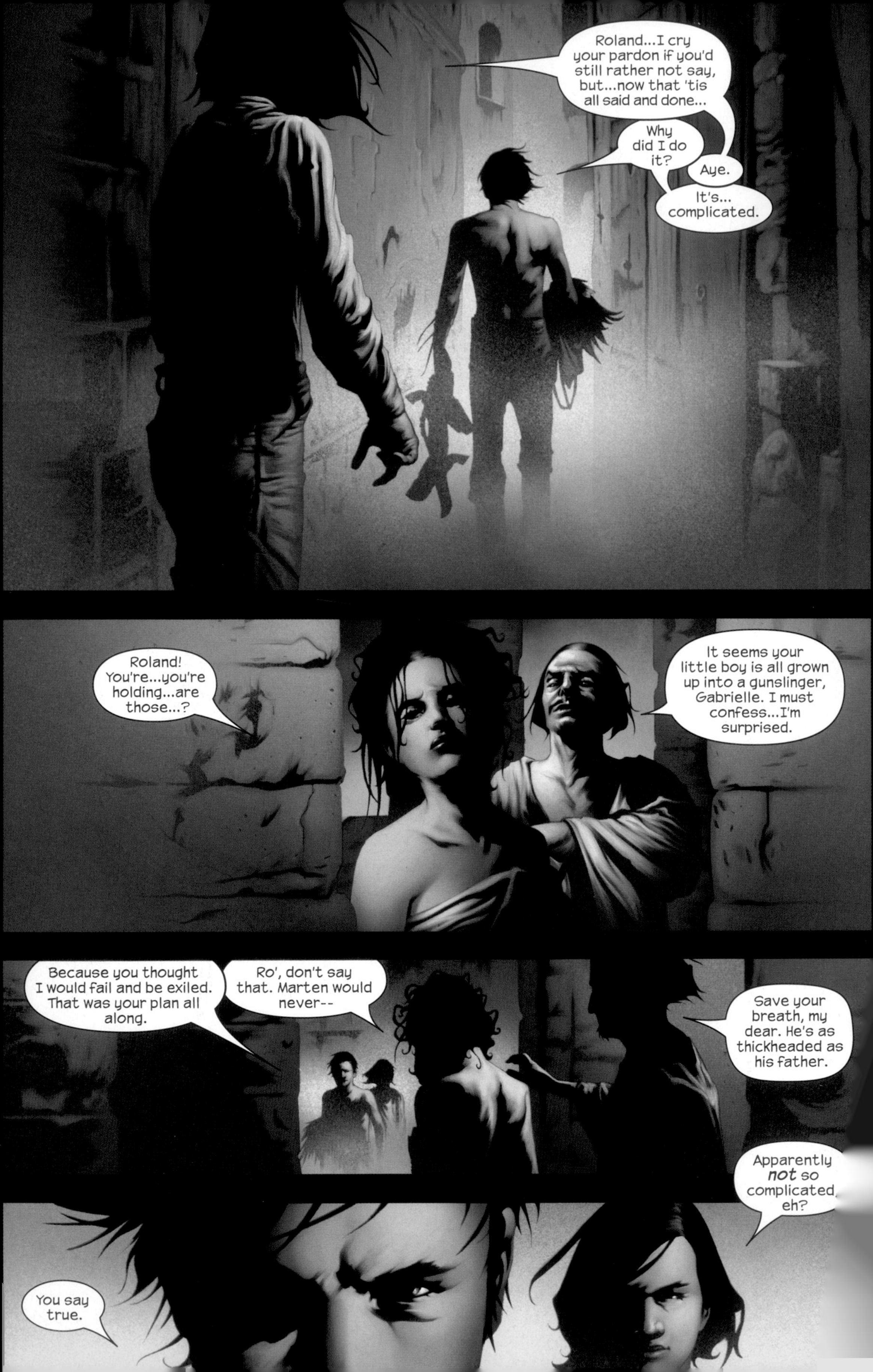

Roland...I cry your pardon if you'd still rather not say, but...now that 'tis all said and done...
Why did I do it?
Aye.
It's... complicated.
Roland! You're...you're holding...are those...?
It seems your little boy is all grown up into a gunslinger, Gabrielle. I must confess...I'm surprised.
Because you thought I would fail and be exiled. That was your plan all along.
Ro', don't say that. Marten would never--
Save your breath, my dear. He's as thickheaded as his father.
Apparently *not* so complicated, eh?
You say true.

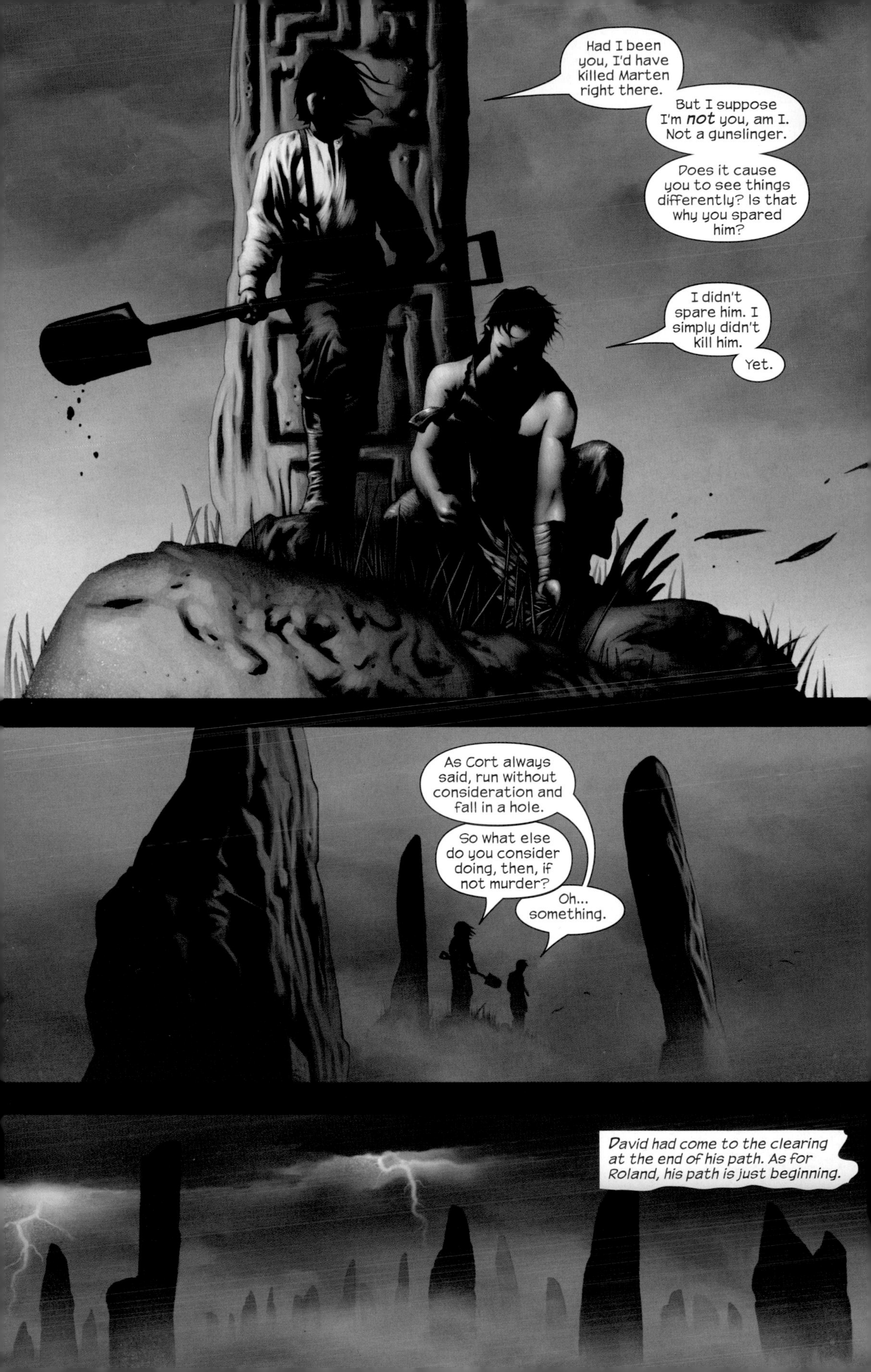
Had I been you, I'd have killed Marten right there.
But I suppose I'm **not** you, am I. Not a gunslinger.
Does it cause you to see things differently? Is that why you spared him?
I didn't spare him. I simply didn't kill him.
Yet.
As Cort always said, run without consideration and fall in a hole.
So what else do you consider doing, then, if not murder?
Oh... something.
David had come to the clearing at the end of his path. As for Roland, his path is just beginning.

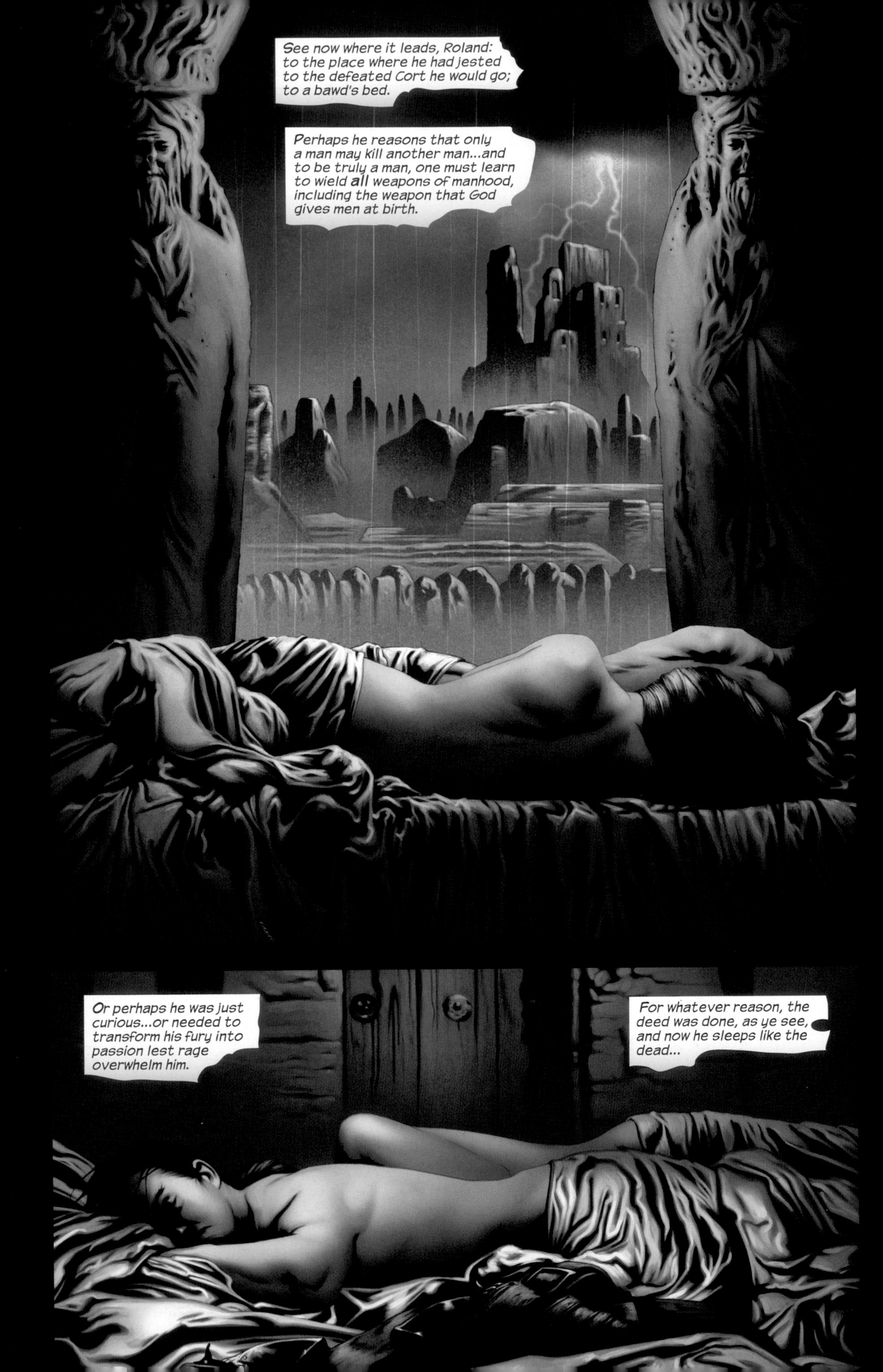
See now where it leads, Roland: to the place where he had jested to the defeated Cort he would go; to a bawd's bed.
Perhaps he reasons that only a man may kill another man...and to be truly a man, one must learn to wield **all** weapons of manhood, including the weapon that God gives men at birth.
Or perhaps he was just curious...or needed to transform his fury into passion lest rage overwhelm him.
For whatever reason, the deed was done, as ye see, and now he sleeps like the dead...

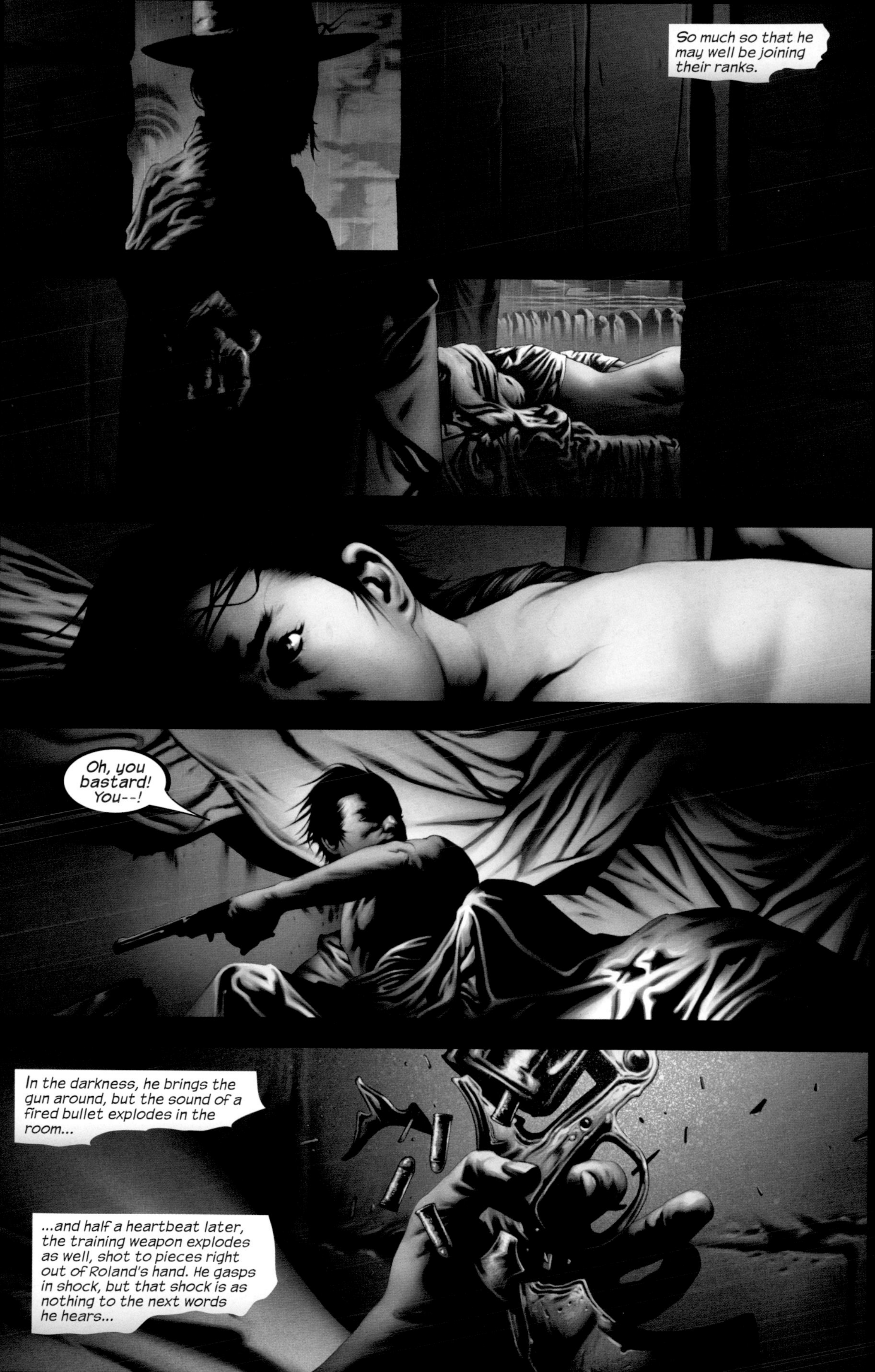
So much so that he may well be joining their ranks.
Oh, you bastard! You--!
In the darkness, he brings the gun around, but the sound of a fired bullet explodes in the room...
...and half a heartbeat later, the training weapon explodes as well, shot to pieces right out of Roland's hand. He gasps in shock, but that shock is as nothing to the next words he hears...

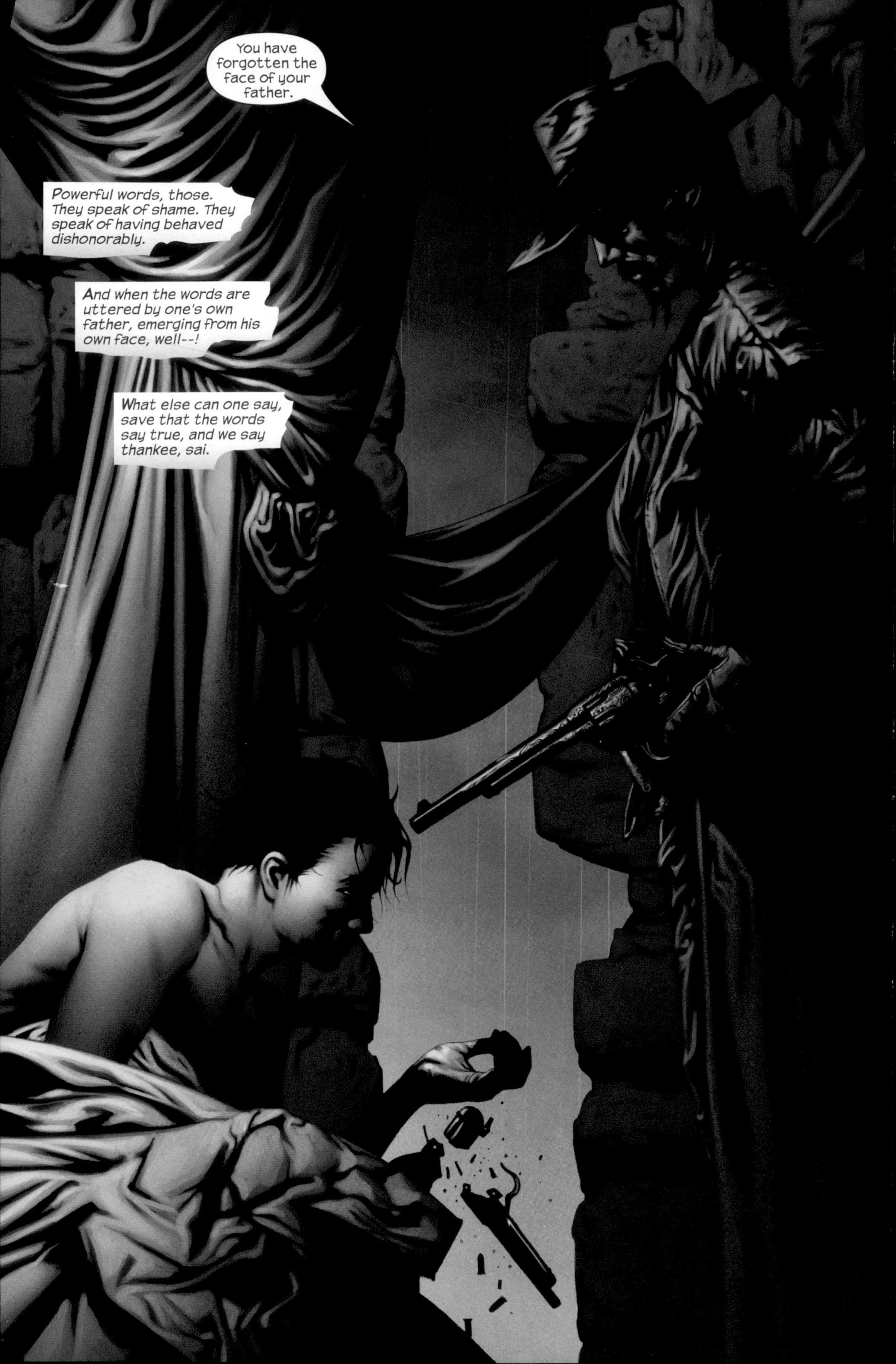
You have forgotten the face of your father.
Powerful words, those. They speak of shame. They speak of having behaved dishonorably.
And when the words are uttered by one's own father, emerging from his own face, well--!
What else can one say, save that the words say true, and we say thankee, sai.

STEPHEN KING

THE DARK TOWER

THE GUNSLINGER BORN

CHAPTER TWO

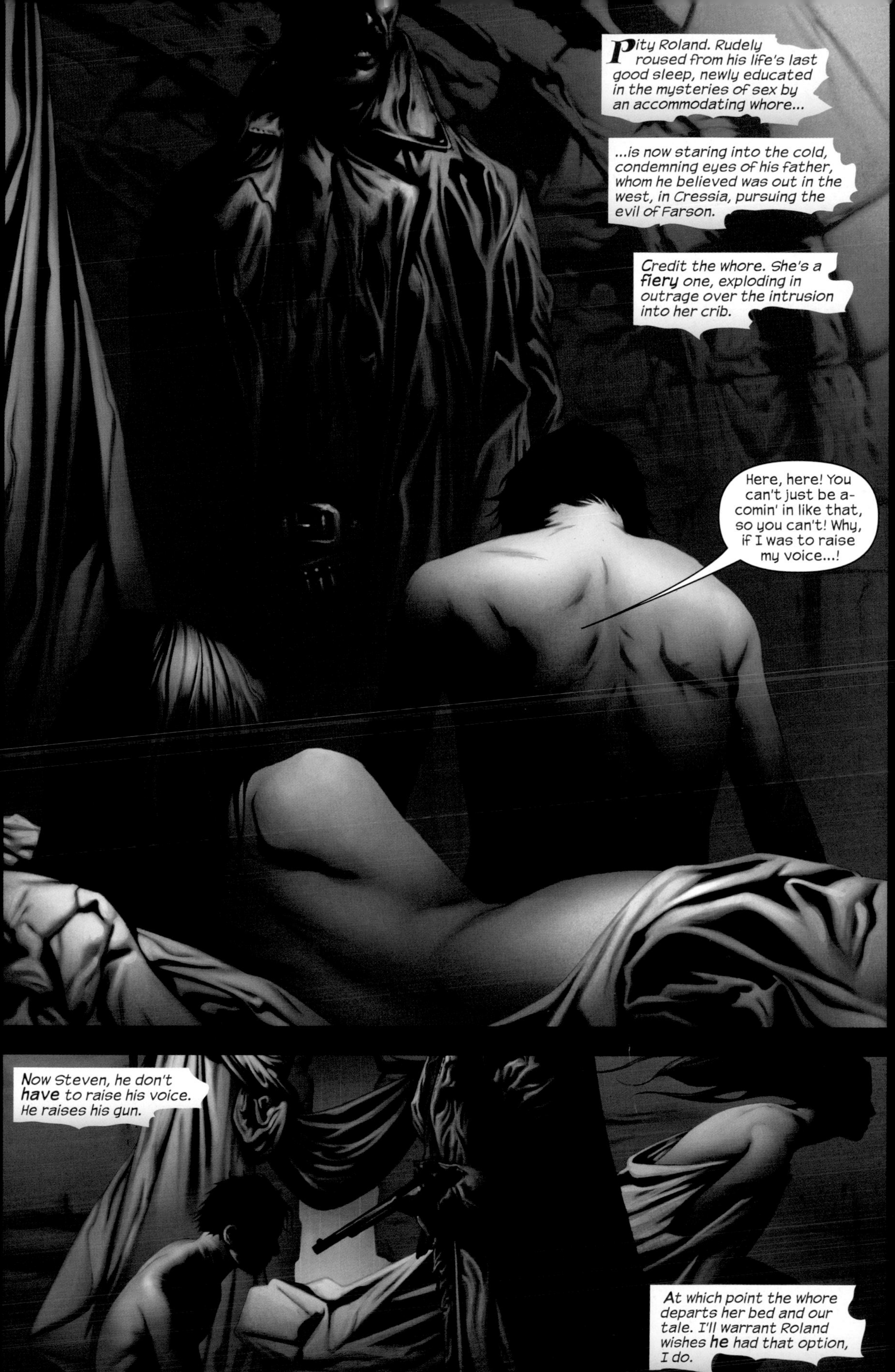
Pity Roland. Rudely roused from his life's last good sleep, newly educated in the mysteries of sex by an accommodating whore...
...is now staring into the cold, condemning eyes of his father, whom he believed was out in the west, in Cressia, pursuing the evil of Farson.
Credit the whore. She's a fiery one, exploding in outrage over the intrusion into her crib.
Here, here! You can't just be a-comin' in like that, so you can't! Why, if I was to raise my voice...!
Now Steven, he don't have to raise his voice. He raises his gun.
At which point the whore departs her bed and our tale. I'll warrant Roland wishes he had that option, I do.

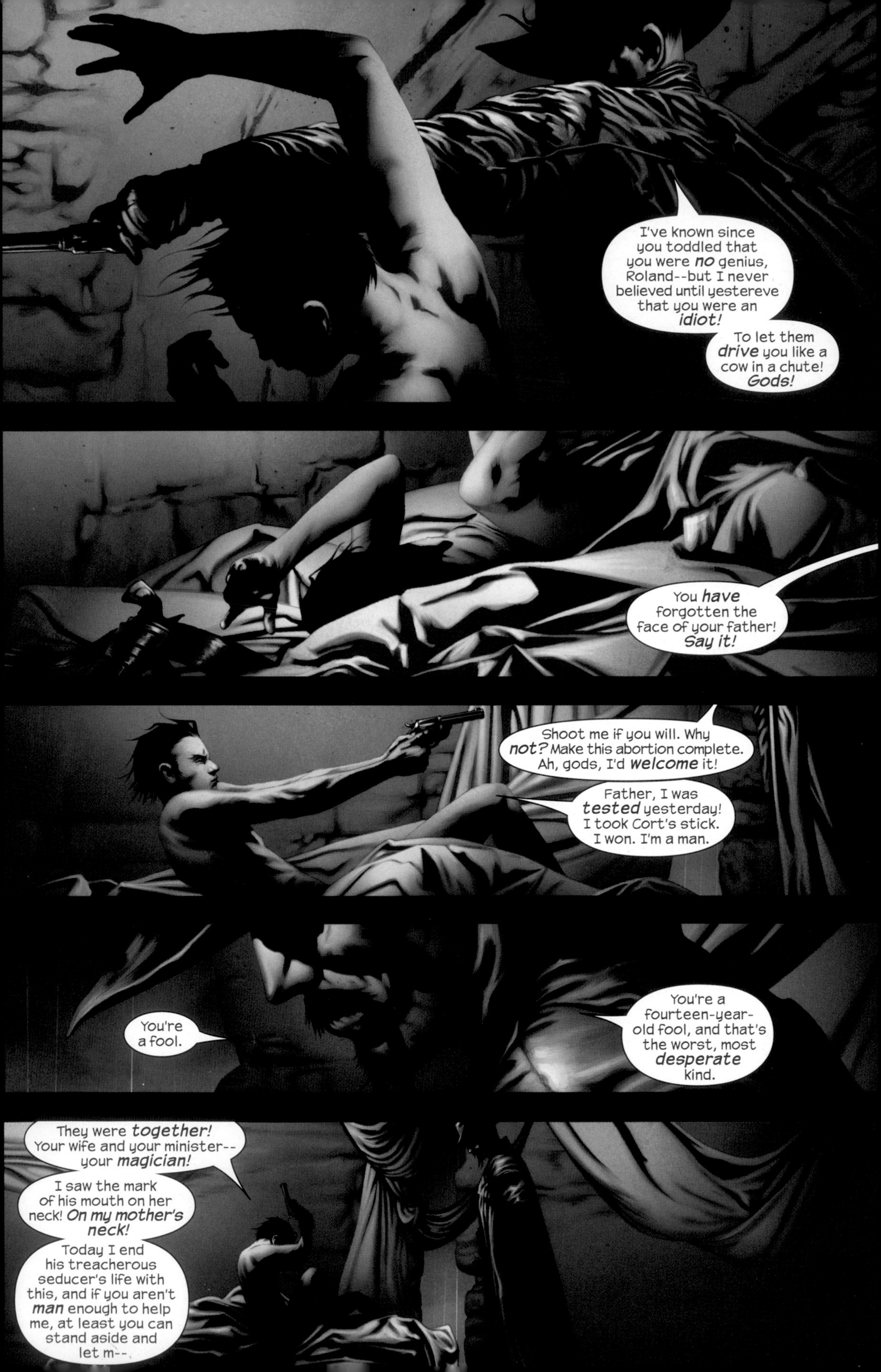
I've known since you toddled that you were *no* genius, Roland--but I never believed until yestereve that you were an *idiot!*
To let them *drive* you like a cow in a chute! *Gods!*
You *have* forgotten the face of your father! *Say it!*
Shoot me if you will. Why *not?* Make this abortion complete. Ah, gods, I'd *welcome* it!
Father, I was *tested* yesterday! I took Cort's stick. I won. I'm a man.
You're a fool.
You're a fourteen-year-old fool, and that's the worst, most *desperate* kind.
They were *together!* Your wife and your minister-- your *magician!*
I saw the mark of his mouth on her neck! *On my mother's neck!*
Today I end his treacherous seducer's life with this, and if you aren't *man* enough to help me, at least you can stand aside and let m--

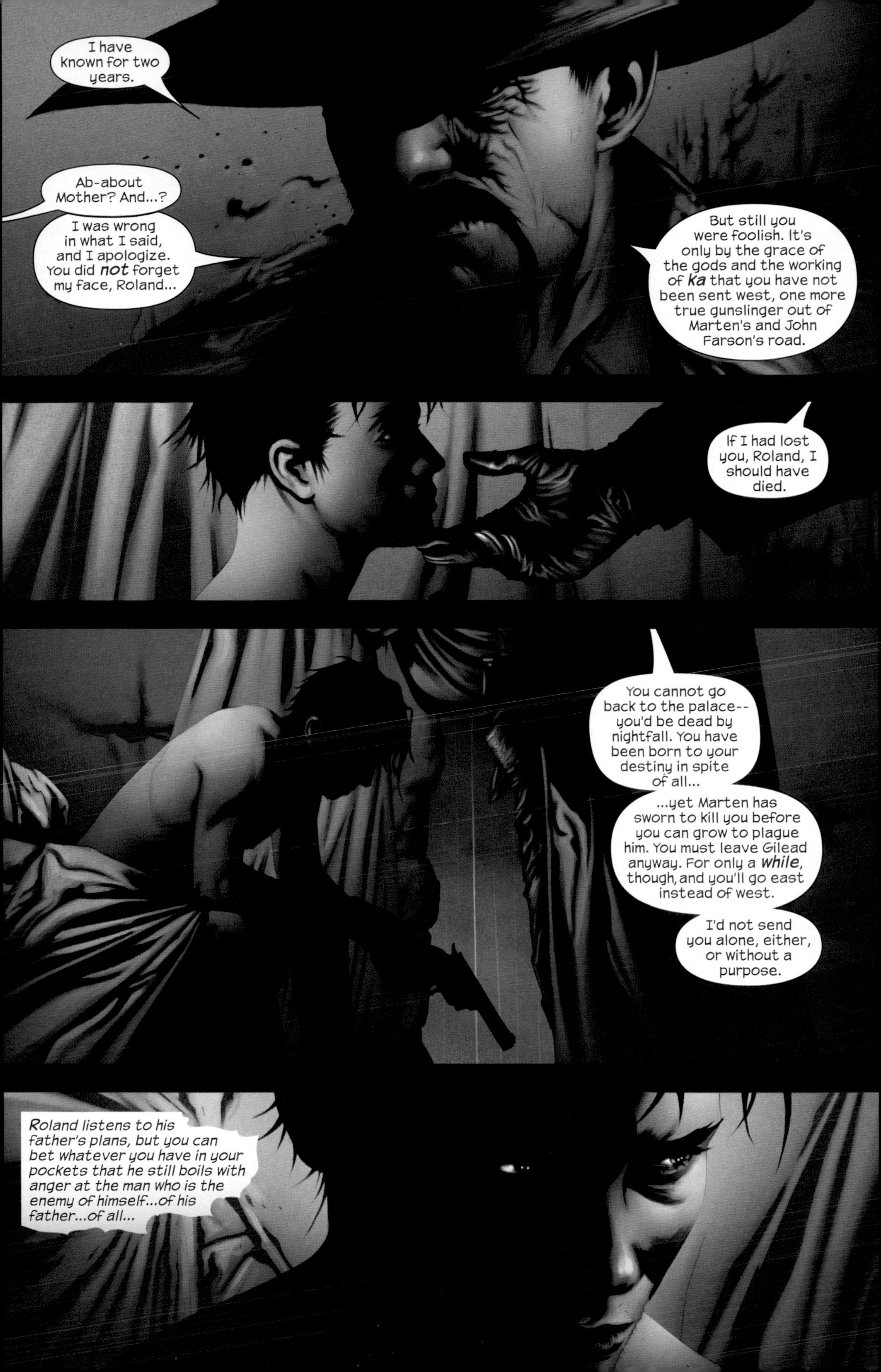

I have known for two years.
Ab-about Mother? And...?
I was wrong in what I said, and I apologize. You did *not* forget my face, Roland...
But still you were foolish. It's only by the grace of the gods and the working of *ka* that you have not been sent west, one more true gunslinger out of Marten's and John Farson's road.
If I had lost you, Roland, I should have died.
You cannot go back to the palace--you'd be dead by nightfall. You have been born to your destiny in spite of all...
...yet Marten has sworn to kill you before you can grow to plague him. You must leave Gilead anyway. For only a *while*, though, and you'll go east instead of west.
I'd not send you alone, either, or without a purpose.
Roland listens to his father's plans, but you can bet whatever you have in your pockets that he still boils with anger at the man who is the enemy of himself...of his father...of all...

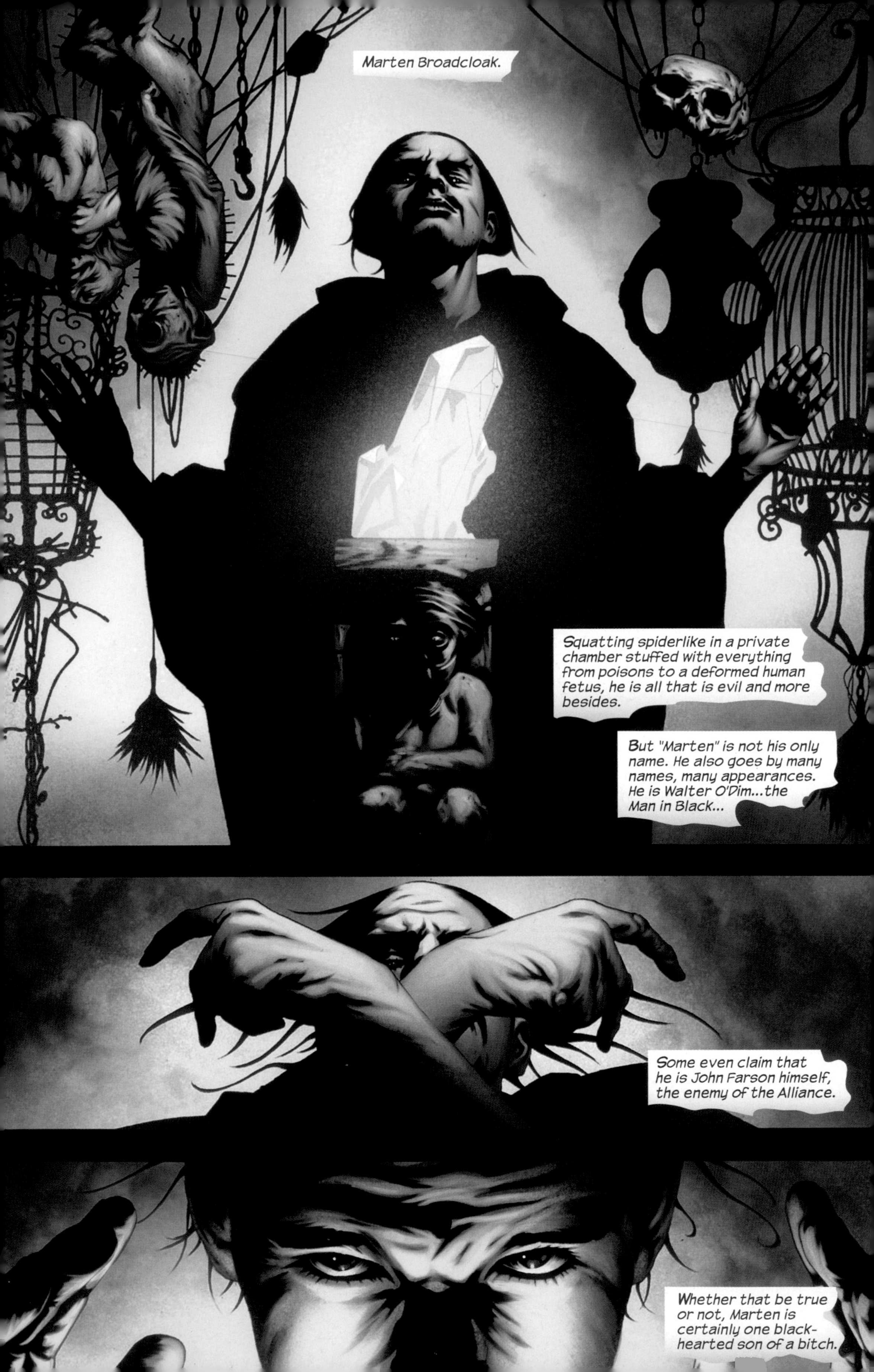
Marten Broadcloak.
Squatting spiderlike in a private chamber stuffed with everything from poisons to a deformed human fetus, he is all that is evil and more besides.
But "Marten" is not his only name. He also goes by many names, many appearances. He is Walter O'Dim...the Man in Black...
Some even claim that he is John Farson himself, the enemy of the Alliance.
Whether that be true or not, Marten is certainly one black-hearted son of a bitch.

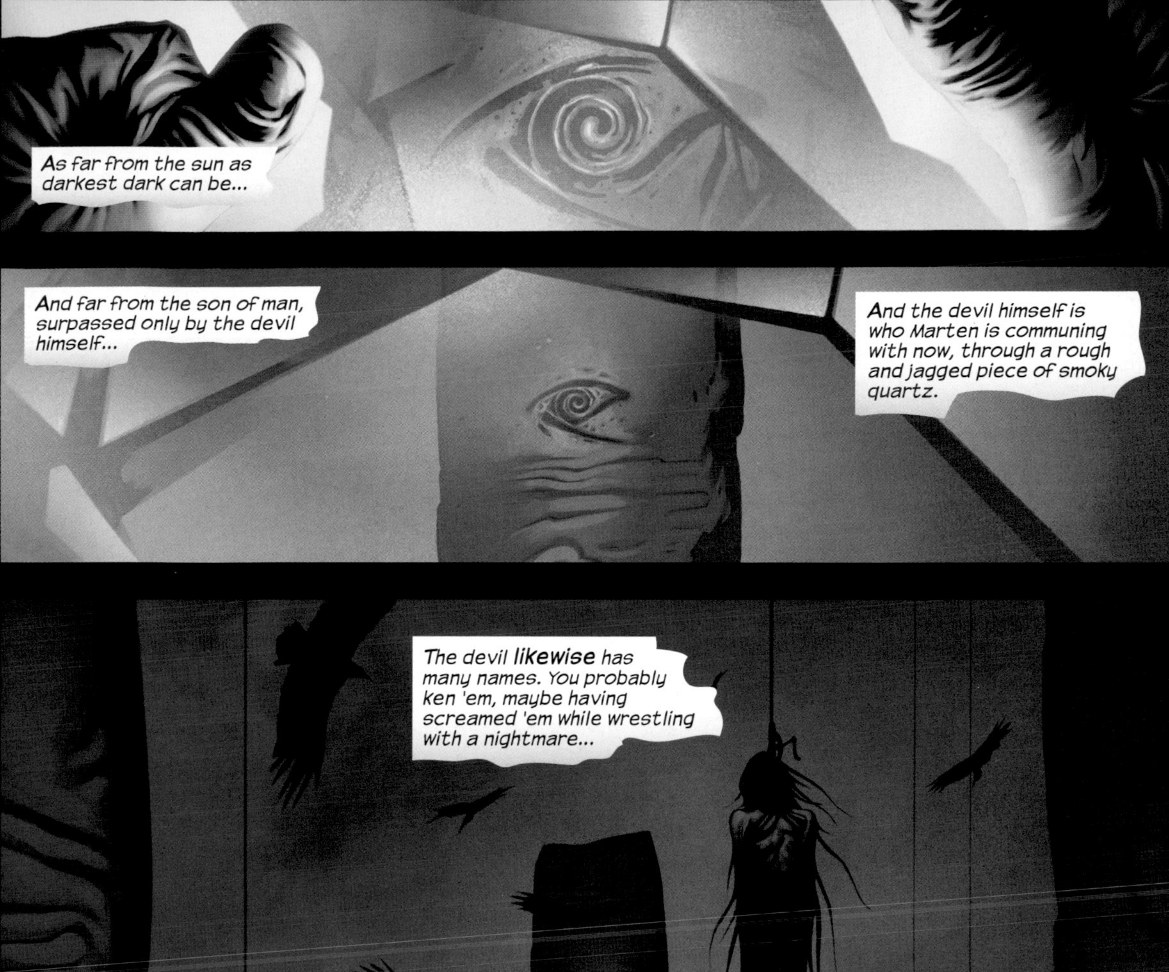
As far from the sun as darkest dark can be...
And far from the son of man, surpassed only by the devil himself...
And the devil himself is who Marten is communing with now, through a rough and jagged piece of smoky quartz.
The devil likewise has many names. You probably ken 'em, maybe having screamed 'em while wrestling with a nightmare...

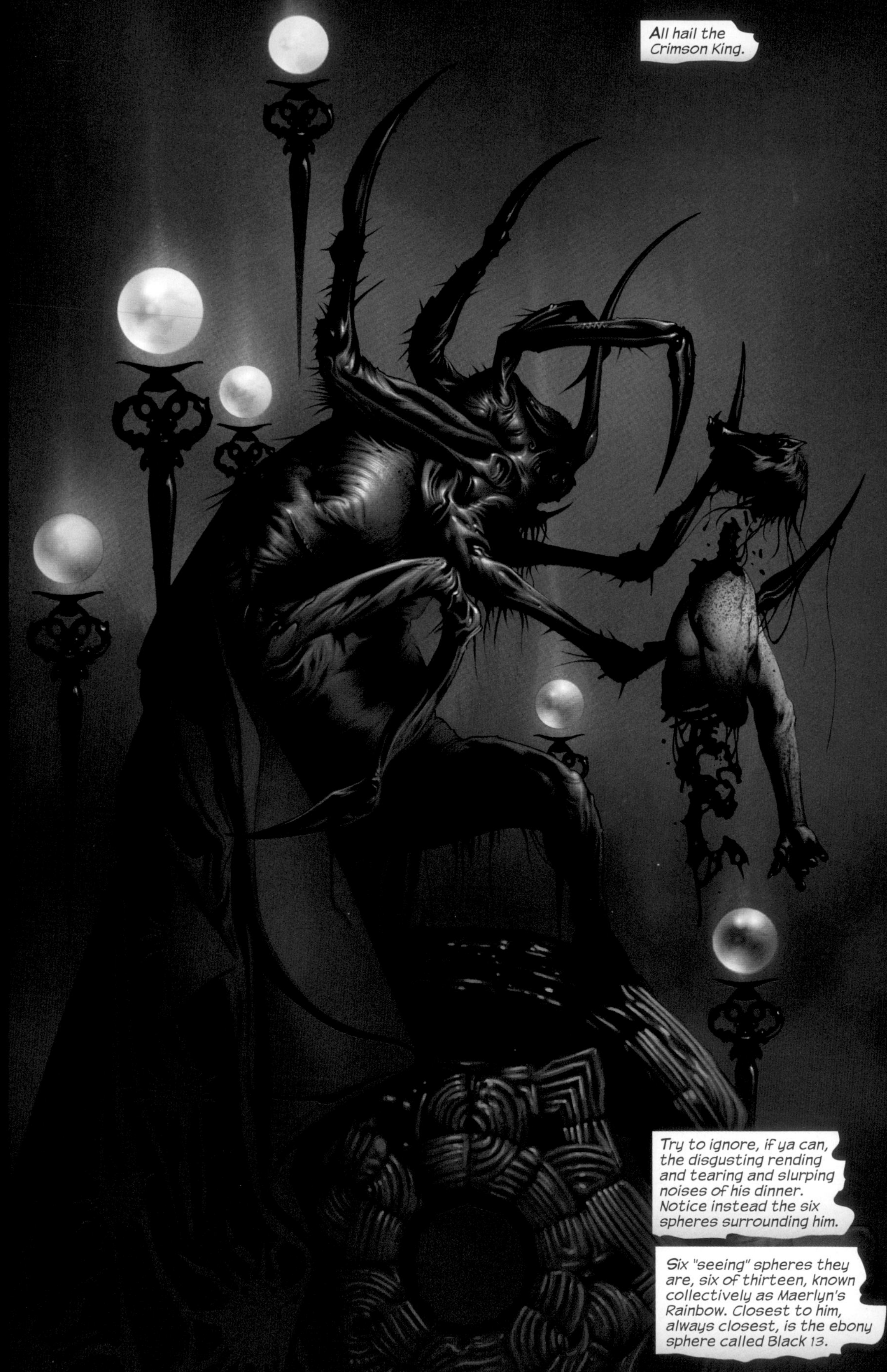
All hail the Crimson King.
Try to ignore, if ya can, the disgusting rending and tearing and slurping noises of his dinner. Notice instead the six spheres surrounding him.
Six "seeing" spheres they are, six of thirteen, known collectively as Maerlyn's Rainbow. Closest to him, always closest, is the ebony sphere called Black 13.

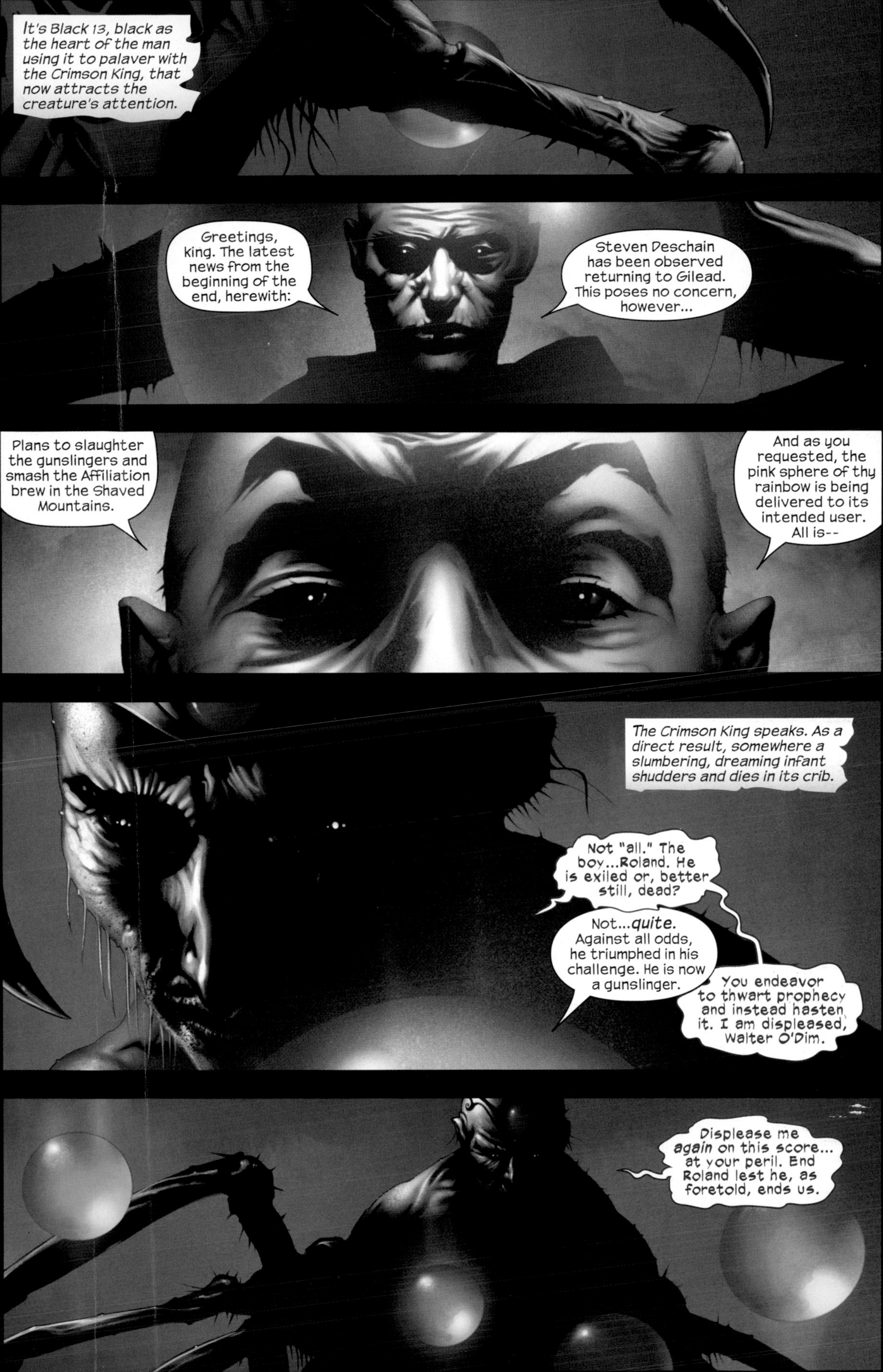
It's Black 13, black as the heart of the man using it to palaver with the Crimson King, that now attracts the creature's attention.
Greetings, King. The latest news from the beginning of the end, herewith:
Steven Deschain has been observed returning to Gilead. This poses no concern, however...
Plans to slaughter the gunslingers and smash the Affiliation brew in the Shaved Mountains.
And as you requested, the pink sphere of thy rainbow is being delivered to its intended user. All is--
The Crimson King speaks. As a direct result, somewhere a slumbering, dreaming infant shudders and dies in its crib.
Not "all." The boy...Roland. He is exiled or, better still, dead?
Not...*quite.* Against all odds, he triumphed in his challenge. He is now a gunslinger.
You endeavor to thwart prophecy and instead hasten it. I am displeased, Walter O'Dim.
Displease me *again* on this score... at your peril. End Roland lest he, as foretold, ends us.

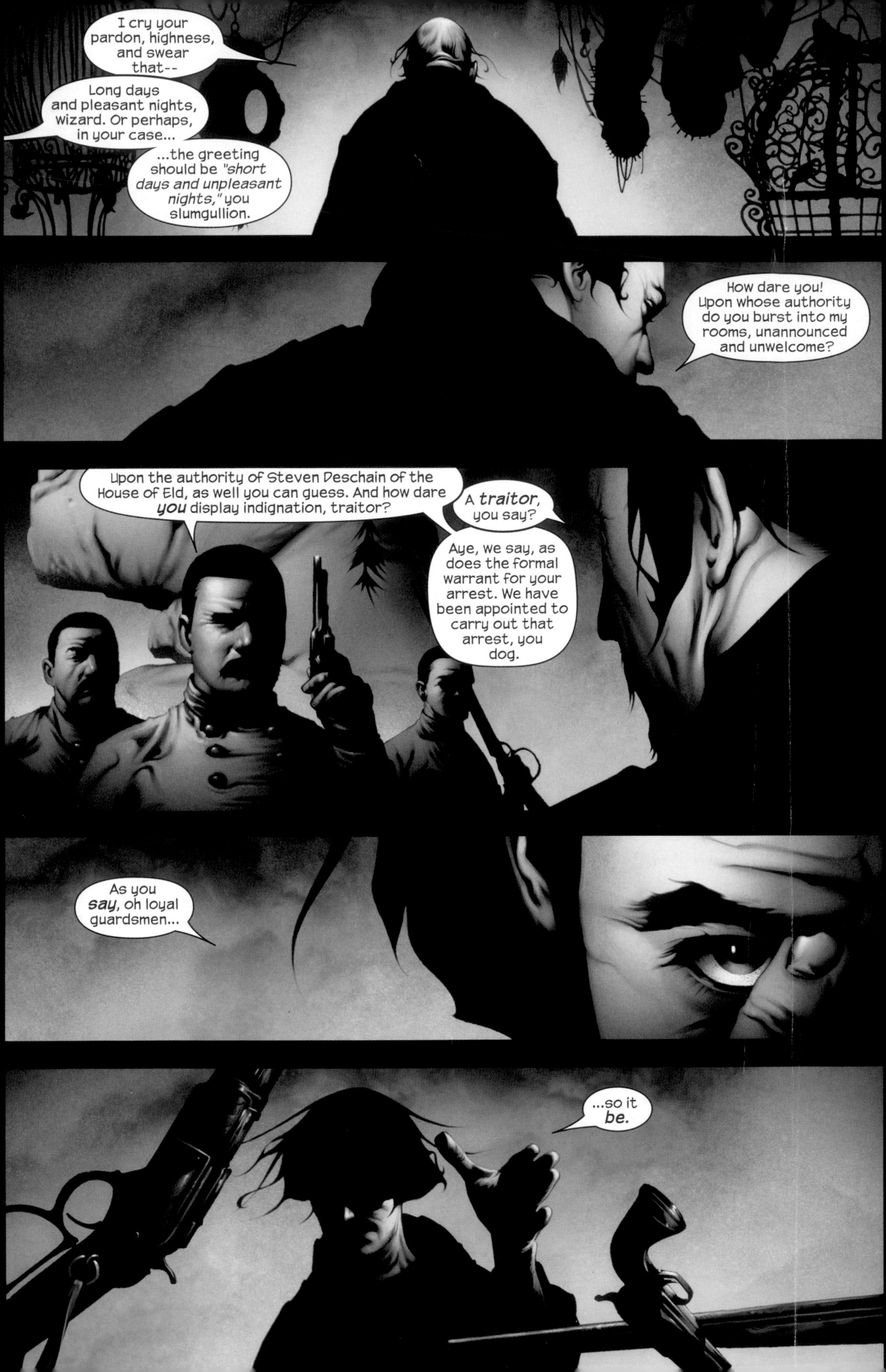
I cry your pardon, highness, and swear that--
Long days and pleasant nights, wizard. Or perhaps, in your case...
...the greeting should be "short days and unpleasant nights," you slumgullion.
How dare you! Upon whose authority do you burst into my rooms, unannounced and unwelcome?
Upon the authority of Steven Deschain of the House of Eld, as well you can guess. And how dare you display indignation, traitor?
A traitor, you say?
Aye, we say, as does the formal warrant for your arrest. We have been appointed to carry out that arrest, you dog.
As you say, oh loyal guardsmen...
...so it be.

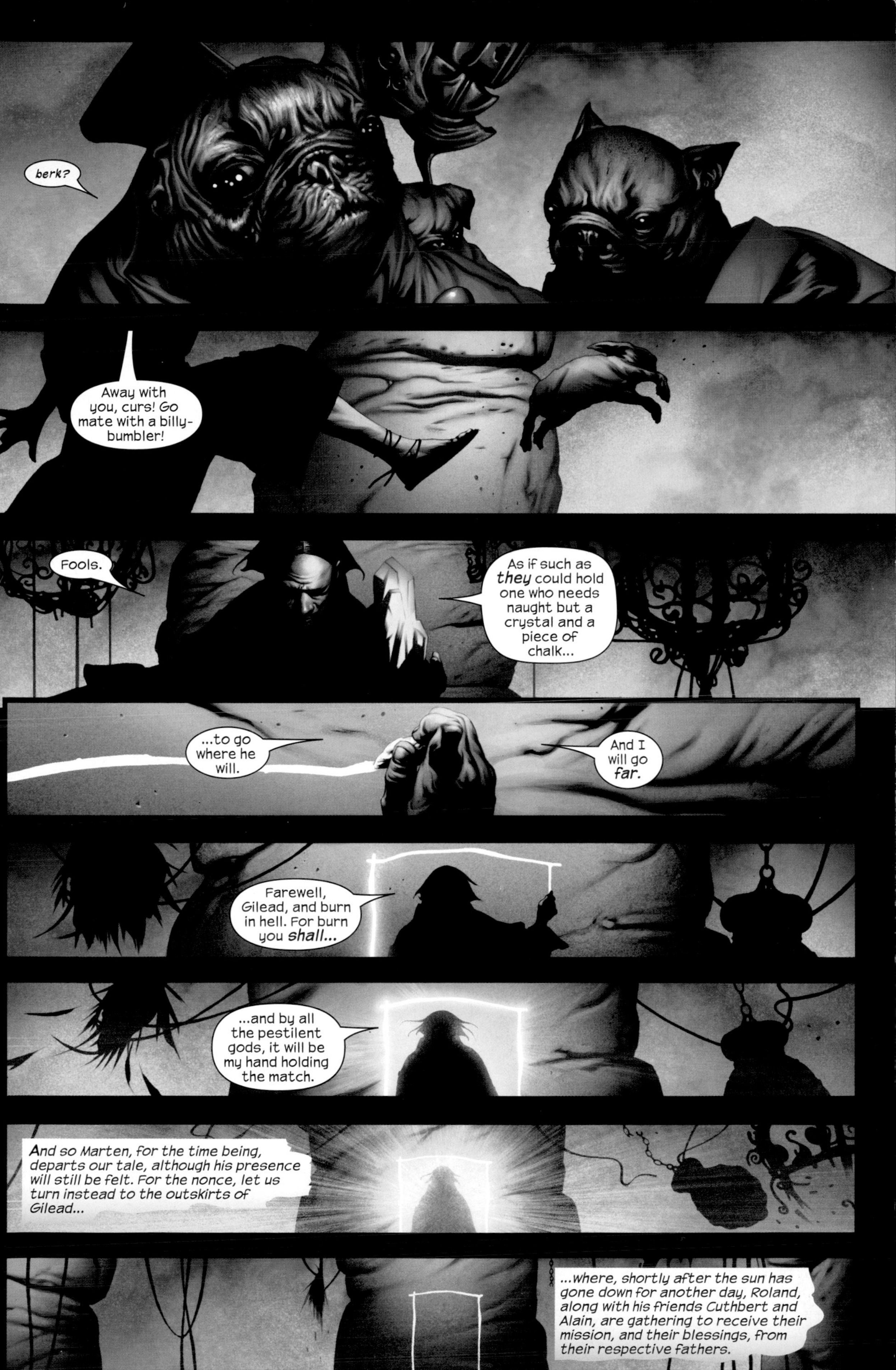
berk?
Away with you, curs! Go mate with a billy-bumbler!
Fools.
As if such as *they* could hold one who needs naught but a crystal and a piece of chalk...
...to go where he will.
And I will go *far.*
Farewell, Gilead, and burn in hell. For burn you *shall...*
...and by all the pestilent gods, it will be my hand holding the match.
And so Marten, for the time being, departs our tale, although his presence will still be felt. For the nonce, let us turn instead to the outskirts of Gilead...
...where, shortly after the sun has gone down for another day, Roland, along with his friends Cuthbert and Alain, are gathering to receive their mission, and their blessings, from their respective fathers.

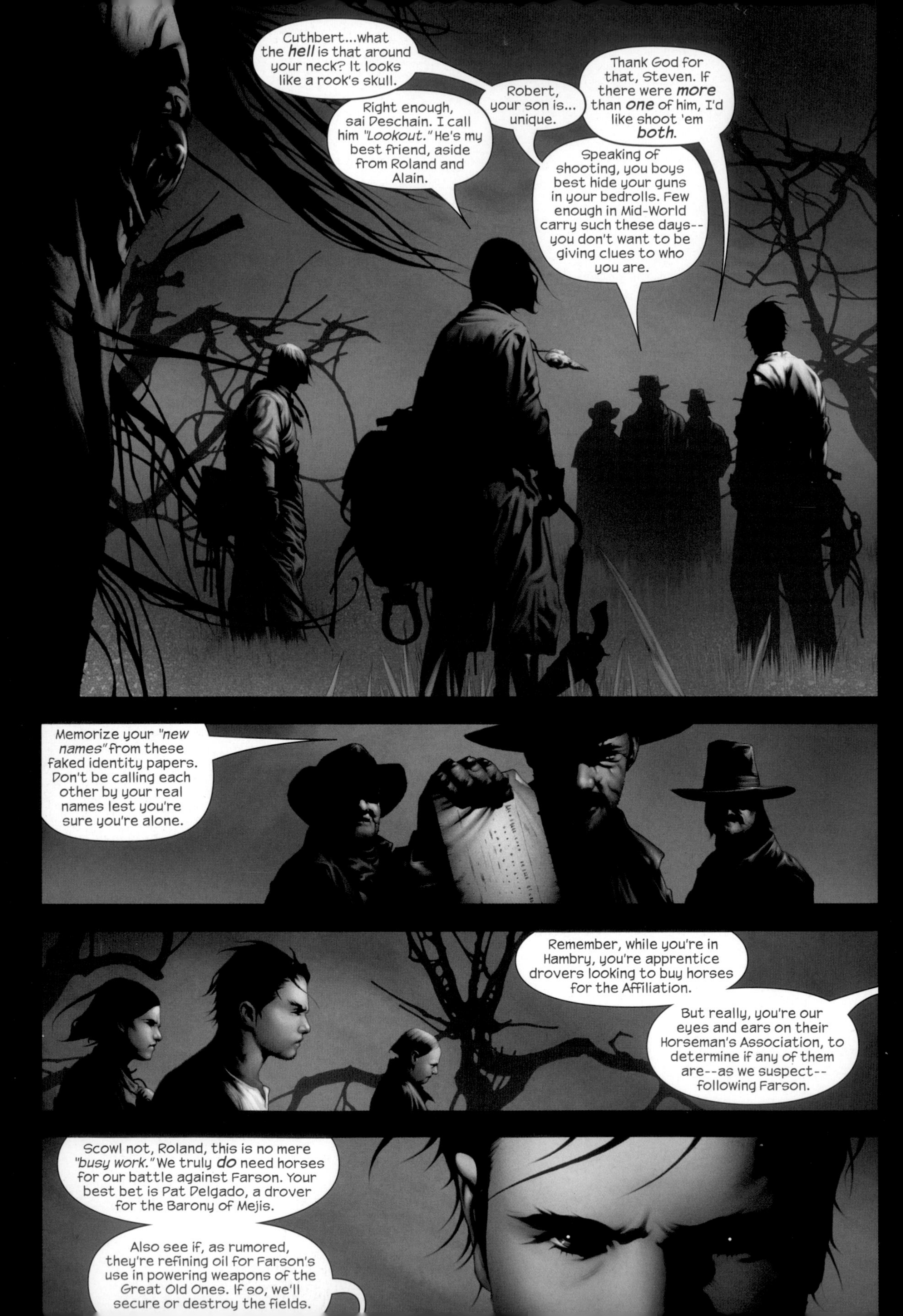

Cuthbert...what the *hell* is that around your neck? It looks like a rook's skull.
Right enough, sai Deschain. I call him *"Lookout."* He's my best friend, aside from Roland and Alain.
Robert, your son is... unique.
Thank God for that, Steven. If there were *more* than *one* of him, I'd like shoot 'em *both*.
Speaking of shooting, you boys best hide your guns in your bedrolls. Few enough in Mid-World carry such these days--you don't want to be giving clues to who you are.
Memorize your *"new names"* from these faked identity papers. Don't be calling each other by your real names lest you're sure you're alone.
Remember, while you're in Hambry, you're apprentice drovers looking to buy horses for the Affiliation.
But really, you're our eyes and ears on their Horseman's Association, to determine if any of them are--as we suspect--following Farson.
Scowl not, Roland, this is no mere *"busy work."* We truly *do* need horses for our battle against Farson. Your best bet is Pat Delgado, a drover for the Barony of Mejis.
Also see if, as rumored, they're refining oil for Farson's use in powering weapons of the Great Old Ones. If so, we'll secure or destroy the fields.

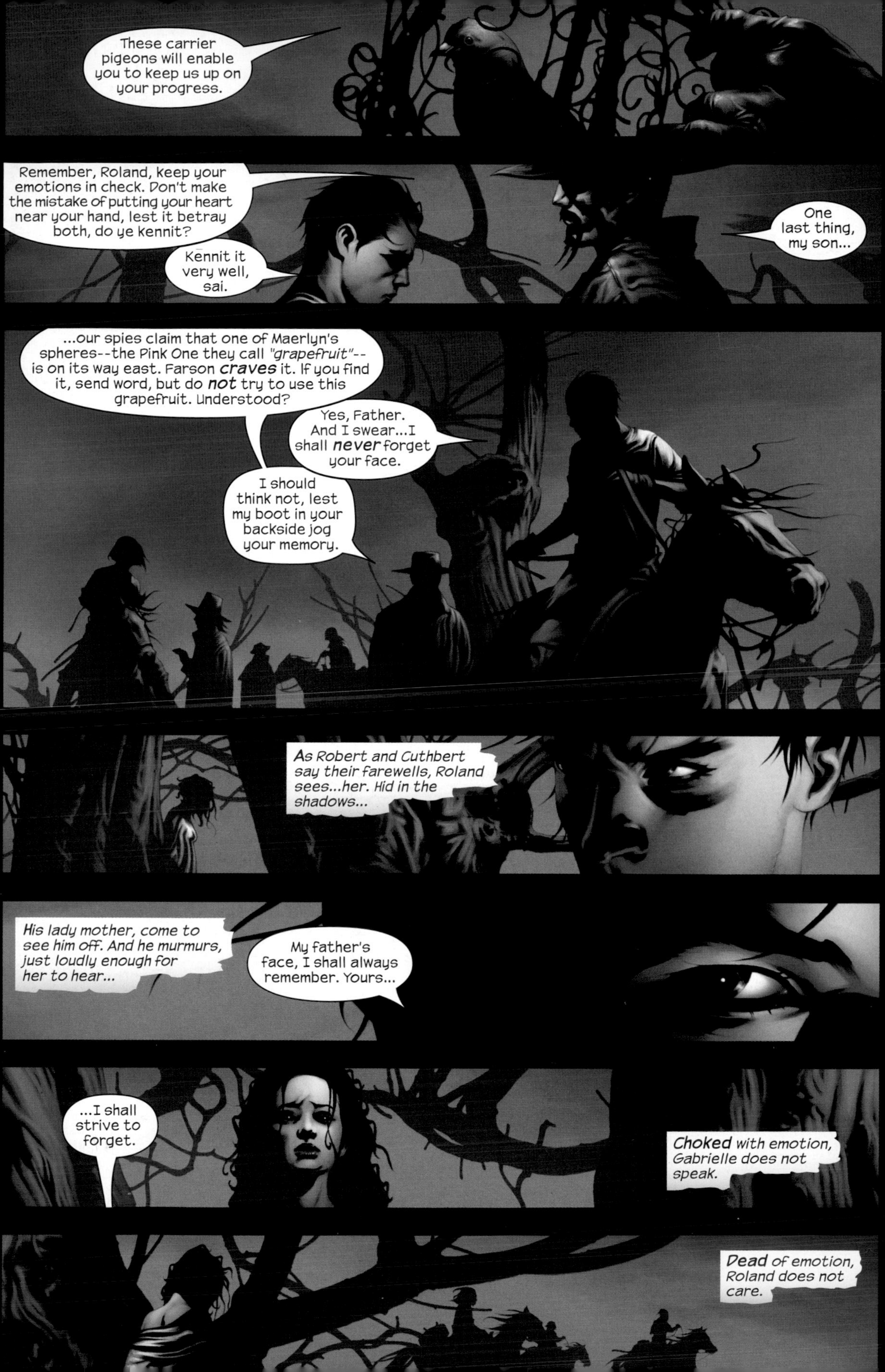

These carrier pigeons will enable you to keep us up on your progress.
Remember, Roland, keep your emotions in check. Don't make the mistake of putting your heart near your hand, lest it betray both, do ye kennit?
Kennit it very well, sai.
One last thing, my son...
...our spies claim that one of Maerlyn's spheres--the Pink One they call "grapefruit"--is on its way east. Farson craves it. If you find it, send word, but do not try to use this grapefruit. Understood?
Yes, Father. And I swear...I shall never forget your face.
I should think not, lest my boot in your backside jog your memory.
As Robert and Cuthbert say their farewells, Roland sees...her. Hid in the shadows...
His lady mother, come to see him off. And he murmurs, just loudly enough for her to hear...
My father's face, I shall always remember. Yours...
...I shall strive to forget.
Choked with emotion, Gabrielle does not speak.
Dead of emotion, Roland does not care.

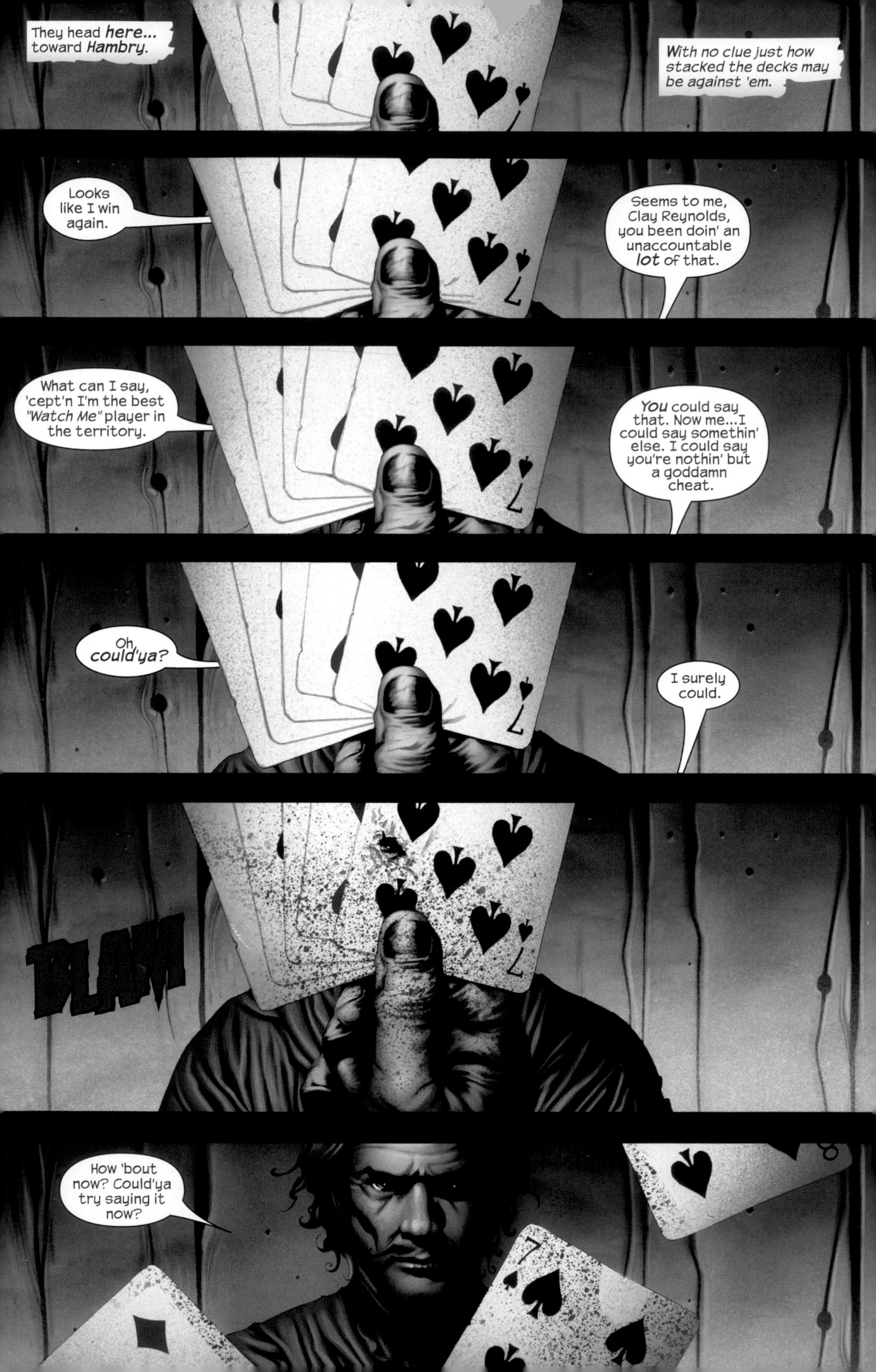

They head here... toward Hambry.
With no clue just how stacked the decks may be against 'em.
Looks like I win again.
Seems to me, Clay Reynolds, you been doin' an unaccountable lot of that.
What can I say, 'cept'n I'm the best "Watch Me" player in the territory.
You could say that. Now me...I could say somethin' else. I could say you're nothin' but a goddamn cheat.
Oh, could'ya?
I surely could.
BLAM
How 'bout now? Could'ya try saying it now?

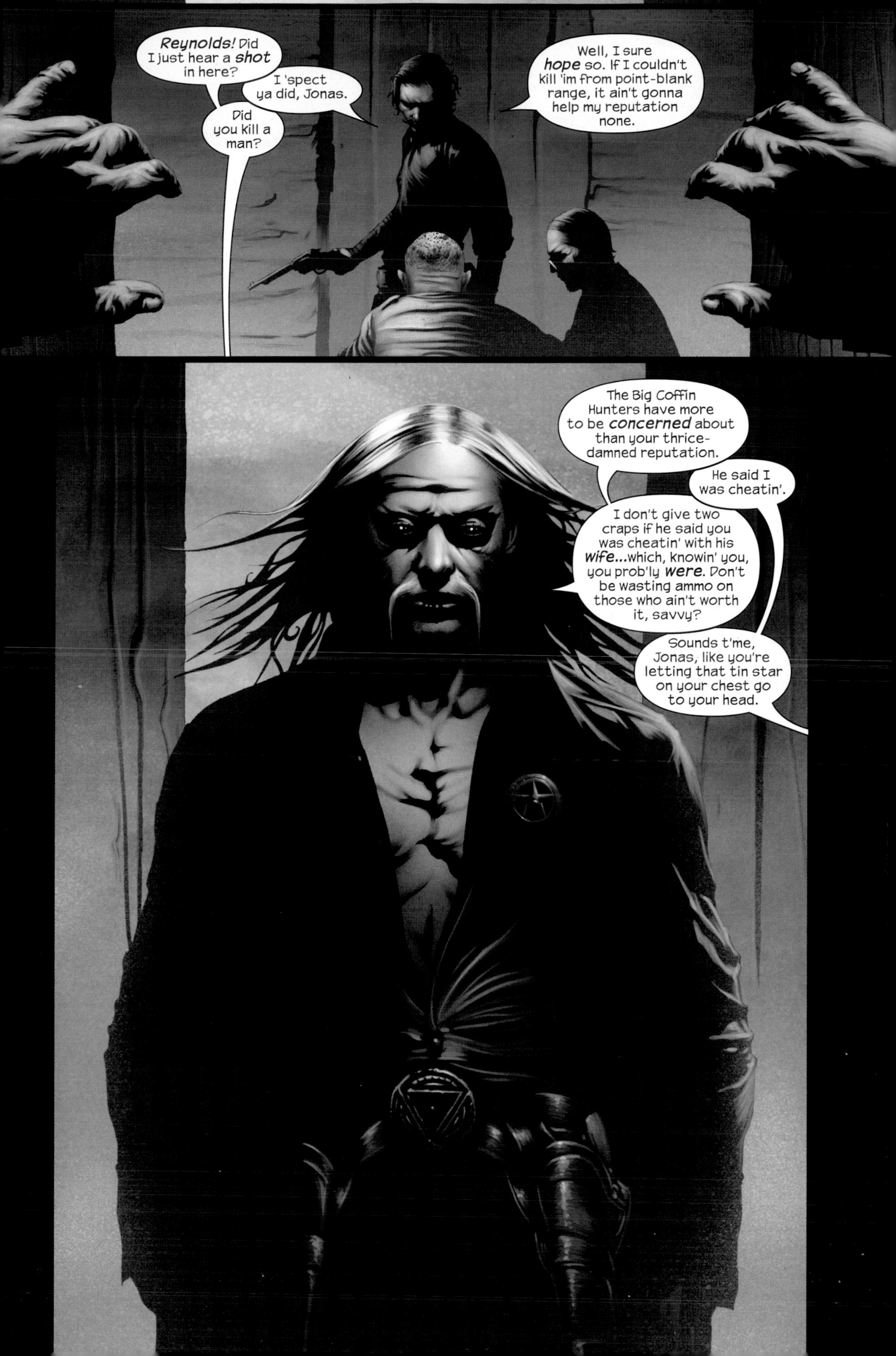
Reynolds! Did I just hear a shot in here?
Did you kill a man?
I 'spect ya did, Jonas.
Well, I sure hope so. If I couldn't kill 'im from point-blank range, it ain't gonna help my reputation none.
The Big Coffin Hunters have more to be concerned about than your thrice-damned reputation.
He said I was cheatin'.
I don't give two craps if he said you was cheatin' with his wife...which, knowin' you, you prob'ly were. Don't be wasting ammo on those who ain't worth it, savvy?
Sounds t'me, Jonas, like you're letting that tin star on your chest go to your head.

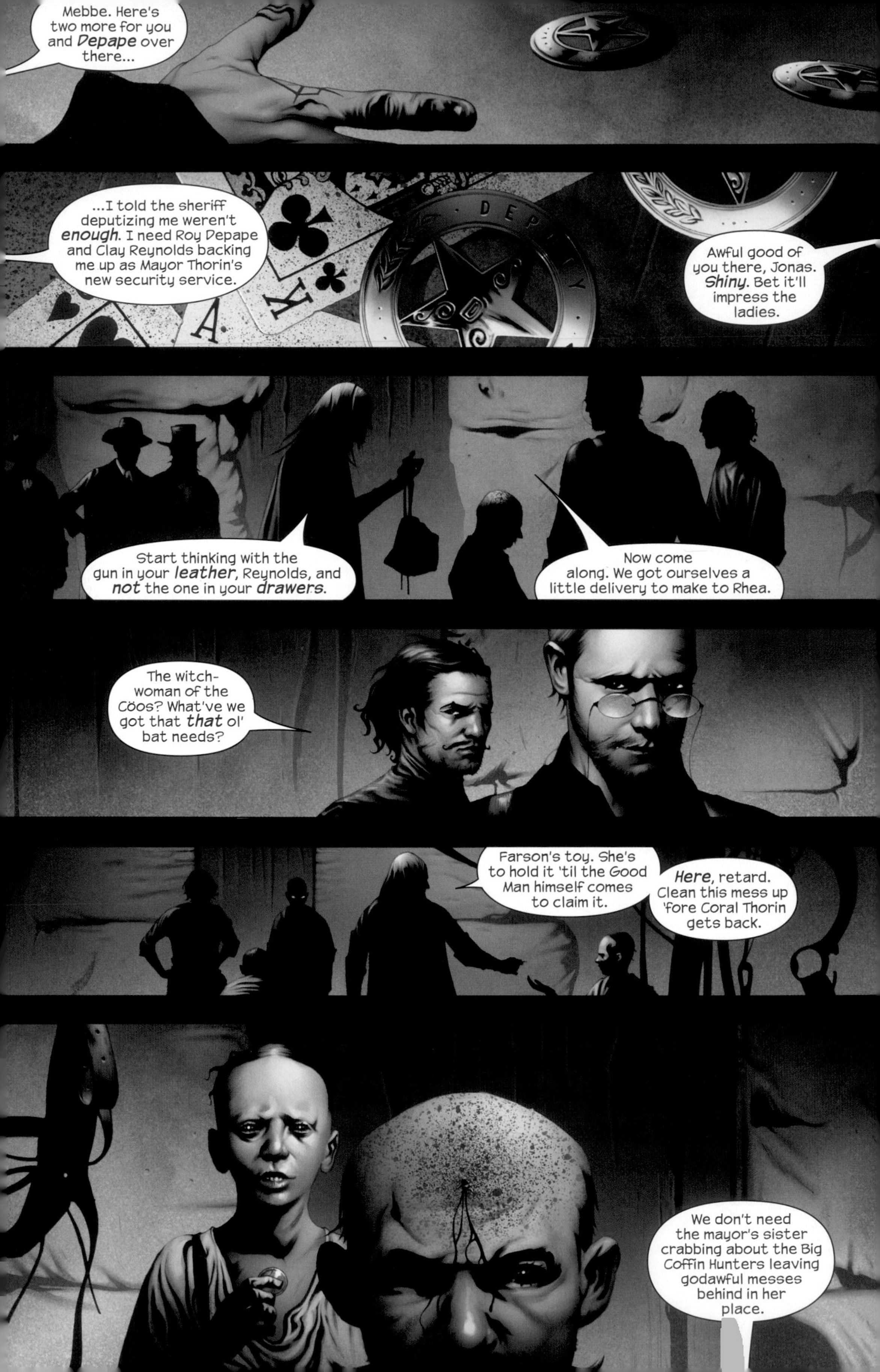
Mebbe. Here's two more for you and *Depape* over there...
...I told the sheriff deputizing me weren't **enough**. I need Roy Depape and Clay Reynolds backing me up as Mayor Thorin's new security service.
DEPUTY
Awful good of you there, Jonas. ***Shiny***. Bet it'll impress the ladies.
Start thinking with the gun in your ***leather***, Reynolds, and ***not*** the one in your ***drawers***.
Now come along. We got ourselves a little delivery to make to Rhea.
The witch-woman of the Cöos? What've we got that ***that*** ol' bat needs?
Farson's toy. She's to hold it 'til the Good Man himself comes to claim it.
Here, retard. Clean this mess up 'fore Coral Thorin gets back.
We don't need the mayor's sister crabbing about the Big Coffin Hunters leaving godawful messes behind in her place.

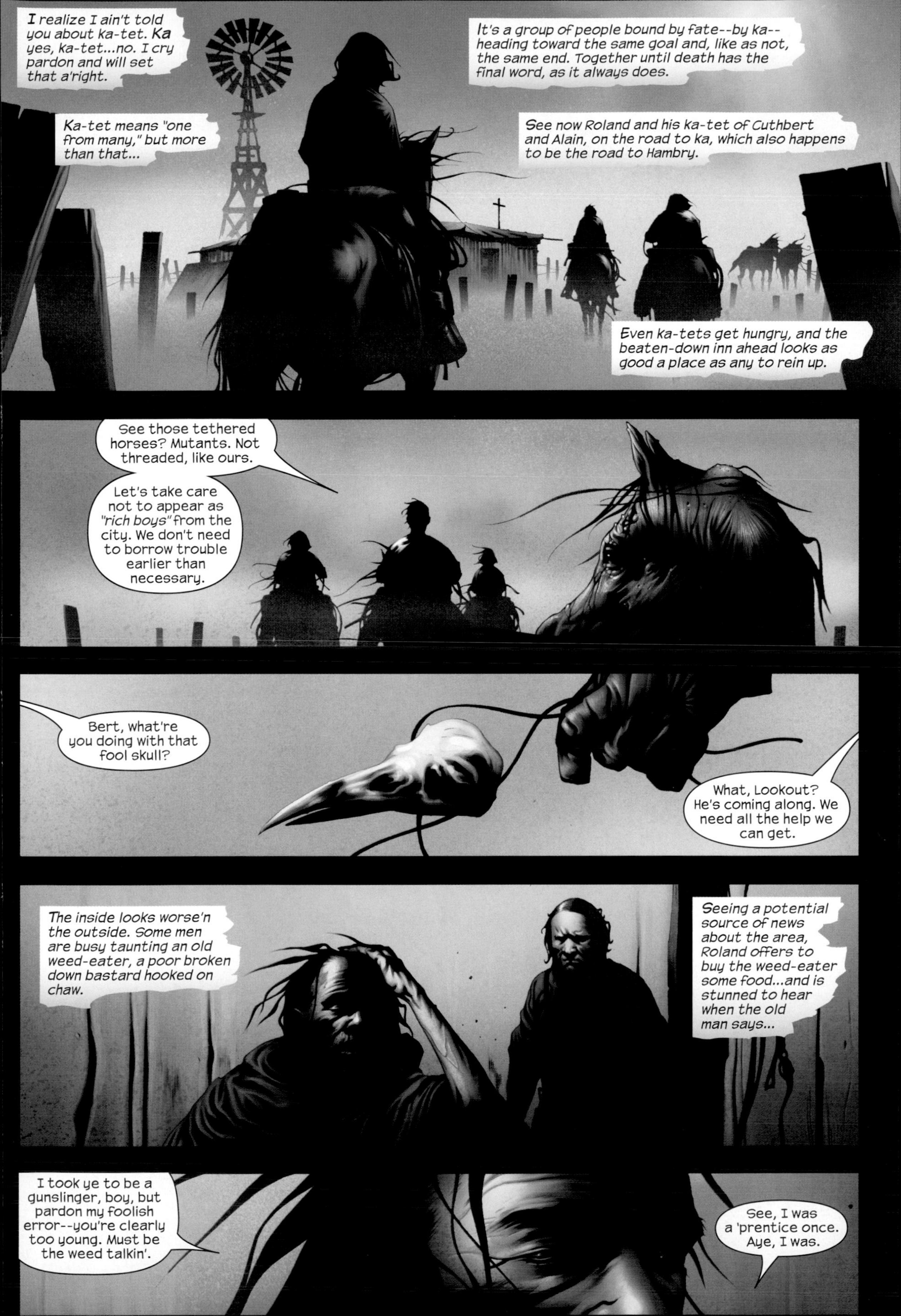
I realize I ain't told you about ka-tet. Ka yes, ka-tet...no. I cry pardon and will set that a'right.
Ka-tet means "one from many," but more than that...
It's a group of people bound by fate--by ka--heading toward the same goal and, like as not, the same end. Together until death has the final word, as it always does.
See now Roland and his ka-tet of Cuthbert and Alain, on the road to ka, which also happens to be the road to Hambry.
Even ka-tets get hungry, and the beaten-down inn ahead looks as good a place as any to rein up.
See those tethered horses? Mutants. Not threaded, like ours.
Let's take care not to appear as "rich boys" from the city. We don't need to borrow trouble earlier than necessary.
Bert, what're you doing with that fool skull?
What, Lookout? He's coming along. We need all the help we can get.
The inside looks worse'n the outside. Some men are busy taunting an old weed-eater, a poor broken down bastard hooked on chaw.
Seeing a potential source of news about the area, Roland offers to buy the weed-eater some food...and is stunned to hear when the old man says...
I took ye to be a gunslinger, boy, but pardon my foolish error--you're clearly too young. Must be the weed talkin'.
See, I was a 'prentice once. Aye, I was.

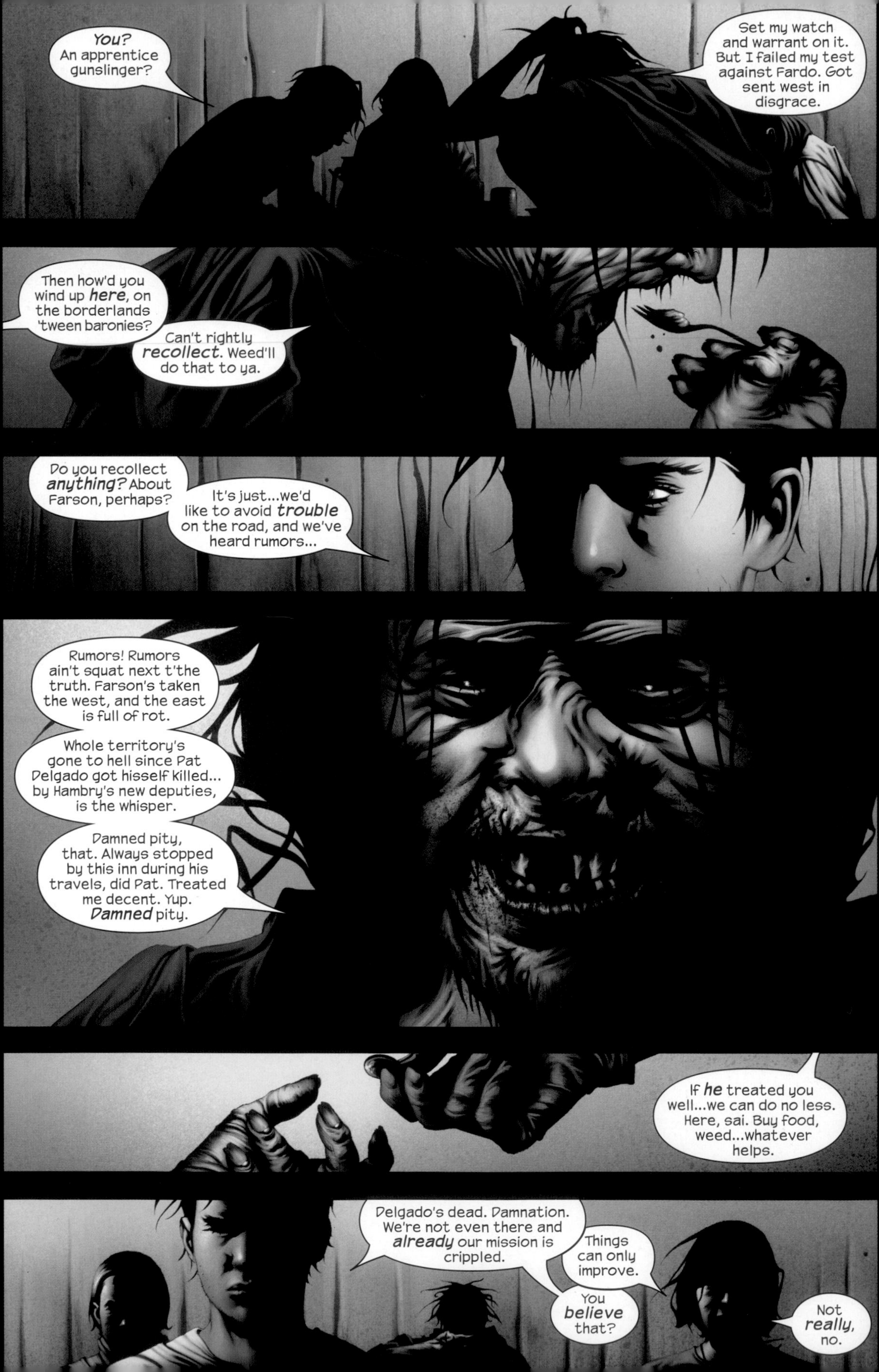
You? An apprentice gunslinger?
Set my watch and warrant on it. But I failed my test against Fardo. Got sent west in disgrace.
Then how'd you wind up here, on the borderlands 'tween baronies?
Can't rightly recollect. Weed'll do that to ya.
Do you recollect anything? About Farson, perhaps?
It's just...we'd like to avoid trouble on the road, and we've heard rumors...
Rumors! Rumors ain't squat next t'the truth. Farson's taken the west, and the east is full of rot.
Whole territory's gone to hell since Pat Delgado got hisself killed... by Hambry's new deputies, is the whisper.
Damned pity, that. Always stopped by this inn during his travels, did Pat. Treated me decent. Yup. Damned pity.
If he treated you well...we can do no less. Here, sai. Buy food, weed...whatever helps.
Delgado's dead. Damnation. We're not even there and already our mission is crippled.
Things can only improve.
You believe that?
Not really, no.

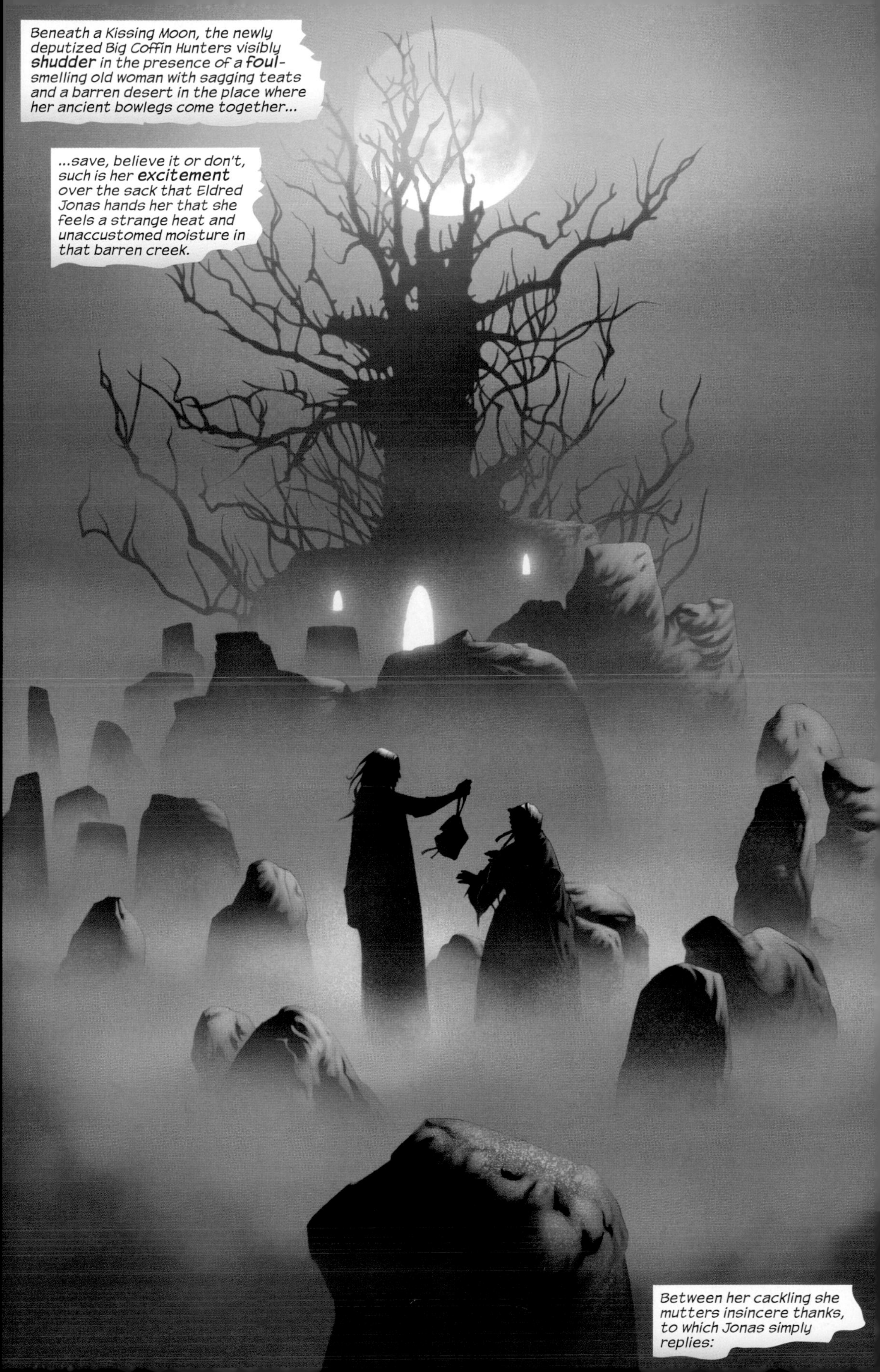
Beneath a Kissing Moon, the newly deputized Big Coffin Hunters visibly **shudder** in the presence of a **foul**-smelling old woman with sagging teats and a barren desert in the place where her ancient bowlegs come together...
...save, believe it or don't, such is her **excitement** over the sack that Eldred Jonas hands her that she feels a strange heat and unaccustomed moisture in that barren creek.
Between her cackling she mutters insincere thanks, to which Jonas simply replies:

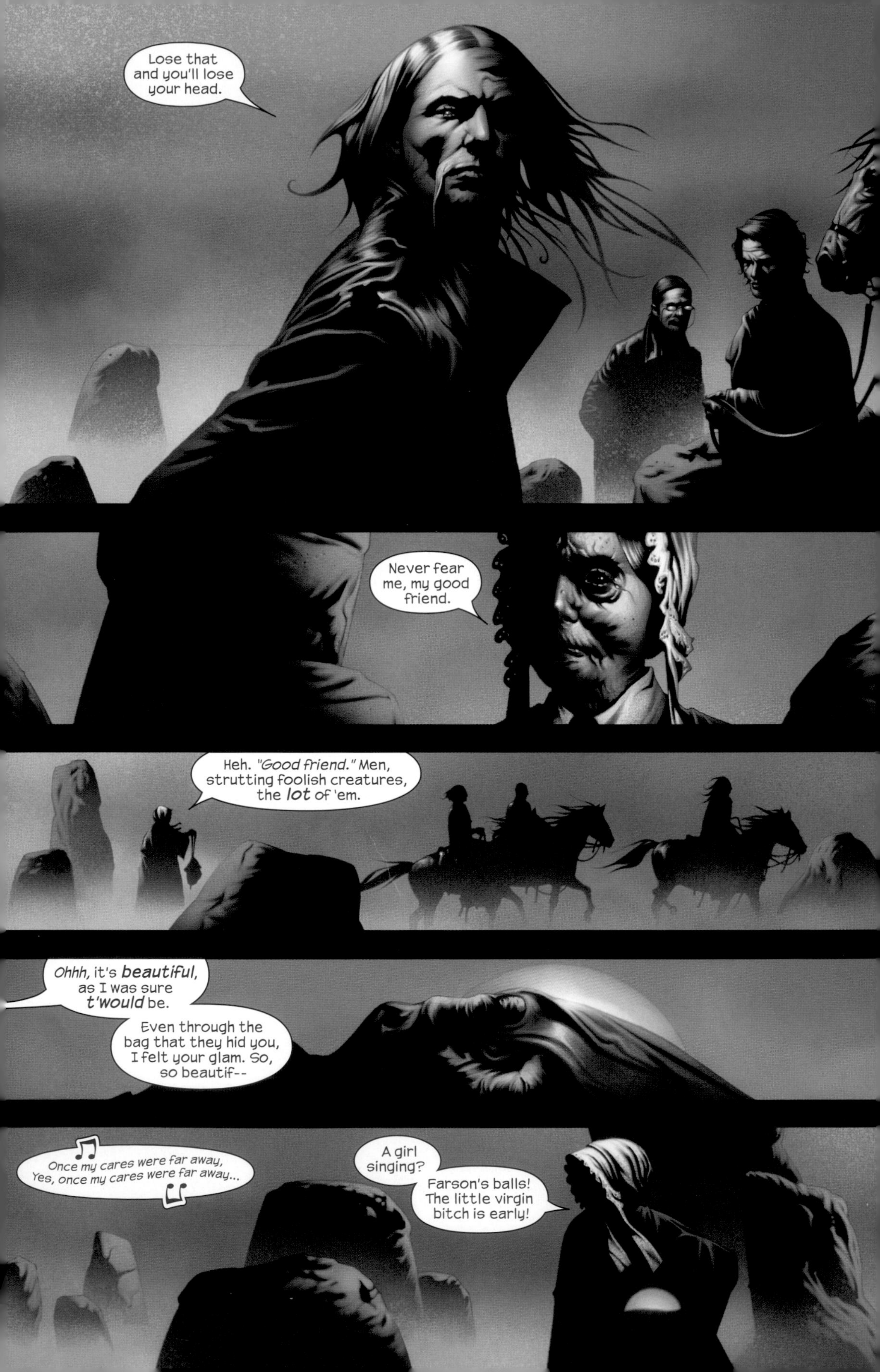
Lose that and you'll lose your head.
Never fear me, my good friend.
Heh. "Good friend." Men, strutting foolish creatures, the lot of 'em.
Ohhh, it's beautiful, as I was sure t'would be.
Even through the bag that they hid you, I felt your glam. So, so beautif--
Once my cares were far away, Yes, once my cares were far away...
A girl singing?
Farson's balls! The little virgin bitch is early!

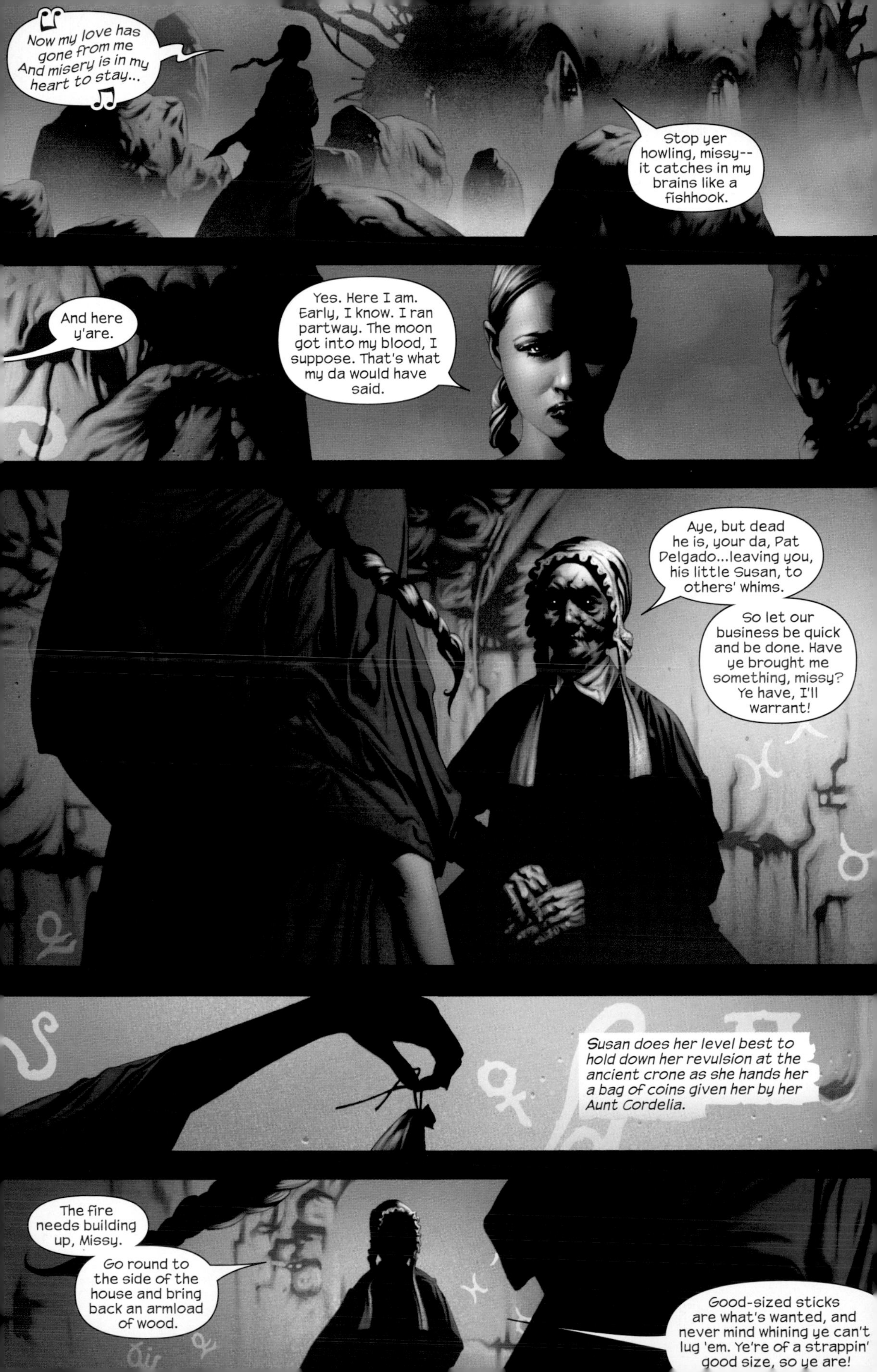
Now my love has gone from me And misery is in my heart to stay...
Stop yer howling, missy-- it catches in my brains like a fishhook.
And here y'are.
Yes. Here I am. Early, I know. I ran partway. The moon got into my blood, I suppose. That's what my da would have said.
Aye, but dead he is, your da, Pat Delgado...leaving you, his little Susan, to others' whims.
So let our business be quick and be done. Have ye brought me something, missy? Ye have, I'll warrant!
Susan does her level best to hold down her revulsion at the ancient crone as she hands her a bag of coins given her by her Aunt Cordelia.
The fire needs building up, Missy.
Go round to the side of the house and bring back an armload of wood.
Good-sized sticks are what's wanted, and never mind whining ye can't lug 'em. Ye're of a strappin' good size, so ye are!

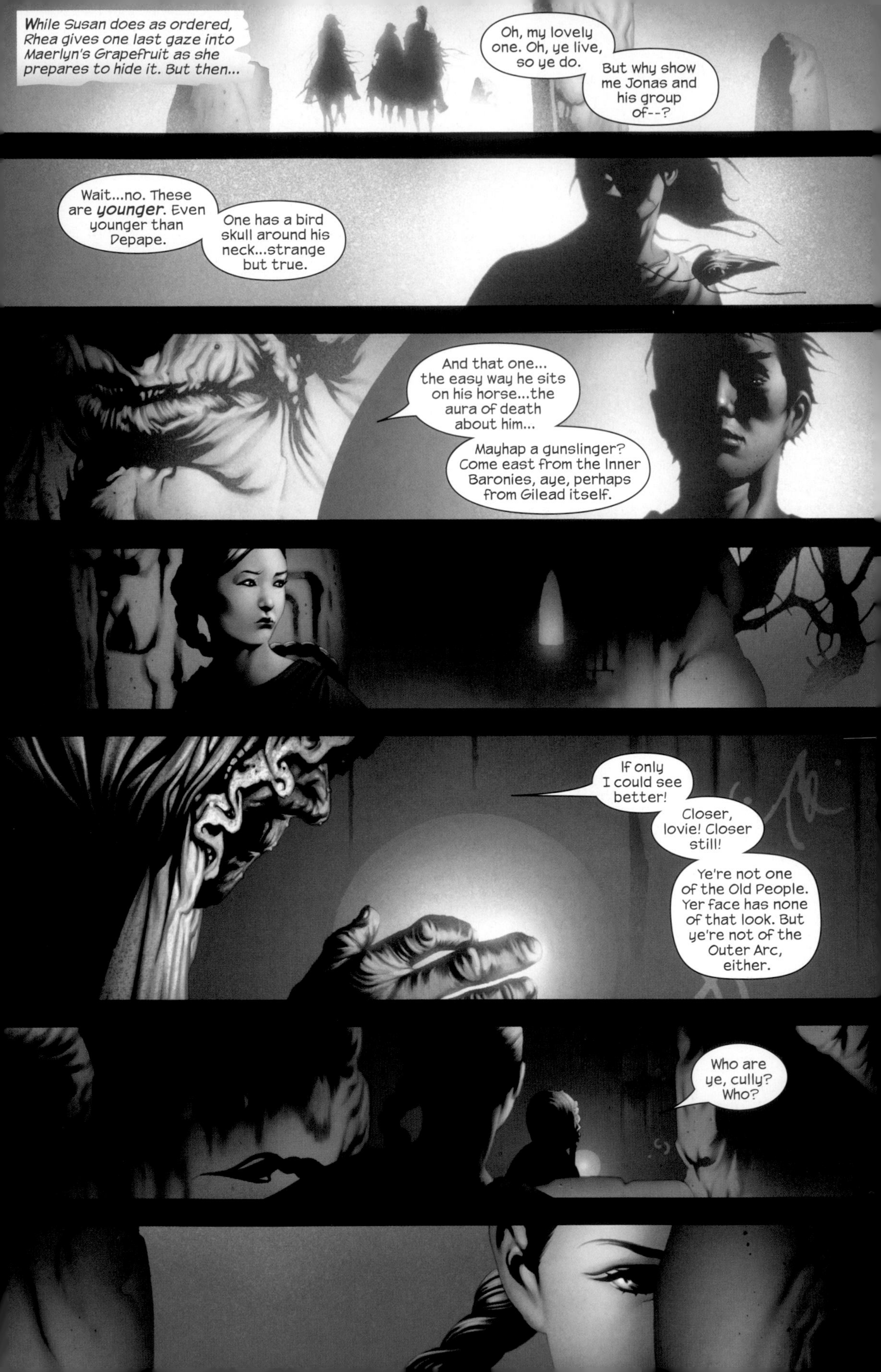
While Susan does as ordered, Rhea gives one last gaze into Maerlyn's Grapefruit as she prepares to hide it. But then...
Oh, my lovely one. Oh, ye live, so ye do.
But why show me Jonas and his group of--?
Wait...no. These are younger. Even younger than Depape.
One has a bird skull around his neck...strange but true.
And that one... the easy way he sits on his horse...the aura of death about him...
Mayhap a gunslinger? Come east from the Inner Baronies, aye, perhaps from Gilead itself.
If only I could see better!
Closer, lovie! Closer still!
Ye're not one of the Old People. Yer face has none of that look. But ye're not of the Outer Arc, either.
Who are ye, cully? Who?

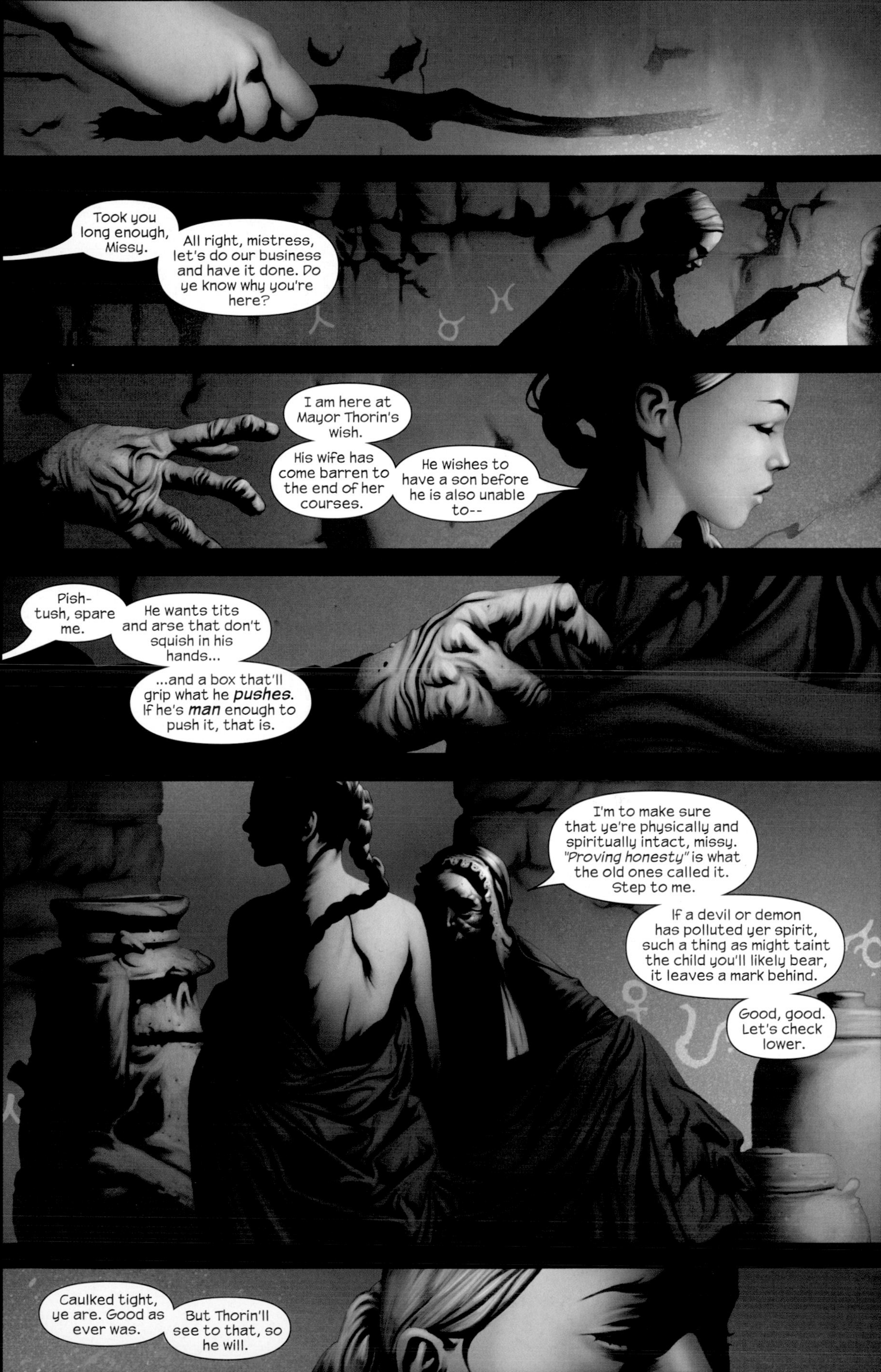
Took you long enough, Missy.
All right, mistress, let's do our business and have it done. Do ye know why you're here?
I am here at Mayor Thorin's wish.
His wife has come barren to the end of her courses.
He wishes to have a son before he is also unable to--
Pish-tush, spare me.
He wants tits and arse that don't squish in his hands...
...and a box that'll grip what he *pushes*. If he's *man* enough to push it, that is.
I'm to make sure that ye're physically and spiritually intact, missy. *"Proving honesty"* is what the old ones called it. Step to me.
If a devil or demon has polluted yer spirit, such a thing as might taint the child you'll likely bear, it leaves a mark behind.
Good, good. Let's check lower.
Caulked tight, ye are. Good as ever was.
But Thorin'll see to that, so he will.

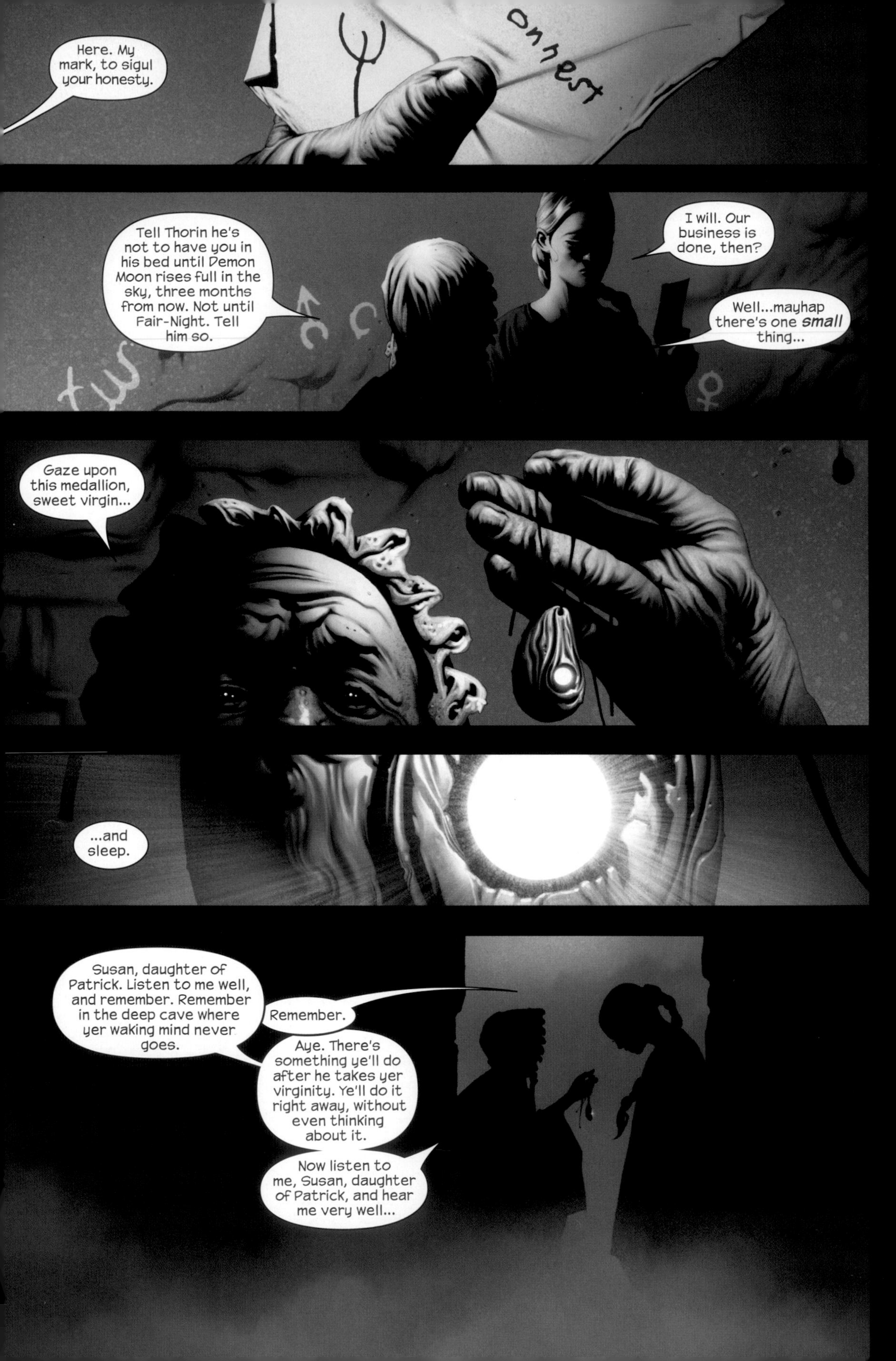
onhest
Here. My mark, to sigul your honesty.
Tell Thorin he's not to have you in his bed until Demon Moon rises full in the sky, three months from now. Not until Fair-Night. Tell him so.
I will. Our business is done, then?
Well...mayhap there's one *small* thing...
Gaze upon this medallion, sweet virgin...
...and sleep.
Susan, daughter of Patrick. Listen to me well, and remember. Remember in the deep cave where yer waking mind never goes.
Remember.
Aye. There's something ye'll do after he takes yer virginity. Ye'll do it right away, without even thinking about it.
Now listen to me, Susan, daughter of Patrick, and hear me very well...

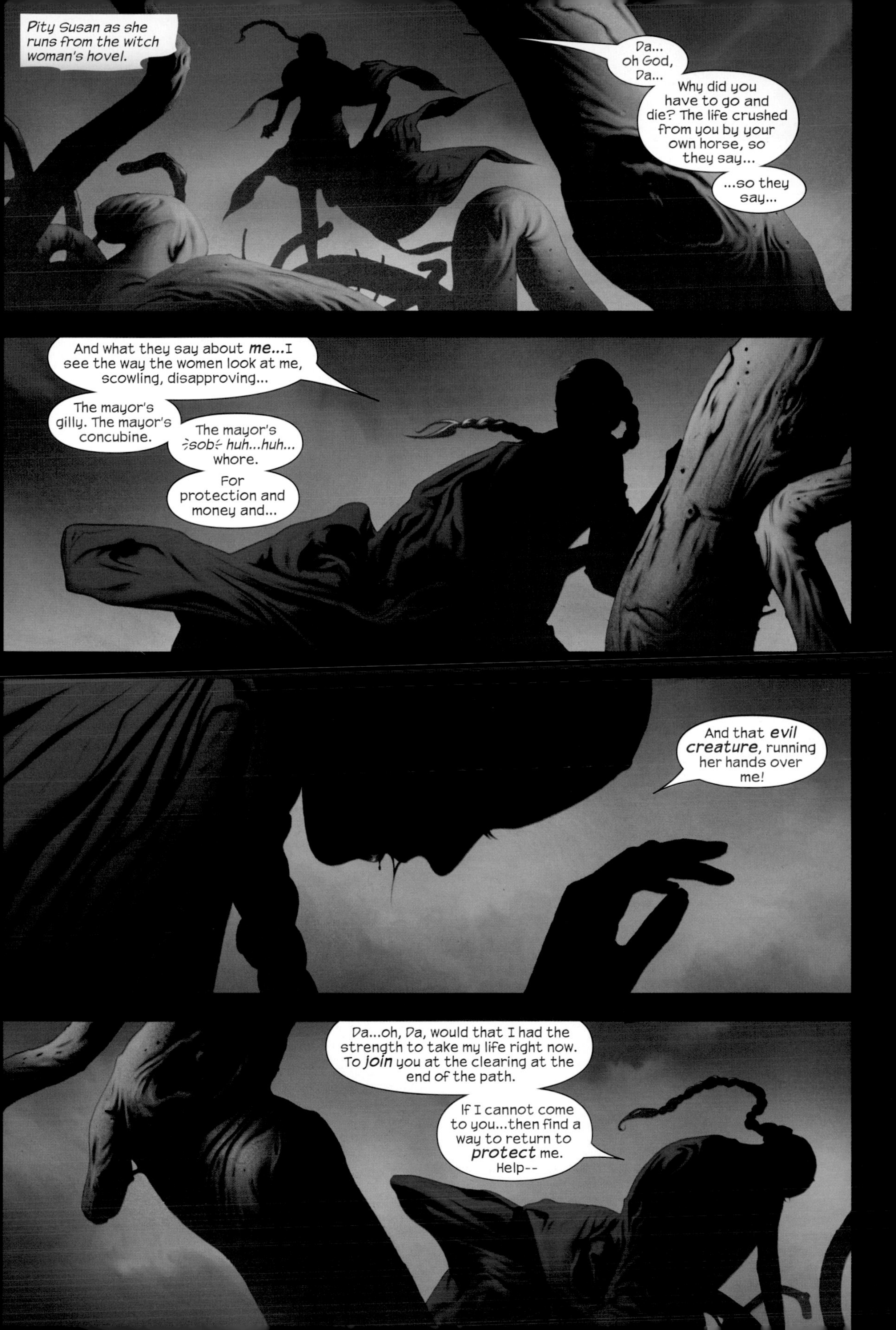
Pity Susan as she runs from the witch woman's hovel.
Da... oh God, Da...
Why did you have to go and die? The life crushed from you by your own horse, so they say...
...so they say...
And what they say about *me...*I see the way the women look at me, scowling, disapproving...
The mayor's gilly. The mayor's concubine.
The mayor's *sob* *huh...huh...* whore.
For protection and money and...
And that *evil creature*, running her hands over me!
Da...oh, Da, would that I had the strength to take my life right now. To *join* you at the clearing at the end of the path.
If I cannot come to you...then find a way to return to *protect* me. Help--

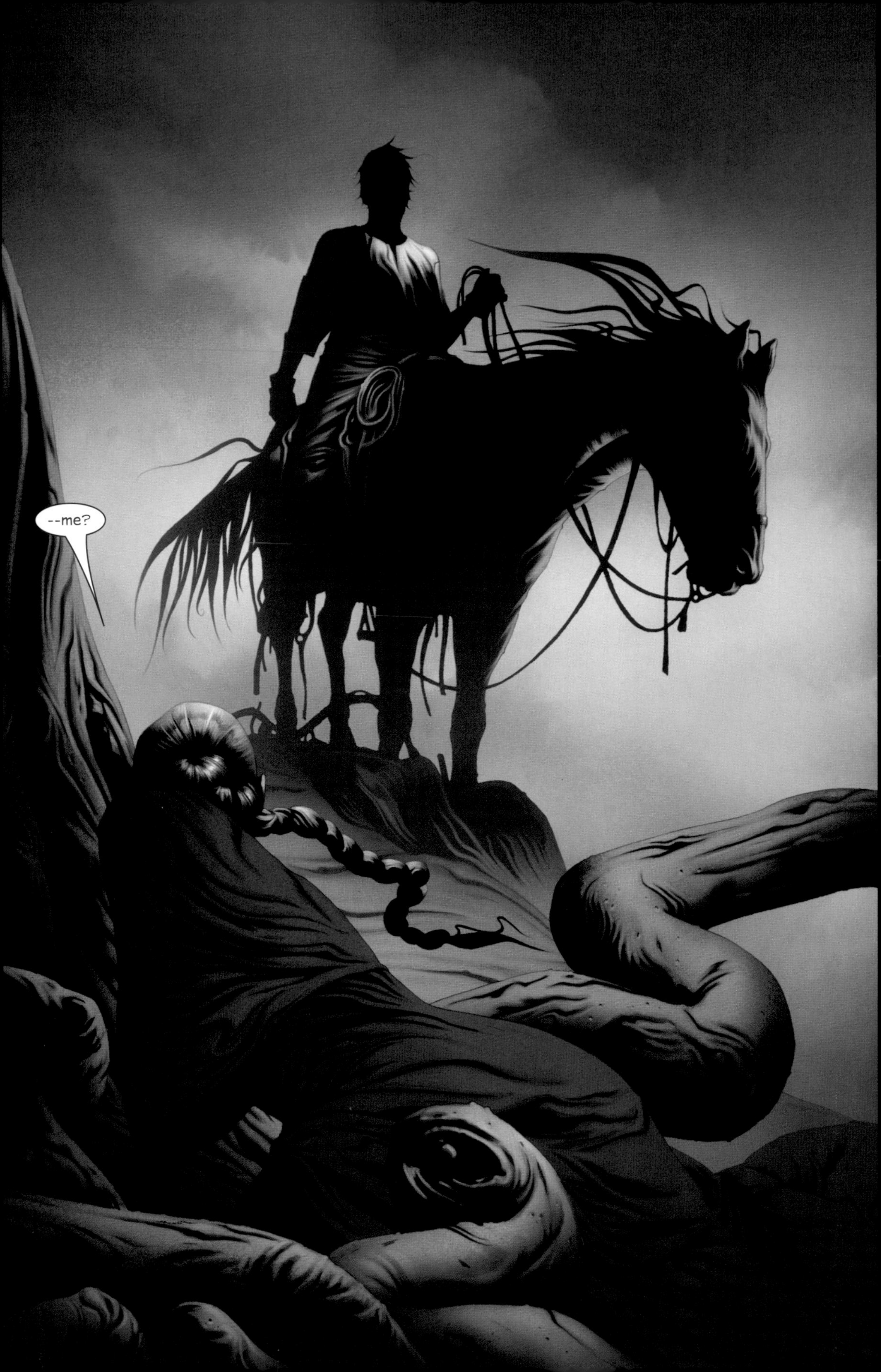
--me?

STEPHEN KING

THE DARK TOWER

THE GUNSLINGER BORN

CHAPTER THREE

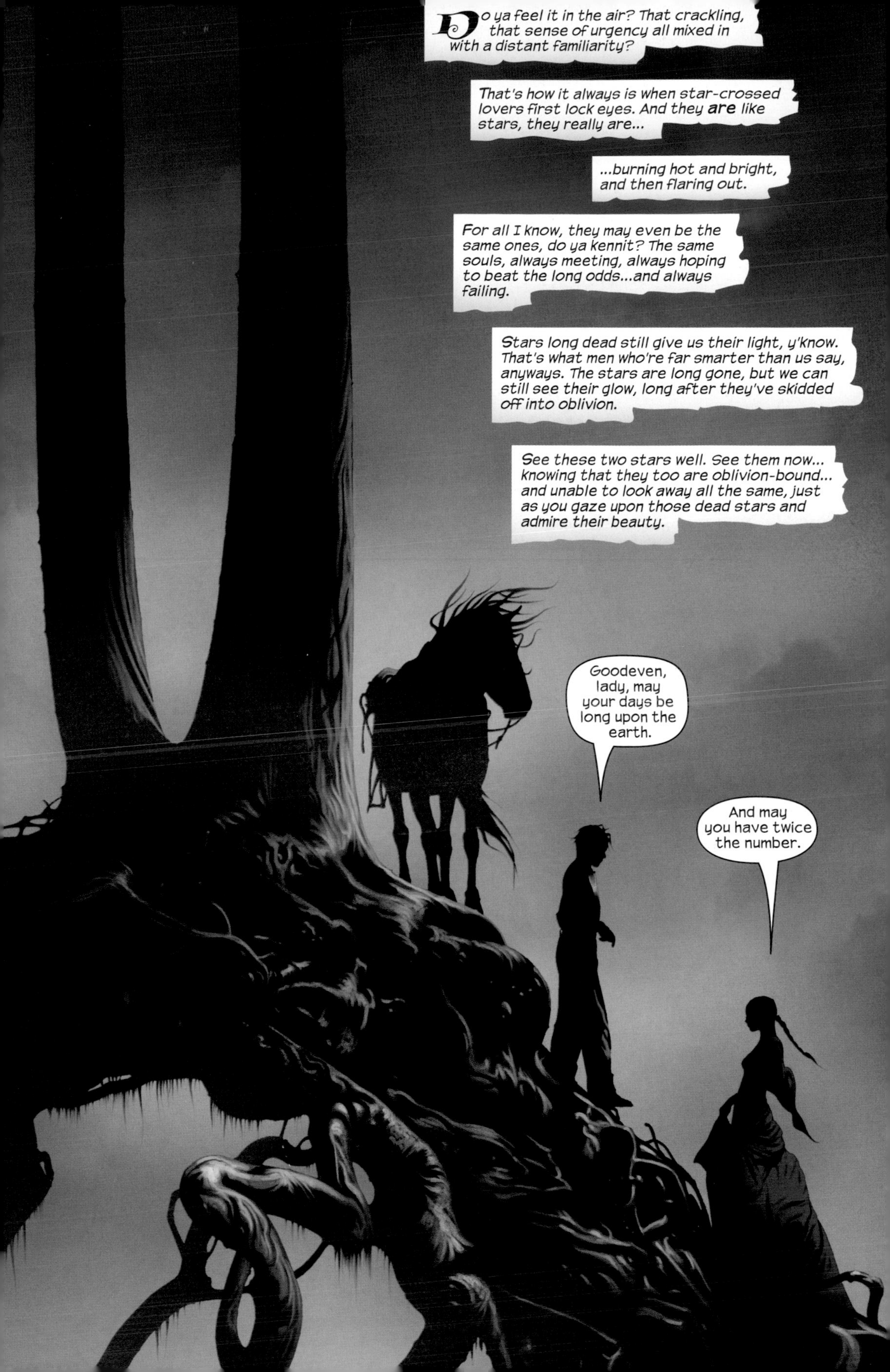
Do ya feel it in the air? That crackling, that sense of urgency all mixed in with a distant familiarity?
That's how it always is when star-crossed lovers first lock eyes. And they **are** like stars, they really are...
...burning hot and bright, and then flaring out.
For all I know, they may even be the same ones, do ya kennit? The same souls, always meeting, always hoping to beat the long odds...and always failing.
Stars long dead still give us their light, y'know. That's what men who're far smarter than us say, anyways. The stars are long gone, but we can still see their glow, long after they've skidded off into oblivion.
See these two stars well. See them now... knowing that they too are oblivion-bound... and unable to look away all the same, just as you gaze upon those dead stars and admire their beauty.
Goodeven, lady, may your days be long upon the earth.
And may you have twice the number.

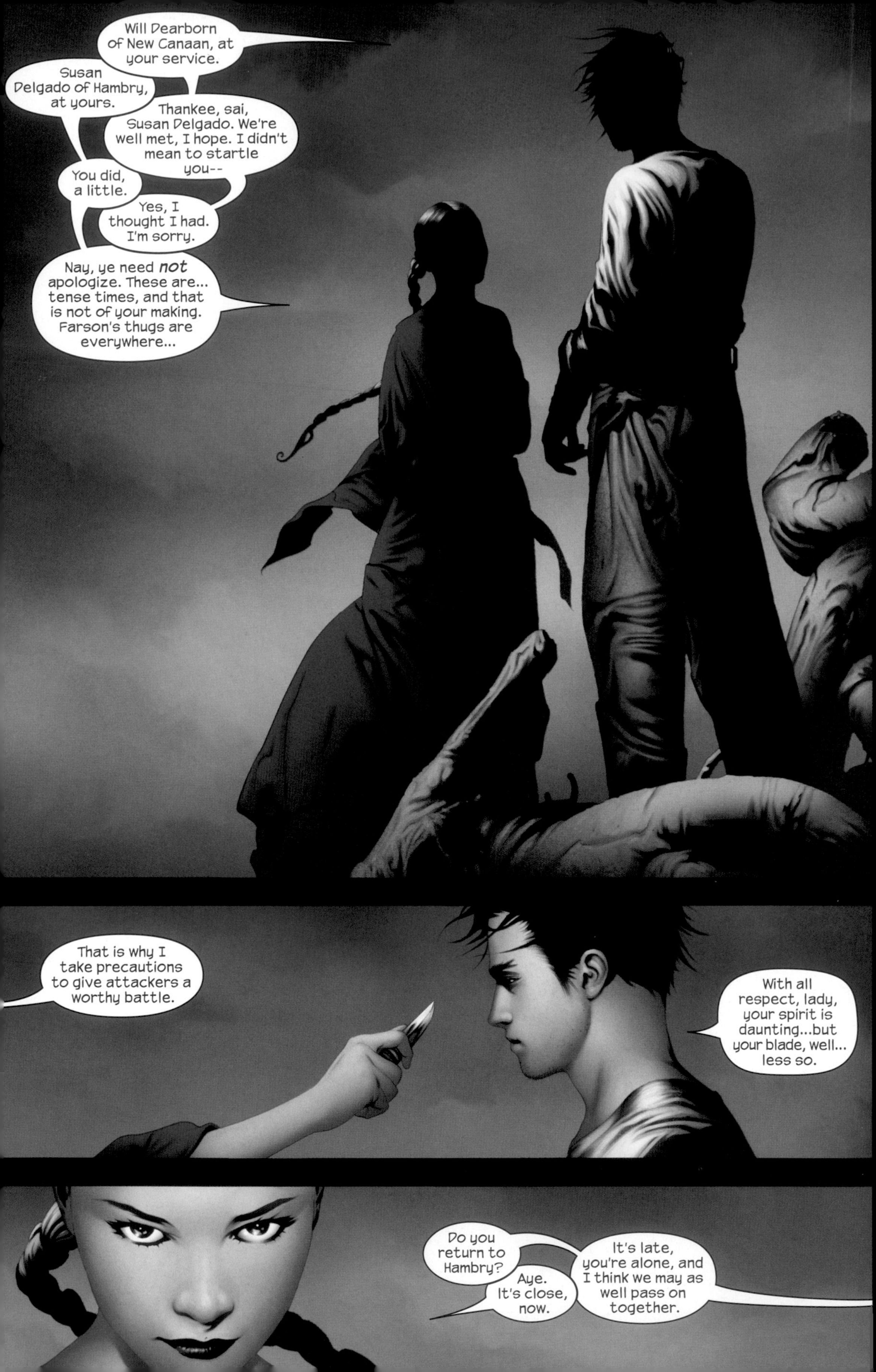
Will Dearborn of New Canaan, at your service.
Susan Delgado of Hambry, at yours.
Thankee, sai, Susan Delgado. We're well met, I hope. I didn't mean to startle you--
You did, a little.
Yes, I thought I had. I'm sorry.
Nay, ye need *not* apologize. These are... tense times, and that is not of your making. Farson's thugs are everywhere...
That is why I take precautions to give attackers a worthy battle.
With all respect, lady, your spirit is daunting...but your blade, well... less so.
Do you return to Hambry?
Aye. It's close, now.
It's late, you're alone, and I think we may as well pass on together.

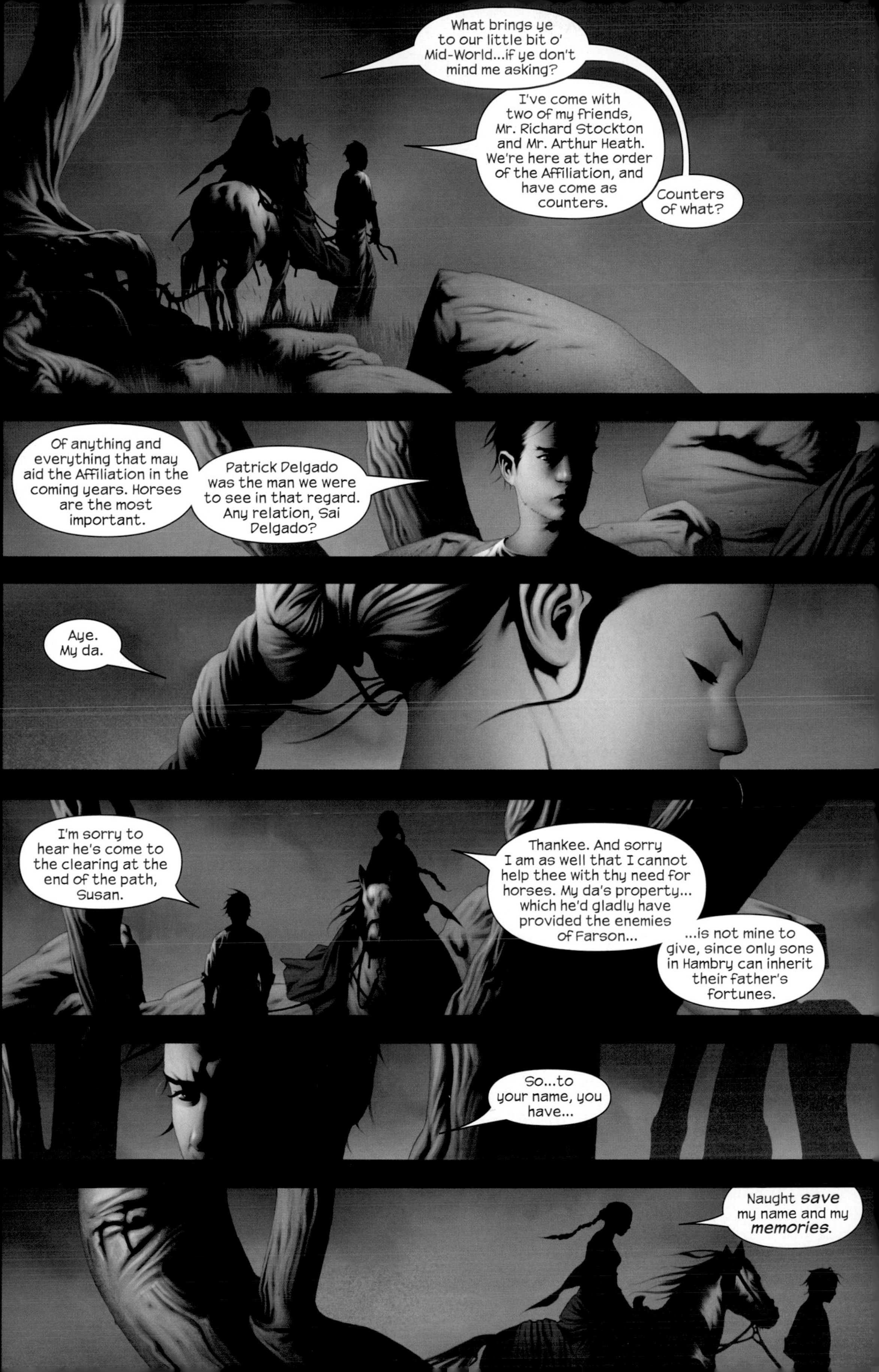
What brings ye to our little bit o' Mid-World...if ye don't mind me asking?
I've come with two of my friends, Mr. Richard Stockton and Mr. Arthur Heath. We're here at the order of the Affiliation, and have come as counters.
Counters of what?
Of anything and everything that may aid the Affiliation in the coming years. Horses are the most important.
Patrick Delgado was the man we were to see in that regard. Any relation, Sai Delgado?
Aye. My da.
I'm sorry to hear he's come to the clearing at the end of the path, Susan.
Thankee. And sorry I am as well that I cannot help thee with thy need for horses. My da's property... which he'd gladly have provided the enemies of Farson...
...is not mine to give, since only sons in Hambry can inherit their father's fortunes.
So...to your name, you have...
Naught *save* my name and my *memories*.

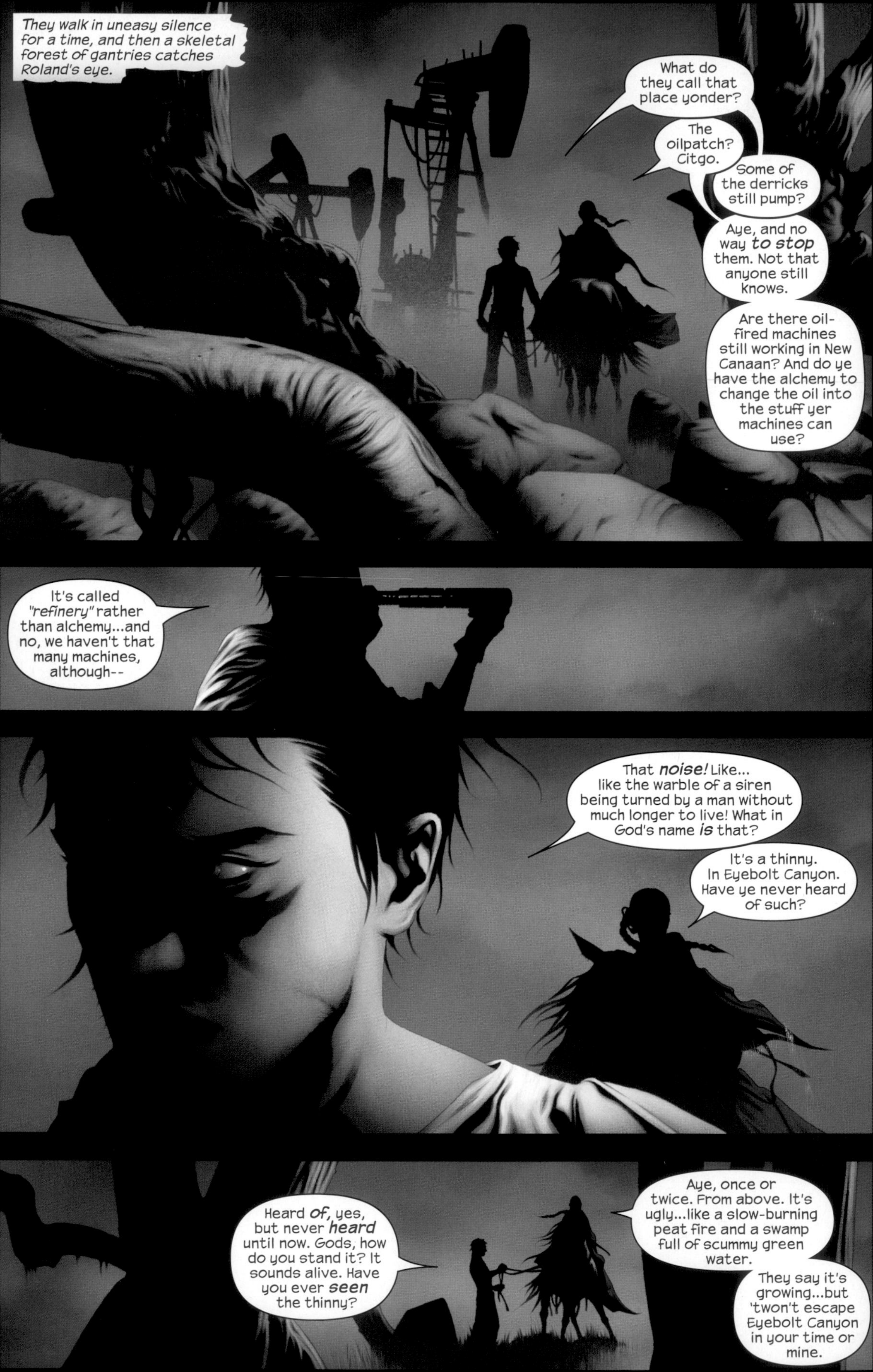
They walk in uneasy silence for a time, and then a skeletal forest of gantries catches Roland's eye.
What do they call that place yonder?
The oilpatch? Citgo.
Some of the derricks still pump?
Aye, and no way to stop them. Not that anyone still knows.
Are there oil-fired machines still working in New Canaan? And do ye have the alchemy to change the oil into the stuff yer machines can use?
It's called "refinery" rather than alchemy...and no, we haven't that many machines, although--
That noise! Like... like the warble of a siren being turned by a man without much longer to live! What in God's name is that?
It's a thinny. In Eyebolt Canyon. Have ye never heard of such?
Heard of, yes, but never heard until now. Gods, how do you stand it? It sounds alive. Have you ever seen the thinny?
Aye, once or twice. From above. It's ugly...like a slow-burning peat fire and a swamp full of scummy green water.
They say it's growing...but 'twon't escape Eyebolt Canyon in your time or mine.

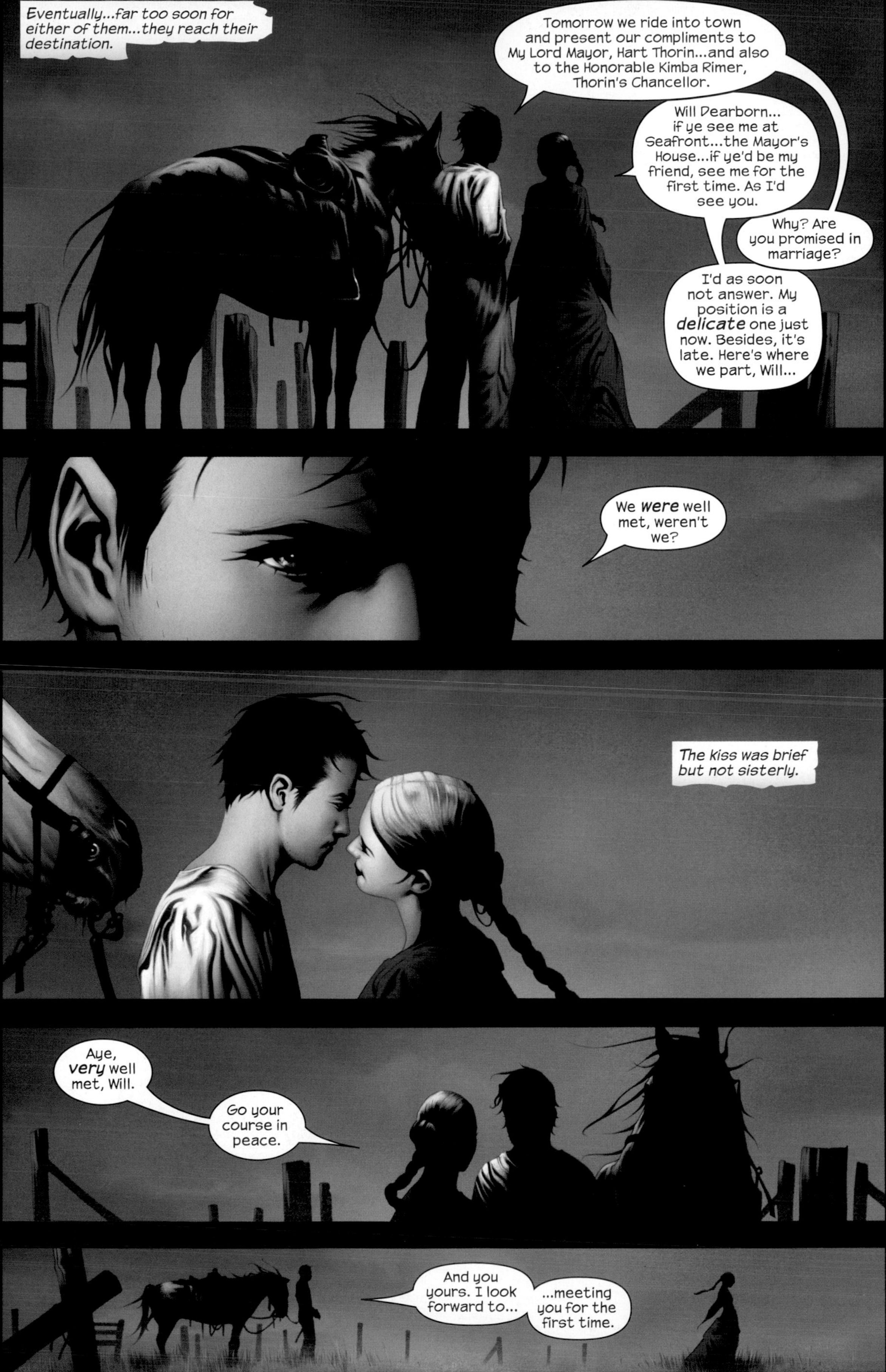
Eventually...far too soon for either of them...they reach their destination.
Tomorrow we ride into town and present our compliments to My Lord Mayor, Hart Thorin...and also to the Honorable Kimba Rimer, Thorin's Chancellor.
Will Dearborn... if ye see me at Seafront...the Mayor's House...if ye'd be my friend, see me for the first time. As I'd see you.
Why? Are you promised in marriage?
I'd as soon not answer. My position is a *delicate* one just now. Besides, it's late. Here's where we part, Will...
We *were* well met, weren't we?
The kiss was brief but not sisterly.
Aye, *very* well met, Will.
Go your course in peace.
And you yours. I look forward to...
...meeting you for the first time.

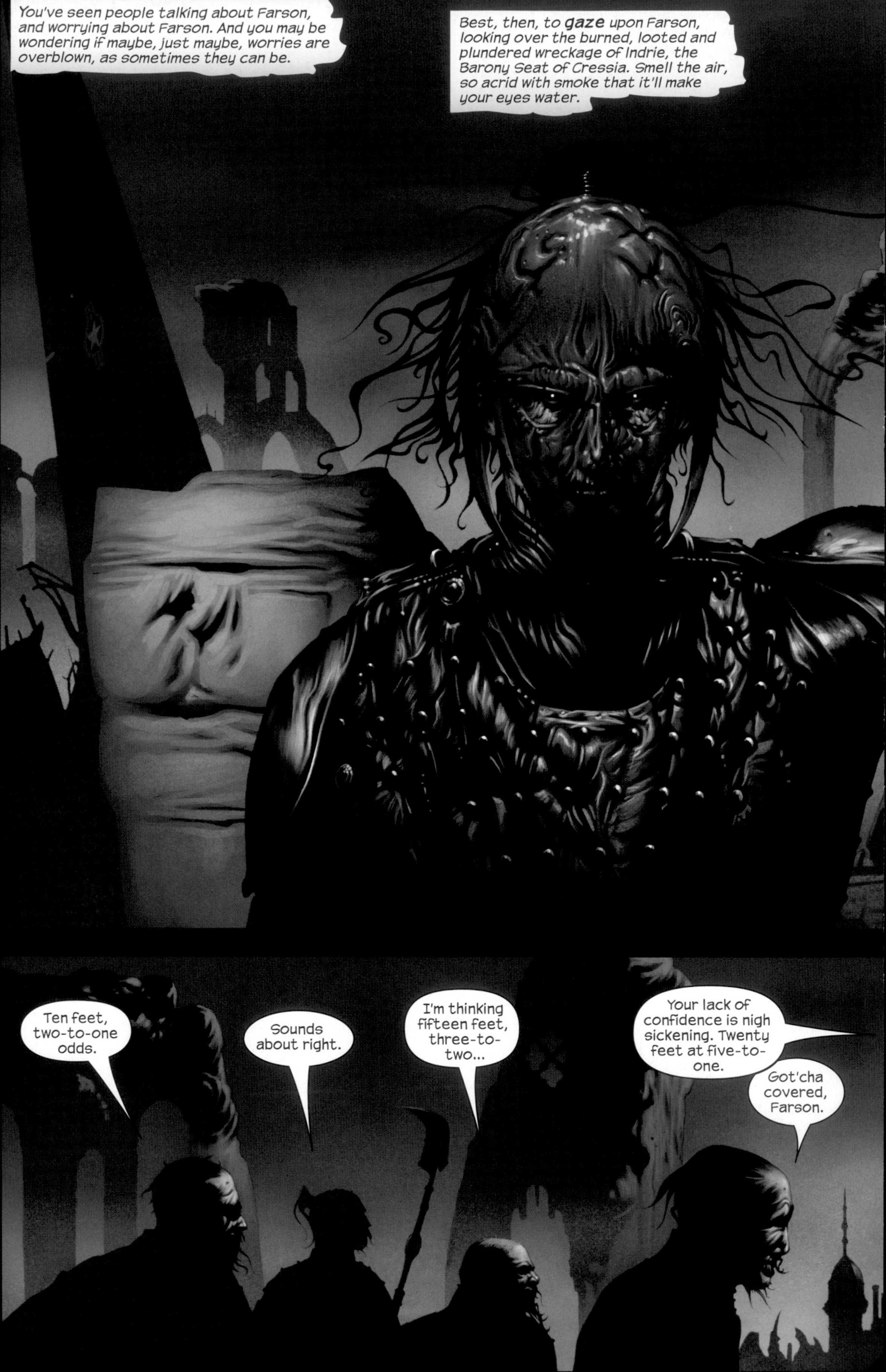
You've seen people talking about Farson, and worrying about Farson. And you may be wondering if maybe, just maybe, worries are overblown, as sometimes they can be.
Best, then, to gaze upon Farson, looking over the burned, looted and plundered wreckage of Indrie, the Barony Seat of Cressia. Smell the air, so acrid with smoke that it'll make your eyes water.
Ten feet, two-to-one odds.
Sounds about right.
I'm thinking fifteen feet, three-to-two...
Your lack of confidence is nigh sickening. Twenty feet at five-to-one.
Got'cha covered, Farson.

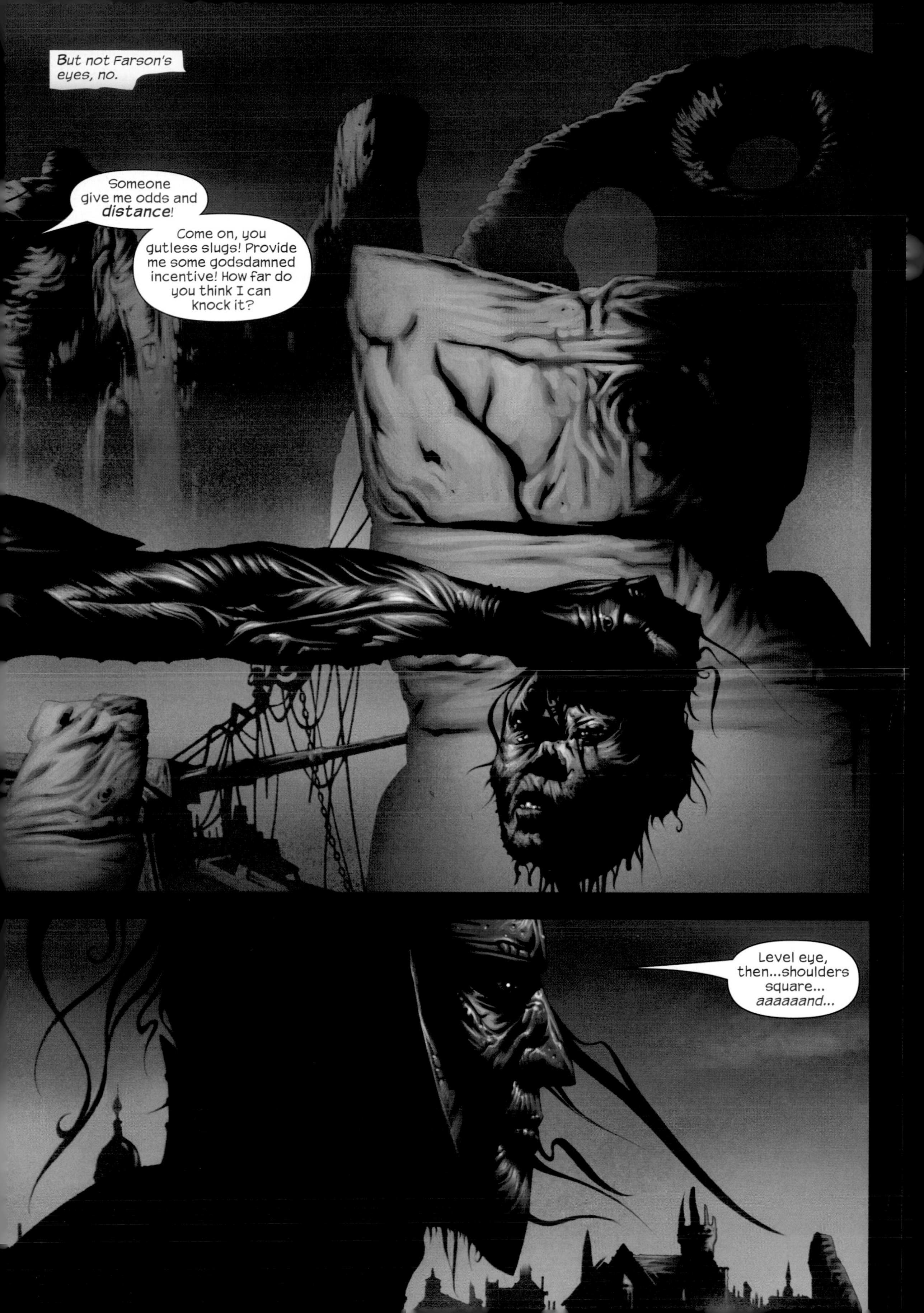
But not Farson's eyes, no.
Someone give me odds and *distance*!
Come on, you gutless slugs! Provide me some godsdamned incentive! How far do you think I can knock it?
Level eye, then...shoulders square... *aaaaaand*...

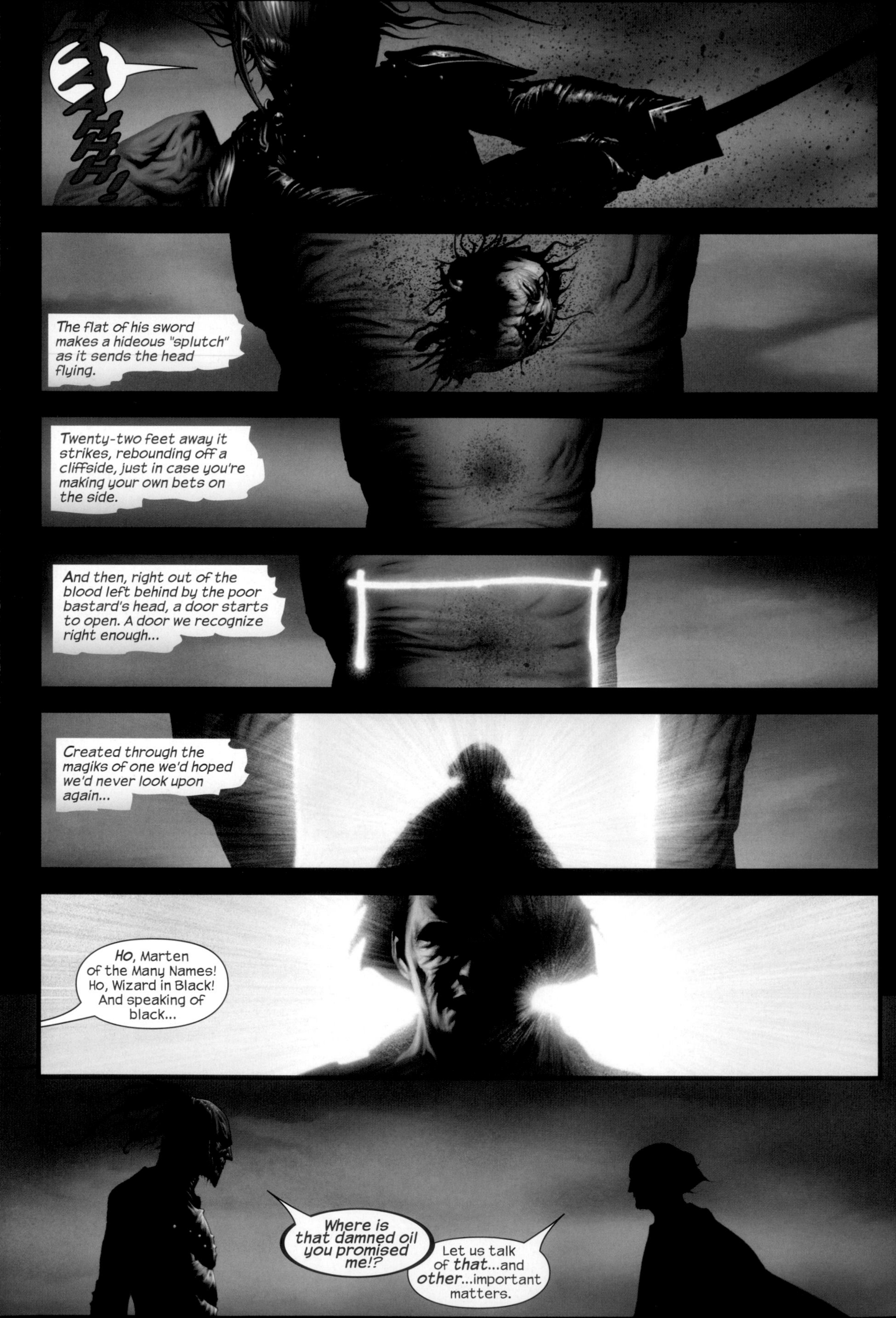
AAAHH!
The flat of his sword makes a hideous "splutch" as it sends the head flying.
Twenty-two feet away it strikes, rebounding off a cliffside, just in case you're making your own bets on the side.
And then, right out of the blood left behind by the poor bastard's head, a door starts to open. A door we recognize right enough...
Created through the magiks of one we'd hoped we'd never look upon again...
HO, Marten of the Many Names! Ho, Wizard in Black! And speaking of black...
Where is that damned oil you promised me!?
Let us talk of that...and other...important matters.

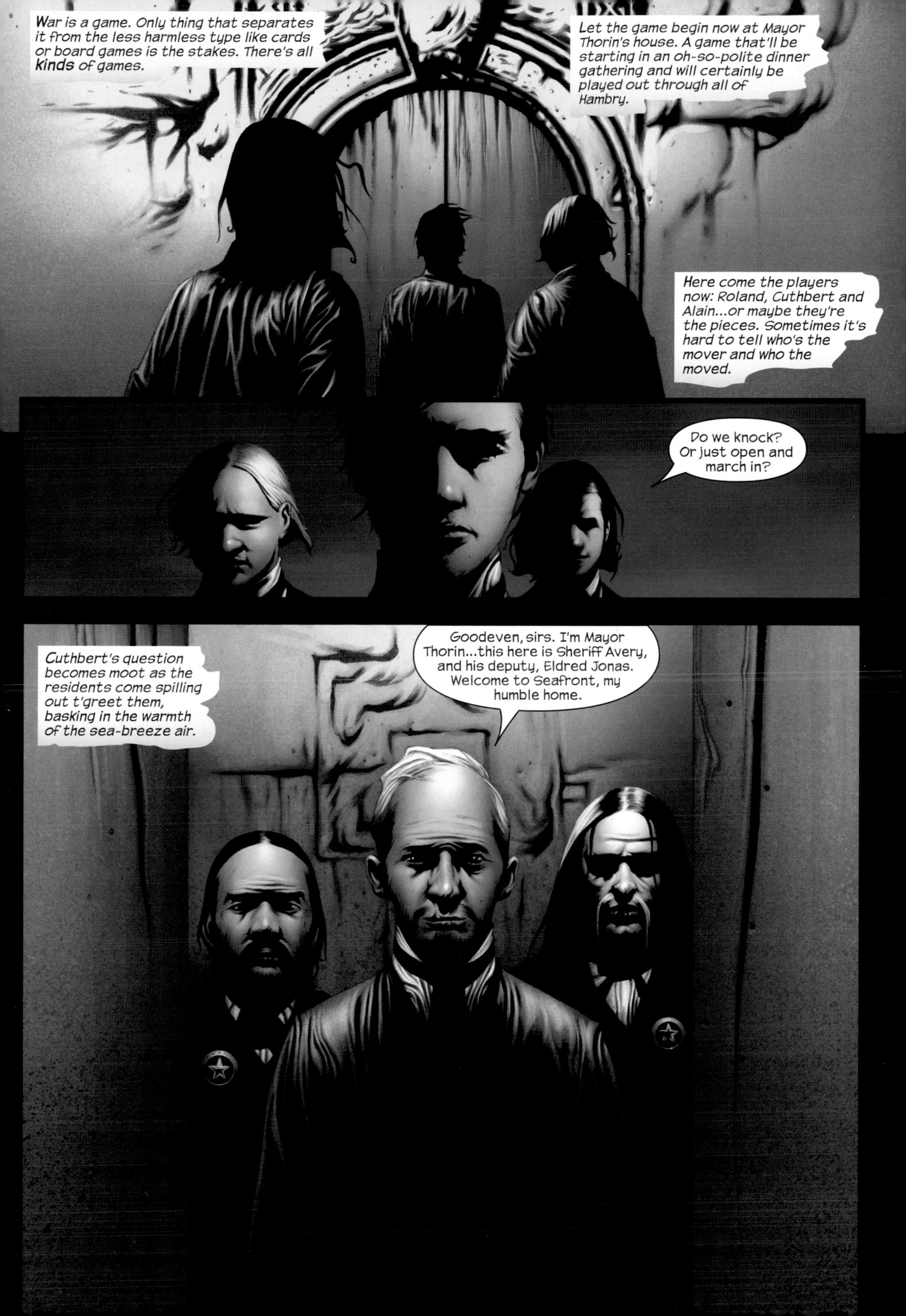

War is a game. Only thing that separates it from the less harmless type like cards or board games is the stakes. There's all **kinds** of games.
Let the game begin now at Mayor Thorin's house. A game that'll be starting in an oh-so-polite dinner gathering and will certainly be played out through all of Hambry.
Here come the players now: Roland, Cuthbert and Alain...or maybe they're the pieces. Sometimes it's hard to tell who's the mover and who the moved.
Do we knock? Or just open and march in?
Cuthbert's question becomes moot as the residents come spilling out t'greet them, basking in the warmth of the sea-breeze air.
Goodeven, sirs. I'm Mayor Thorin...this here is Sheriff Avery, and his deputy, Eldred Jonas. Welcome to Seafront, my humble home.

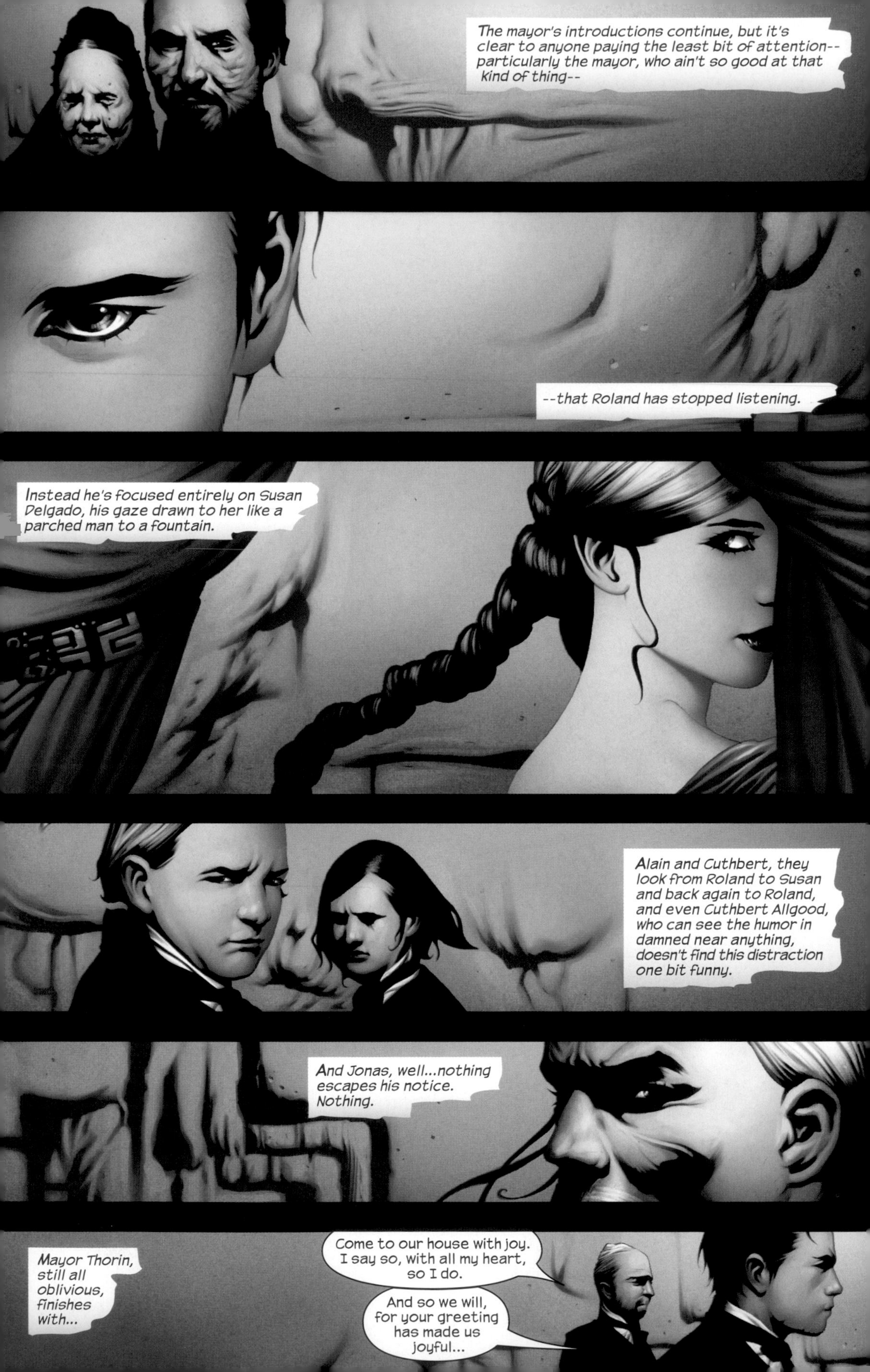
The mayor's introductions continue, but it's clear to anyone paying the least bit of attention-- particularly the mayor, who ain't so good at that kind of thing--
--that Roland has stopped listening.
Instead he's focused entirely on Susan Delgado, his gaze drawn to her like a parched man to a fountain.
Alain and Cuthbert, they look from Roland to Susan and back again to Roland, and even Cuthbert Allgood, who can see the humor in damned near anything, doesn't find this distraction one bit funny.
And Jonas, well...nothing escapes his notice. Nothing.
Mayor Thorin, still all oblivious, finishes with...
Come to our house with joy. I say so, with all my heart, so I do.
And so we will, for your greeting has made us joyful...

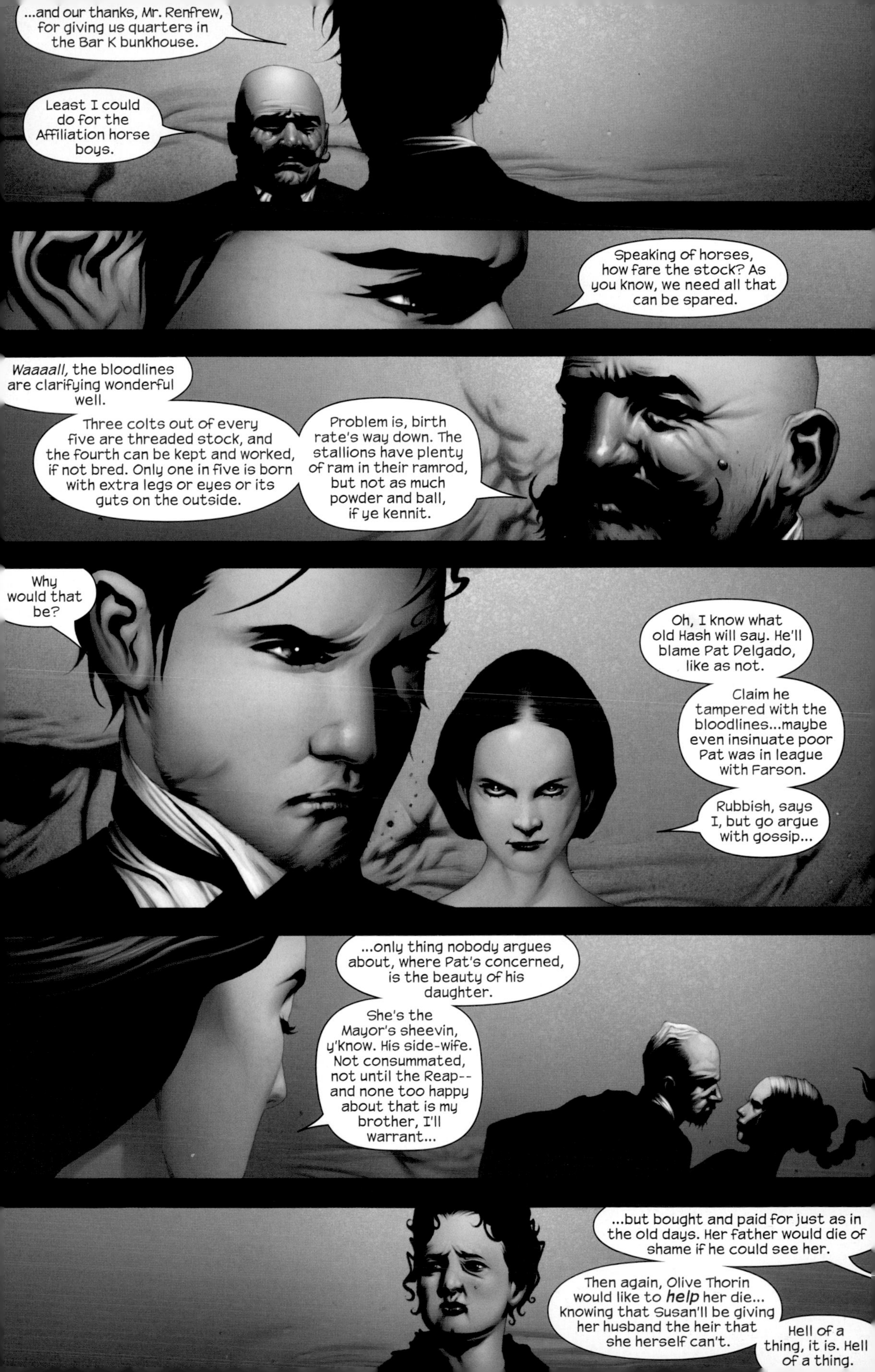

...and our thanks, Mr. Renfrew, for giving us quarters in the Bar K bunkhouse.
Least I could do for the Affiliation horse boys.
Speaking of horses, how fare the stock? As you know, we need all that can be spared.
Waaaall, the bloodlines are clarifying wonderful well.
Three colts out of every five are threaded stock, and the fourth can be kept and worked, if not bred. Only one in five is born with extra legs or eyes or its guts on the outside.
Problem is, birth rate's way down. The stallions have plenty of ram in their ramrod, but not as much powder and ball, if ye kennit.
Why would that be?
Oh, I know what old Hash will say. He'll blame Pat Delgado, like as not.
Claim he tampered with the bloodlines...maybe even insinuate poor Pat was in league with Farson.
Rubbish, says I, but go argue with gossip...
...only thing nobody argues about, where Pat's concerned, is the beauty of his daughter.
She's the Mayor's sheevin, y'know. His side-wife. Not consummated, not until the Reap-- and none too happy about that is my brother, I'll warrant...
...but bought and paid for just as in the old days. Her father would die of shame if he could see her.
Then again, Olive Thorin would like to ***help*** her die... knowing that Susan'll be giving her husband the heir that she herself can't.
Hell of a thing, it is. Hell of a thing.

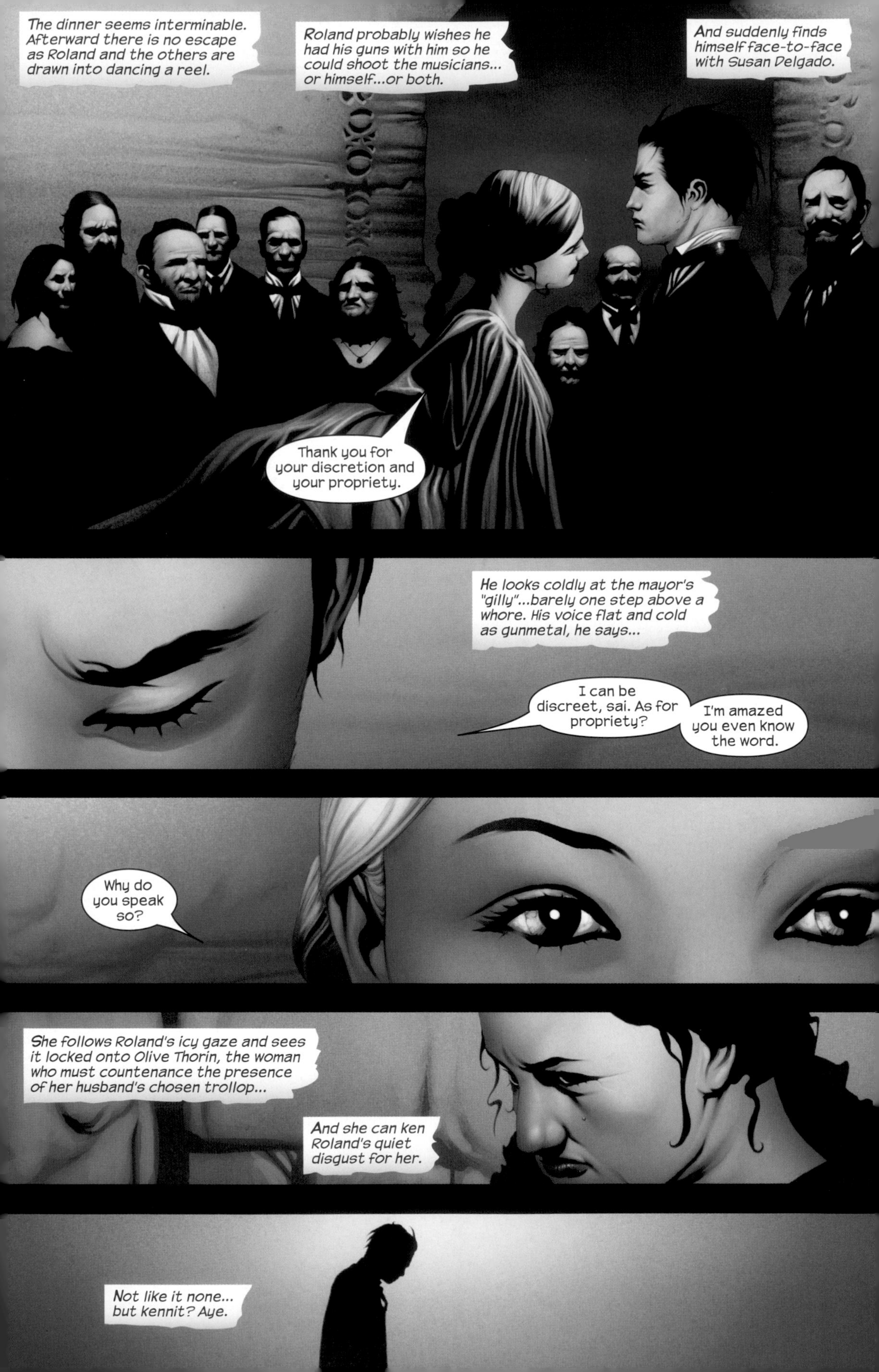
The dinner seems interminable. Afterward there is no escape as Roland and the others are drawn into dancing a reel.
Roland probably wishes he had his guns with him so he could shoot the musicians... or himself...or both.
And suddenly finds himself face-to-face with Susan Delgado.
Thank you for your discretion and your propriety.
He looks coldly at the mayor's "gilly"...barely one step above a whore. His voice flat and cold as gunmetal, he says...
I can be discreet, sai. As for propriety?
I'm amazed you even know the word.
Why do you speak so?
She follows Roland's icy gaze and sees it locked onto Olive Thorin, the woman who must countenance the presence of her husband's chosen trollop...
And she can ken Roland's quiet disgust for her.
Not like it none... but kennit? Aye.

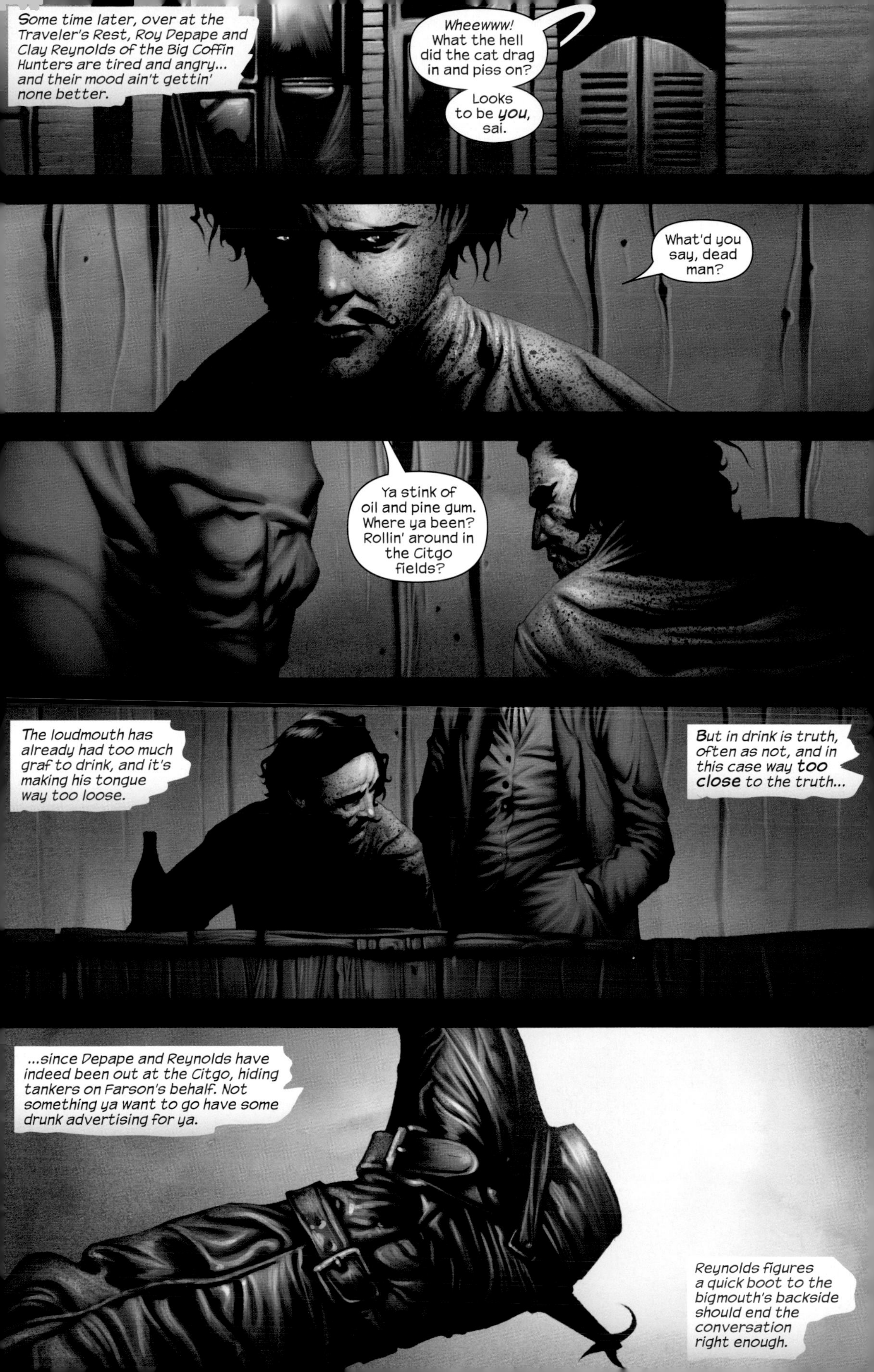
Some time later, over at the Traveler's Rest, Roy Depape and Clay Reynolds of the Big Coffin Hunters are tired and angry... and their mood ain't gettin' none better.
Wheewww! What the hell did the cat drag in and piss on?
Looks to be you, sai.
What'd you say, dead man?
Ya stink of oil and pine gum. Where ya been? Rollin' around in the Citgo fields?
The loudmouth has already had too much graf to drink, and it's making his tongue way too loose.
But in drink is truth, often as not, and in this case way too close to the truth...
...since Depape and Reynolds have indeed been out at the Citgo, hiding tankers on Farson's behalf. Not something ya want to go have some drunk advertising for ya.
Reynolds figures a quick boot to the bigmouth's backside should end the conversation right enough.

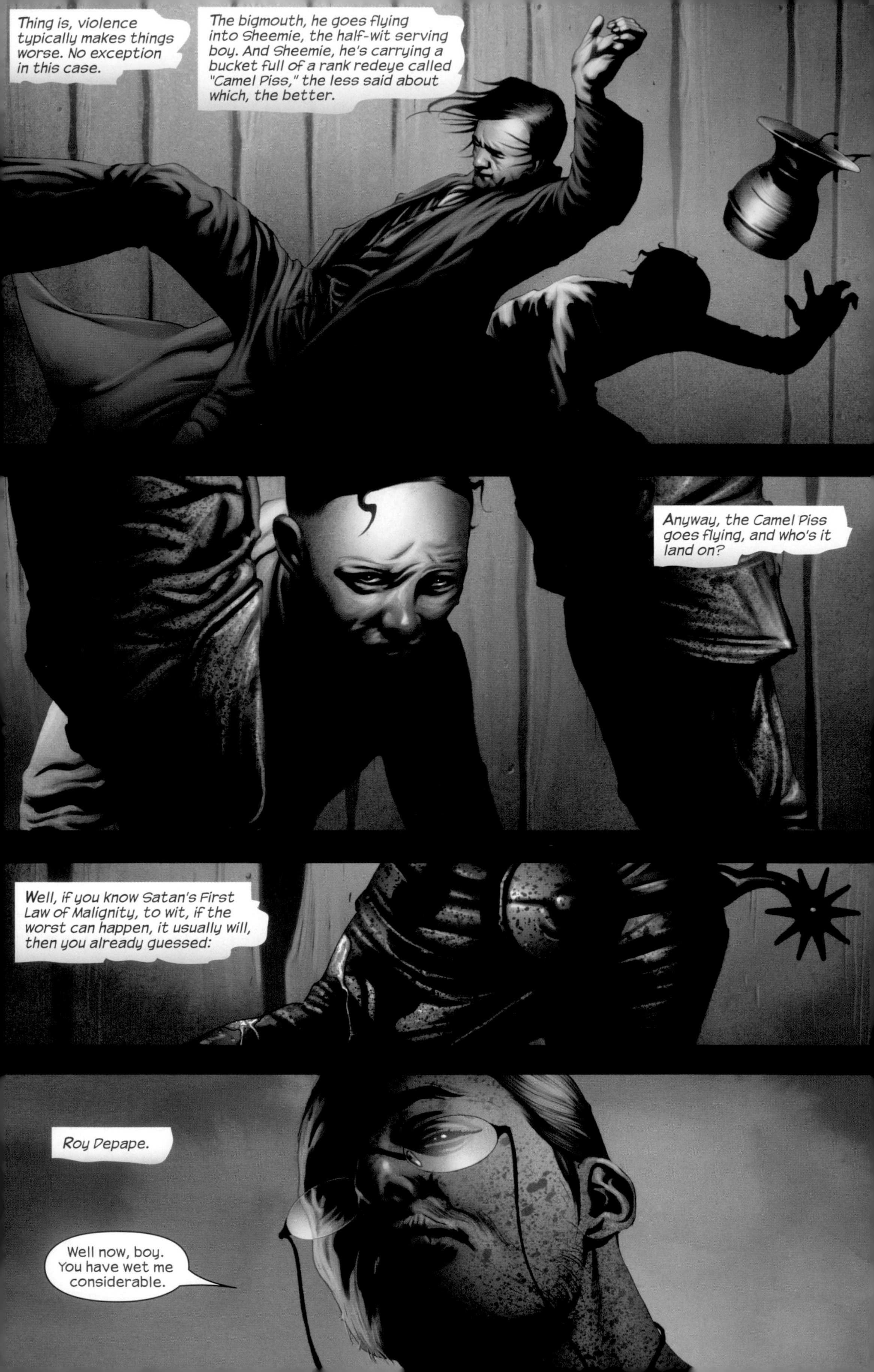
Thing is, violence typically makes things worse. No exception in this case.
The bigmouth, he goes flying into Sheemie, the half-wit serving boy. And Sheemie, he's carrying a bucket full of a rank redeye called "Camel Piss," the less said about which, the better.
Anyway, the Camel Piss goes flying, and who's it land on?
Well, if you know Satan's First Law of Malignity, to wit, if the worst can happen, it usually will, then you already guessed:
Roy Depape.
Well now, boy. You have wet me considerable.

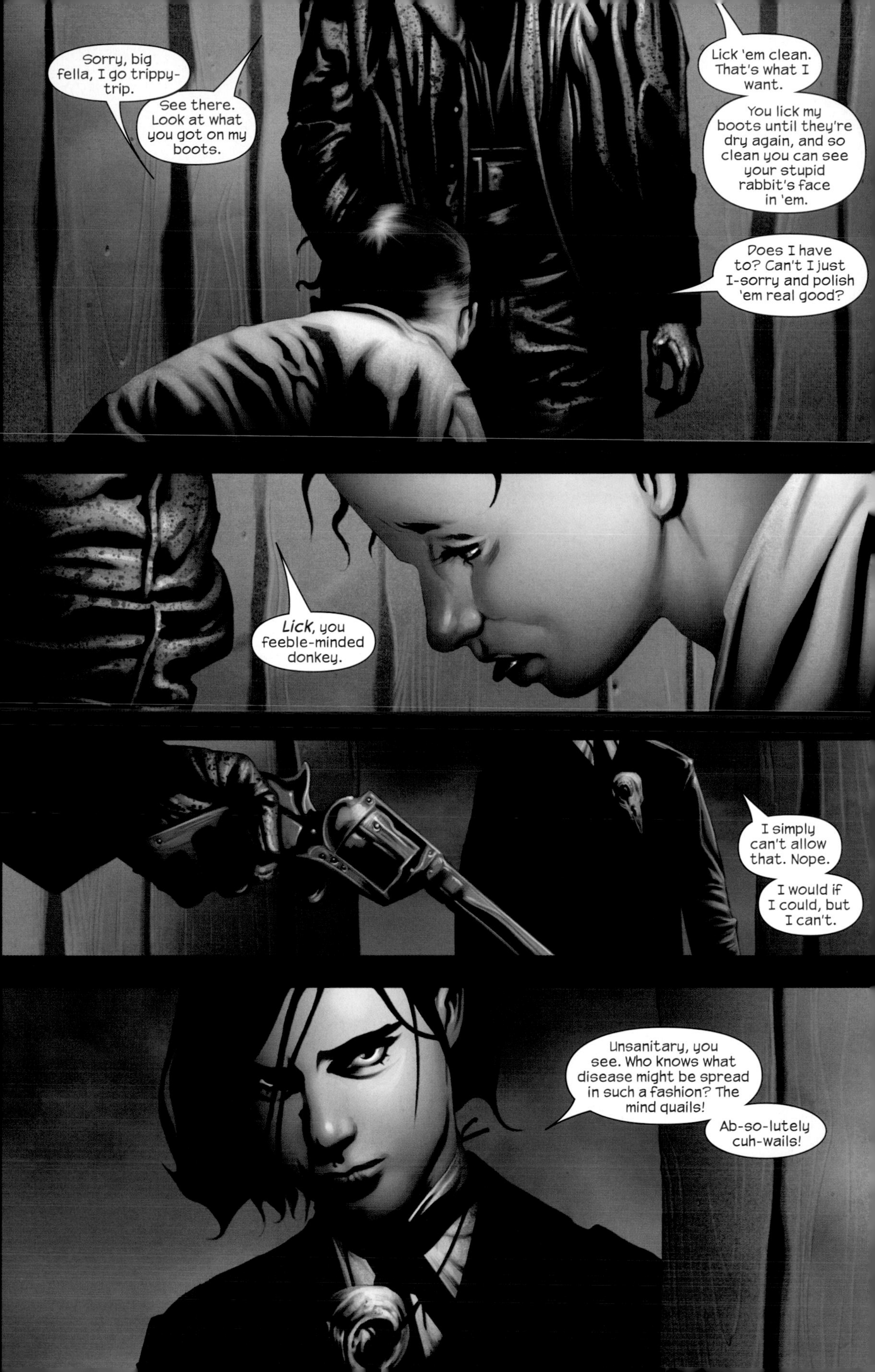

Sorry, big fella, I go trippy-trip.
See there. Look at what you got on my boots.
Lick 'em clean. That's what I want.
You lick my boots until they're dry again, and so clean you can see your stupid rabbit's face in 'em.
Does I have to? Can't I just I-sorry and polish 'em real good?
Lick, you feeble-minded donkey.
I simply can't allow that. Nope.
I would if I could, but I can't.
Unsanitary, you see. Who knows what disease might be spread in such a fashion? The mind quails!
Ab-so-lutely cuh-wails!

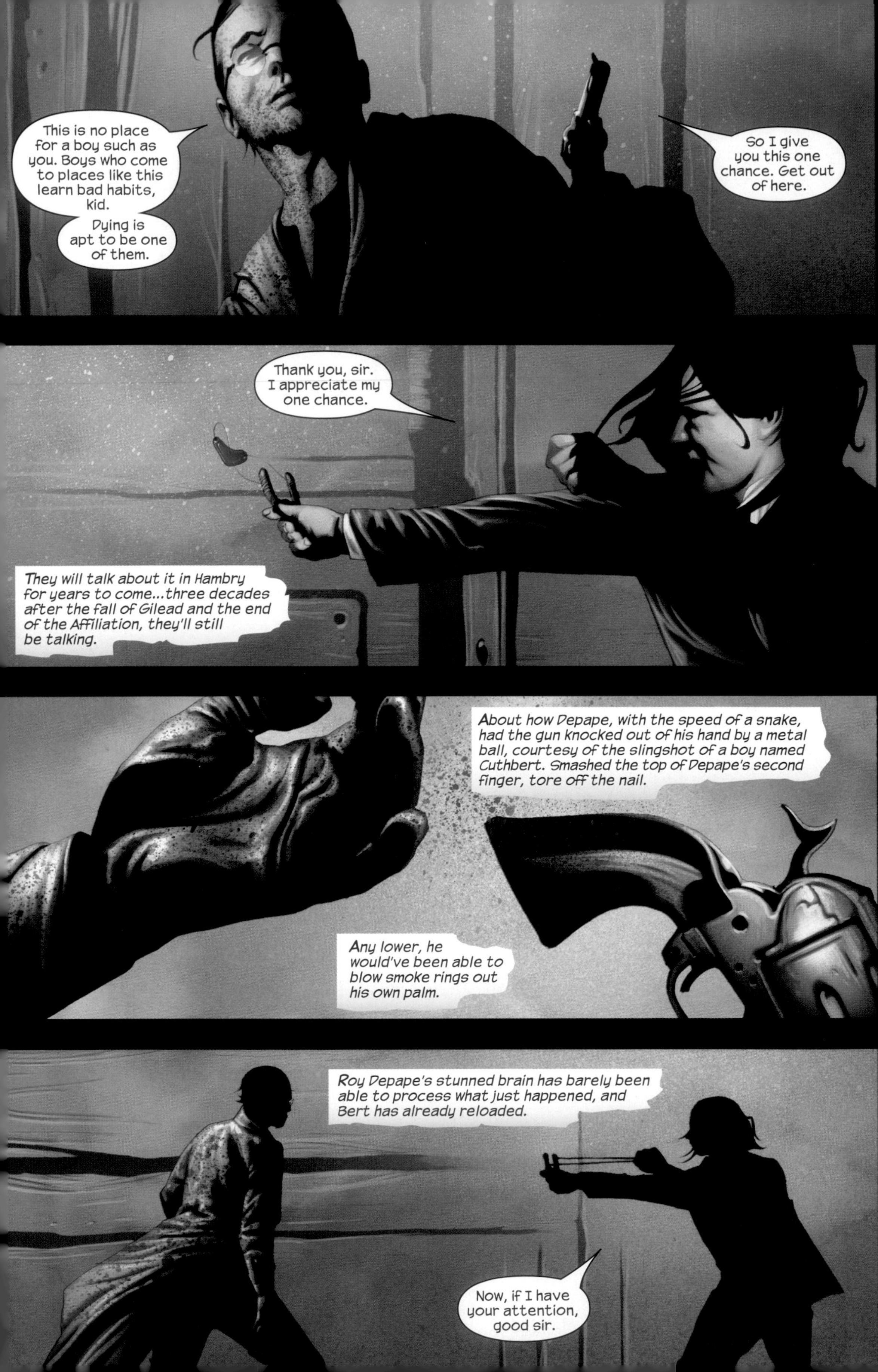
This is no place for a boy such as you. Boys who come to places like this learn bad habits, kid.
Dying is apt to be one of them.
So I give you this one chance. Get out of here.
Thank you, sir. I appreciate my one chance.
They will talk about it in Hambry for years to come...three decades after the fall of Gilead and the end of the Affiliation, they'll still be talking.
About how Depape, with the speed of a snake, had the gun knocked out of his hand by a metal ball, courtesy of the slingshot of a boy named Cuthbert. Smashed the top of Depape's second finger, tore off the nail.
Any lower, he would've been able to blow smoke rings out his own palm.
Roy Depape's stunned brain has barely been able to process what just happened, and Bert has already reloaded.
Now, if I have your attention, good sir.

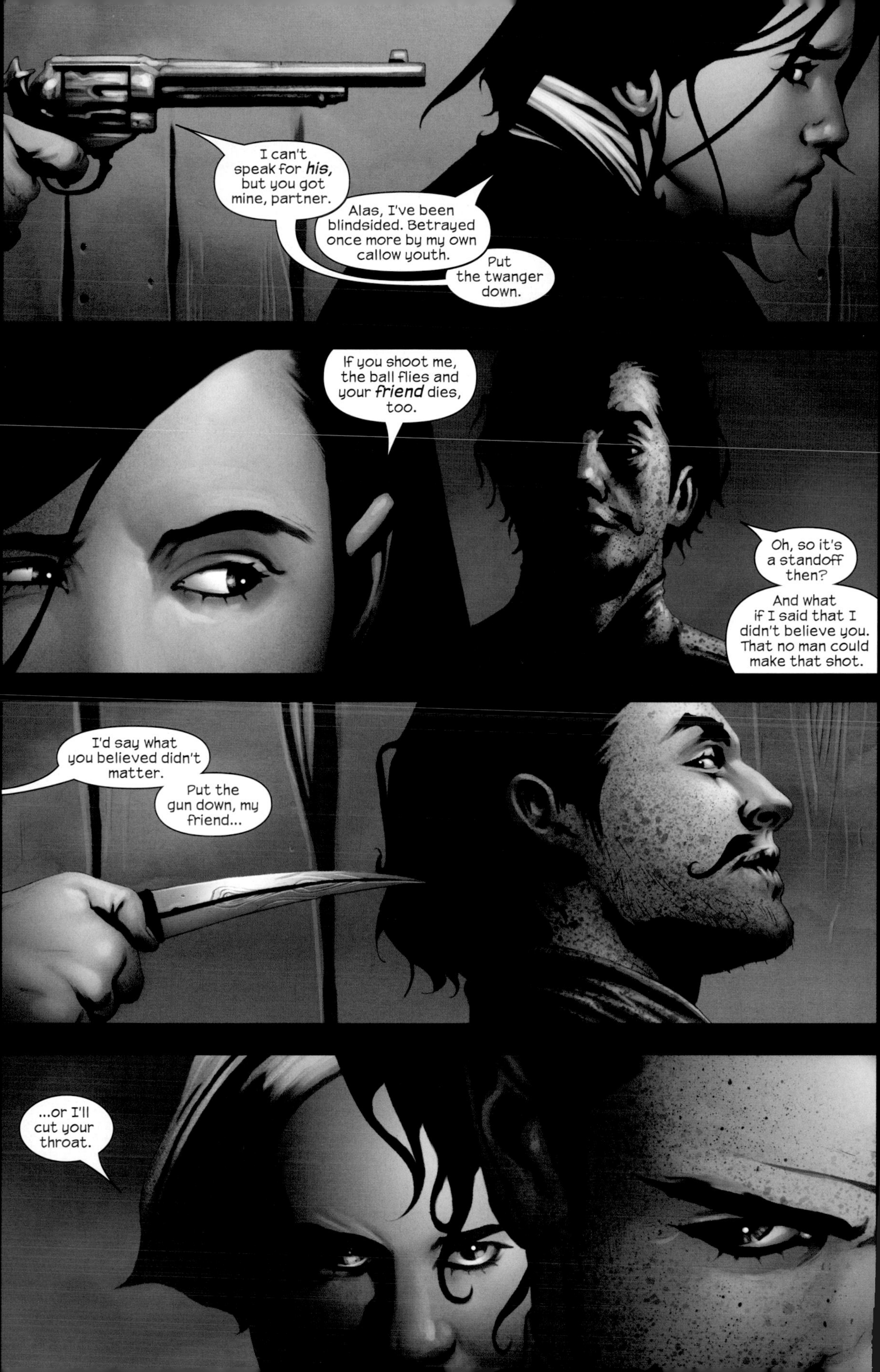
I can't speak for *his*, but you got mine, partner.
Alas, I've been blindsided. Betrayed once more by my own callow youth.
Put the twanger down.
If you shoot me, the ball flies and your *friend* dies, too.
Oh, so it's a standoff then?
And what if I said that I didn't believe you. That no man could make that shot.
I'd say what you believed didn't matter.
Put the gun down, my friend...
...or I'll cut your throat.

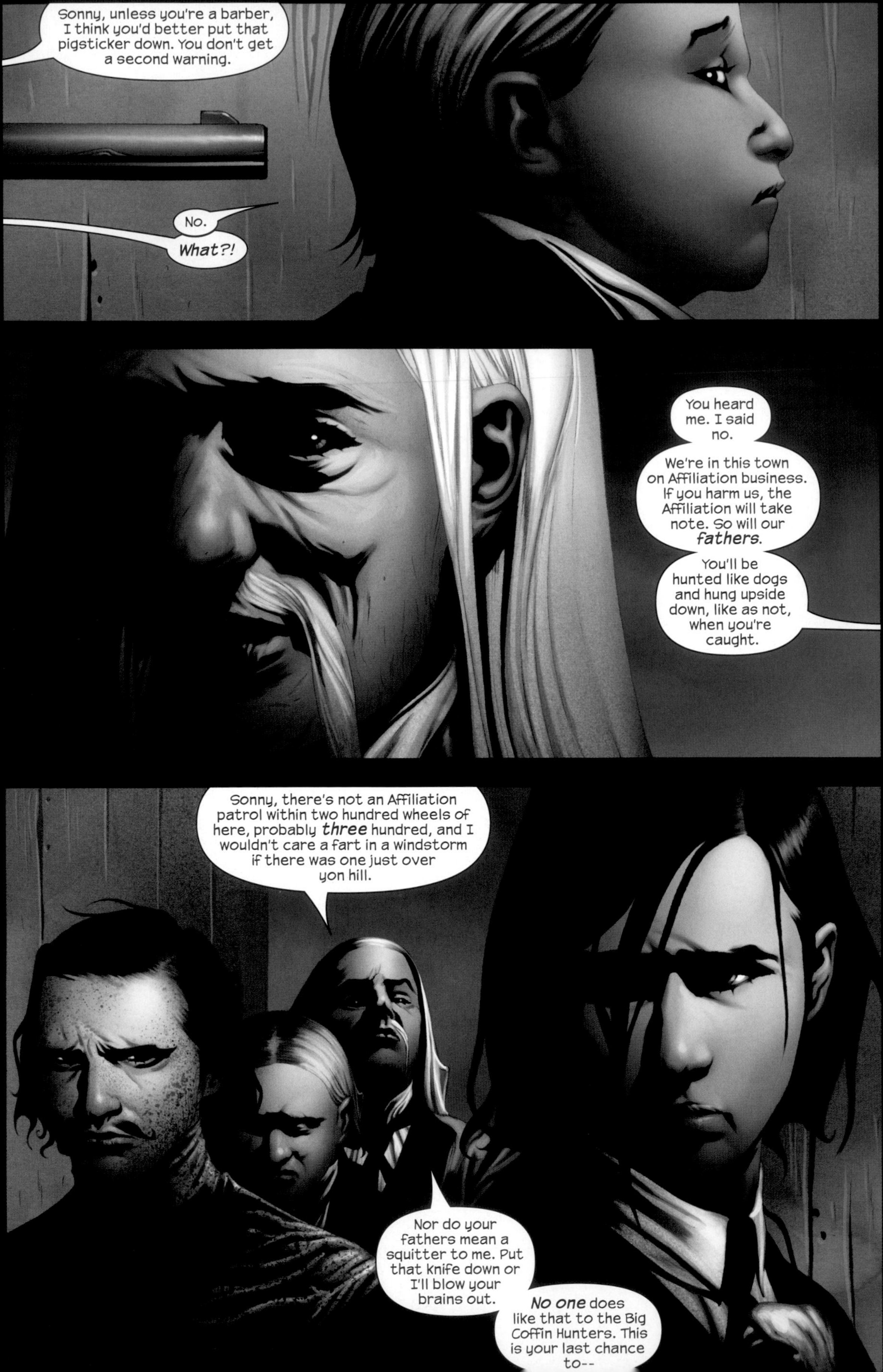
Sonny, unless you're a barber, I think you'd better put that pigsticker down. You don't get a second warning.
No.
What?!
You heard me. I said no.
We're in this town on Affiliation business. If you harm us, the Affiliation will take note. So will our fathers.
You'll be hunted like dogs and hung upside down, like as not, when you're caught.
Sonny, there's not an Affiliation patrol within two hundred wheels of here, probably three hundred, and I wouldn't care a fart in a windstorm if there was one just over yon hill.
Nor do your fathers mean a squitter to me. Put that knife down or I'll blow your brains out.
No one does like that to the Big Coffin Hunters. This is your last chance to--

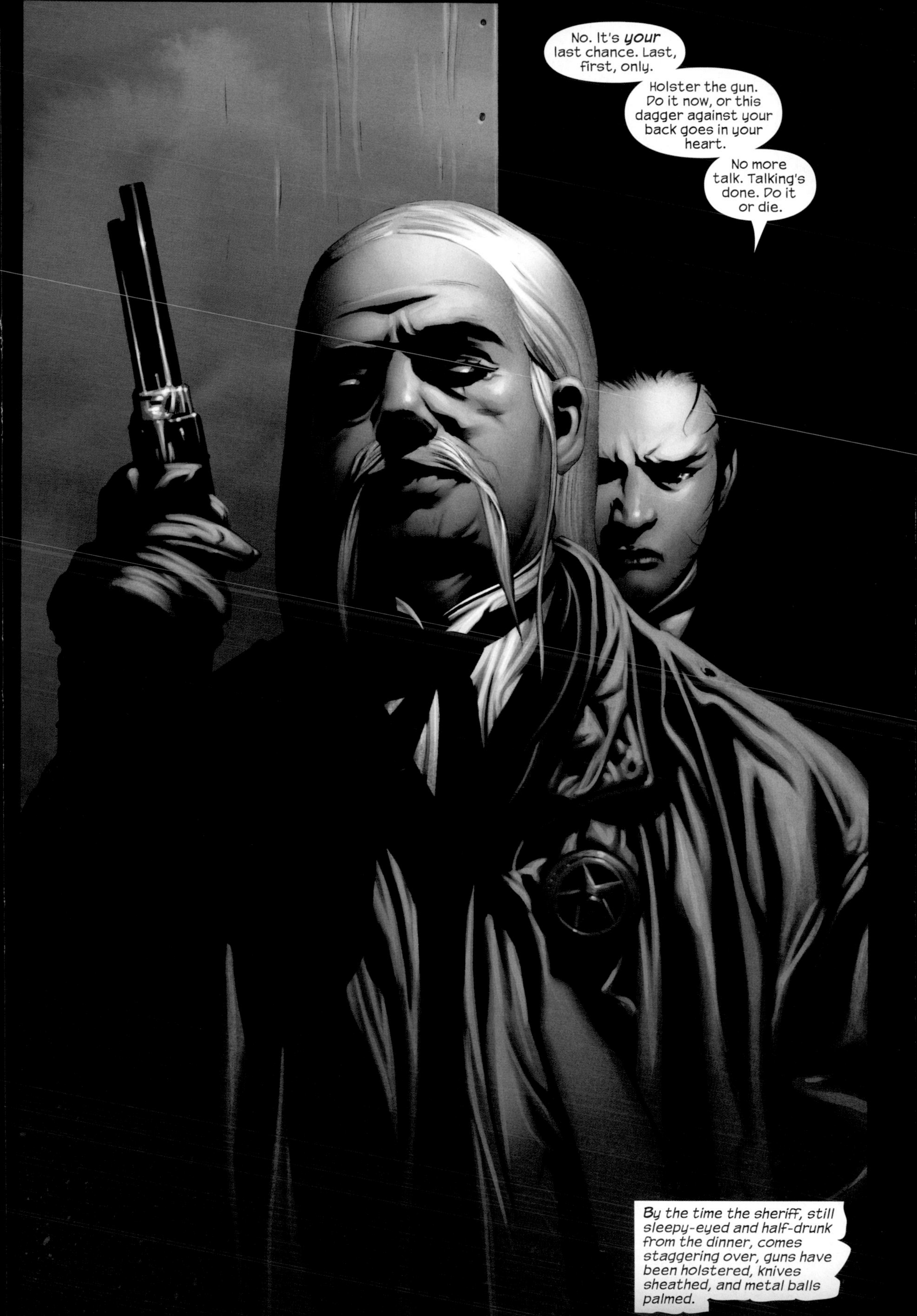
No. It's *your* last chance. Last, first, only.
Holster the gun. Do it now, or this dagger against your back goes in your heart.
No more talk. Talking's done. Do it or die.
By the time the sheriff, still sleepy-eyed and half-drunk from the dinner, comes staggering over, guns have been holstered, knives sheathed, and metal balls palmed.

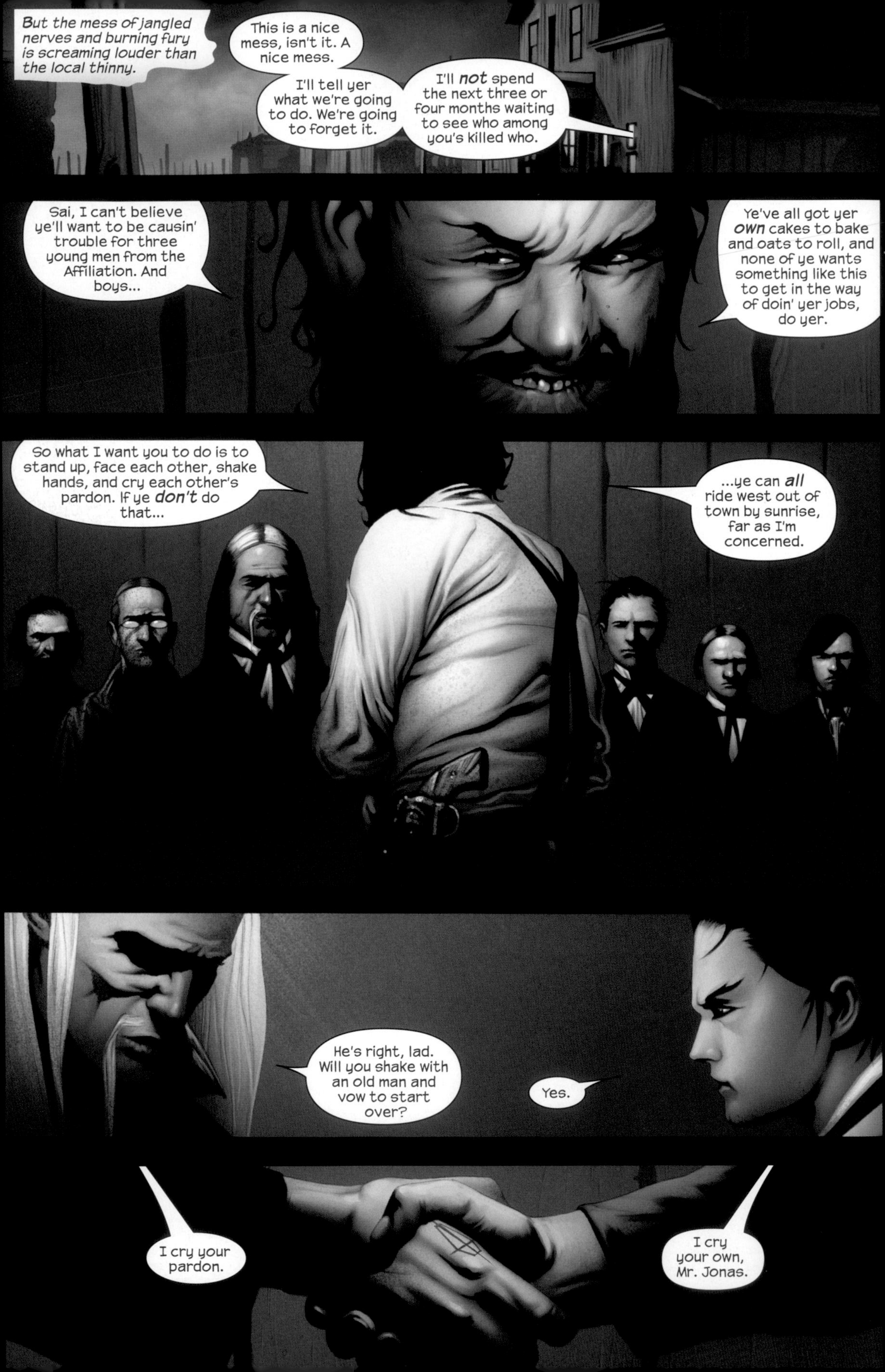

But the mess of jangled nerves and burning fury is screaming louder than the local thinny.
This is a nice mess, isn't it. A nice mess.
I'll tell yer what we're going to do. We're going to forget it.
I'll not spend the next three or four months waiting to see who among you's killed who.
Sai, I can't believe ye'll want to be causin' trouble for three young men from the Affiliation. And boys...
Ye've all got yer own cakes to bake and oats to roll, and none of ye wants something like this to get in the way of doin' yer jobs, do yer.
So what I want you to do is to stand up, face each other, shake hands, and cry each other's pardon. If ye don't do that...
...ye can all ride west out of town by sunrise, far as I'm concerned.
He's right, lad. Will you shake with an old man and vow to start over?
Yes.
I cry your pardon.
I cry your own, Mr. Jonas.

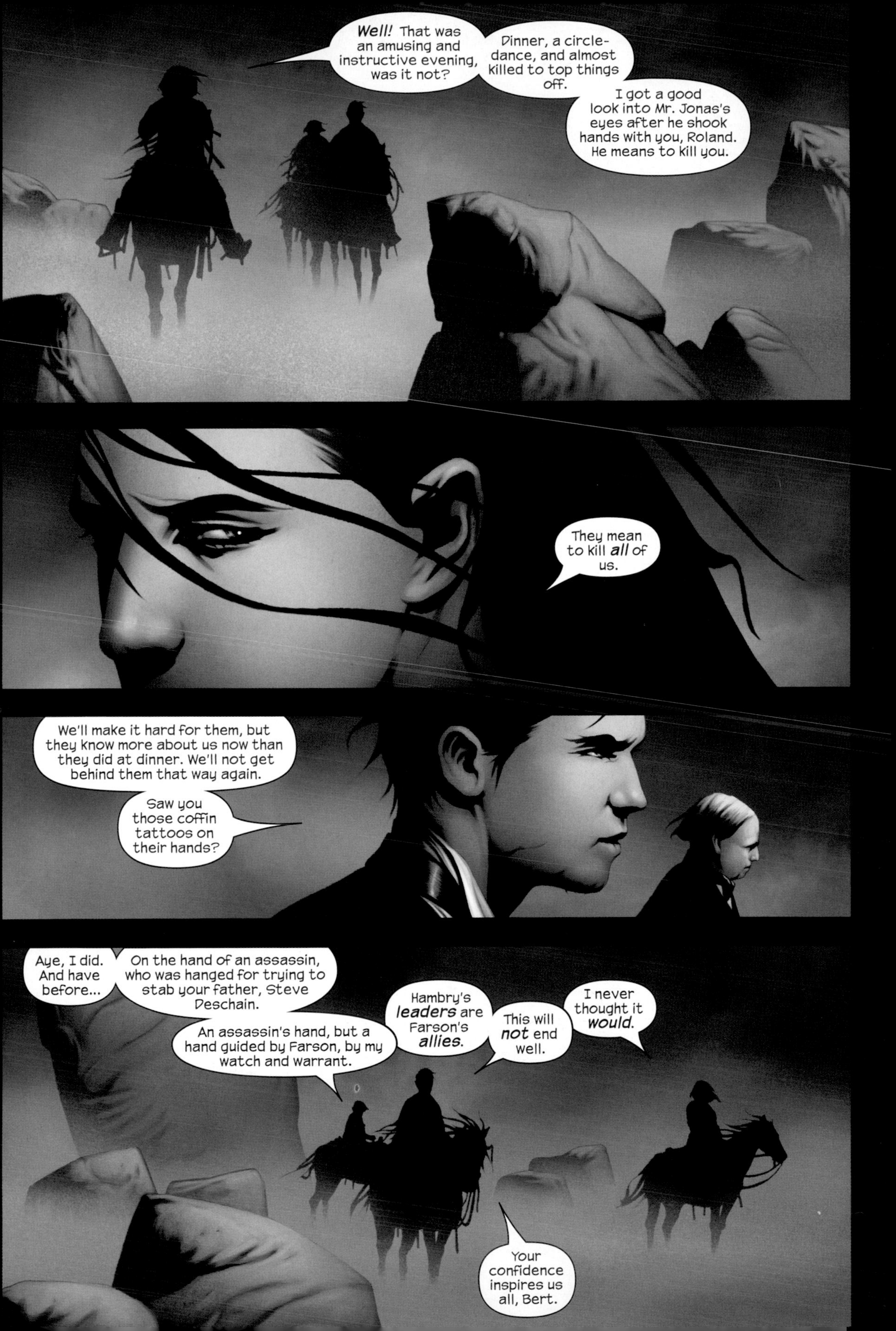
Well! That was an amusing and instructive evening, was it not?
Dinner, a circle-dance, and almost killed to top things off.
I got a good look into Mr. Jonas's eyes after he shook hands with you, Roland. He means to kill you.
They mean to kill all of us.
We'll make it hard for them, but they know more about us now than they did at dinner. We'll not get behind them that way again.
Saw you those coffin tattoos on their hands?
Aye, I did. And have before...
On the hand of an assassin, who was hanged for trying to stab your father, Steve Deschain.
An assassin's hand, but a hand guided by Farson, by my watch and warrant.
Hambry's leaders are Farson's allies.
This will not end well.
I never thought it would.
Your confidence inspires us all, Bert.

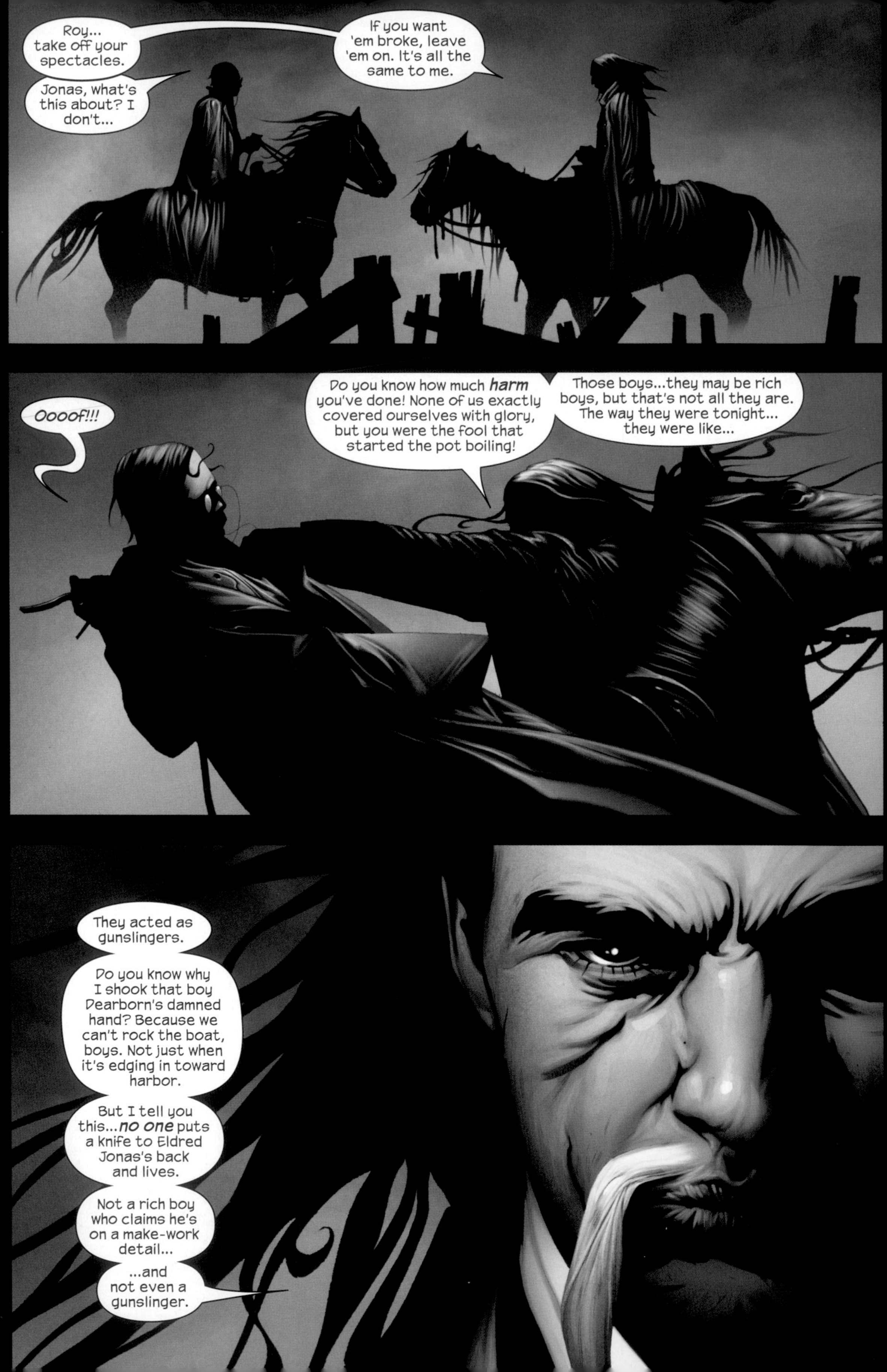
Roy... take off your spectacles.
If you want 'em broke, leave 'em on. It's all the same to me.
Jonas, what's this about? I don't...
Ooooof!!!
Do you know how much harm you've done! None of us exactly covered ourselves with glory, but you were the fool that started the pot boiling!
Those boys...they may be rich boys, but that's not all they are. The way they were tonight... they were like...
They acted as gunslingers.
Do you know why I shook that boy Dearborn's damned hand? Because we can't rock the boat, boys. Not just when it's edging in toward harbor.
But I tell you this...no one puts a knife to Eldred Jonas's back and lives.
Not a rich boy who claims he's on a make-work detail...
...and not even a gunslinger.

STEPHEN KING

THE DARK TOWER

THE GUNSLINGER BORN

CHAPTER FOUR

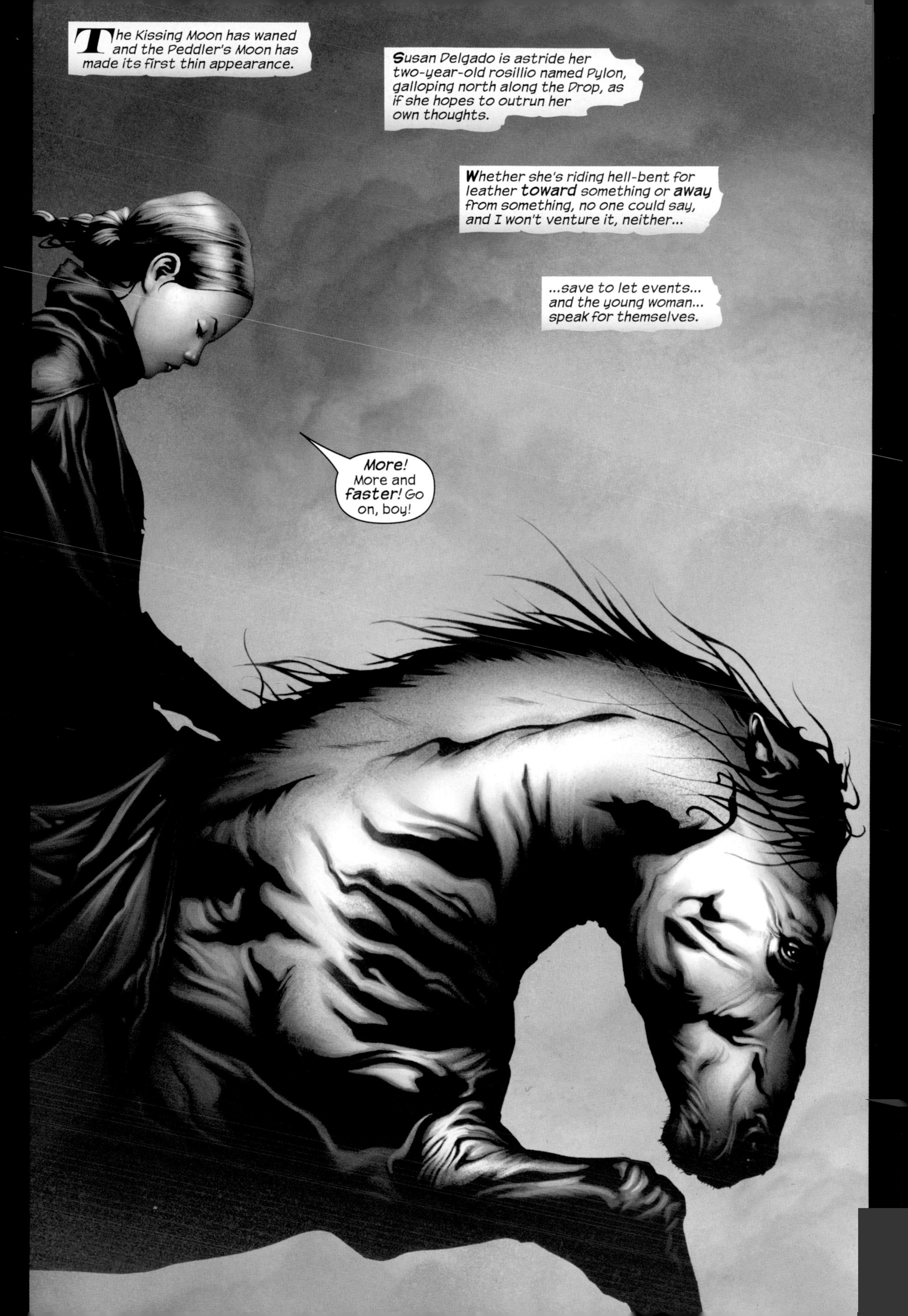
The Kissing Moon has waned and the Peddler's Moon has made its first thin appearance.
Susan Delgado is astride her two-year-old rosillio named Pylon, galloping north along the Drop, as if she hopes to outrun her own thoughts.
Whether she's riding hell-bent for leather toward something or away from something, no one could say, and I won't venture it, neither...
...save to let events... and the young woman... speak for themselves.
More! More and faster! Go on, boy!

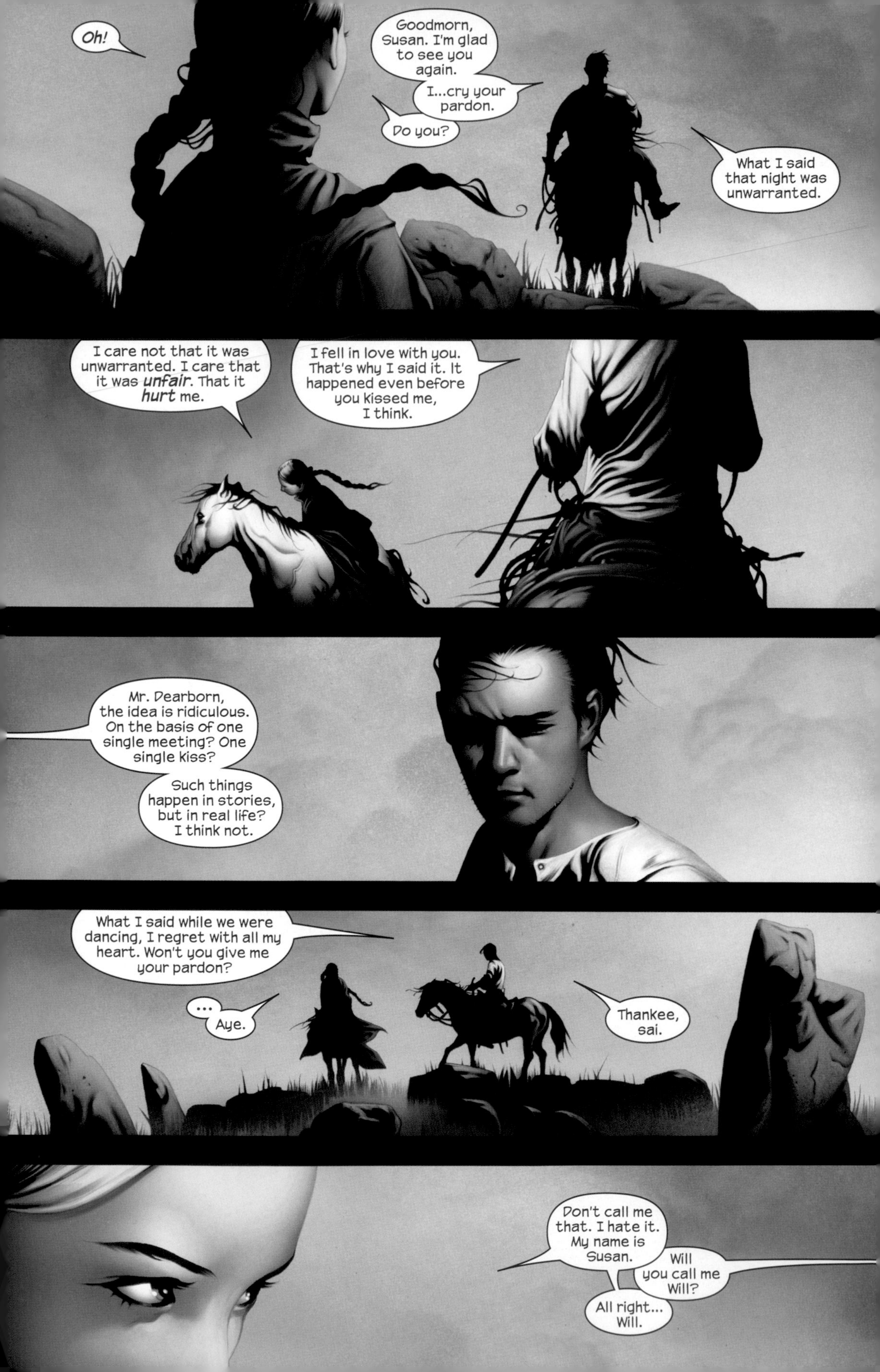
Oh!
Goodmorn, Susan. I'm glad to see you again.
I...cry your pardon.
Do you?
What I said that night was unwarranted.
I care not that it was unwarranted. I care that it was *unfair*. That it *hurt* me.
I fell in love with you. That's why I said it. It happened even before you kissed me, I think.
Mr. Dearborn, the idea is ridiculous. On the basis of one single meeting? One single kiss?
Such things happen in stories, but in real life? I think not.
What I said while we were dancing, I regret with all my heart. Won't you give me your pardon?
... Aye.
Thankee, sai.
Don't call me that. I hate it. My name is Susan.
Will you call me Will?
All right... Will.

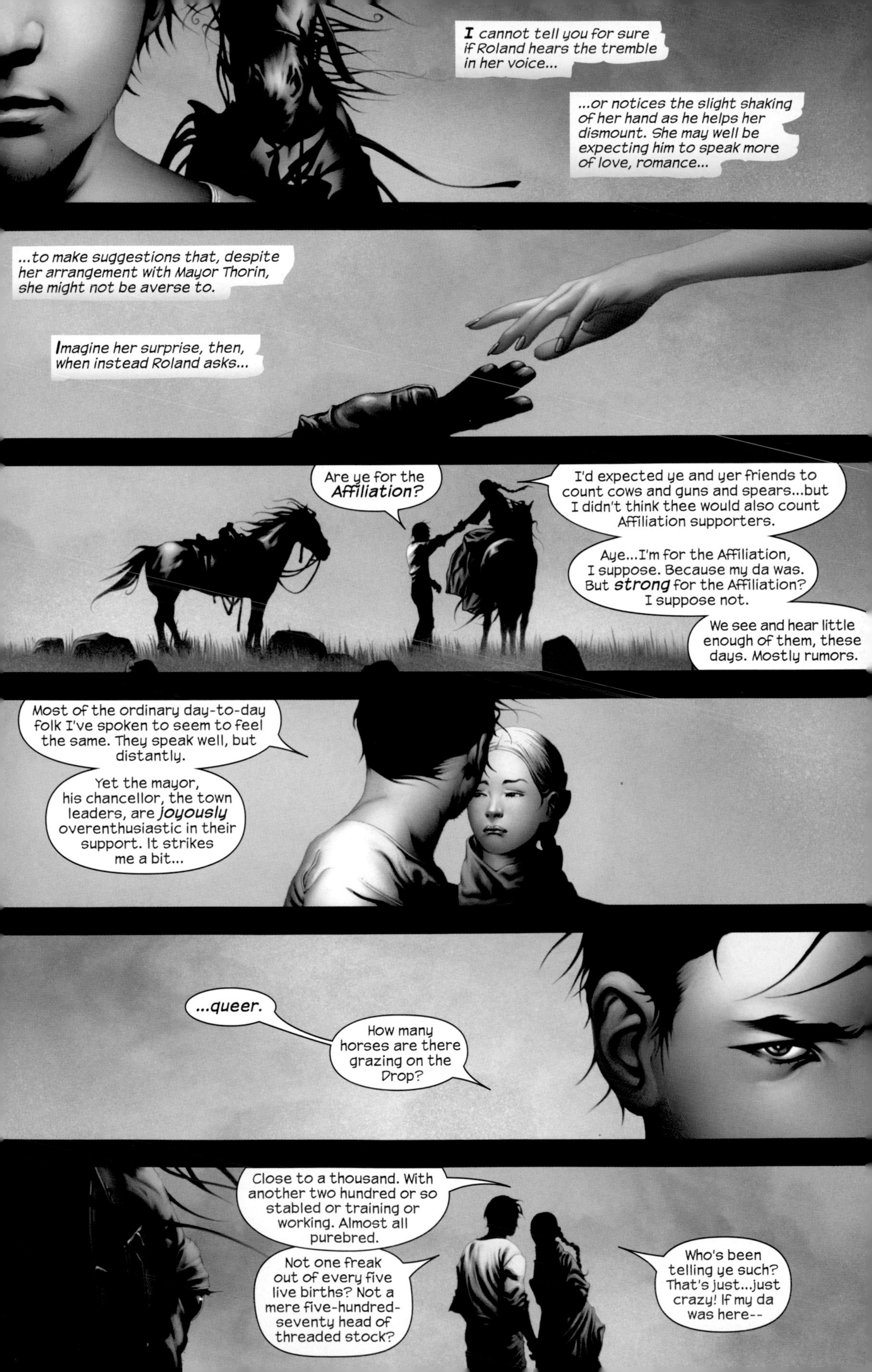
I cannot tell you for sure if Roland hears the tremble in her voice...
...or notices the slight shaking of her hand as he helps her dismount. She may well be expecting him to speak more of love, romance...
...to make suggestions that, despite her arrangement with Mayor Thorin, she might not be averse to.
Imagine her surprise, then, when instead Roland asks...
Are ye for the Affiliation?
I'd expected ye and yer friends to count cows and guns and spears...but I didn't think thee would also count Affiliation supporters.
Aye...I'm for the Affiliation, I suppose. Because my da was. But strong for the Affiliation? I suppose not.
We see and hear little enough of them, these days. Mostly rumors.
Most of the ordinary day-to-day folk I've spoken to seem to feel the same. They speak well, but distantly.
Yet the mayor, his chancellor, the town leaders, are joyously overenthusiastic in their support. It strikes me a bit...
...queer.
How many horses are there grazing on the Drop?
Close to a thousand. With another two hundred or so stabled or training or working. Almost all purebred.
Not one freak out of every five live births? Not a mere five-hundred-seventy head of threaded stock?
Who's been telling ye such? That's just...just crazy! If my da was here--

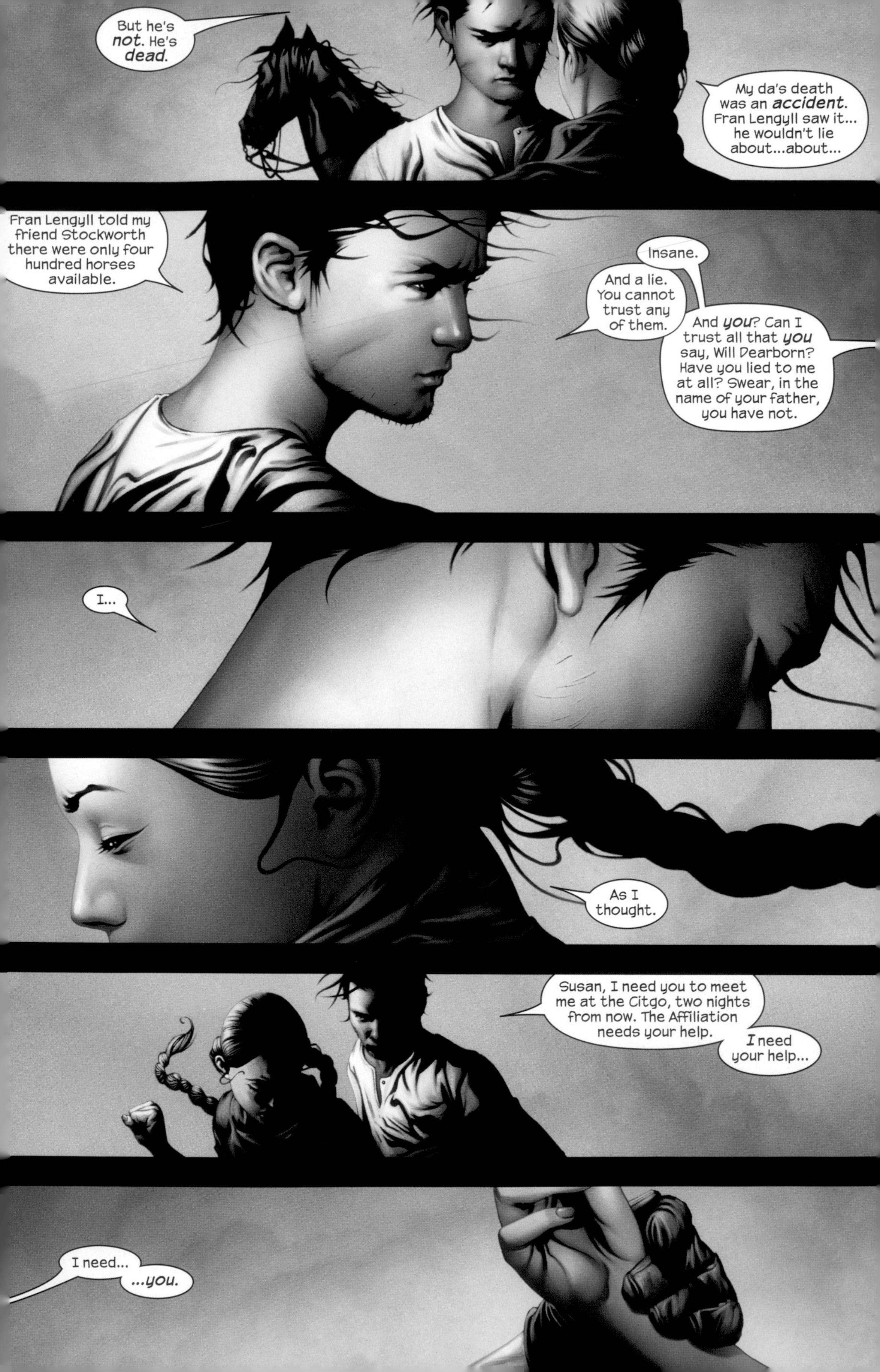
But he's *not*. He's *dead*.
My da's death was an *accident*. Fran Lengyll saw it... he wouldn't lie about...about...
Fran Lengyll told my friend Stockworth there were only four hundred horses available.
Insane.
And a lie. You cannot trust any of them.
And *you*? Can I trust all that *you* say, Will Dearborn? Have you lied to me at all? Swear, in the name of your father, you have not.
I...
As I thought.
Susan, I need you to meet me at the Citgo, two nights from now. The Affiliation needs your help.
I need your help...
I need...
...*you*.

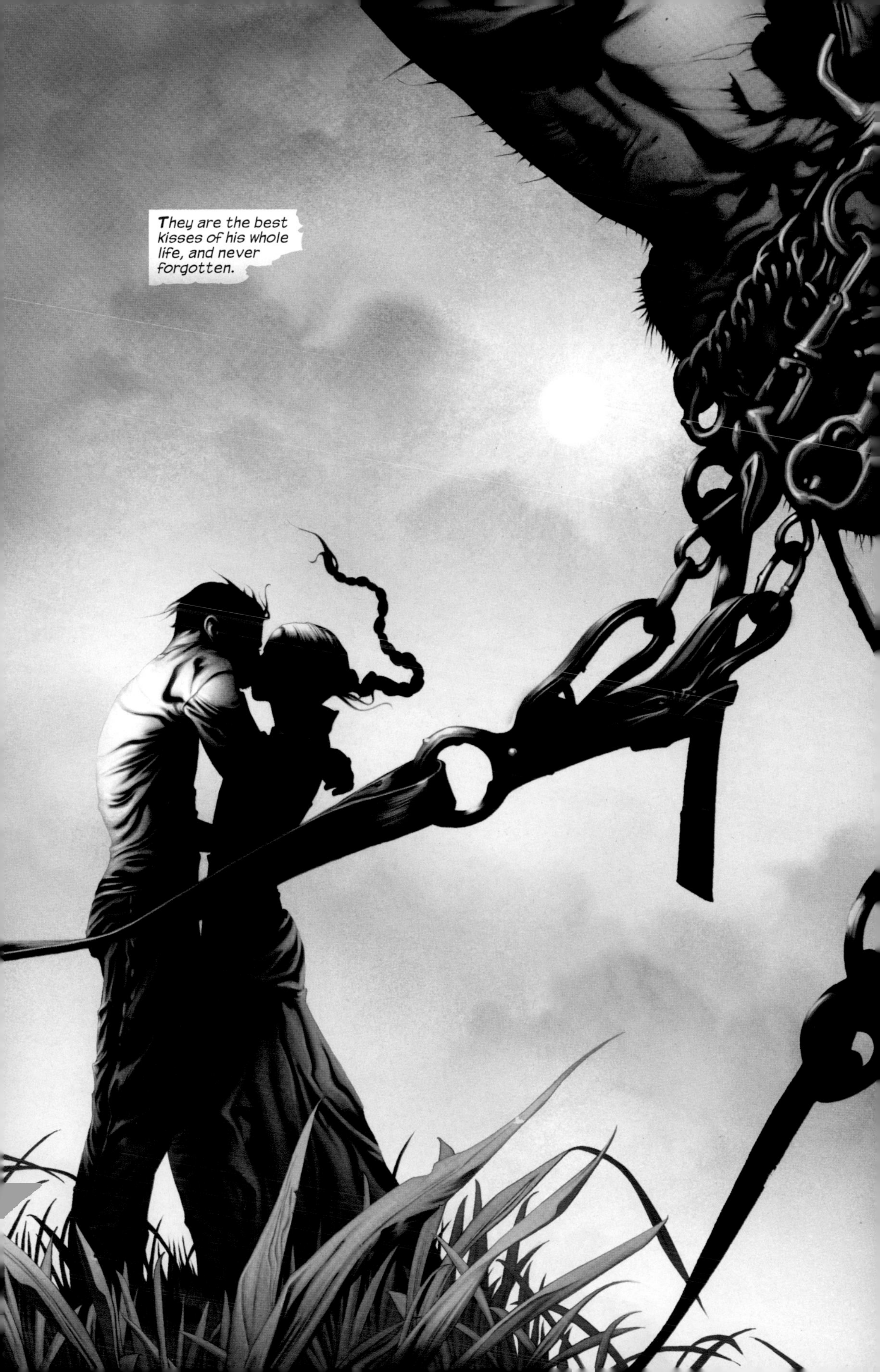
They are the best kisses of his whole life, and never forgotten.

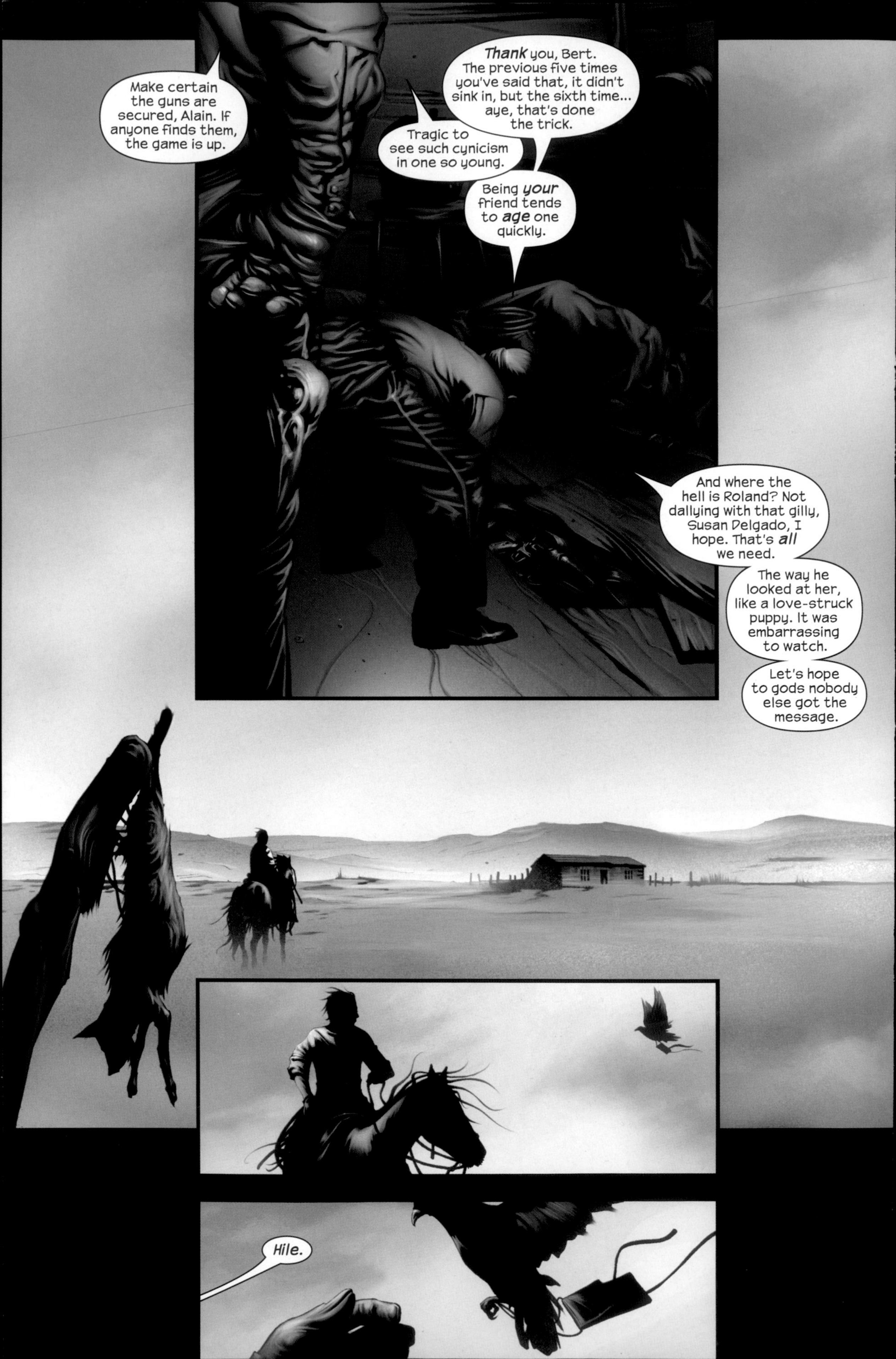
Make certain the guns are secured, Alain. If anyone finds them, the game is up.
Thank you, Bert. The previous five times you've said that, it didn't sink in, but the sixth time... aye, that's done the trick.
Tragic to see such cynicism in one so young.
Being your friend tends to age one quickly.
And where the hell is Roland? Not dallying with that gilly, Susan Delgado, I hope. That's all we need.
The way he looked at her, like a love-struck puppy. It was embarrassing to watch.
Let's hope to gods nobody else got the message.
Hile.

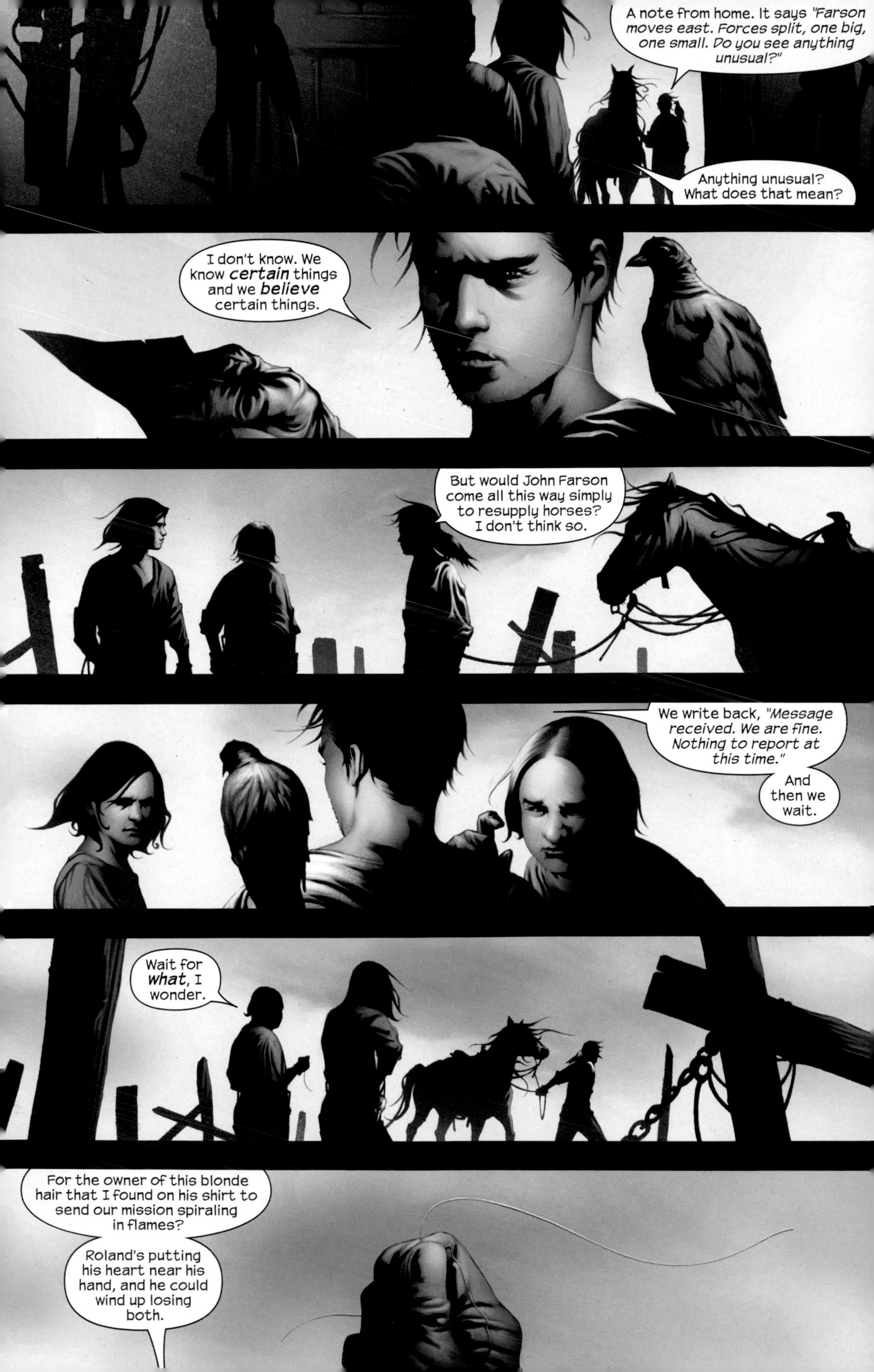
A note from home. It says "Farson moves east. Forces split, one big, one small. Do you see anything unusual?"
Anything unusual? What does that mean?
I don't know. We know *certain* things and we *believe* certain things.
But would John Farson come all this way simply to resupply horses? I don't think so.
We write back, "Message received. We are fine. Nothing to report at this time."
And then we wait.
Wait for *what*, I wonder.
For the owner of this blonde hair that I found on his shirt to send our mission spiraling in flames?
Roland's putting his heart near his hand, and he could wind up losing both.

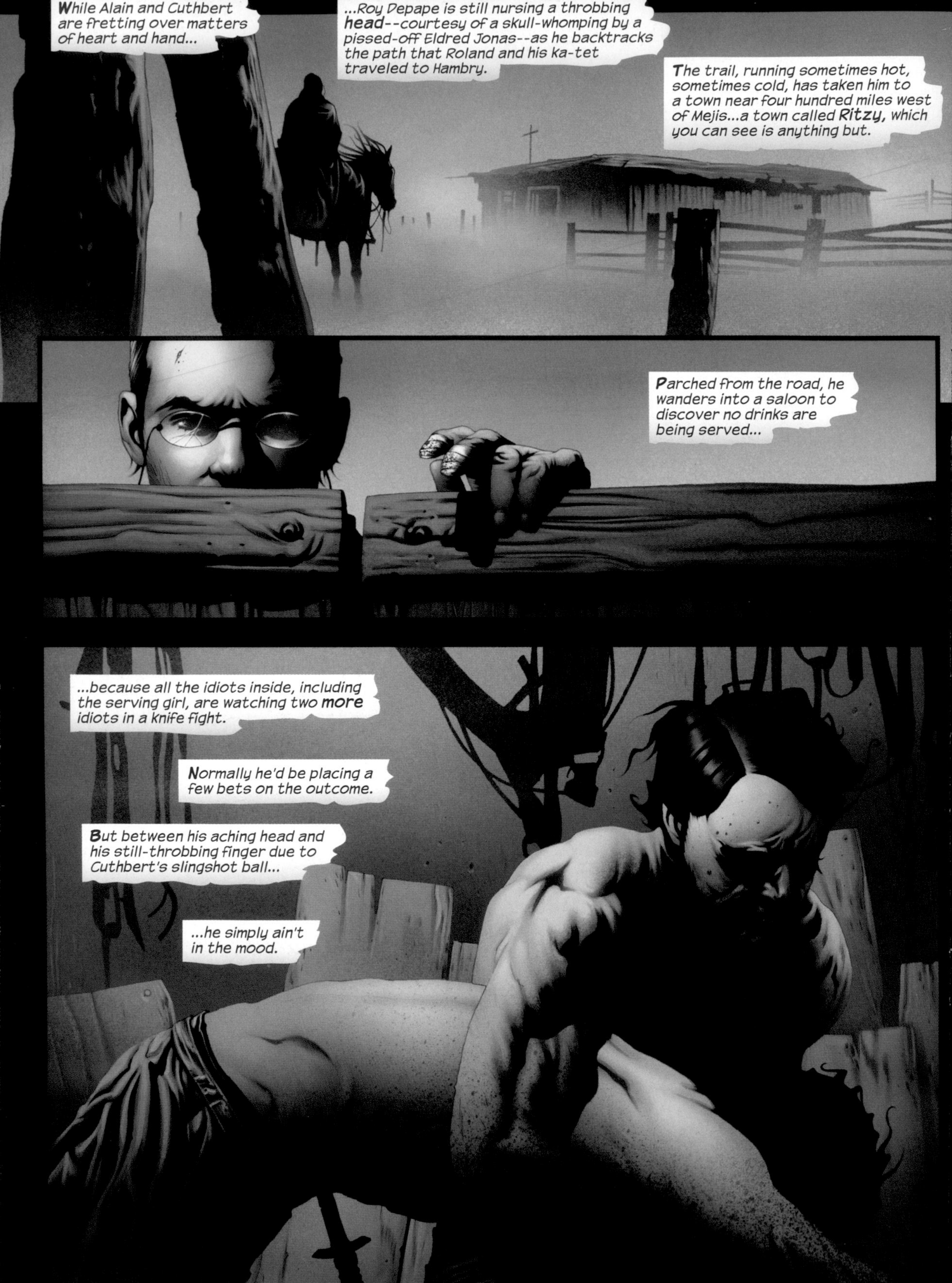
While Alain and Cuthbert are fretting over matters of heart and hand...
...Roy Depape is still nursing a throbbing head--courtesy of a skull-whomping by a pissed-off Eldred Jonas--as he backtracks the path that Roland and his ka-tet traveled to Hambry.
The trail, running sometimes hot, sometimes cold, has taken him to a town near four hundred miles west of Mejis...a town called Ritzy, which you can see is anything but.
Parched from the road, he wanders into a saloon to discover no drinks are being served...
...because all the idiots inside, including the serving girl, are watching two more idiots in a knife fight.
Normally he'd be placing a few bets on the outcome.
But between his aching head and his still-throbbing finger due to Cuthbert's slingshot ball...
...he simply ain't in the mood.

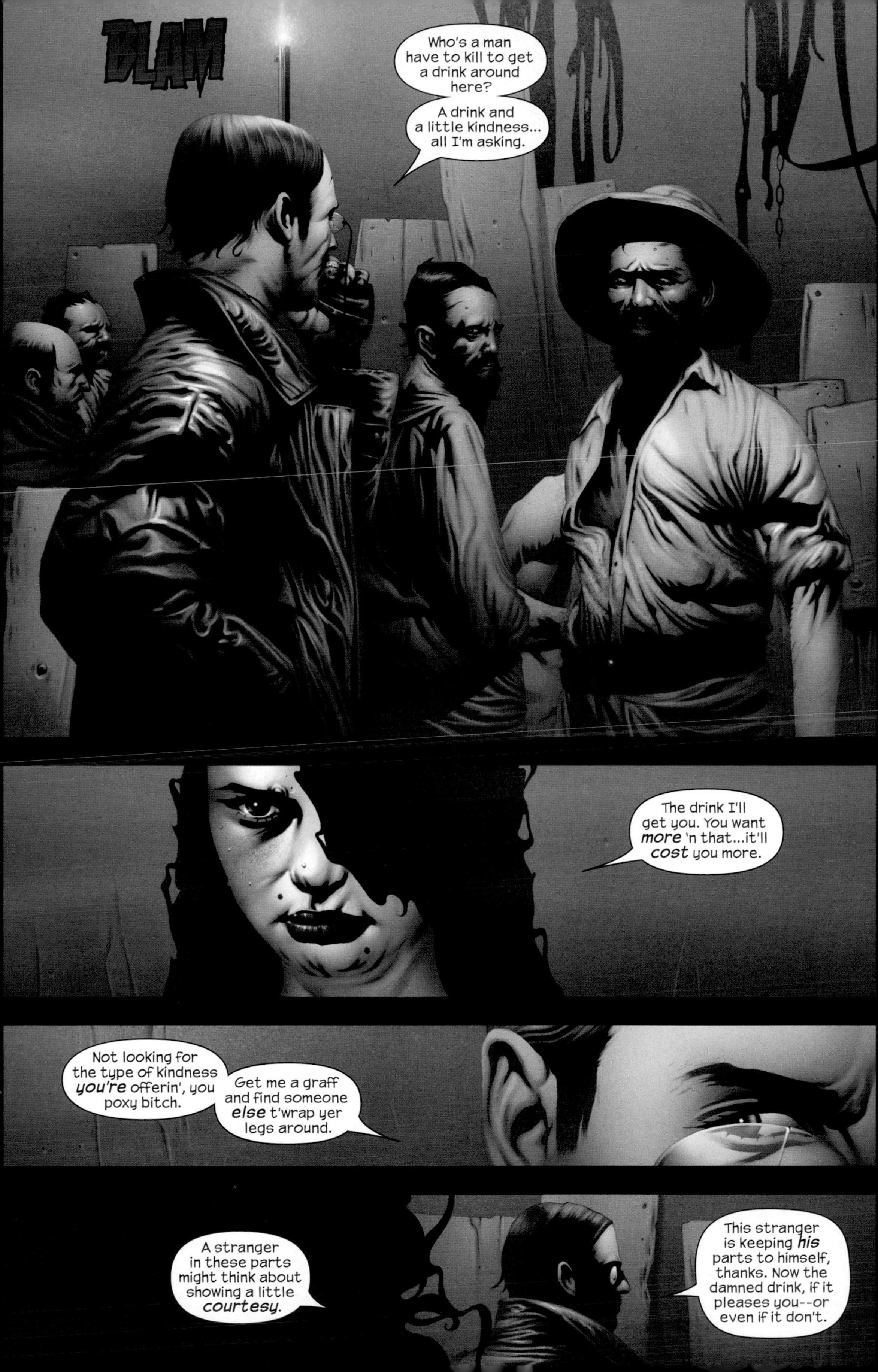
BLAM
Who's a man have to kill to get a drink around here?
A drink and a little kindness... all I'm asking.
The drink I'll get you. You want *more* 'n that...it'll *cost* you more.
Not looking for the type of kindness *you're* offerin', you poxy bitch.
Get me a graff and find someone *else* t'wrap yer legs around.
A stranger in these parts might think about showing a little *courtesy*.
This stranger is keeping *his* parts to himself, thanks. Now the damned drink, if it pleases you--or even if it don't.

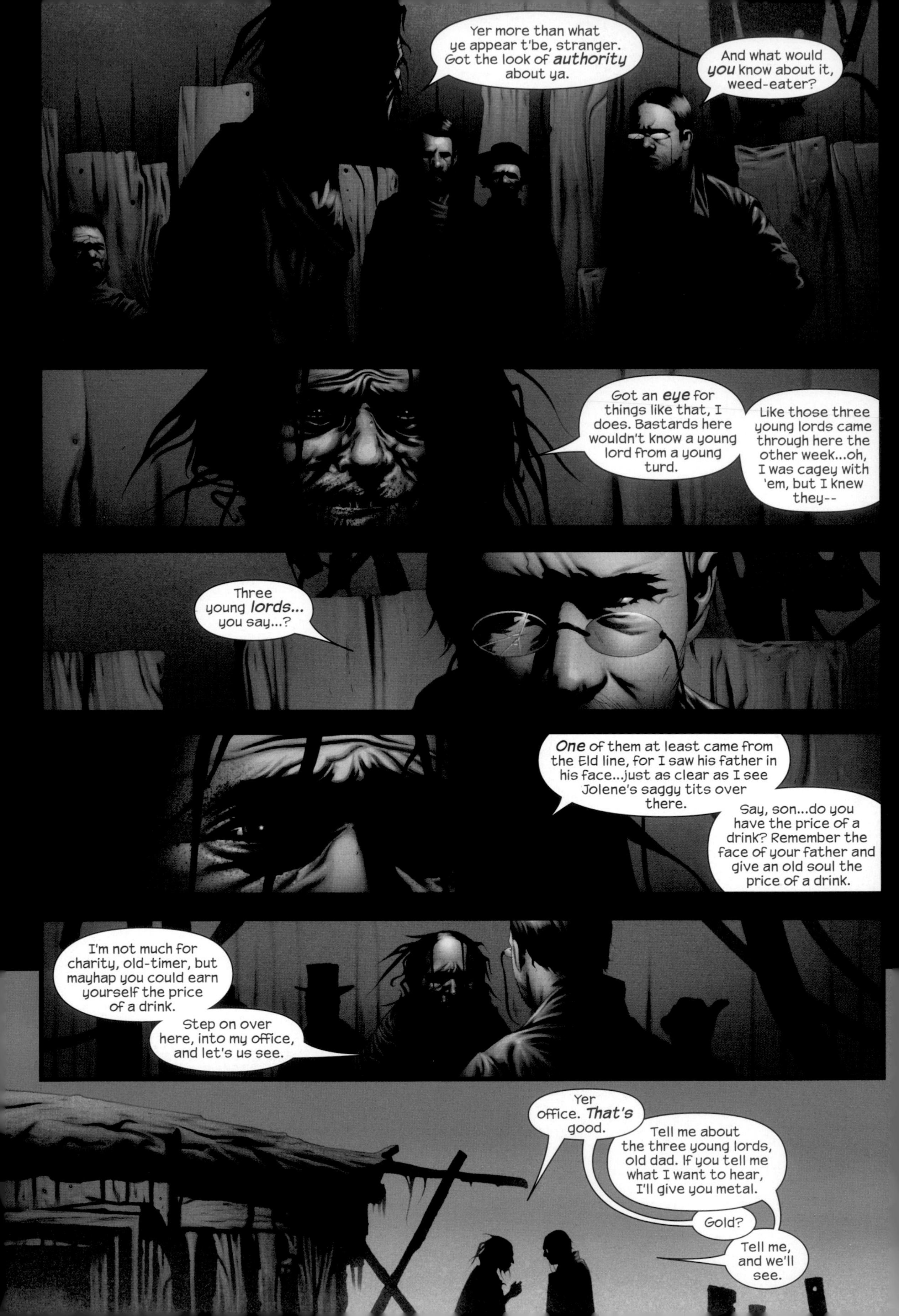
Yer more than what ye appear t'be, stranger. Got the look of *authority* about ya.
And what would *you* know about it, weed-eater?
Got an *eye* for things like that, I does. Bastards here wouldn't know a young lord from a young turd.
Like those three young lords came through here the other week...oh, I was cagey with 'em, but I knew they--
Three young *lords*... you say...?
One of them at least came from the Eld line, for I saw his father in his face...just as clear as I see Jolene's saggy tits over there.
Say, son...do you have the price of a drink? Remember the face of your father and give an old soul the price of a drink.
I'm not much for charity, old-timer, but mayhap you could earn yourself the price of a drink.
Step on over here, into my office, and let's us see.
Yer office. *That's* good.
Tell me about the three young lords, old dad. If you tell me what I want to hear, I'll give you metal.
Gold?
Tell me, and we'll see.

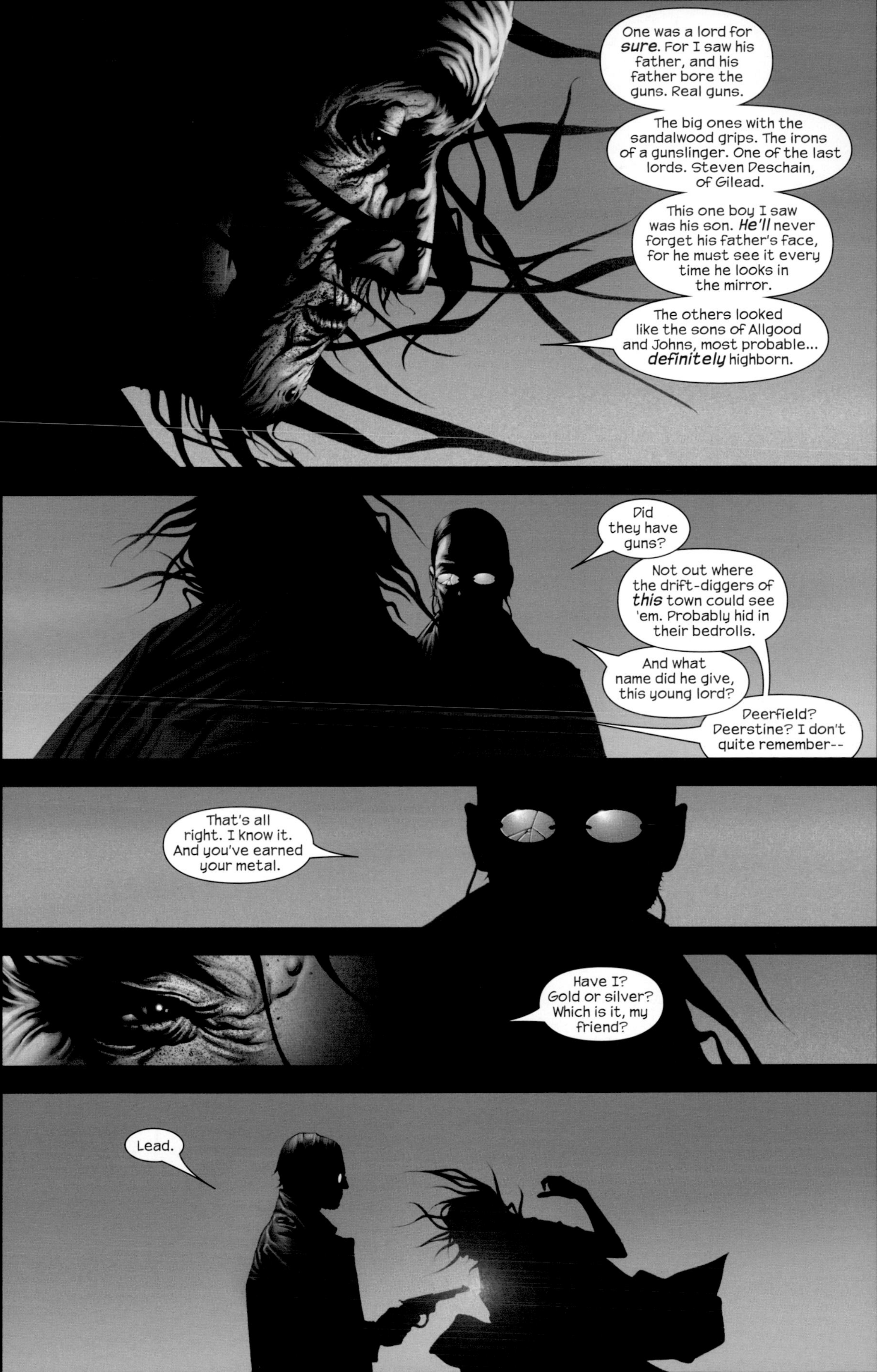
One was a lord for *sure*. For I saw his father, and his father bore the guns. Real guns.
The big ones with the sandalwood grips. The irons of a gunslinger. One of the last lords. Steven Deschain, of Gilead.
This one boy I saw was his son. *He'll* never forget his father's face, for he must see it every time he looks in the mirror.
The others looked like the sons of Allgood and Johns, most probable... *definitely* highborn.
Did they have guns?
Not out where the drift-diggers of *this* town could see 'em. Probably hid in their bedrolls.
And what name did he give, this young lord?
Deerfield? Deerstine? I don't quite remember--
That's all right. I know it. And you've earned your metal.
Have I? Gold or silver? Which is it, my friend?
Lead.

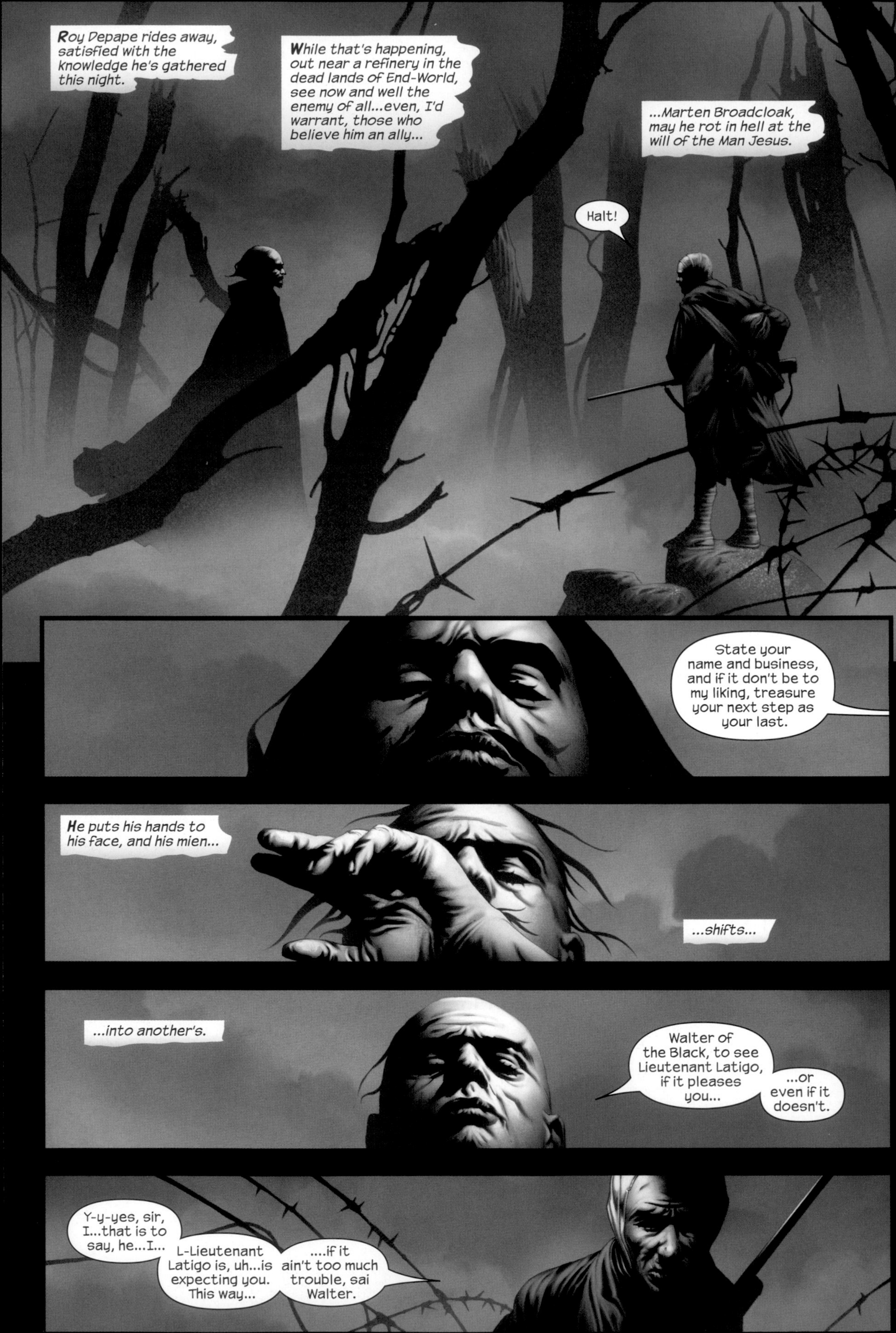
Roy Depape rides away, satisfied with the knowledge he's gathered this night.
While that's happening, out near a refinery in the dead lands of End-World, see now and well the enemy of all...even, I'd warrant, those who believe him an ally...
...Marten Broadcloak, may he rot in hell at the will of the Man Jesus.
Halt!
State your name and business, and if it don't be to my liking, treasure your next step as your last.
He puts his hands to his face, and his mien...
...shifts...
...into another's.
Walter of the Black, to see Lieutenant Latigo, if it pleases you...
...or even if it doesn't.
Y-y-yes, sir, I...that is to say, he...I...
L-Lieutenant Latigo is, uh...is expecting you. This way...
....if it ain't too much trouble, sai Walter.

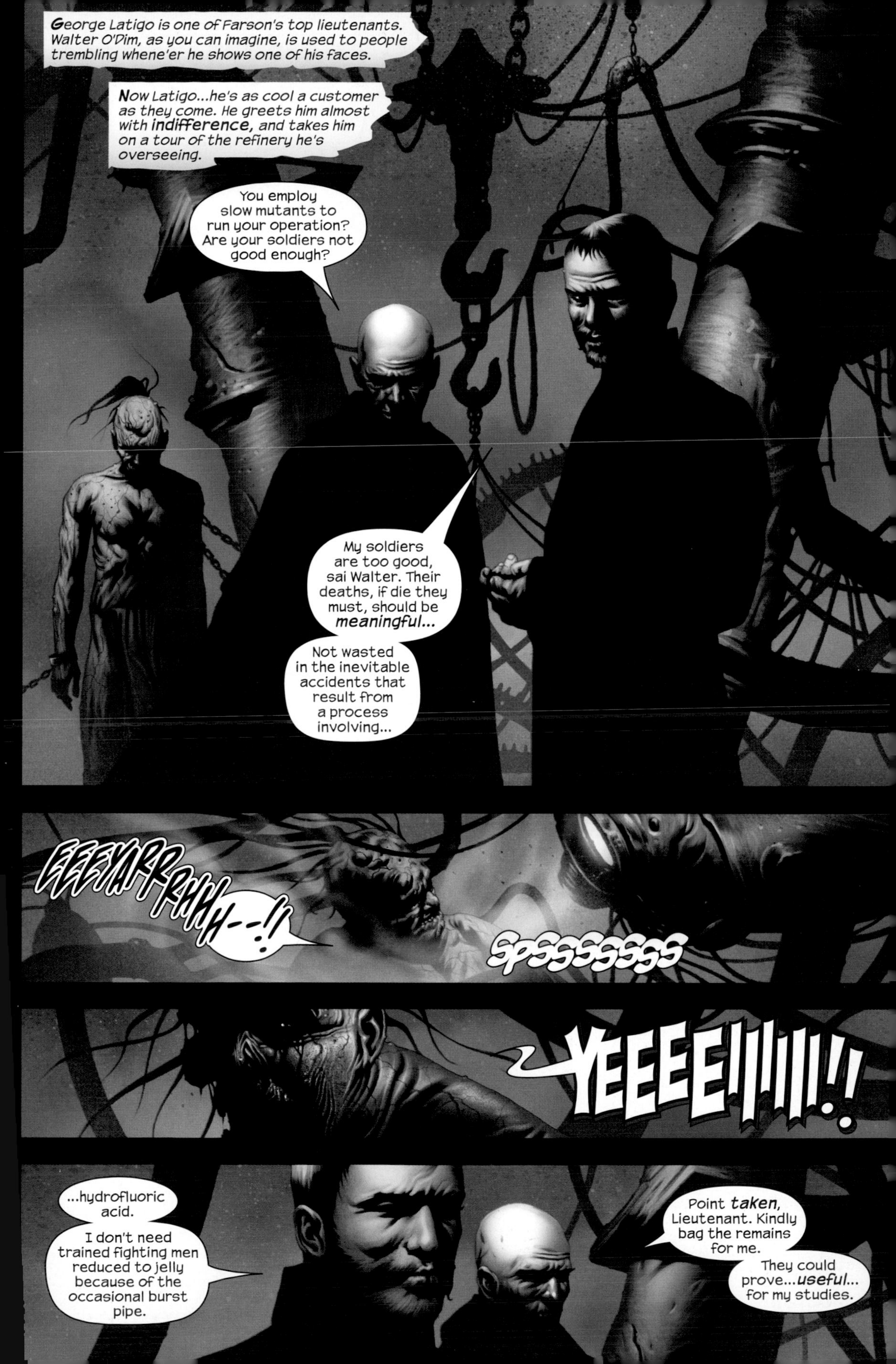
George Latigo is one of Farson's top lieutenants. Walter O'Dim, as you can imagine, is used to people trembling whene'er he shows one of his faces.
Now Latigo...he's as cool a customer as they come. He greets him almost with indifference, and takes him on a tour of the refinery he's overseeing.
You employ slow mutants to run your operation? Are your soldiers not good enough?
My soldiers are too good, sai Walter. Their deaths, if die they must, should be meaningful...
Not wasted in the inevitable accidents that result from a process involving...
EEEYARRRHHH--!!
SPSSSSSSS
YEEEEIIIIII!!
...hydrofluoric acid.
I don't need trained fighting men reduced to jelly because of the occasional burst pipe.
Point taken, Lieutenant. Kindly bag the remains for me.
They could prove...useful... for my studies.

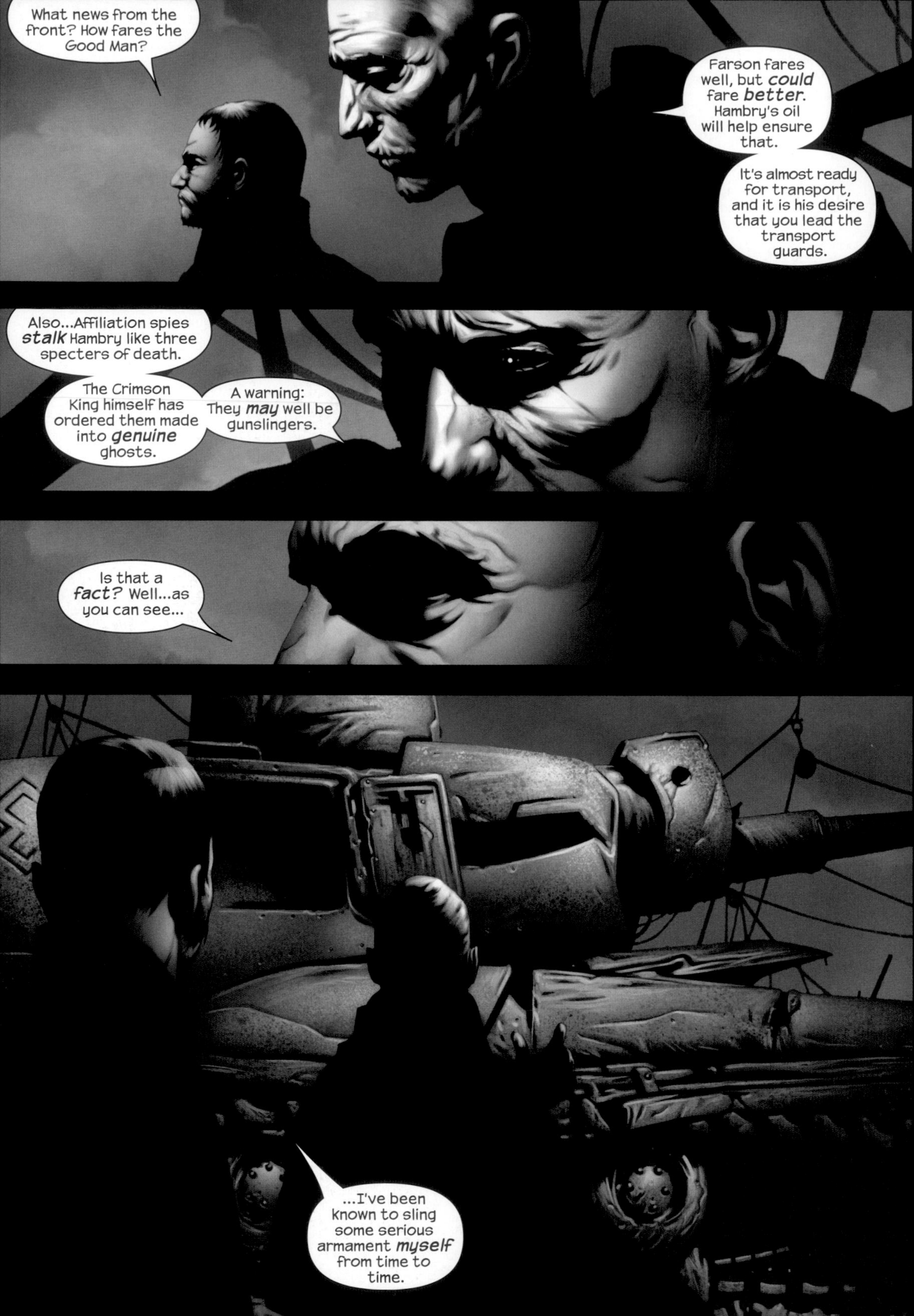

What news from the front? How fares the Good Man?
Farson fares well, but *could* fare *better*. Hambry's oil will help ensure that.
It's almost ready for transport, and it is his desire that you lead the transport guards.
Also...Affiliation spies *stalk* Hambry like three specters of death.
The Crimson King himself has ordered them made into *genuine* ghosts.
A warning: They *may* well be gunslingers.
Is that a *fact?* Well...as you can see...
...I've been known to sling some serious armament *myself* from time to time.

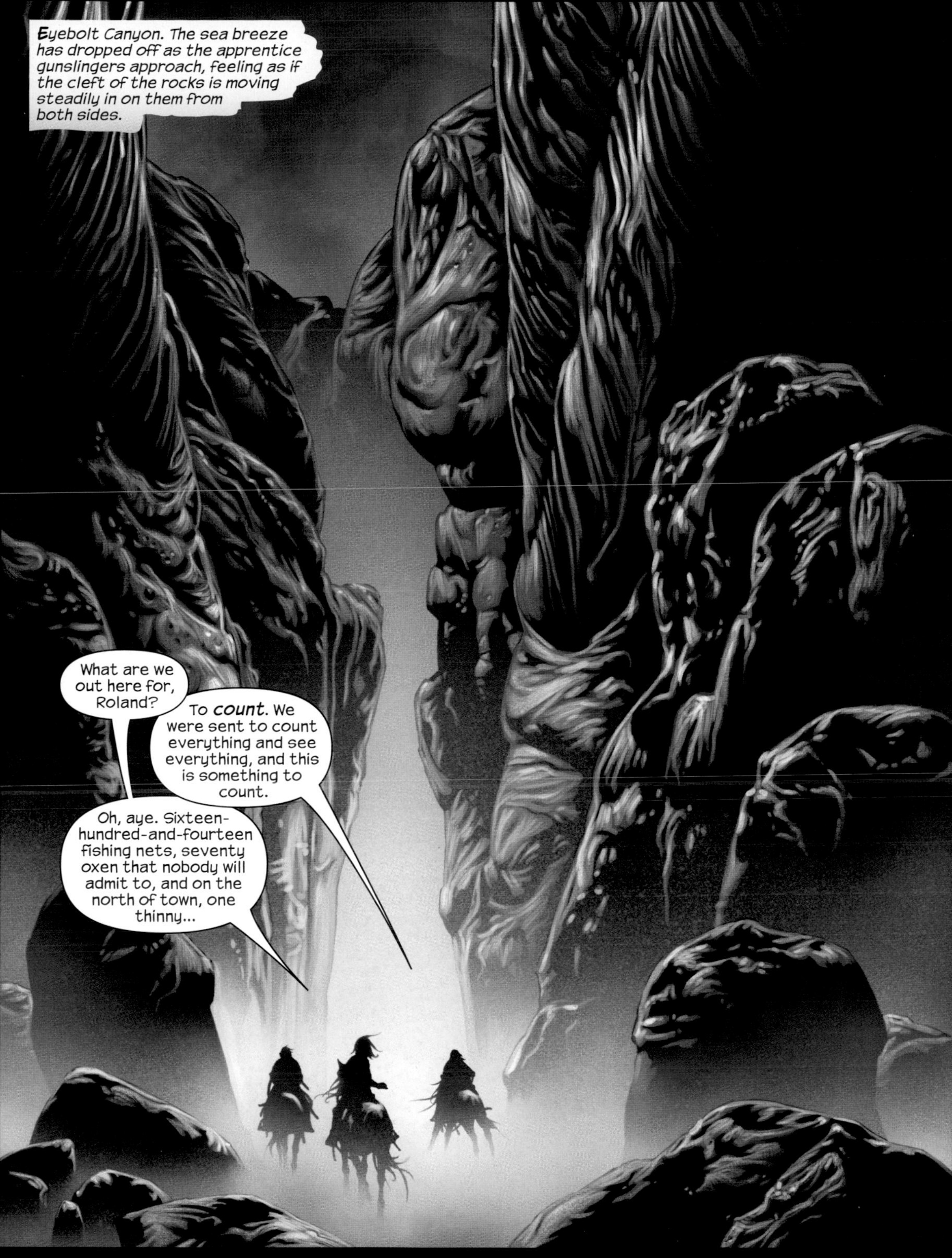
Eyebolt Canyon. The sea breeze has dropped off as the apprentice gunslingers approach, feeling as if the cleft of the rocks is moving steadily in on them from both sides.
What are we out here for, Roland?
To *count*. We were sent to count everything and see everything, and this is something to count.
Oh, aye. Sixteen-hundred-and-fourteen fishing nets, seventy oxen that nobody will admit to, and on the north of town, one thinny...

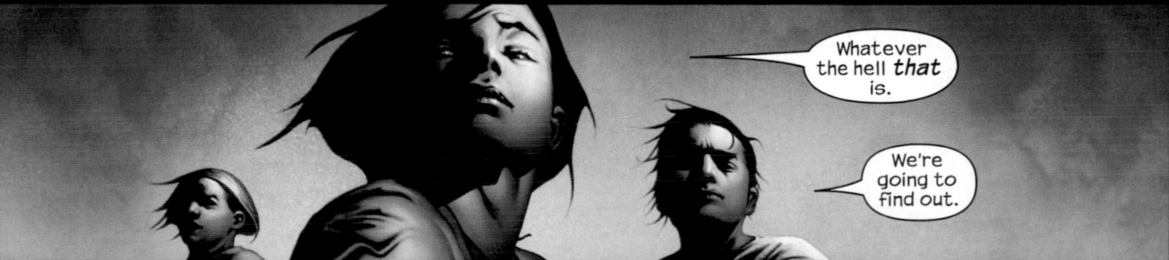
Whatever the hell *that* is.
We're going to find out.

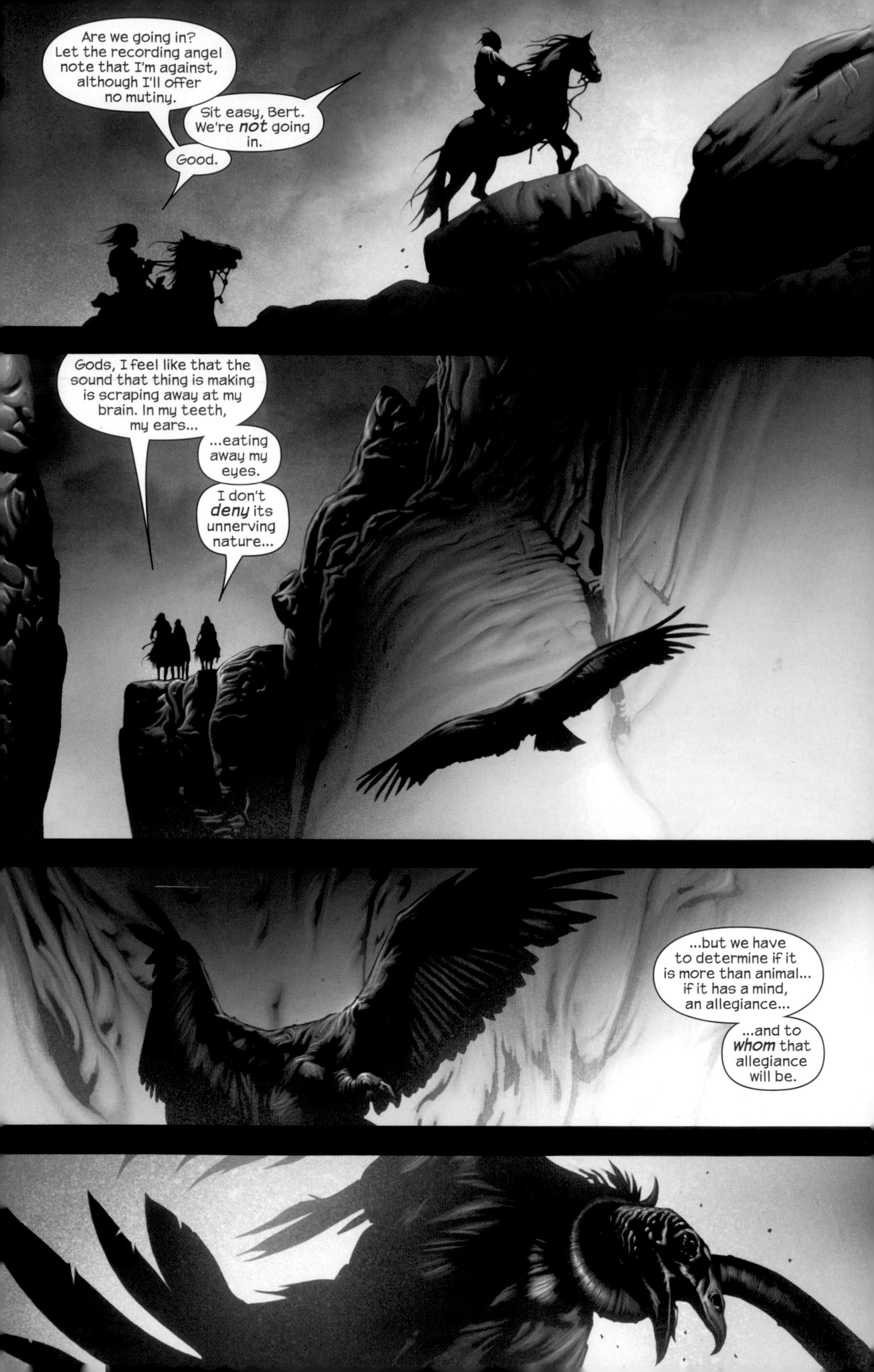
Are we going in? Let the recording angel note that I'm against, although I'll offer no mutiny.
Sit easy, Bert. We're not going in.
Good.
Gods, I feel like that the sound that thing is making is scraping away at my brain. In my teeth, my ears...
...eating away my eyes.
I don't deny its unnerving nature...
...but we have to determine if it is more than animal... if it has a mind, an allegiance...
...and to whom that allegiance will be.

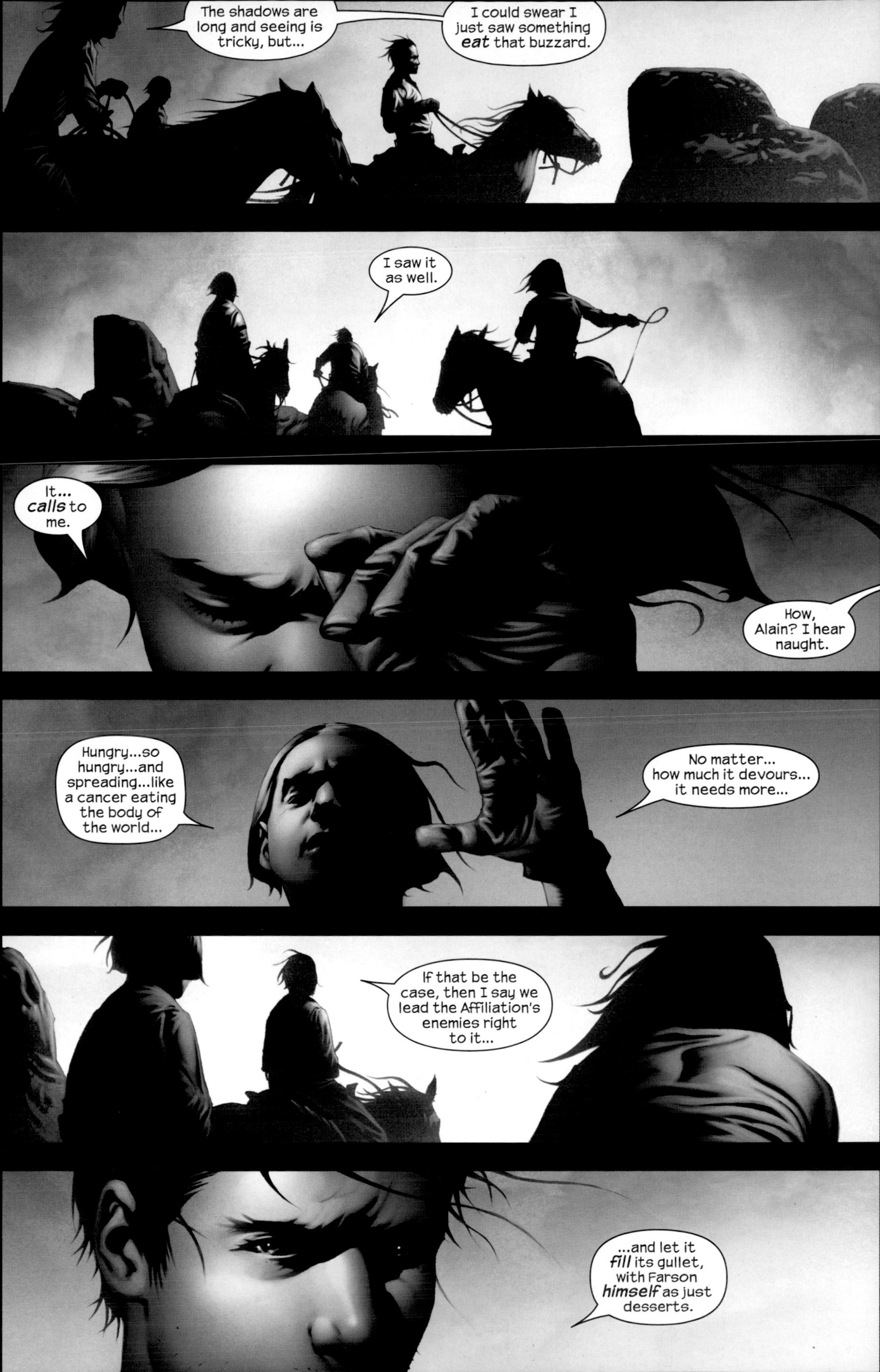
The shadows are long and seeing is tricky, but...
I could swear I just saw something *eat* that buzzard.
I saw it as well.
It... *calls* to me.
How, Alain? I hear naught.
Hungry...so hungry...and spreading...like a cancer eating the body of the world...
No matter... how much it devours... it needs more...
If that be the case, then I say we lead the Affiliation's enemies right to it...
...and let it *fill* its gullet, with Farson *himself* as just desserts.

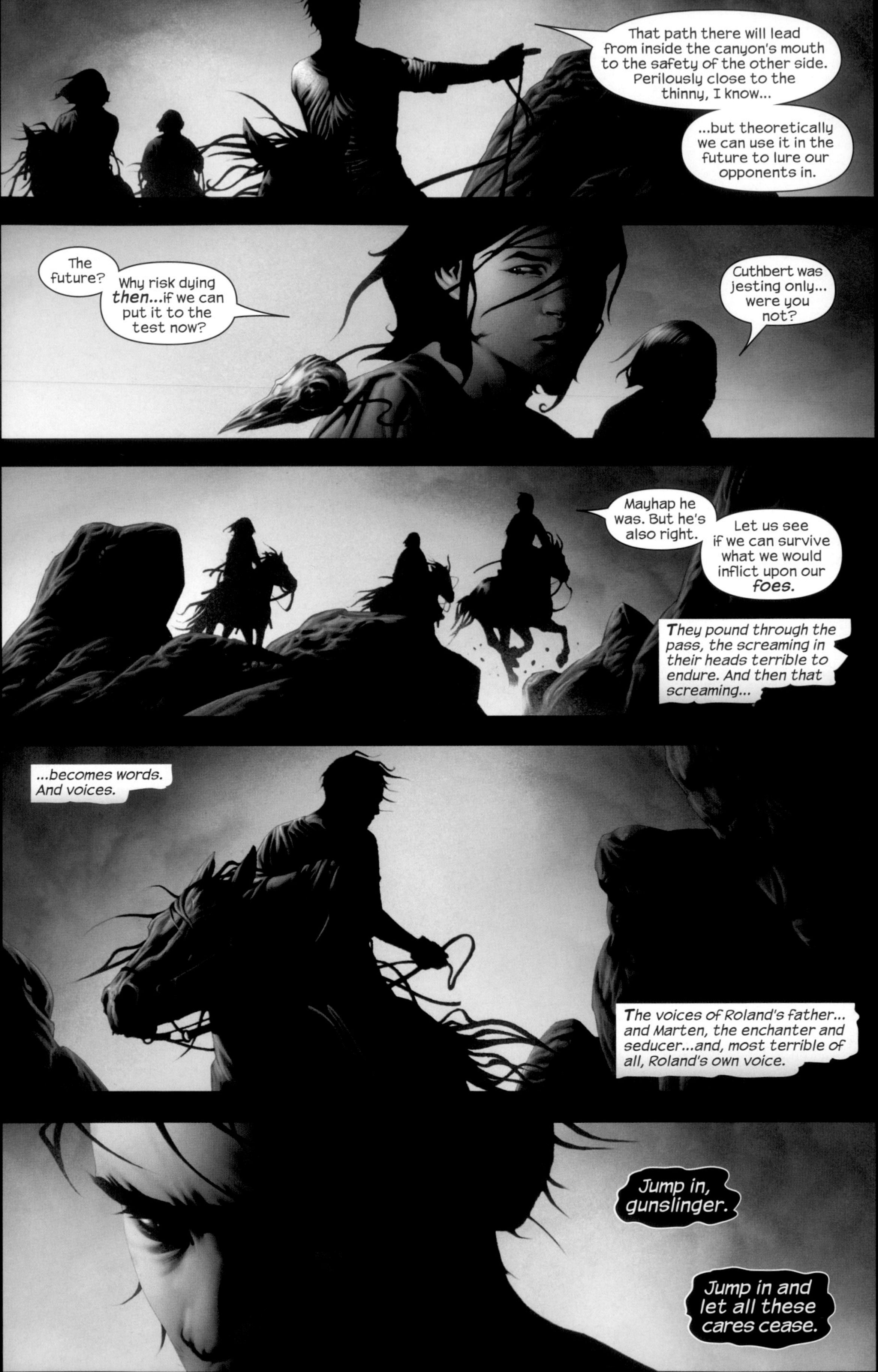
That path there will lead from inside the canyon's mouth to the safety of the other side. Perilously close to the thinny, I know...
...but theoretically we can use it in the future to lure our opponents in.
The future?
Why risk dying *then*...if we can put it to the test now?
Cuthbert was jesting only... were you not?
Mayhap he was. But he's also right.
Let us see if we can survive what we would inflict upon our *foes.*
They pound through the pass, the screaming in their heads terrible to endure. And then that screaming...
...becomes words. And voices.
The voices of Roland's father... and Marten, the enchanter and seducer...and, most terrible of all, Roland's own voice.
Jump in, gunslinger.
Jump in and let all these cares cease.

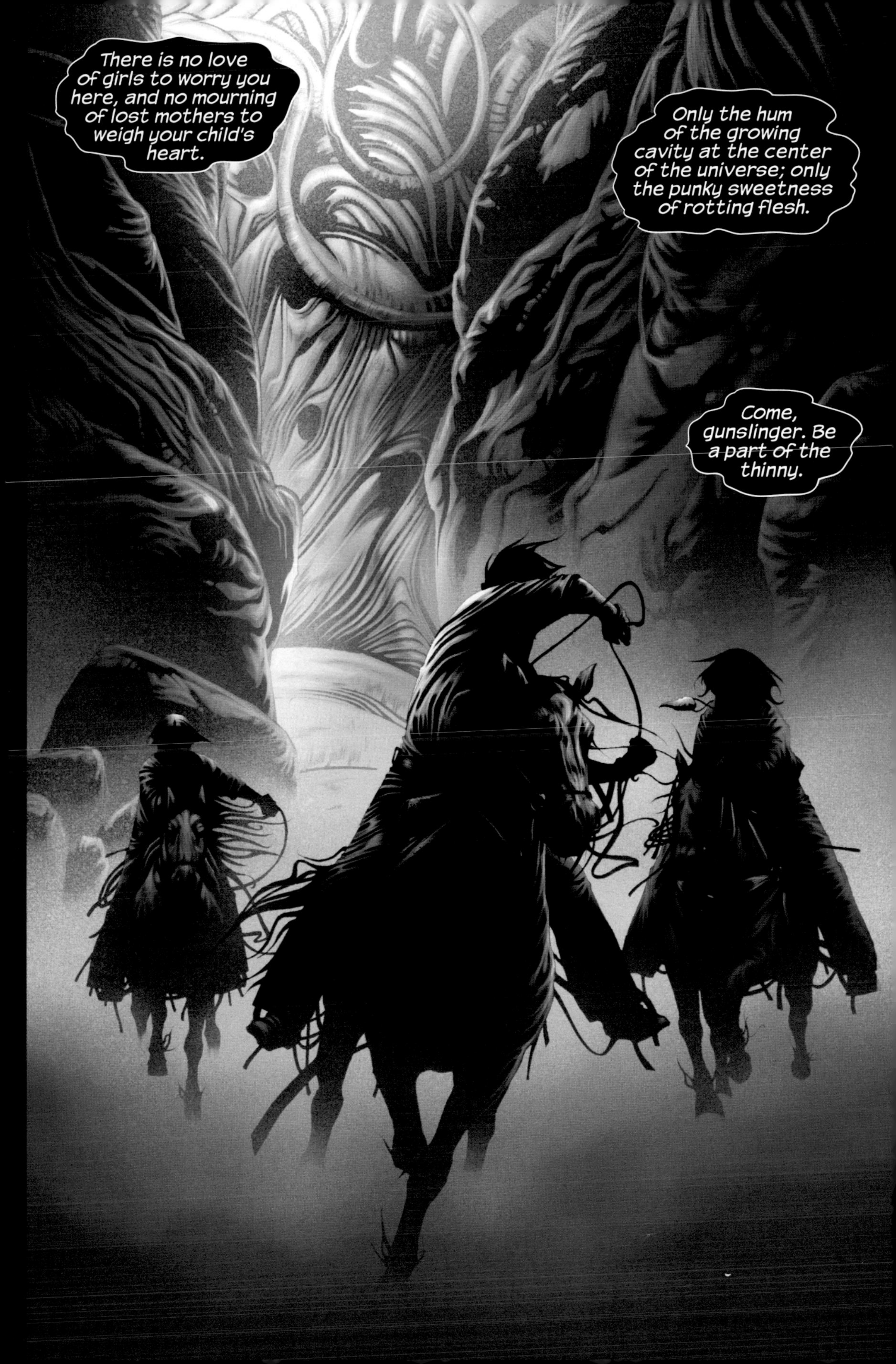
There is no love of girls to worry you here, and no mourning of lost mothers to weigh your child's heart.
Only the hum of the growing cavity at the center of the universe; only the punky sweetness of rotting flesh.
Come, gunslinger. Be a part of the thinny.

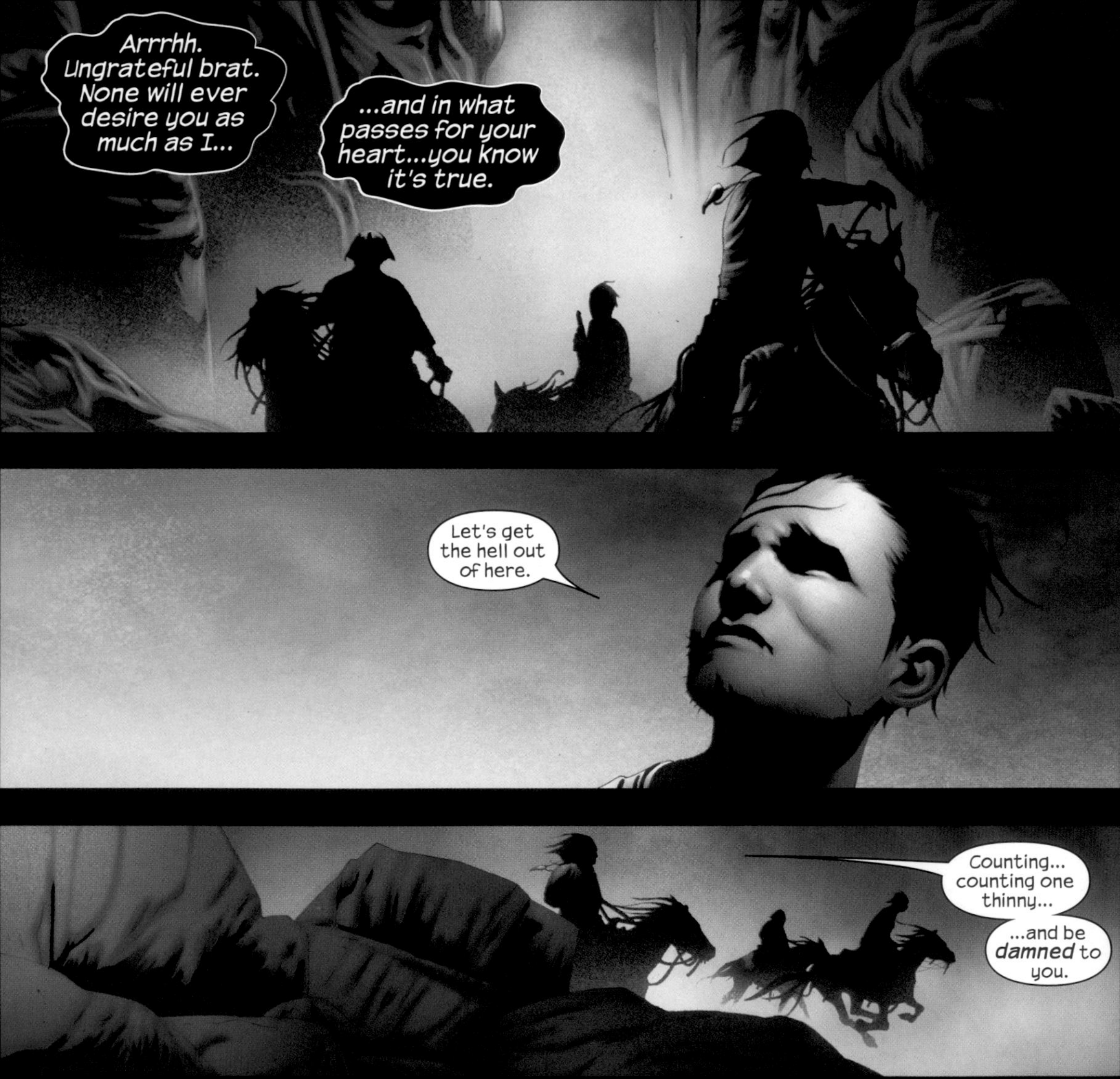
Arrrhh. Ungrateful brat. None will ever desire you as much as I...
...and in what passes for your heart...you know it's true.
Let's get the hell out of here.
Counting... counting one thinny...
...and be *damned* to you.

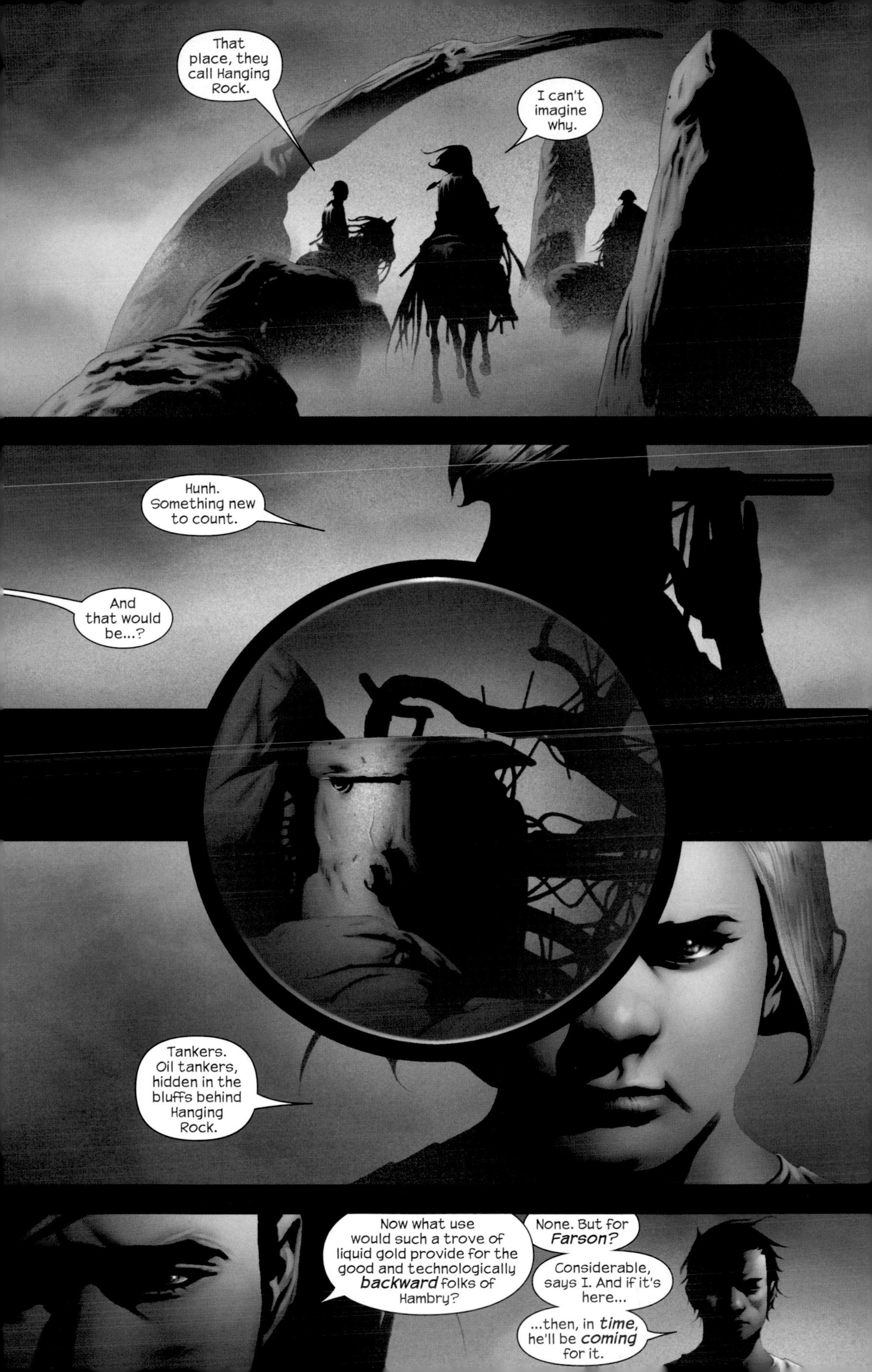

That place, they call Hanging Rock.
I can't imagine why.
Hunh. Something new to count.
And that would be...?
Tankers. Oil tankers, hidden in the bluffs behind Hanging Rock.
Now what use would such a trove of liquid gold provide for the good and technologically *backward* folks of Hambry?
None. But for *Farson?*
Considerable, says I. And if it's here...
...then, in *time,* he'll be *coming* for it.

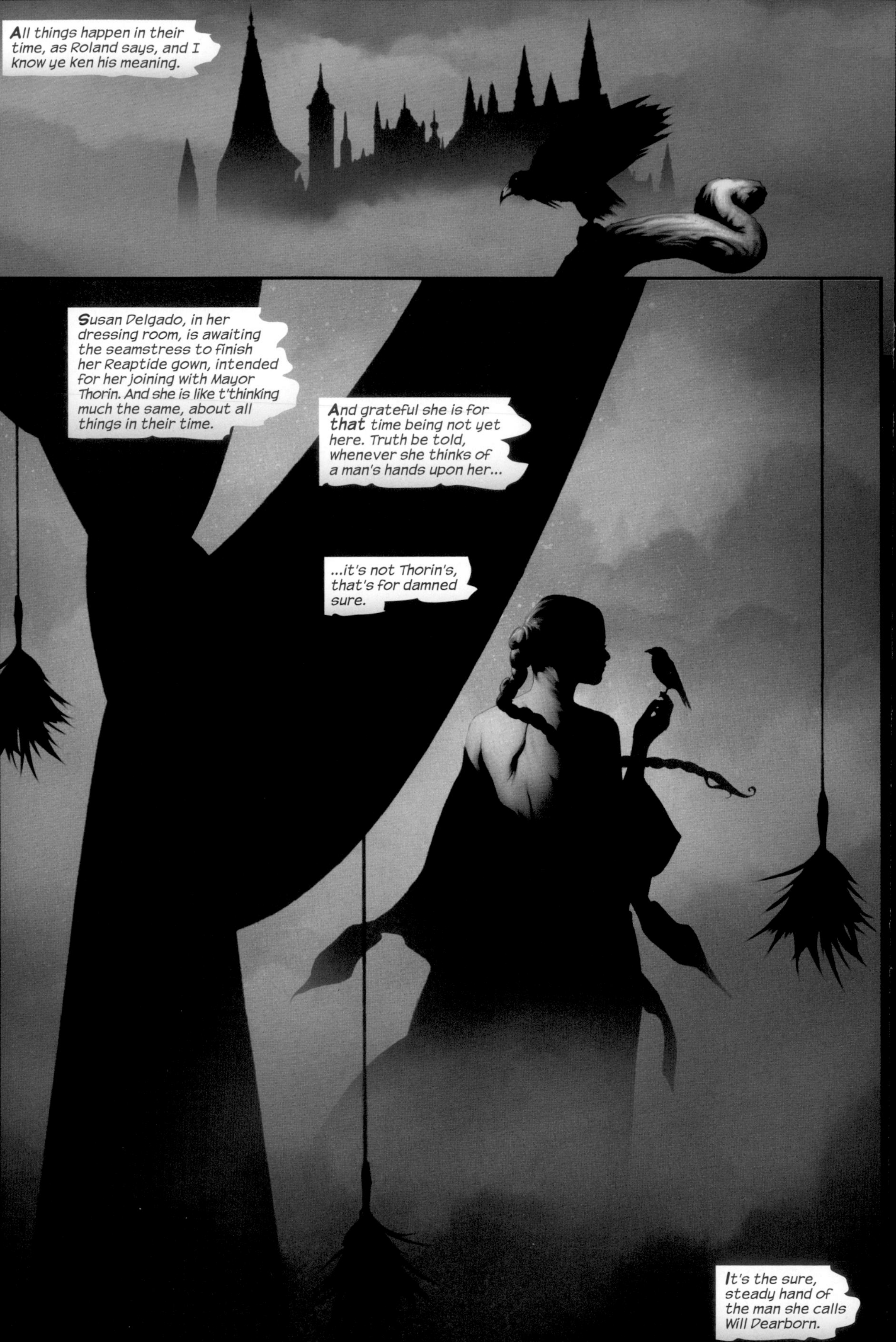
All things happen in their time, as Roland says, and I know ye ken his meaning.
Susan Delgado, in her dressing room, is awaiting the seamstress to finish her Reaptide gown, intended for her joining with Mayor Thorin. And she is like t'thinking much the same, about all things in their time.
And grateful she is for **that** time being not yet here. Truth be told, whenever she thinks of a man's hands upon her...
...it's not Thorin's, that's for damned sure.
It's the sure, steady hand of the man she calls Will Dearborn.

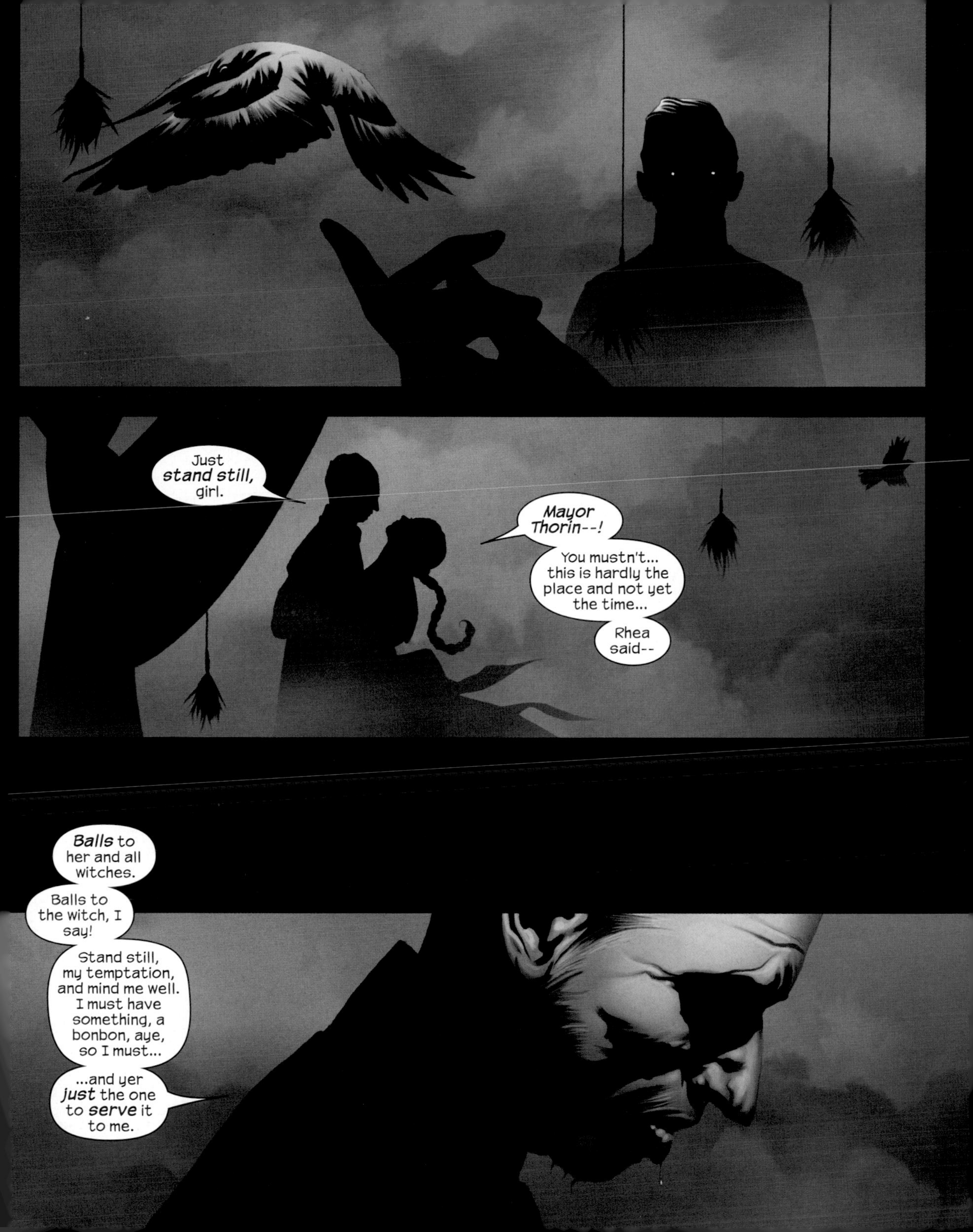
Just *stand still,* girl.
Mayor Thorin--!
You mustn't... this is hardly the place and not yet the time...
Rhea said--
Balls to her and all witches.
Balls to the witch, I say!
Stand still, my temptation, and mind me well. I must have something, a bonbon, aye, so I must...
...and yer *just* the one to *serve* it to me.

STEPHEN KING

THE DARK TOWER

THE GUNSLINGER BORN

CHAPTER FIVE

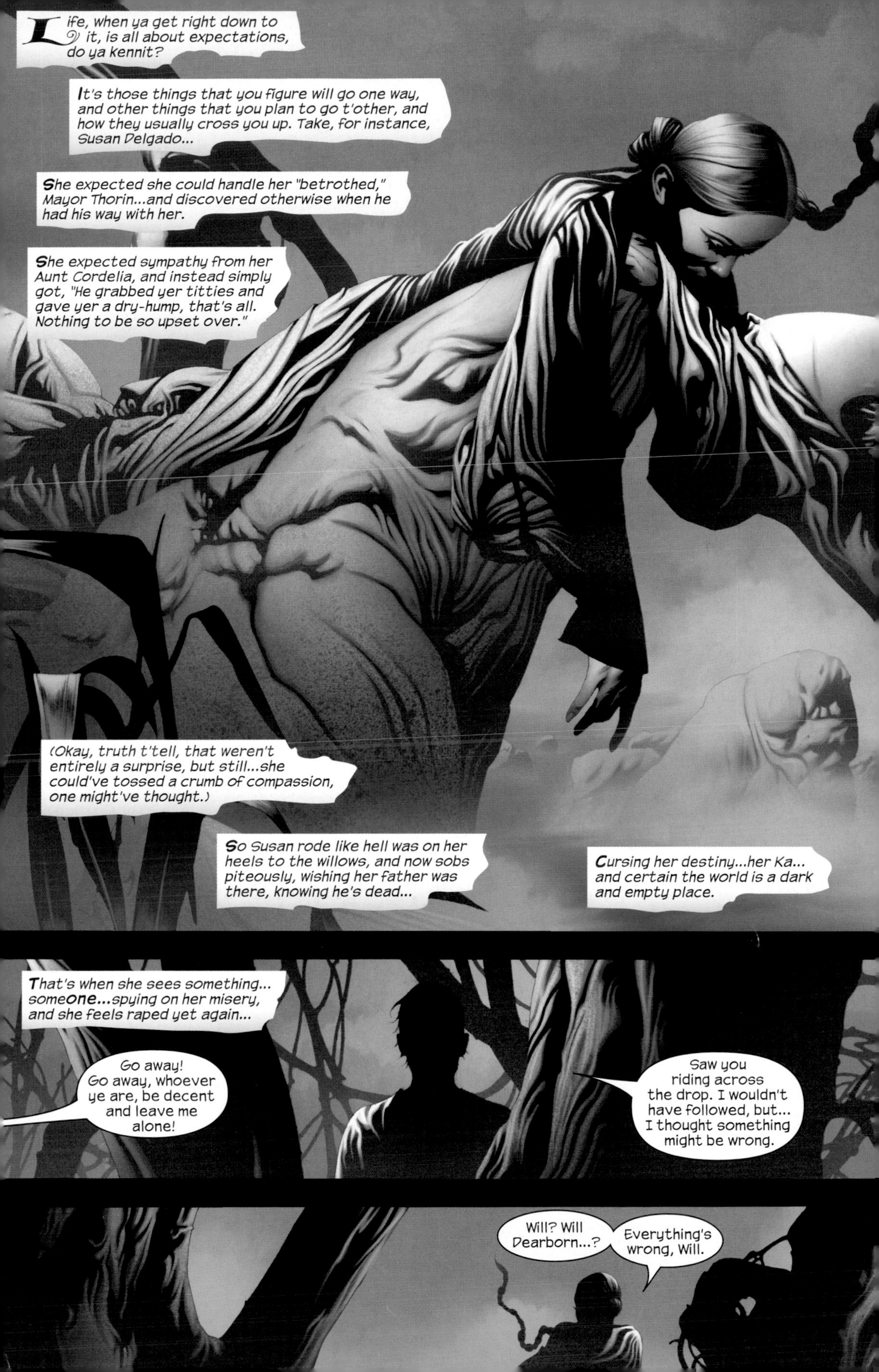
Life, when ya get right down to it, is all about expectations, do ya kennit?
It's those things that you figure will go one way, and other things that you plan to go t'other, and how they usually cross you up. Take, for instance, Susan Delgado...
She expected she could handle her "betrothed," Mayor Thorin...and discovered otherwise when he had his way with her.
She expected sympathy from her Aunt Cordelia, and instead simply got, "He grabbed yer titties and gave yer a dry-hump, that's all. Nothing to be so upset over."
(Okay, truth t'tell, that weren't entirely a surprise, but still...she could've tossed a crumb of compassion, one might've thought.)
So Susan rode like hell was on her heels to the willows, and now sobs piteously, wishing her father was there, knowing he's dead...
Cursing her destiny...her Ka... and certain the world is a dark and empty place.
That's when she sees something... someONE...spying on her misery, and she feels raped yet again...
Go away! Go away, whoever ye are, be decent and leave me alone!
Saw you riding across the drop. I wouldn't have followed, but... I thought something might be wrong.
Will? Will Dearborn...?
Everything's wrong, Will.

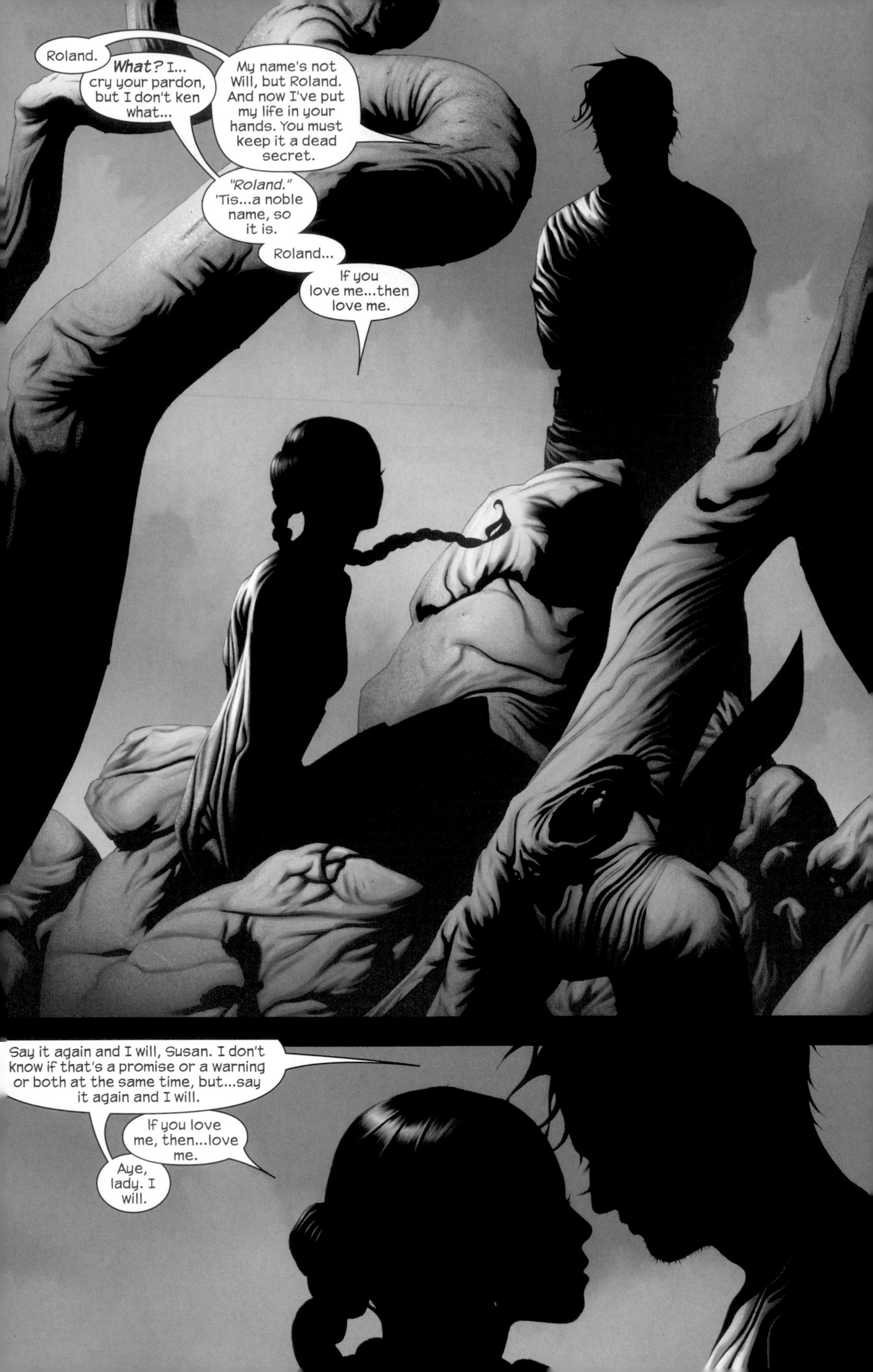
Roland.
What? I... cry your pardon, but I don't ken what...
My name's not Will, but Roland. And now I've put my life in your hands. You must keep it a dead secret.
"Roland." 'Tis...a noble name, so it is.
Roland...
If you love me...then love me.
Say it again and I will, Susan. I don't know if that's a promise or a warning or both at the same time, but...say it again and I will.
If you love me, then...love me.
Aye, lady. I will.

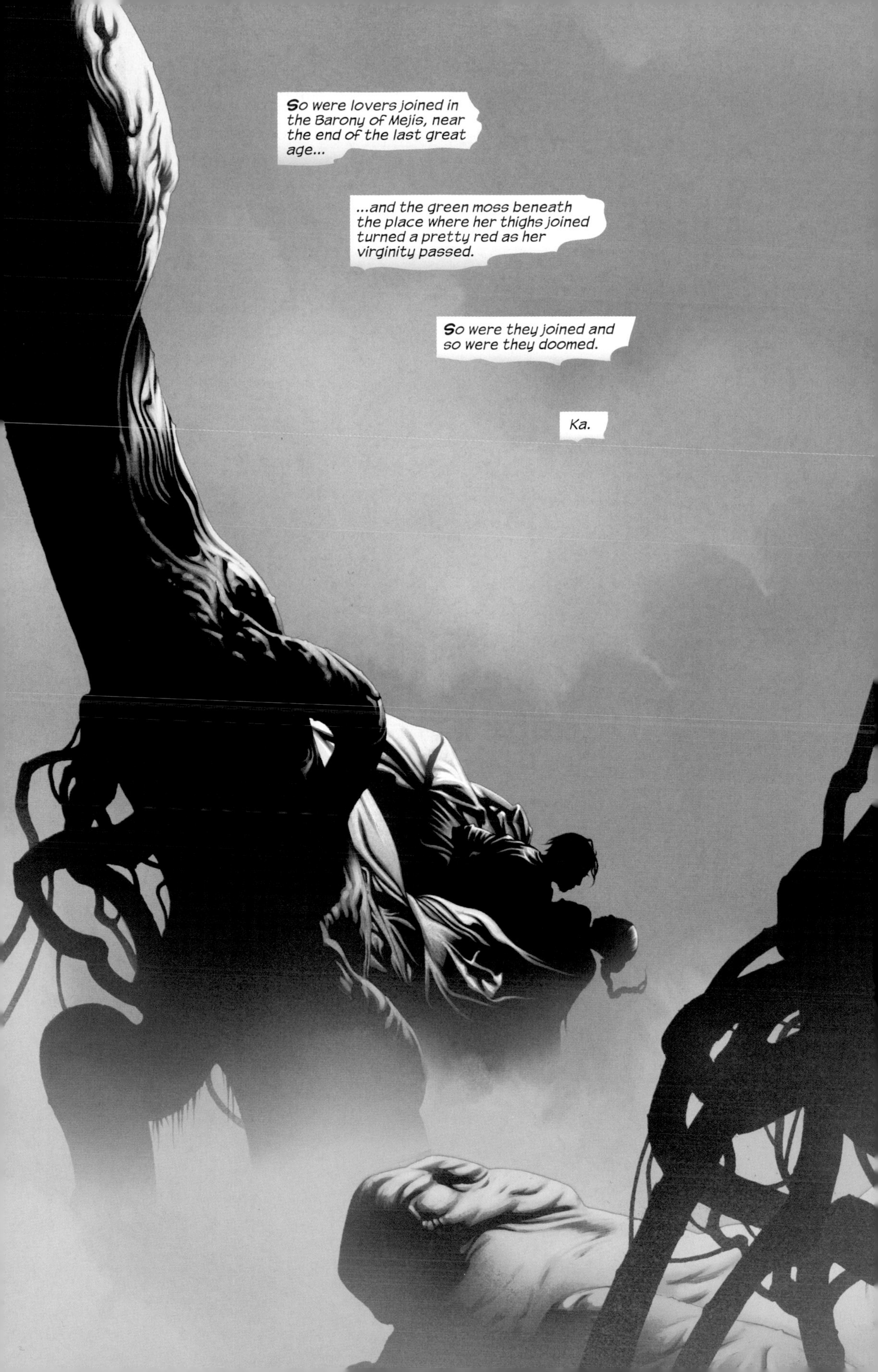
So were lovers joined in the Barony of Mejis, near the end of the last great age...
...and the green moss beneath the place where her thighs joined turned a pretty red as her virginity passed.
So were they joined and so were they doomed.
Ka.

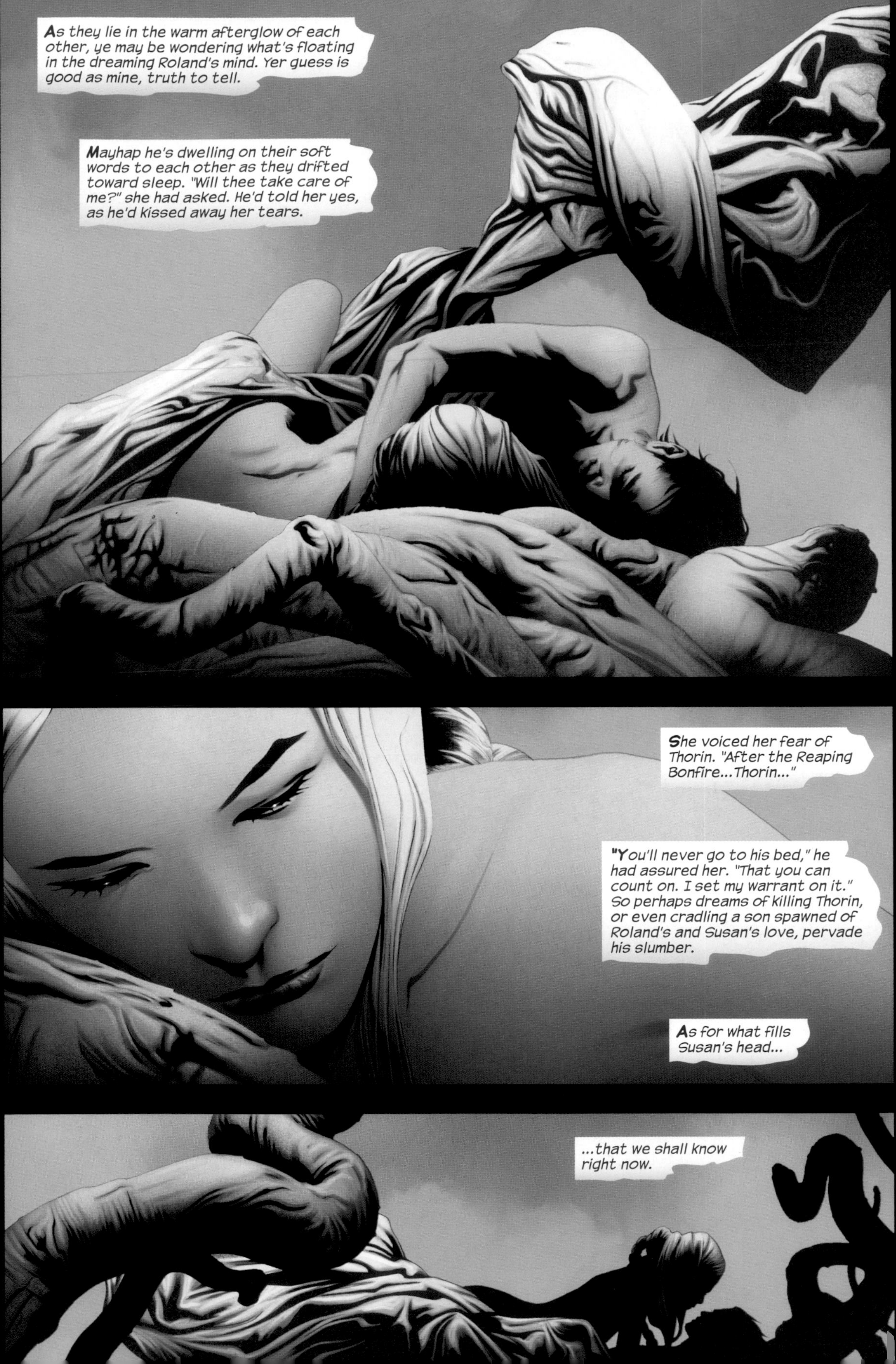
As they lie in the warm afterglow of each other, ye may be wondering what's floating in the dreaming Roland's mind. Yer guess is good as mine, truth to tell.
Mayhap he's dwelling on their soft words to each other as they drifted toward sleep. "Will thee take care of me?" she had asked. He'd told her yes, as he'd kissed away her tears.
She voiced her fear of Thorin. "After the Reaping Bonfire...Thorin..."
"You'll never go to his bed," he had assured her. "That you can count on. I set my warrant on it." So perhaps dreams of killing Thorin, or even cradling a son spawned of Roland's and Susan's love, pervade his slumber.
As for what fills Susan's head...
...that we shall know right now.

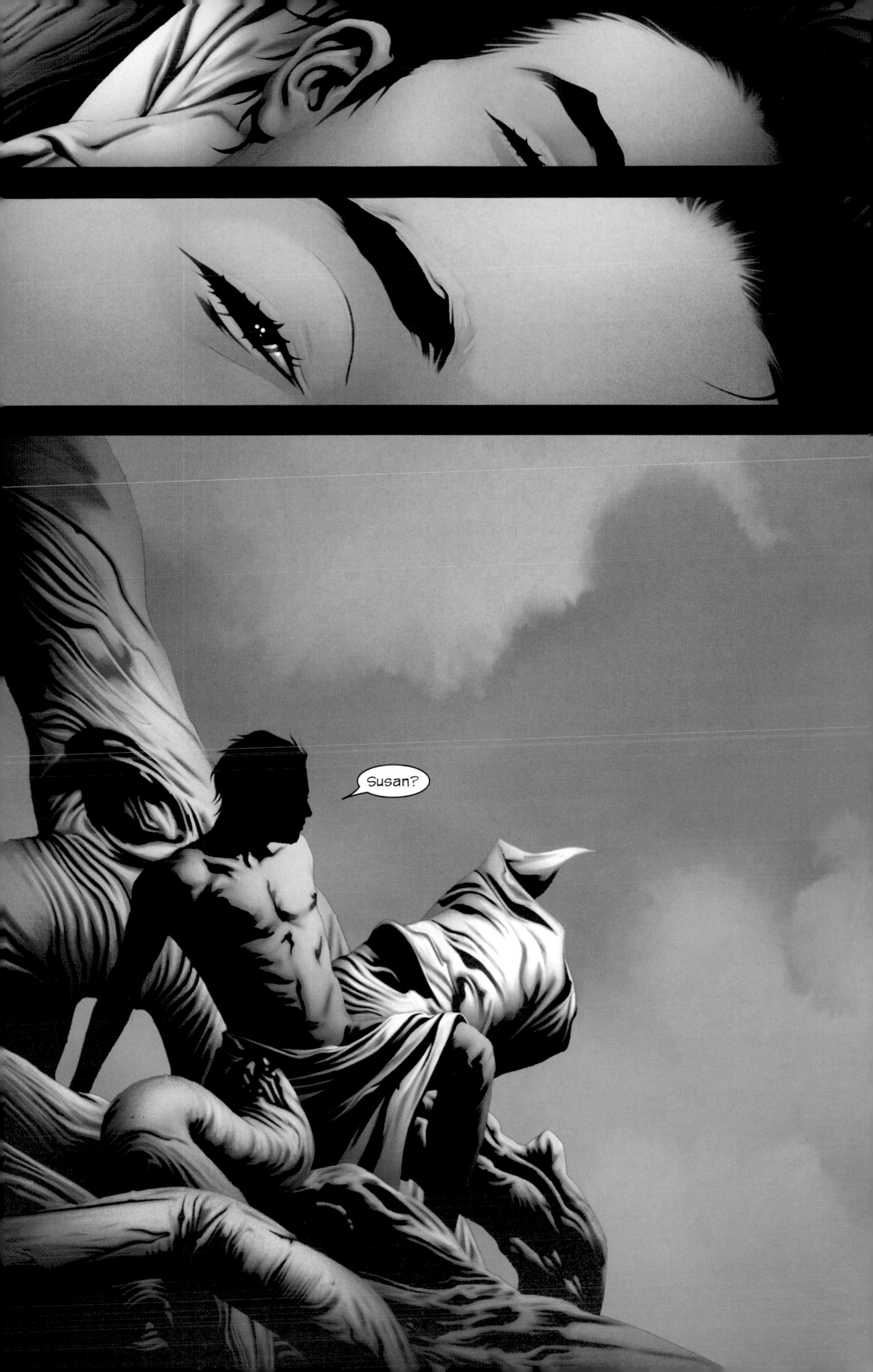
Susan?

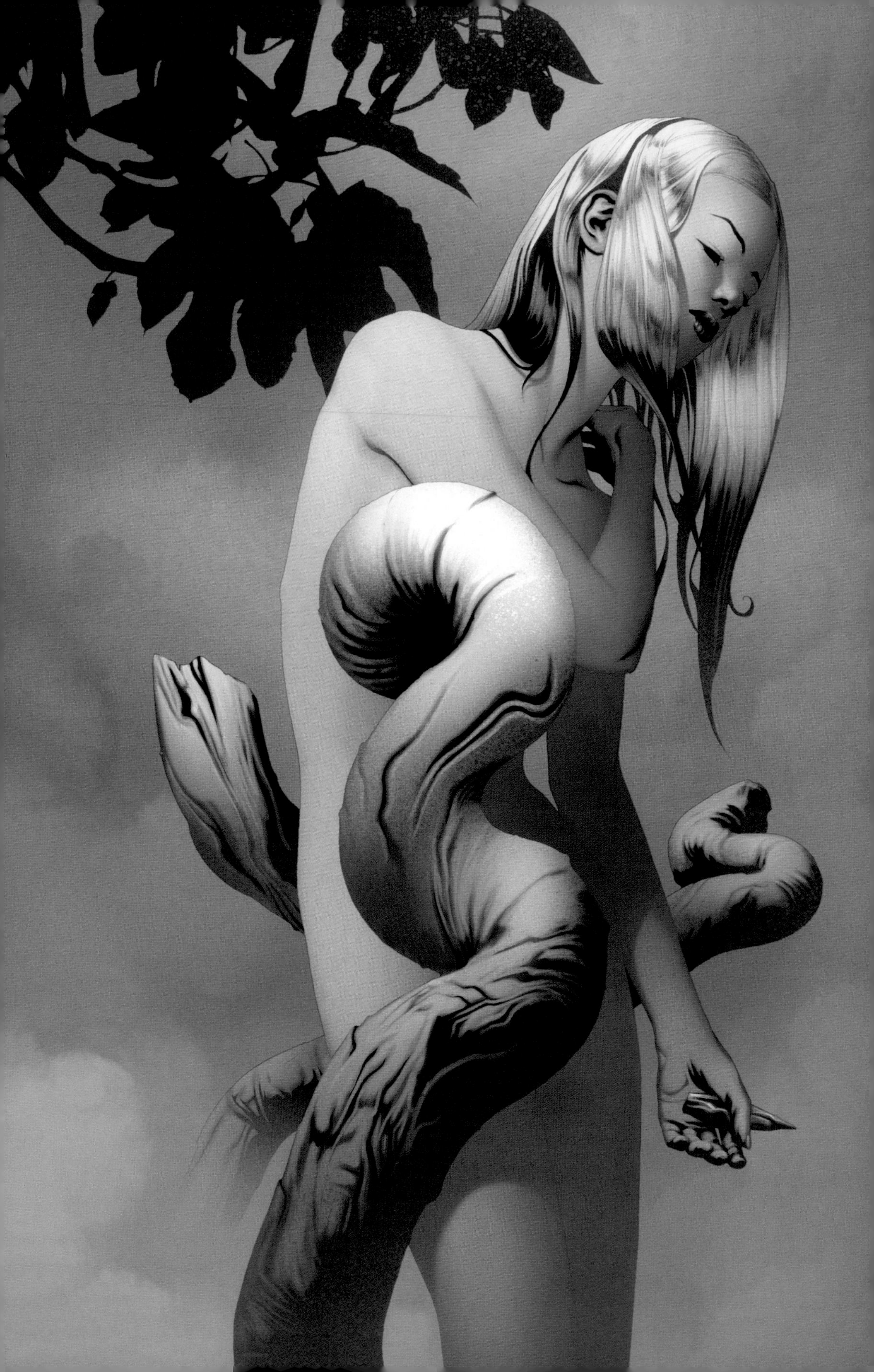

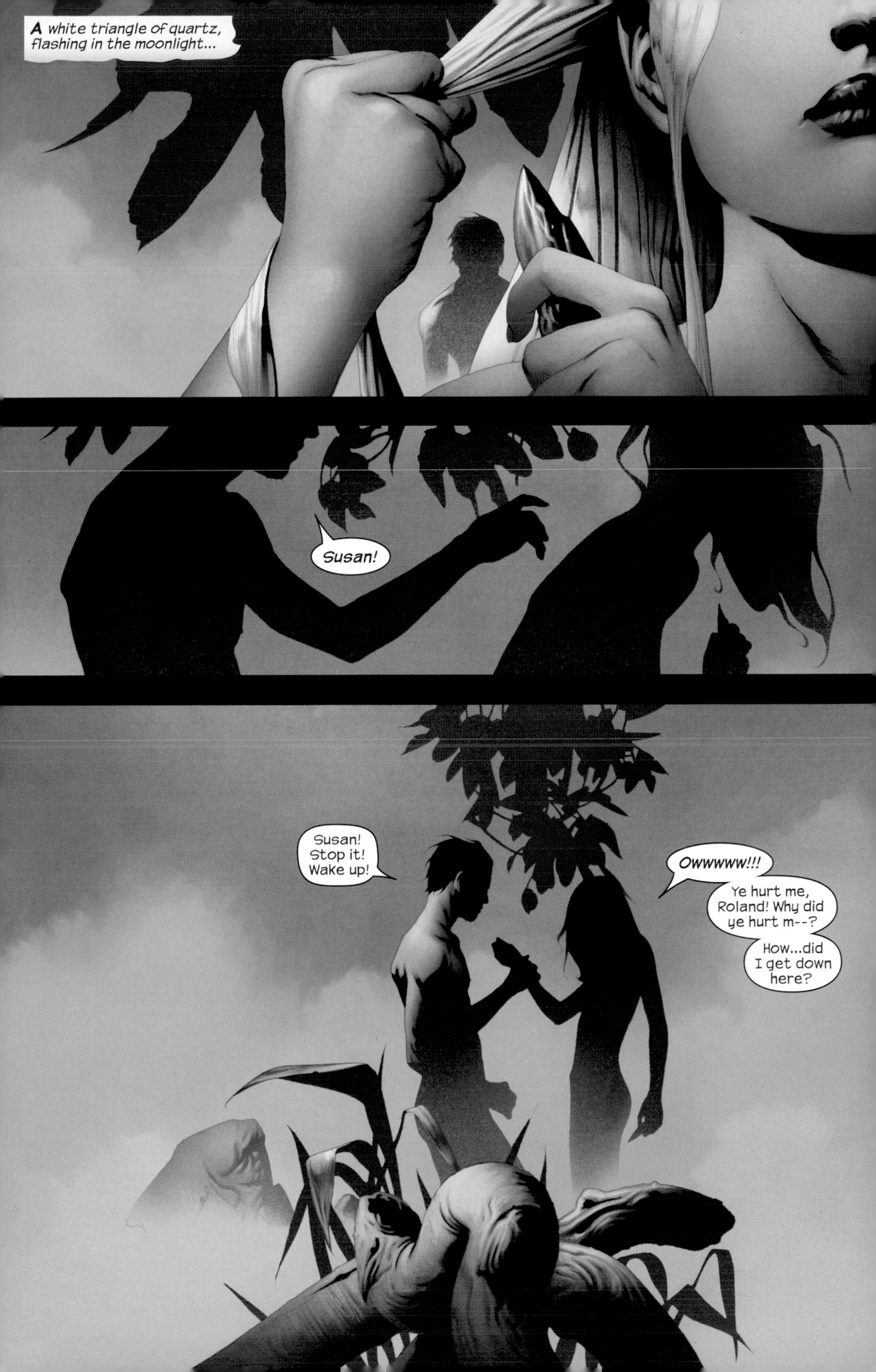
A white triangle of quartz, flashing in the moonlight...
Susan!
Susan! Stop it! Wake up!
Owwwww!!!
Ye hurt me, Roland! Why did ye hurt m--?
How...did I get down here?

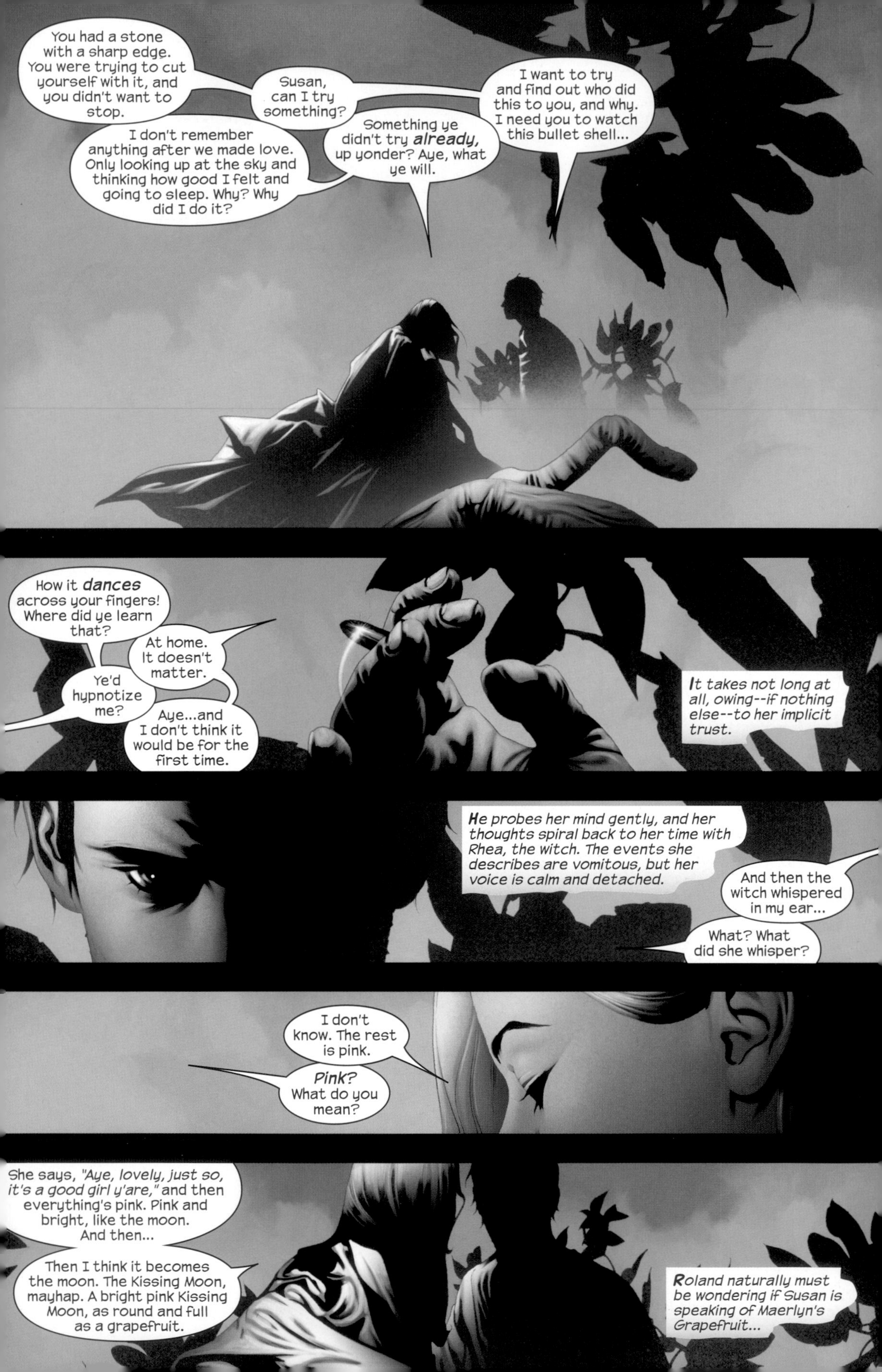

You had a stone with a sharp edge. You were trying to cut yourself with it, and you didn't want to stop.
Susan, can I try something?
I want to try and find out who did this to you, and why. I need you to watch this bullet shell...
I don't remember anything after we made love. Only looking up at the sky and thinking how good I felt and going to sleep. Why? Why did I do it?
Something ye didn't try *already,* up yonder? Aye, what ye will.
How it *dances* across your fingers! Where did ye learn that?
At home. It doesn't matter.
Ye'd hypnotize me?
Aye...and I don't think it would be for the first time.
It takes not long at all, owing--if nothing else--to her implicit trust.
He probes her mind gently, and her thoughts spiral back to her time with Rhea, the witch. The events she describes are vomitous, but her voice is calm and detached.
And then the witch whispered in my ear...
What? What did she whisper?
I don't know. The rest is pink.
Pink? What do you mean?
She says, *"Aye, lovely, just so, it's a good girl y'are,"* and then everything's pink. Pink and bright, like the moon. And then...
Then I think it becomes the moon. The Kissing Moon, mayhap. A bright pink Kissing Moon, as round and full as a grapefruit.
Roland naturally must be wondering if Susan is speaking of Maerlyn's Grapefruit...

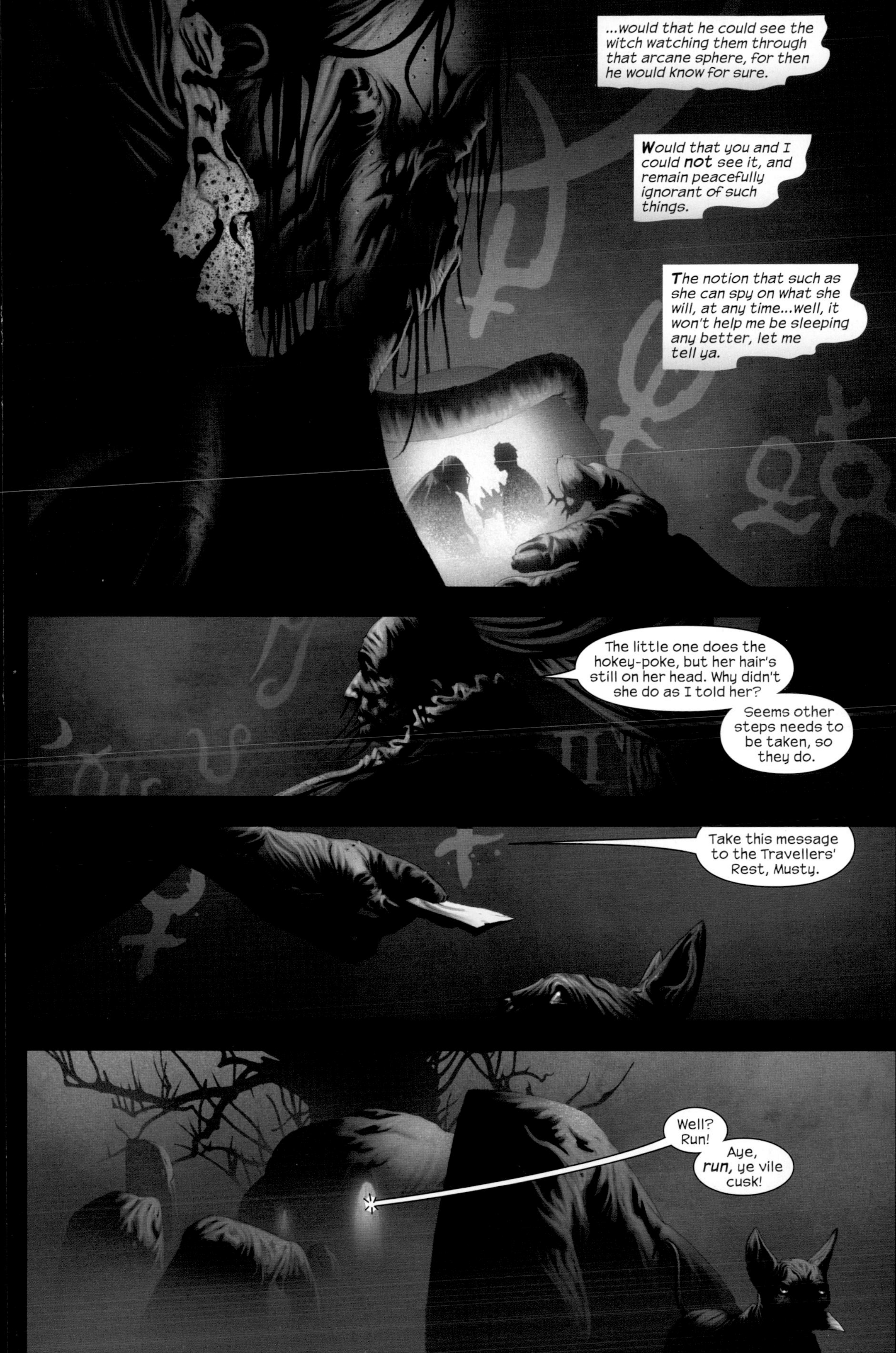
...would that he could see the witch watching them through that arcane sphere, for then he would know for sure.
Would that you and I could **not** see it, and remain peacefully ignorant of such things.
The notion that such as she can spy on what she will, at any time...well, it won't help me be sleeping any better, let me tell ya.
The little one does the hokey-poke, but her hair's still on her head. Why didn't she do as I told her?
Seems other steps needs to be taken, so they do.
Take this message to the Travellers' Rest, Musty.
Well? Run!
Aye, **run,** ye vile cusk!

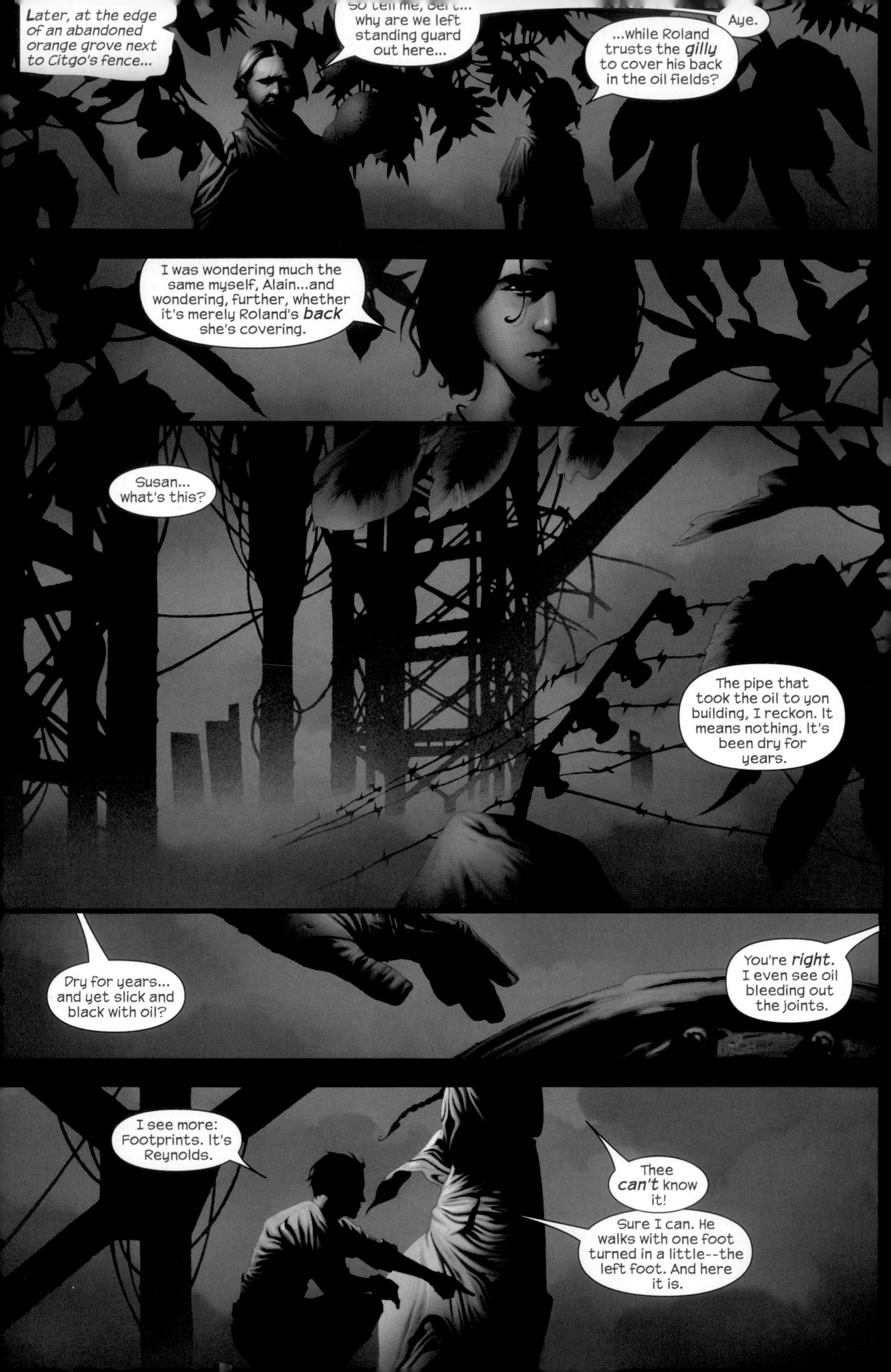
Later, at the edge of an abandoned orange grove next to Citgo's fence...
why are we left standing guard out here...
Aye.
...while Roland trusts the gilly to cover his back in the oil fields?
I was wondering much the same myself, Alain...and wondering, further, whether it's merely Roland's back she's covering.
Susan... what's this?
The pipe that took the oil to yon building, I reckon. It means nothing. It's been dry for years.
Dry for years... and yet slick and black with oil?
You're right. I even see oil bleeding out the joints.
I see more: Footprints. It's Reynolds.
Thee can't know it!
Sure I can. He walks with one foot turned in a little--the left foot. And here it is.

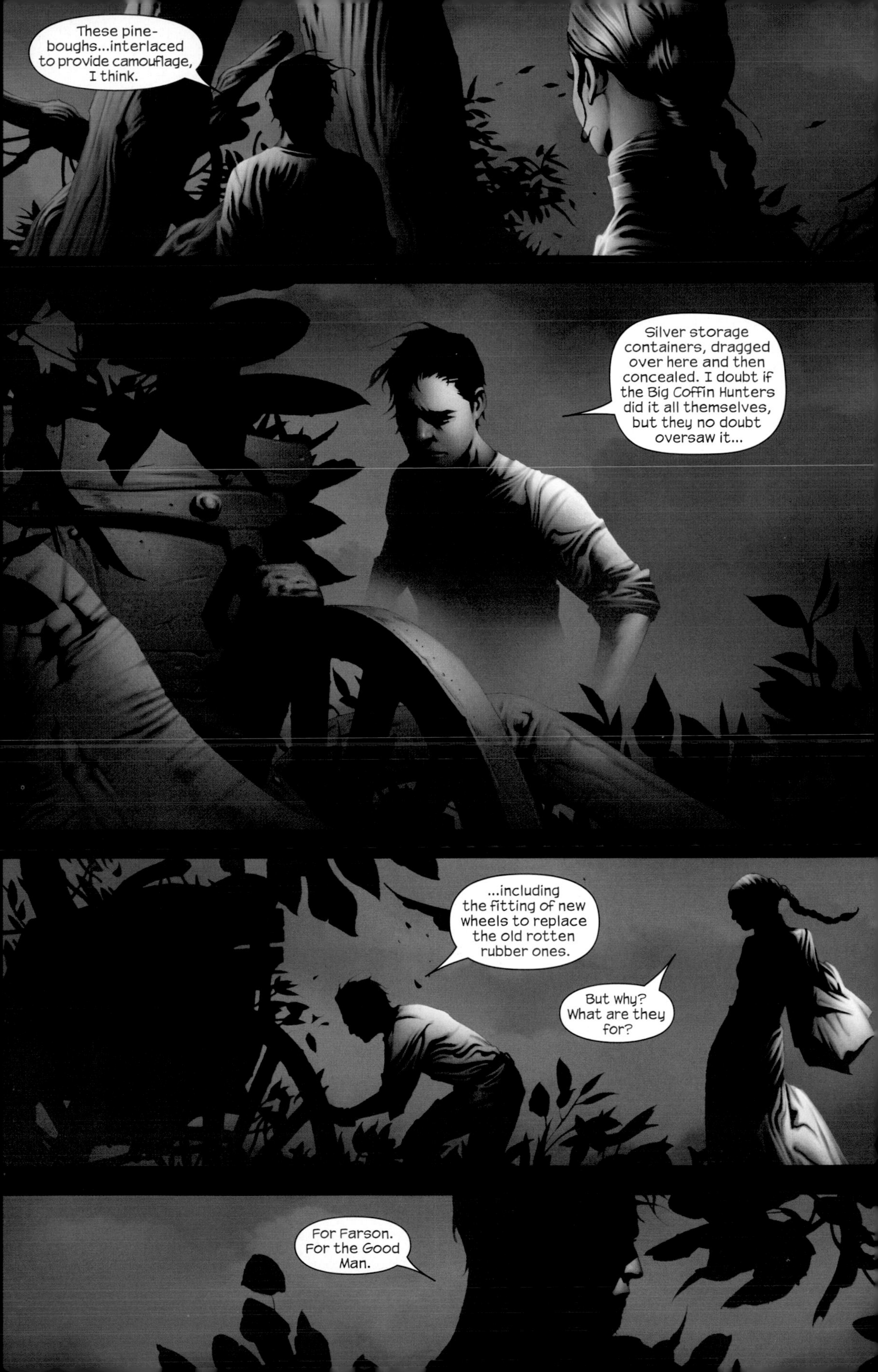
These pine-boughs...interlaced to provide camouflage, I think.
Silver storage containers, dragged over here and then concealed. I doubt if the Big Coffin Hunters did it all themselves, but they no doubt oversaw it...
...including the fitting of new wheels to replace the old rotten rubber ones.
But why? What are they for?
For Farson. For the Good Man.

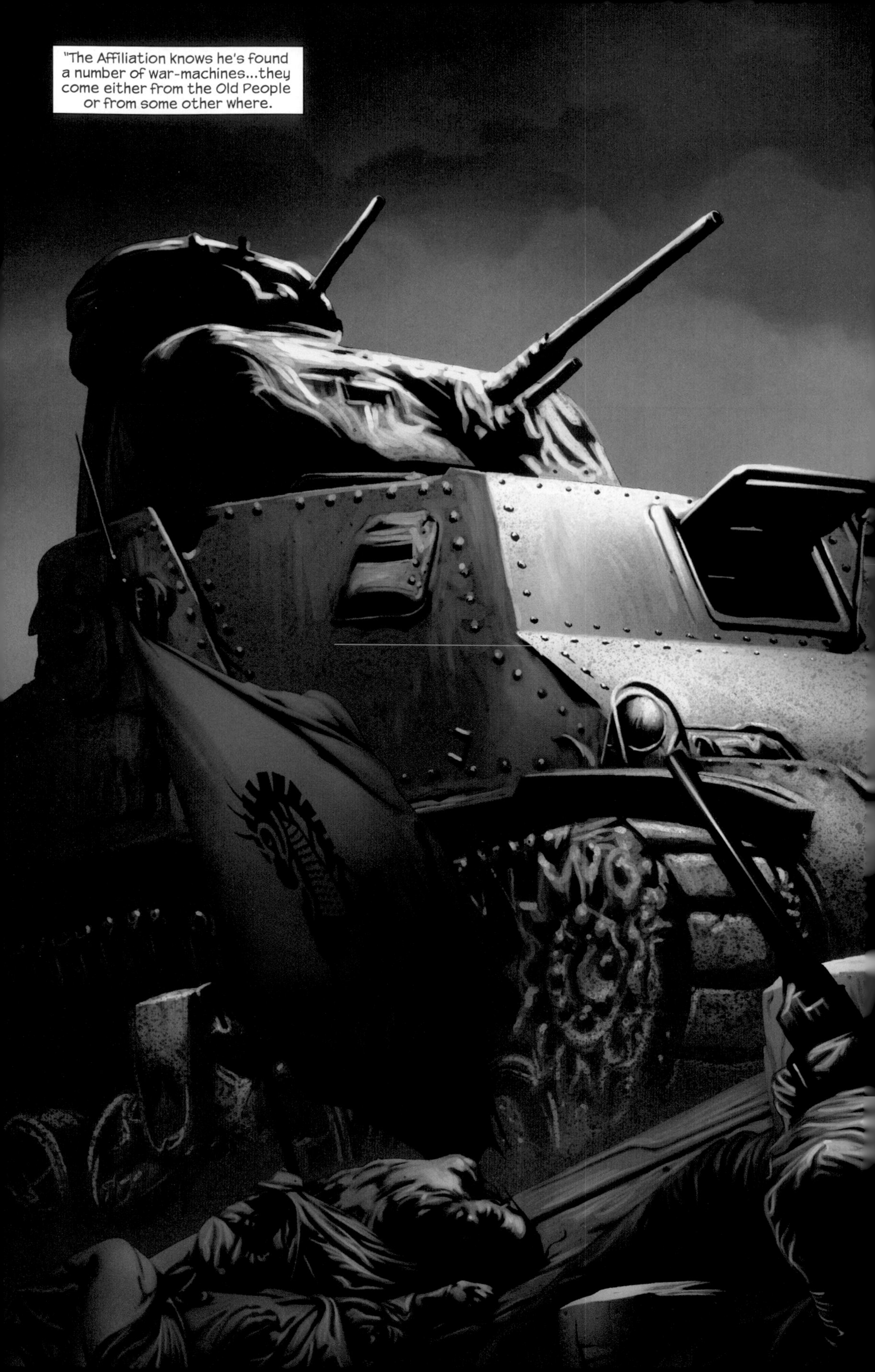
"The Affiliation knows he's found a number of war-machines...they come either from the Old People or from some other where.

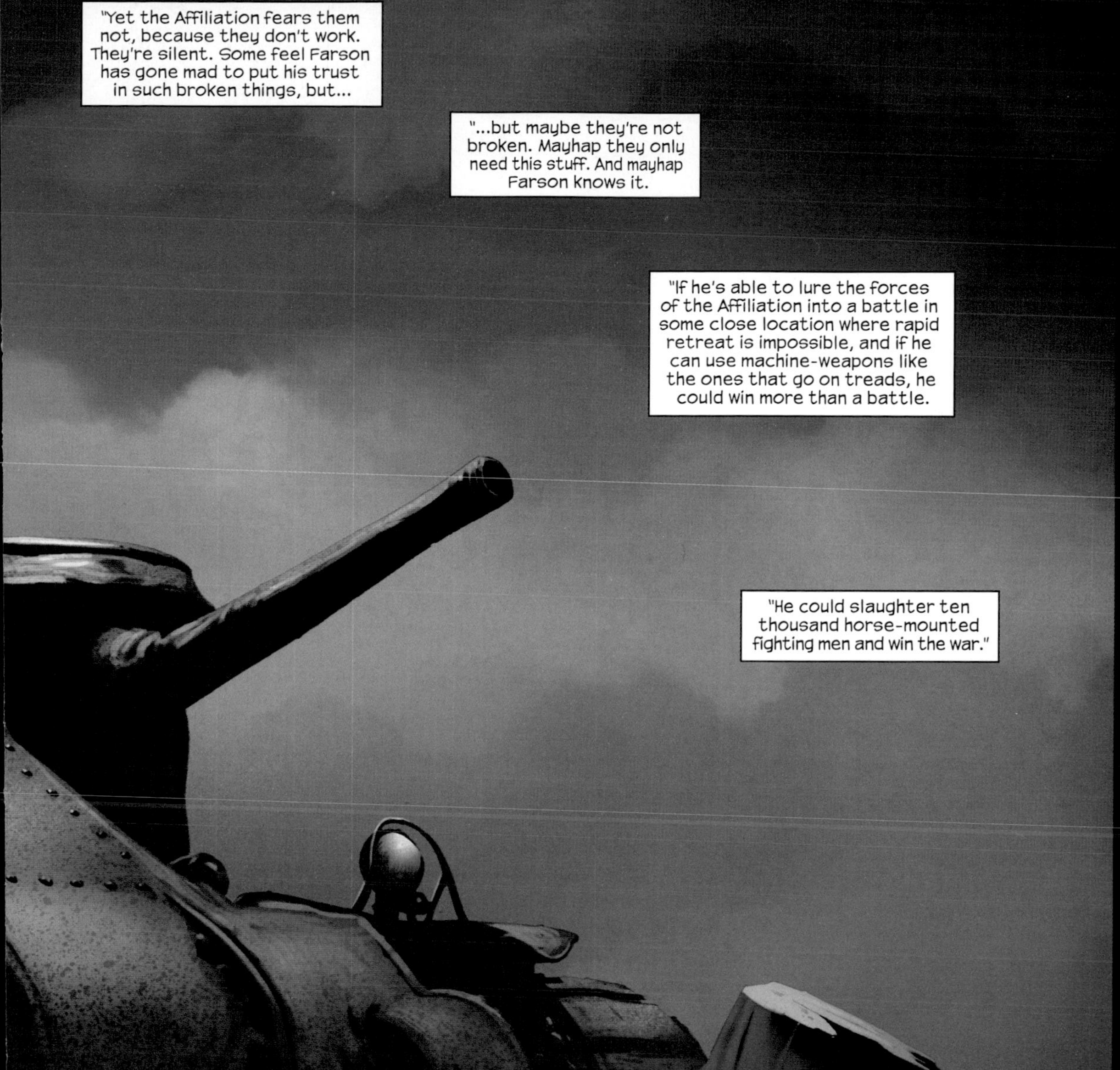
"Yet the Affiliation fears them not, because they don't work. They're silent. Some feel Farson has gone mad to put his trust in such broken things, but...
"...but maybe they're not broken. Mayhap they only need this stuff. And mayhap Farson knows it.
"If he's able to lure the forces of the Affiliation into a battle in some close location where rapid retreat is impossible, and if he can use machine-weapons like the ones that go on treads, he could win more than a battle.
"He could slaughter ten thousand horse-mounted fighting men and win the war."

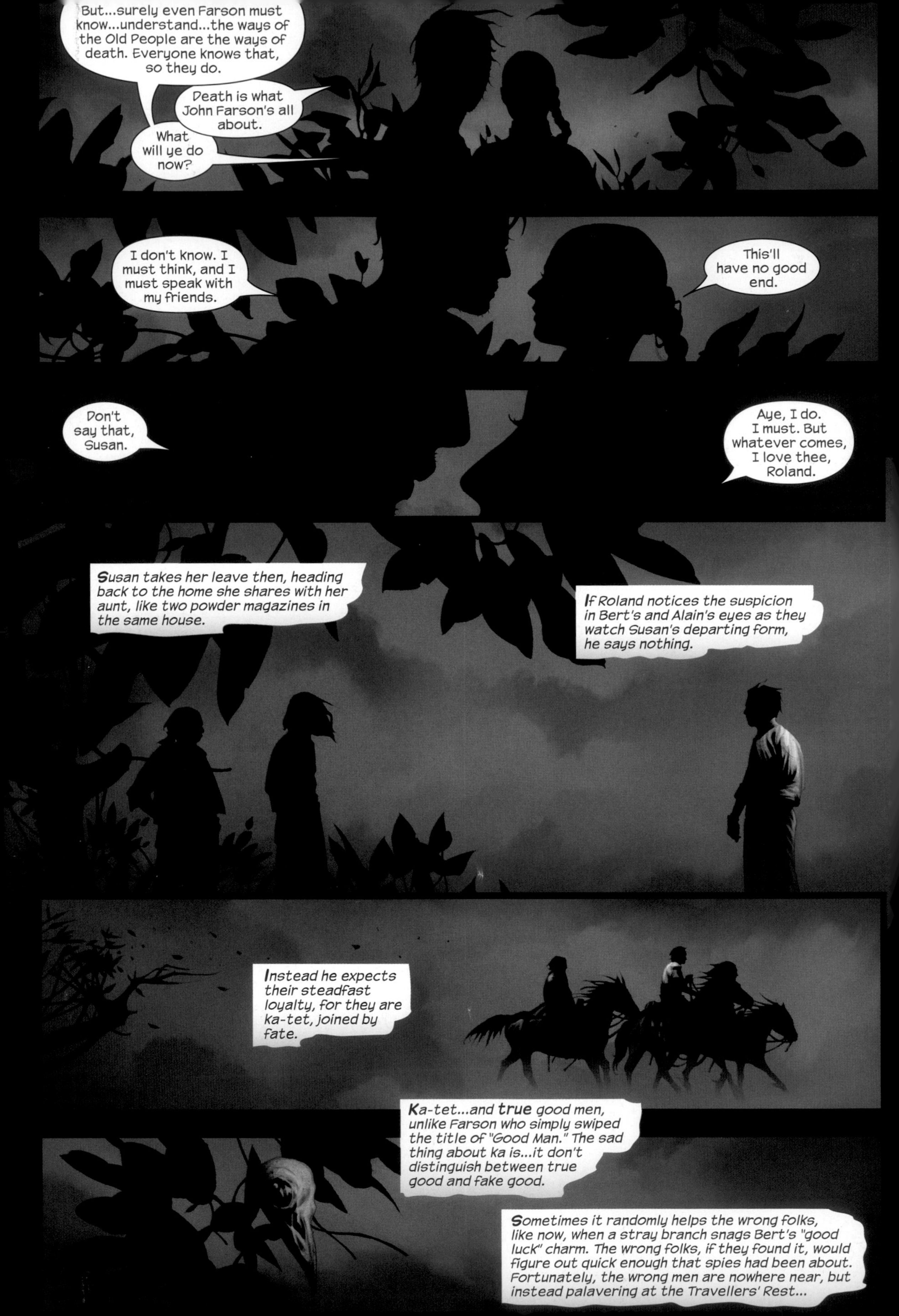

But...surely even Farson must know...understand...the ways of the Old People are the ways of death. Everyone knows that, so they do.
Death is what John Farson's all about.
What will ye do now?
I don't know. I must think, and I must speak with my friends.
This'll have no good end.
Don't say that, Susan.
Aye, I do. I must. But whatever comes, I love thee, Roland.
Susan takes her leave then, heading back to the home she shares with her aunt, like two powder magazines in the same house.
If Roland notices the suspicion in Bert's and Alain's eyes as they watch Susan's departing form, he says nothing.
Instead he expects their steadfast loyalty, for they are ka-tet, joined by fate.
Ka-tet...and true good men, unlike Farson who simply swiped the title of "Good Man." The sad thing about ka is...it don't distinguish between true good and fake good.
Sometimes it randomly helps the wrong folks, like now, when a stray branch snags Bert's "good luck" charm. The wrong folks, if they found it, would figure out quick enough that spies had been about. Fortunately, the wrong men are nowhere near, but instead palavering at the Travellers' Rest...

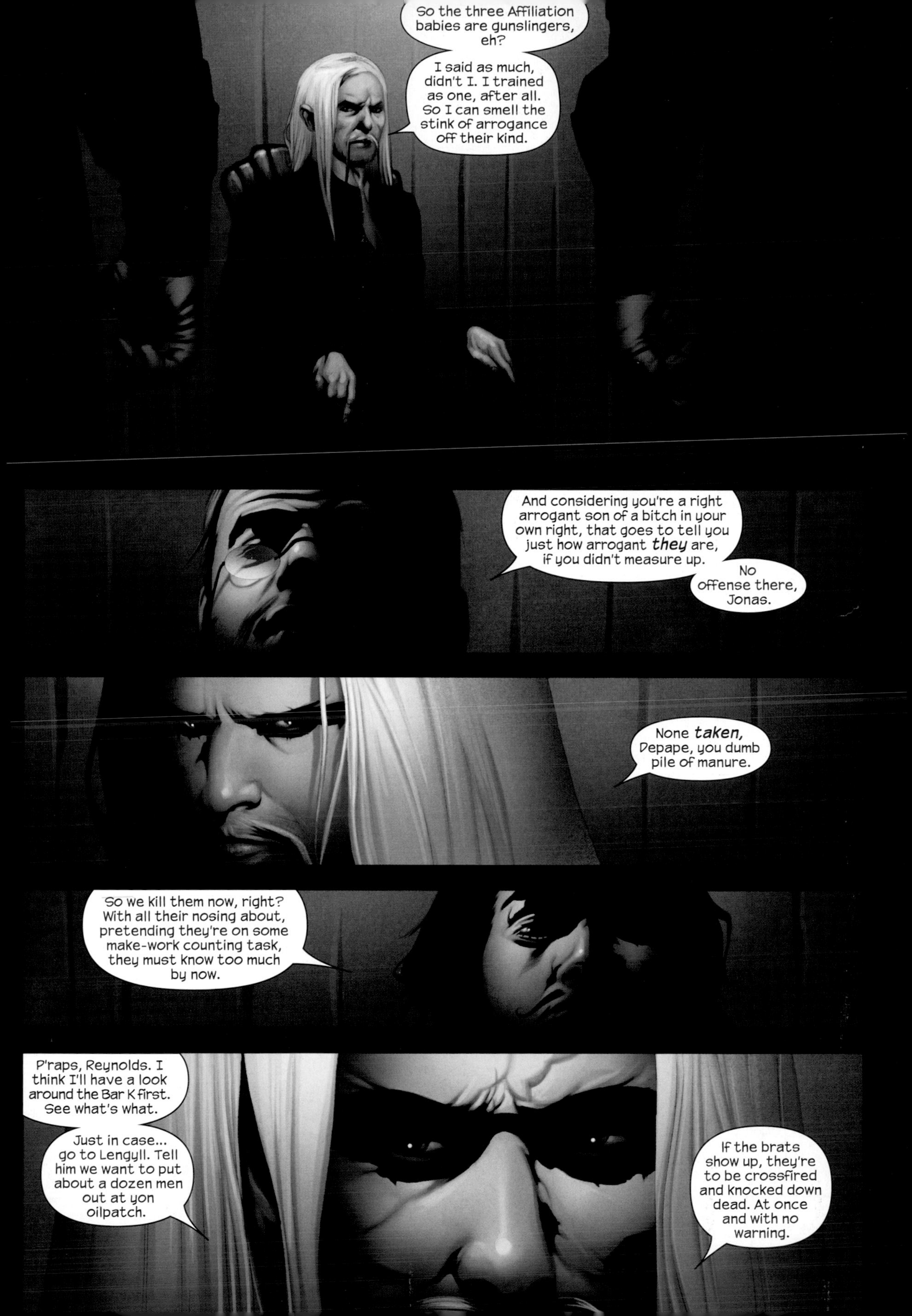

So the three Affiliation babies are gunslingers, eh?
I said as much, didn't I. I trained as one, after all. So I can smell the stink of arrogance off their kind.
And considering you're a right arrogant son of a bitch in your own right, that goes to tell you just how arrogant *they* are, if you didn't measure up.
No offense there, Jonas.
None *taken,* Depape, you dumb pile of manure.
So we kill them now, right? With all their nosing about, pretending they're on some make-work counting task, they must know too much by now.
P'raps, Reynolds. I think I'll have a look around the Bar K first. See what's what.
Just in case... go to Lengyll. Tell him we want to put about a dozen men out at yon oilpatch.
If the brats show up, they're to be crossfired and knocked down dead. At once and with no warning.

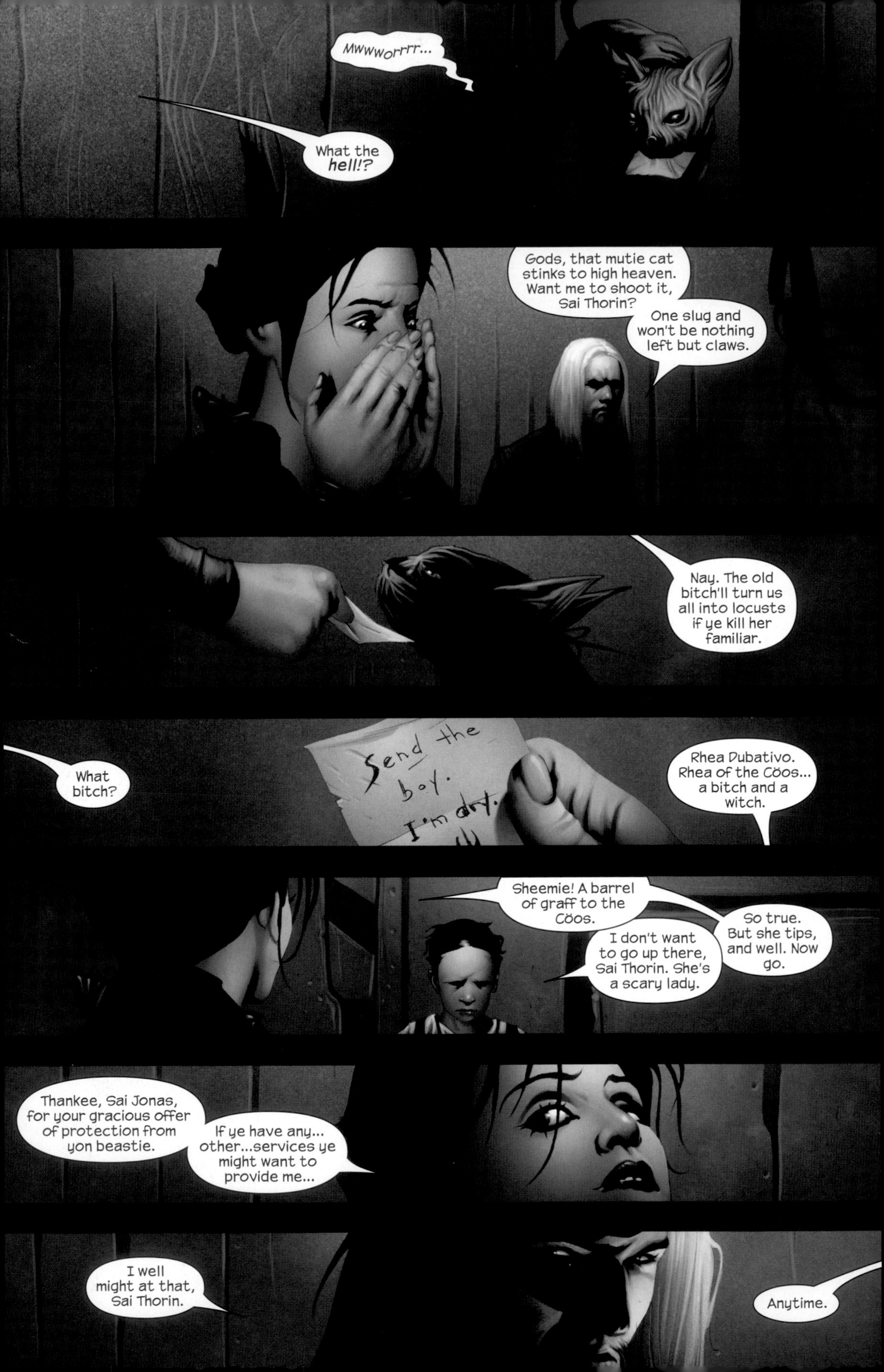
Mwwworrrr...
What the *hell!?*
Gods, that mutie cat stinks to high heaven. Want me to shoot it, Sai Thorin?
One slug and won't be nothing left but claws.
Nay. The old bitch'll turn us all into locusts if ye kill her familiar.
What bitch?
Send the boy. I'm dry.
Rhea Dubativo. Rhea of the Cöos... a bitch and a witch.
Sheemie! A barrel of graff to the Cöos.
I don't want to go up there, Sai Thorin. She's a scary lady.
So true. But she tips, and well. Now go.
Thankee, Sai Jonas, for your gracious offer of protection from yon beastie.
If ye have any... other...services ye might want to provide me...
I well might at that, Sai Thorin.
Anytime.

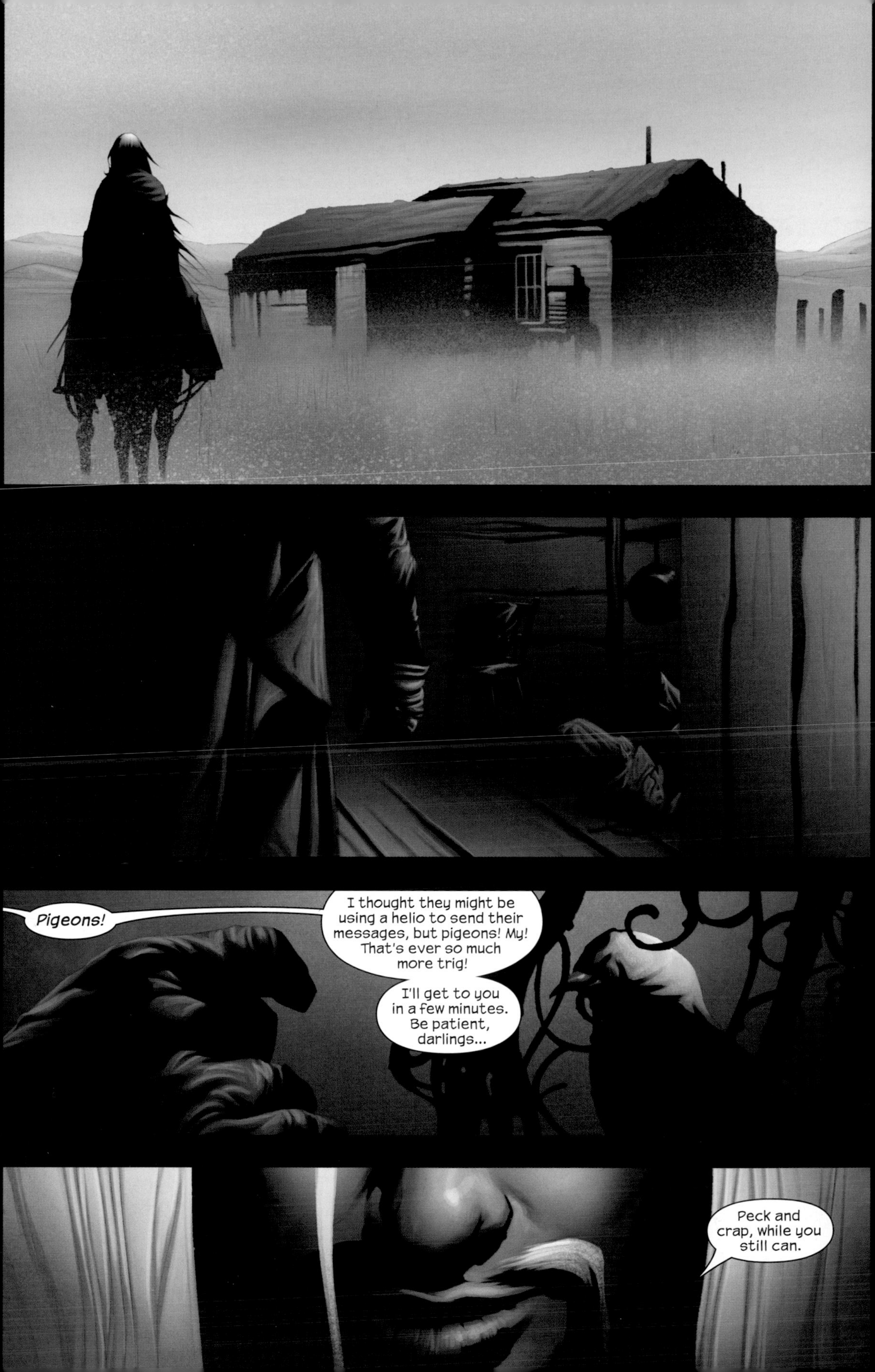
Pigeons!
I thought they might be using a helio to send their messages, but pigeons! My! That's ever so much more trig!
I'll get to you in a few minutes. Be patient, darlings...
Peck and crap, while you still can.

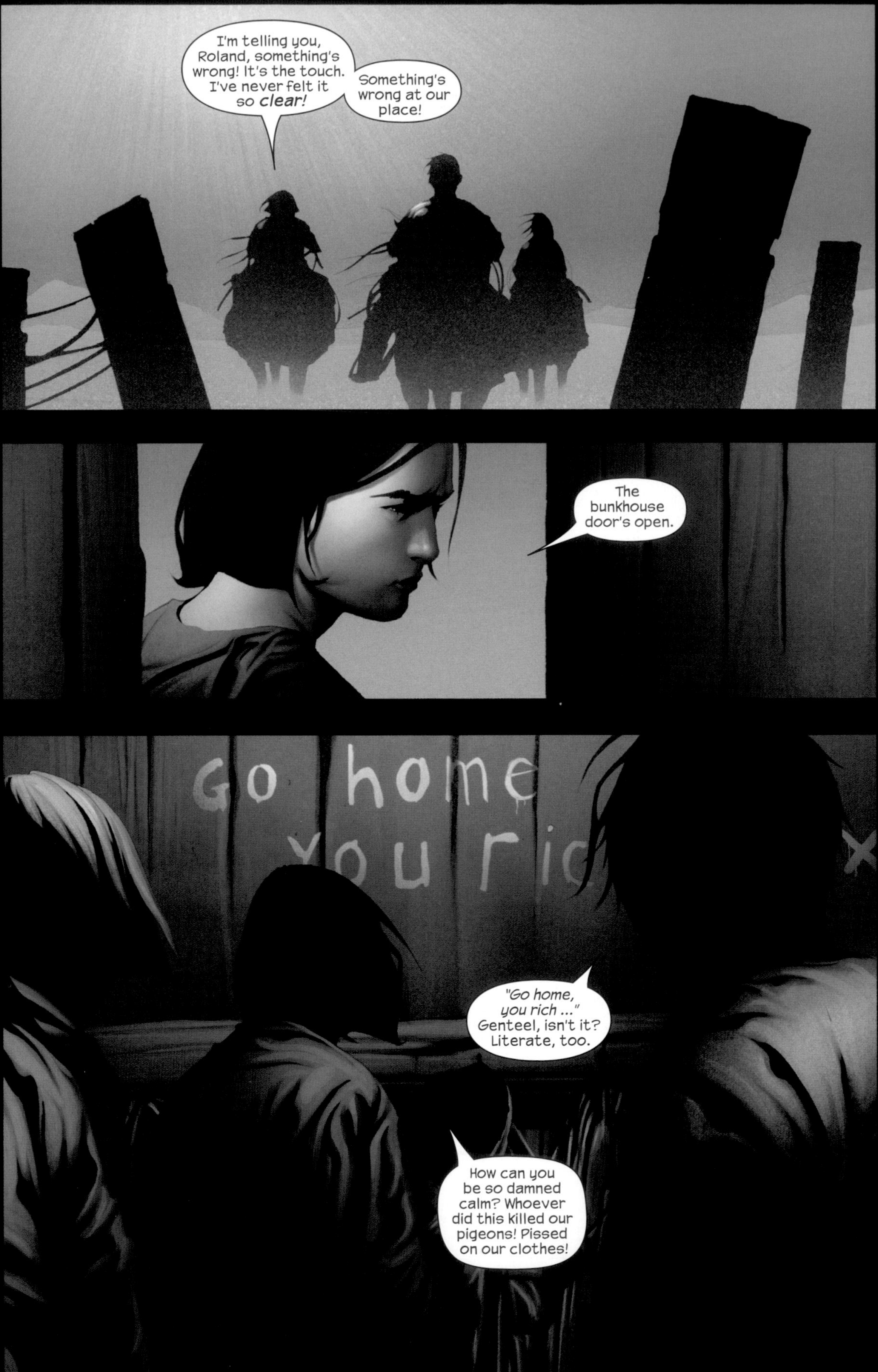
I'm telling you, Roland, something's wrong! It's the touch. I've never felt it so *clear!*
Something's wrong at our place!
The bunkhouse door's open.
Go home you ric
"Go home, you rich ..." Genteel, isn't it? Literate, too.
How can you be so damned calm? Whoever did this killed our pigeons! Pissed on our clothes!

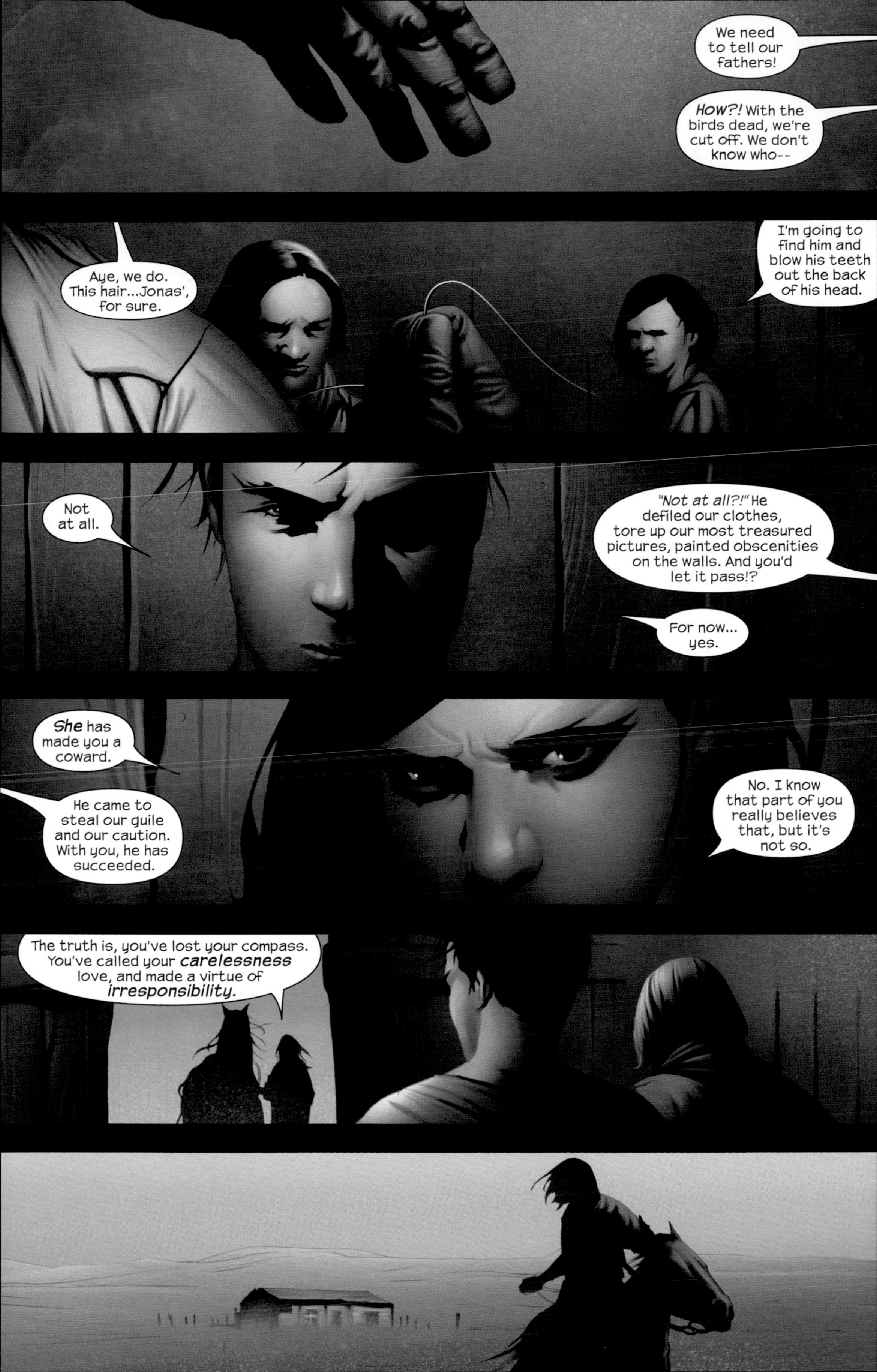
We need to tell our fathers!
HOW?! With the birds dead, we're cut off. We don't know who--
Aye, we do. This hair...Jonas', for sure.
I'm going to find him and blow his teeth out the back of his head.
Not at all.
"Not at all?!" He defiled our clothes, tore up our most treasured pictures, painted obscenities on the walls. And you'd let it pass!?
For now... yes.
She has made you a coward.
He came to steal our guile and our caution. With you, he has succeeded.
No. I know that part of you really believes that, but it's not so.
The truth is, you've lost your compass. You've called your ***carelessness*** love, and made a virtue of ***irresponsibility.***

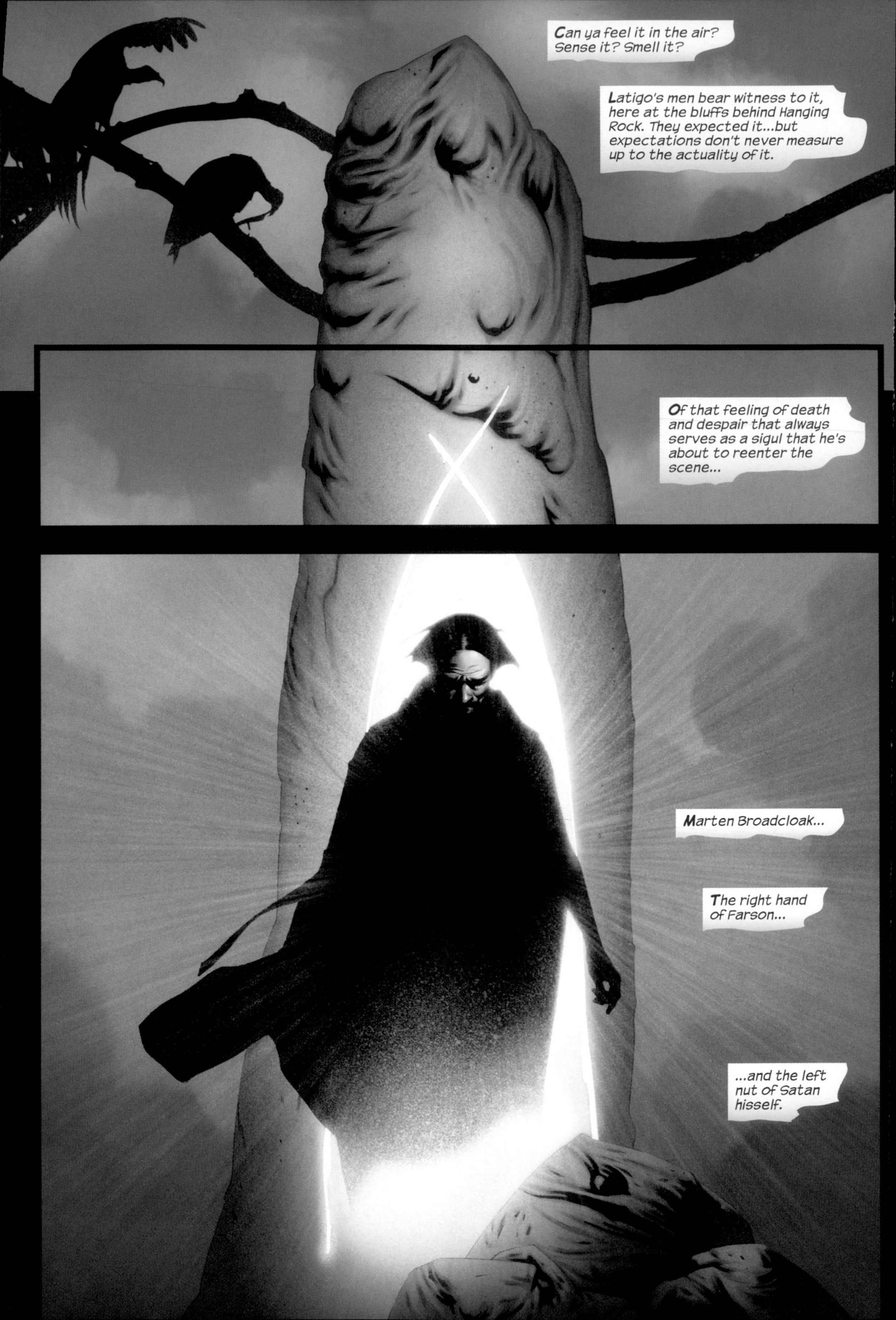
Can ya feel it in the air? Sense it? Smell it?
Latigo's men bear witness to it, here at the bluffs behind Hanging Rock. They expected it...but expectations don't never measure up to the actuality of it.
Of that feeling of death and despair that always serves as a sigul that he's about to reenter the scene...
Marten Broadcloak...
The right hand of Farson...
...and the left nut of Satan hisself.

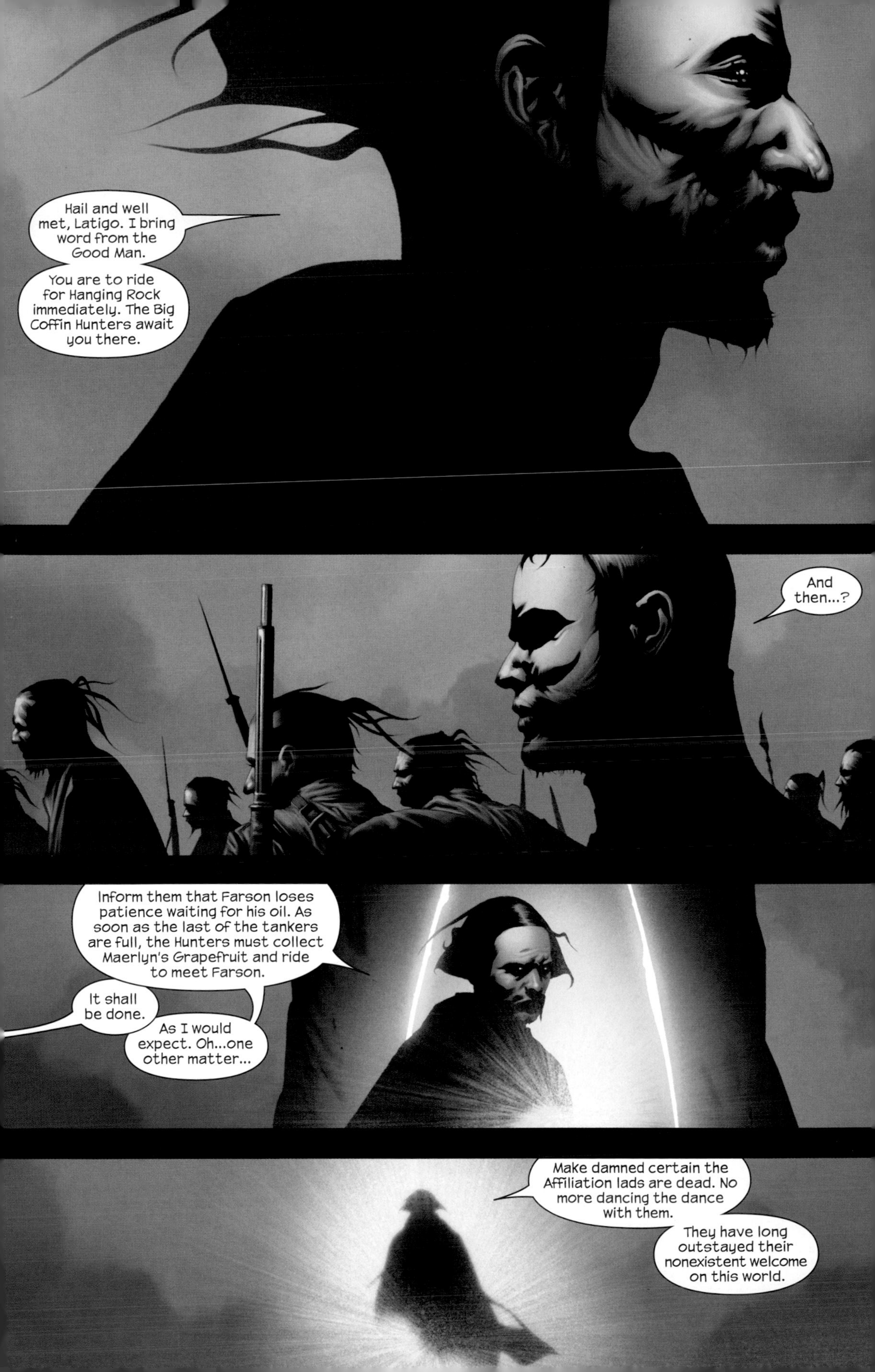
Hail and well met, Latigo. I bring word from the Good Man.
You are to ride for Hanging Rock immediately. The Big Coffin Hunters await you there.
And then...?
Inform them that Farson loses patience waiting for his oil. As soon as the last of the tankers are full, the Hunters must collect Maerlyn's Grapefruit and ride to meet Farson.
It shall be done.
As I would expect. Oh...one other matter...
Make damned certain the Affiliation lads are dead. No more dancing the dance with them.
They have long outstayed their nonexistent welcome on this world.

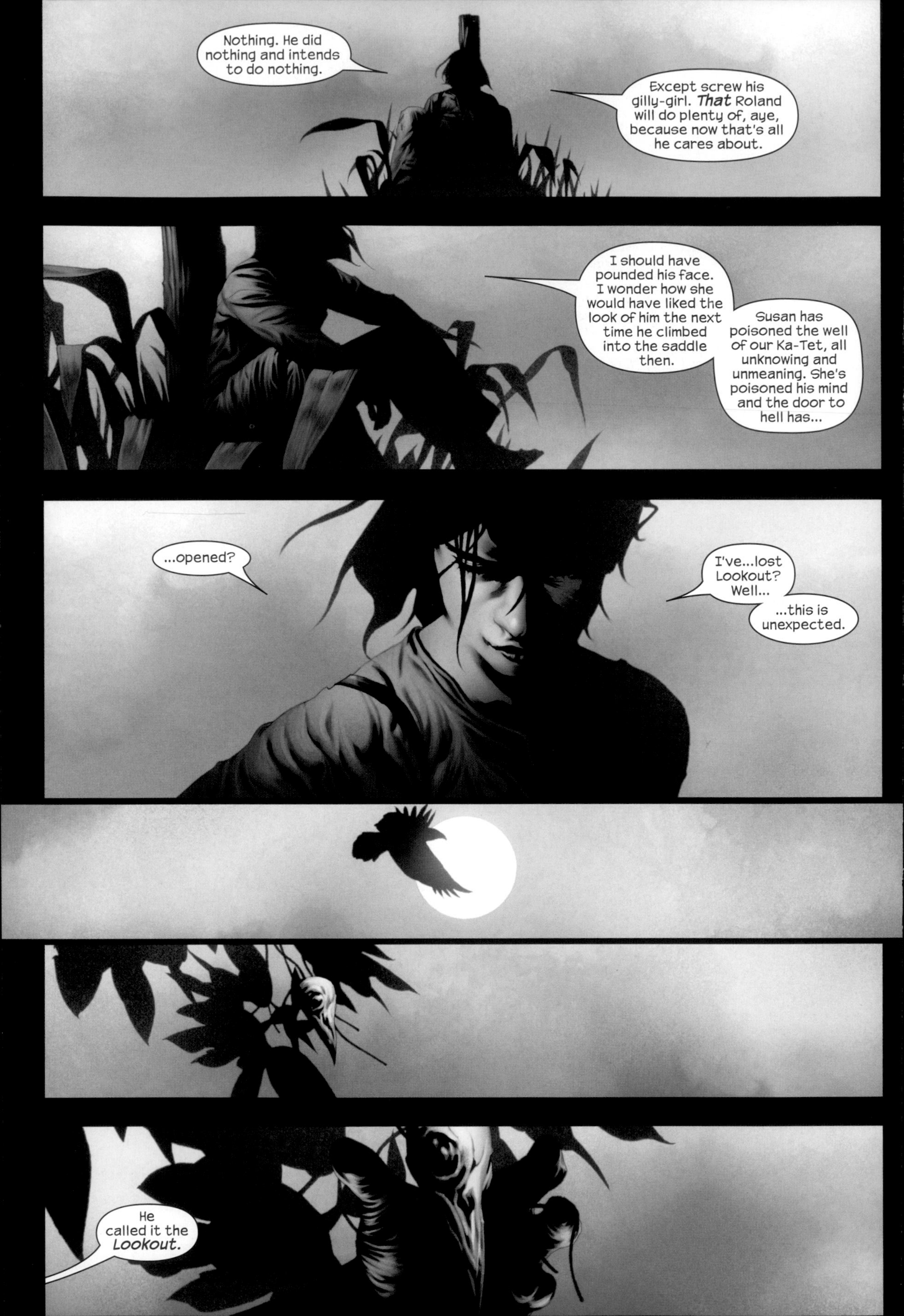

Nothing. He did nothing and intends to do nothing.
Except screw his gilly-girl. *That* Roland will do plenty of, aye, because now that's all he cares about.
I should have pounded his face. I wonder how she would have liked the look of him the next time he climbed into the saddle then.
Susan has poisoned the well of our Ka-Tet, all unknowing and unmeaning. She's poisoned his mind and the door to hell has...
...opened?
I've...lost Lookout? Well...
...this is unexpected.
He called it the *Lookout.*

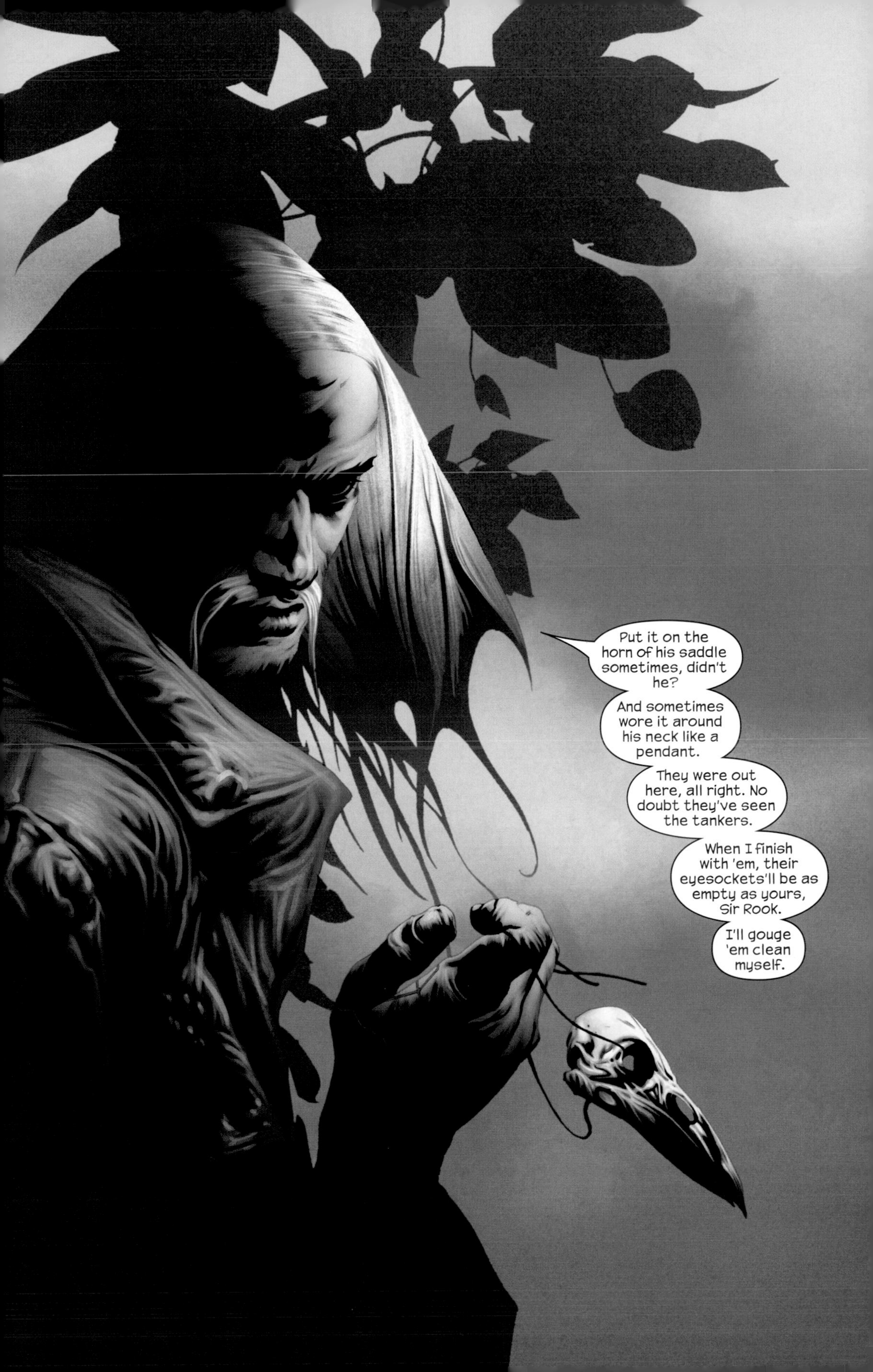
Put it on the horn of his saddle sometimes, didn't he?
And sometimes wore it around his neck like a pendant.
They were out here, all right. No doubt they've seen the tankers.
When I finish with 'em, their eyesockets'll be as empty as yours, Sir Rook.
I'll gouge 'em clean myself.

STEPHEN KING

THE DARK TOWER

THE GUNSLINGER BORN

CHAPTER SIX

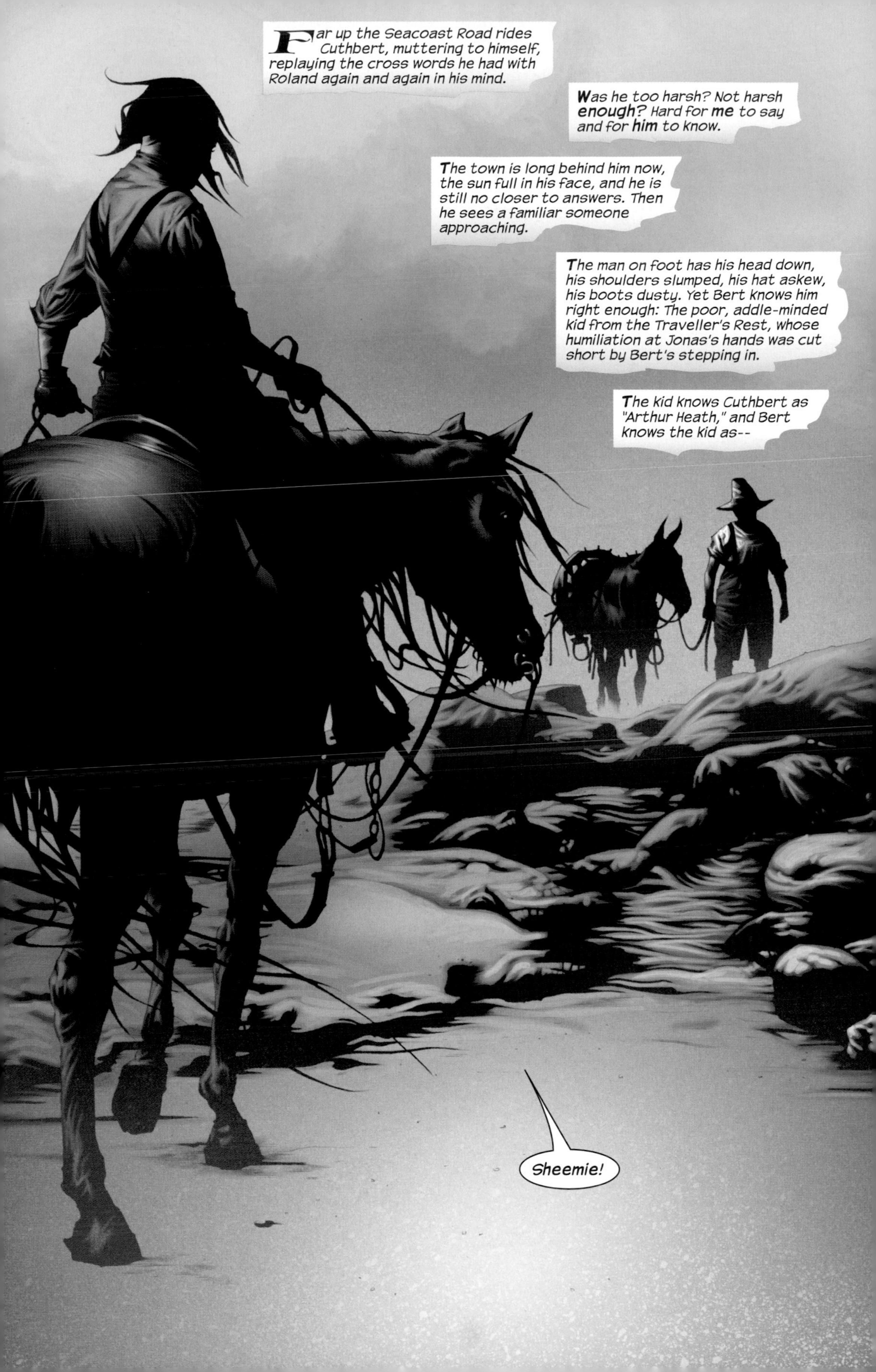
Far up the Seacoast Road rides Cuthbert, muttering to himself, replaying the cross words he had with Roland again and again in his mind.
Was he too harsh? Not harsh enough? Hard for me to say and for him to know.
The town is long behind him now, the sun full in his face, and he is still no closer to answers. Then he sees a familiar someone approaching.
The man on foot has his head down, his shoulders slumped, his hat askew, his boots dusty. Yet Bert knows him right enough: The poor, addle-minded kid from the Traveller's Rest, whose humiliation at Jonas's hands was cut short by Bert's stepping in.
The kid knows Cuthbert as "Arthur Heath," and Bert knows the kid as--
Sheemie!

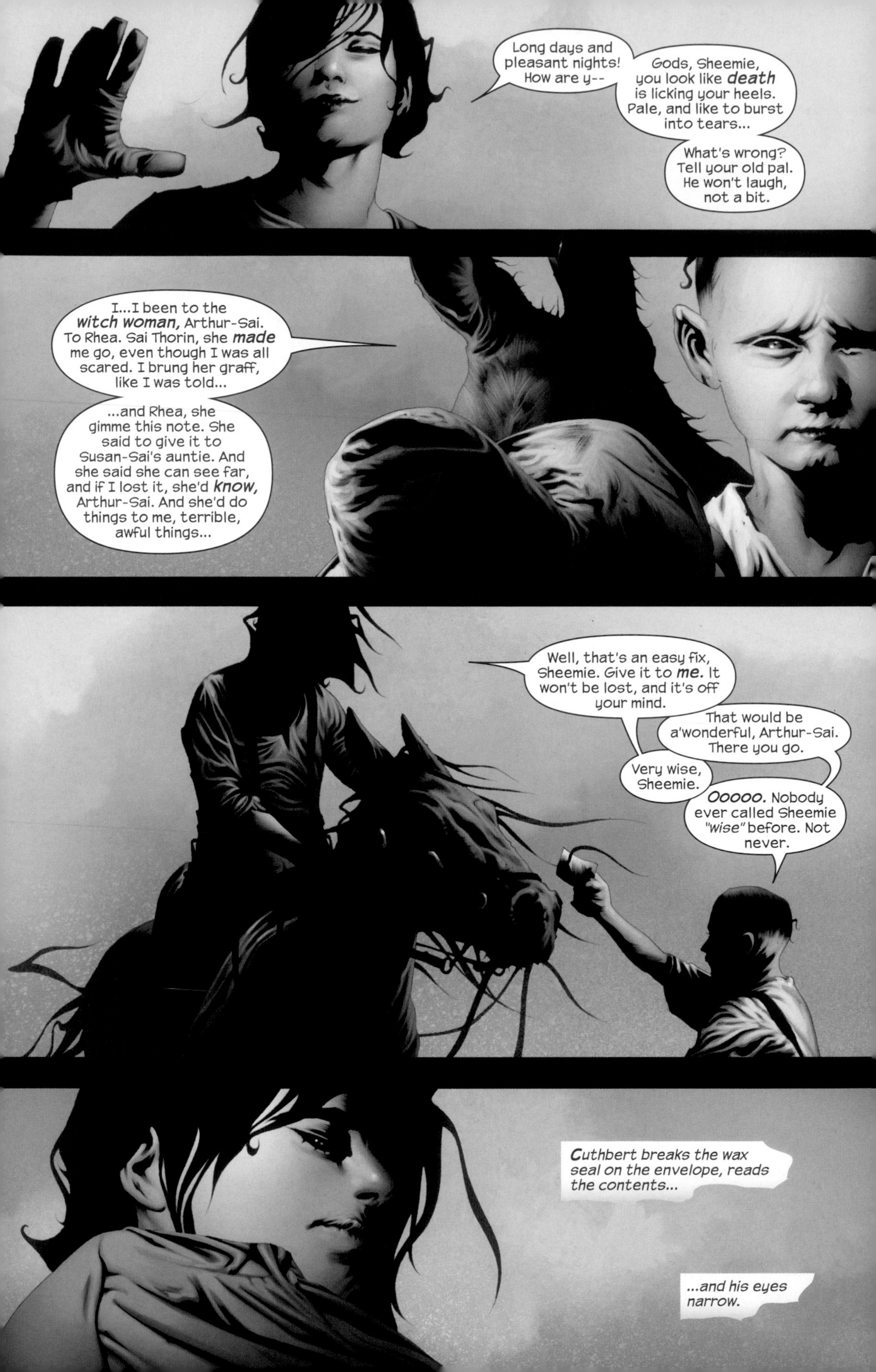
Long days and pleasant nights! How are y--
Gods, Sheemie, you look like **death** is licking your heels. Pale, and like to burst into tears...
What's wrong? Tell your old pal. He won't laugh, not a bit.
I...I been to the **witch woman,** Arthur-Sai. To Rhea. Sai Thorin, she **made** me go, even though I was all scared. I brung her graff, like I was told...
...and Rhea, she gimme this note. She said to give it to Susan-Sai's auntie. And she said she can see far, and if I lost it, she'd **know,** Arthur-Sai. And she'd do things to me, terrible, awful things...
Well, that's an easy fix, Sheemie. Give it to **me.** It won't be lost, and it's off your mind.
That would be a'wonderful, Arthur-Sai. There you go.
Very wise, Sheemie.
Ooooo. Nobody ever called Sheemie *"wise"* before. Not never.
Cuthbert breaks the wax seal on the envelope, reads the contents...
...and his eyes narrow.

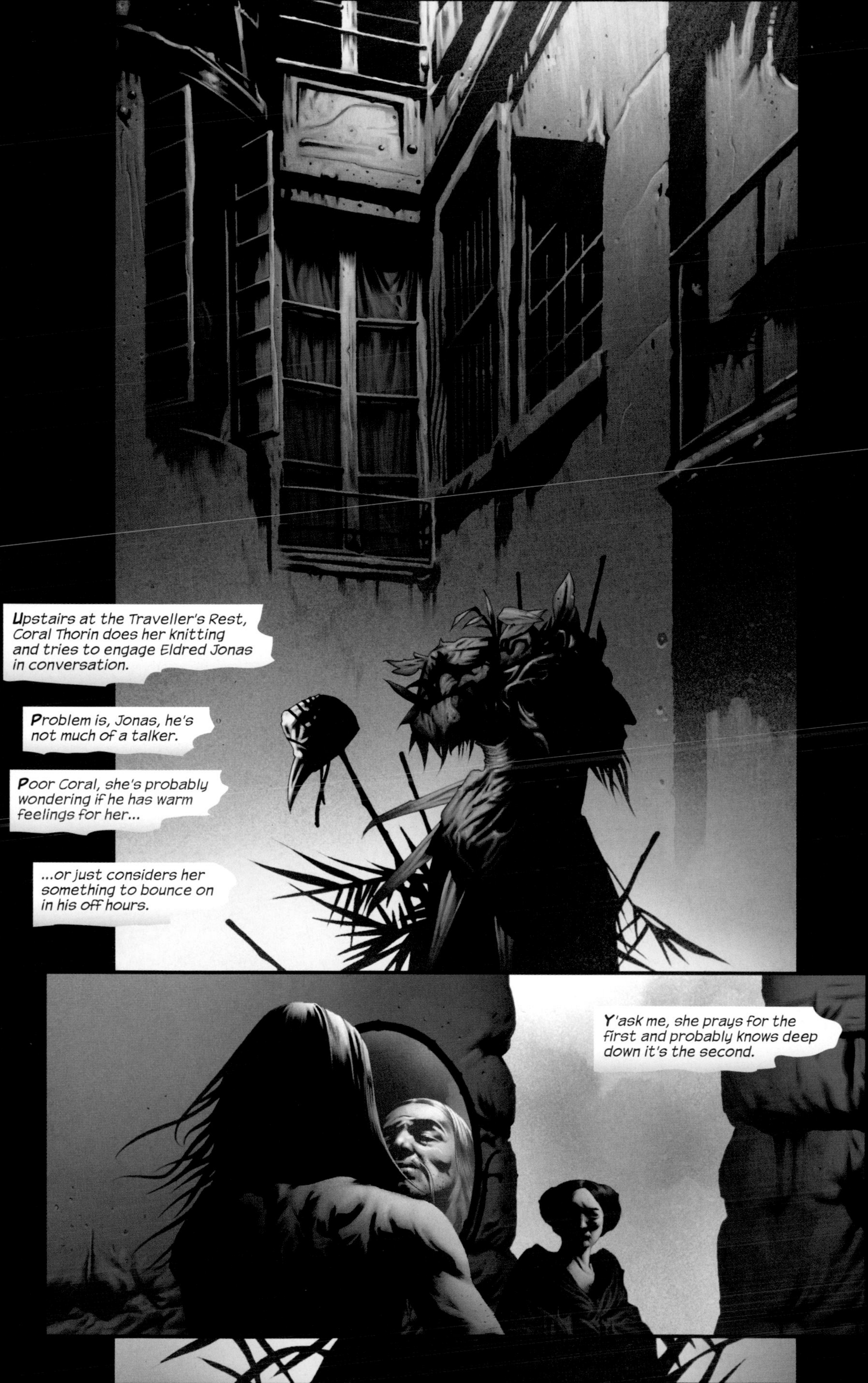

Upstairs at the Traveller's Rest, Coral Thorin does her knitting and tries to engage Eldred Jonas in conversation.
Problem is, Jonas, he's not much of a talker.
Poor Coral, she's probably wondering if he has warm feelings for her...
...or just considers her something to bounce on in his off hours.
Y'ask me, she prays for the first and probably knows deep down it's the second.

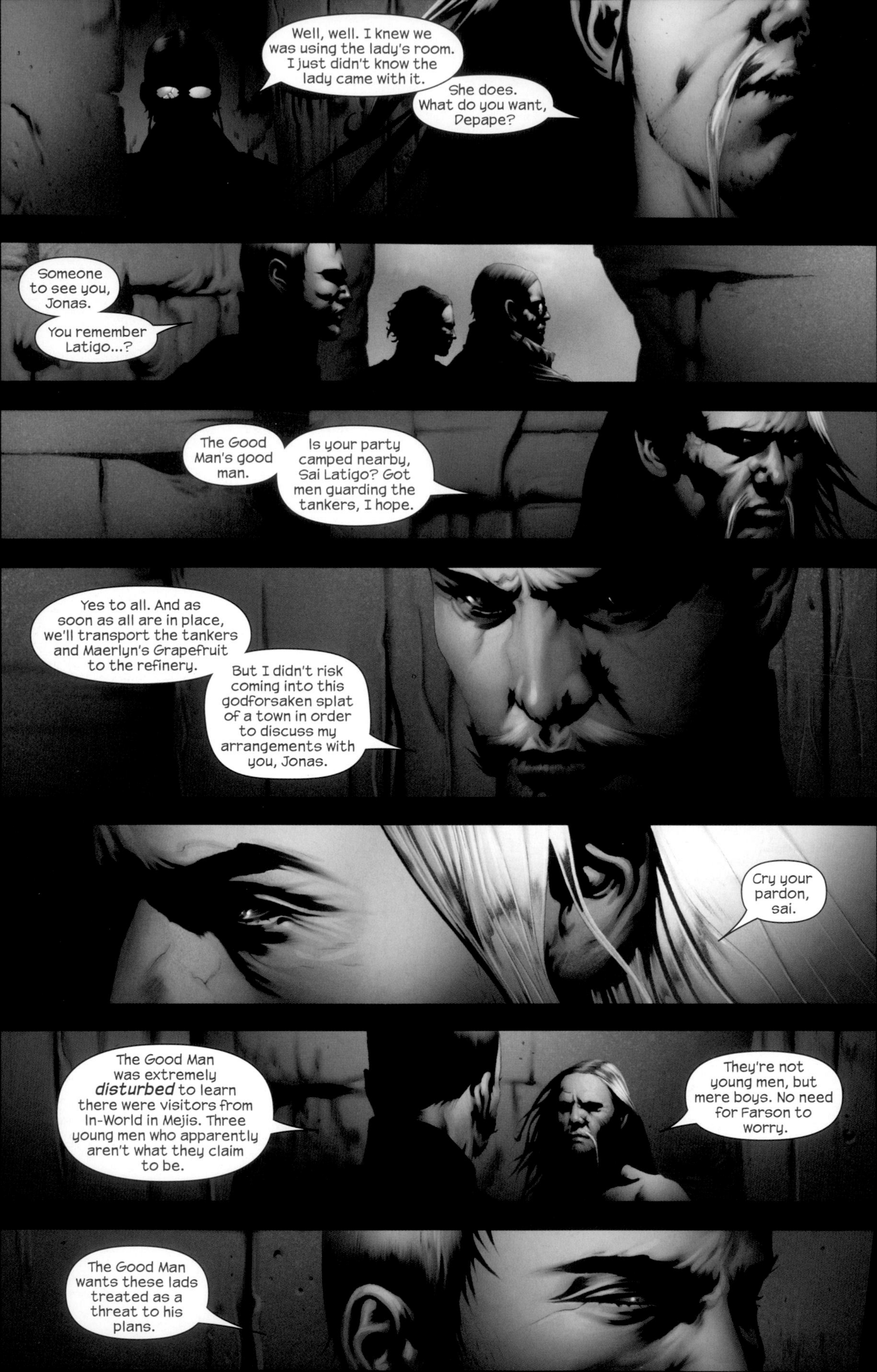

Well, well. I knew we was using the lady's room. I just didn't know the lady came with it.
She does. What do you want, Depape?
Someone to see you, Jonas.
You remember Latigo...?
The Good Man's good man.
Is your party camped nearby, Sai Latigo? Got men guarding the tankers, I hope.
Yes to all. And as soon as all are in place, we'll transport the tankers and Maerlyn's Grapefruit to the refinery.
But I didn't risk coming into this godforsaken splat of a town in order to discuss my arrangements with you, Jonas.
Cry your pardon, sai.
The Good Man was extremely *disturbed* to learn there were visitors from In-World in Mejis. Three young men who apparently aren't what they claim to be.
They're not young men, but mere boys. No need for Farson to worry.
The Good Man wants these lads treated as a threat to his plans.

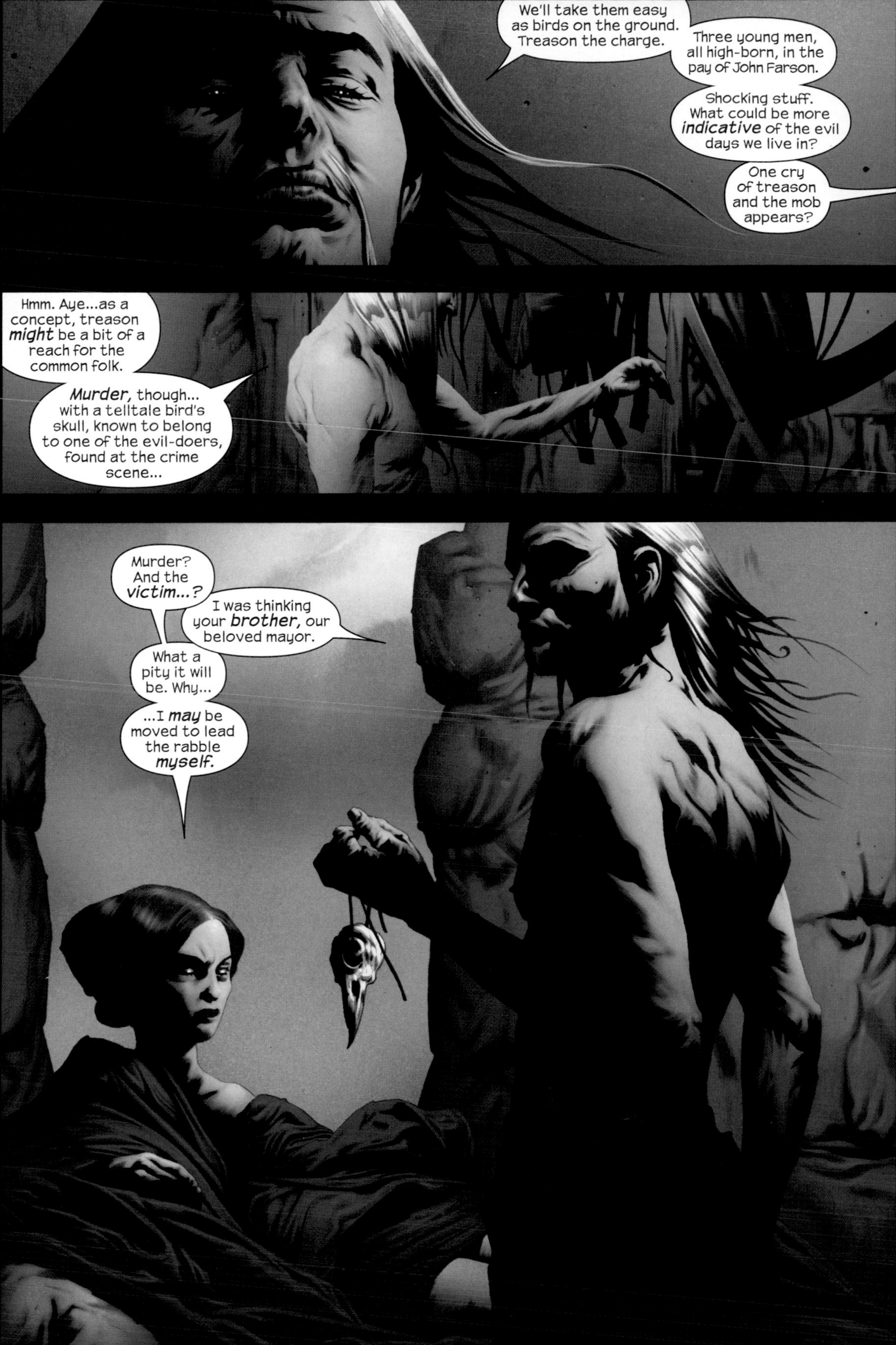
We'll take them easy as birds on the ground. Treason the charge.
Three young men, all high-born, in the pay of John Farson.
Shocking stuff. What could be more *indicative* of the evil days we live in?
One cry of treason and the mob appears?
Hmm. Aye...as a concept, treason *might* be a bit of a reach for the common folk.
Murder, though... with a telltale bird's skull, known to belong to one of the evil-doers, found at the crime scene...
Murder? And the *victim...?*
I was thinking your *brother,* our beloved mayor.
What a pity it will be. Why...
...I *may* be moved to lead the rabble *myself.*

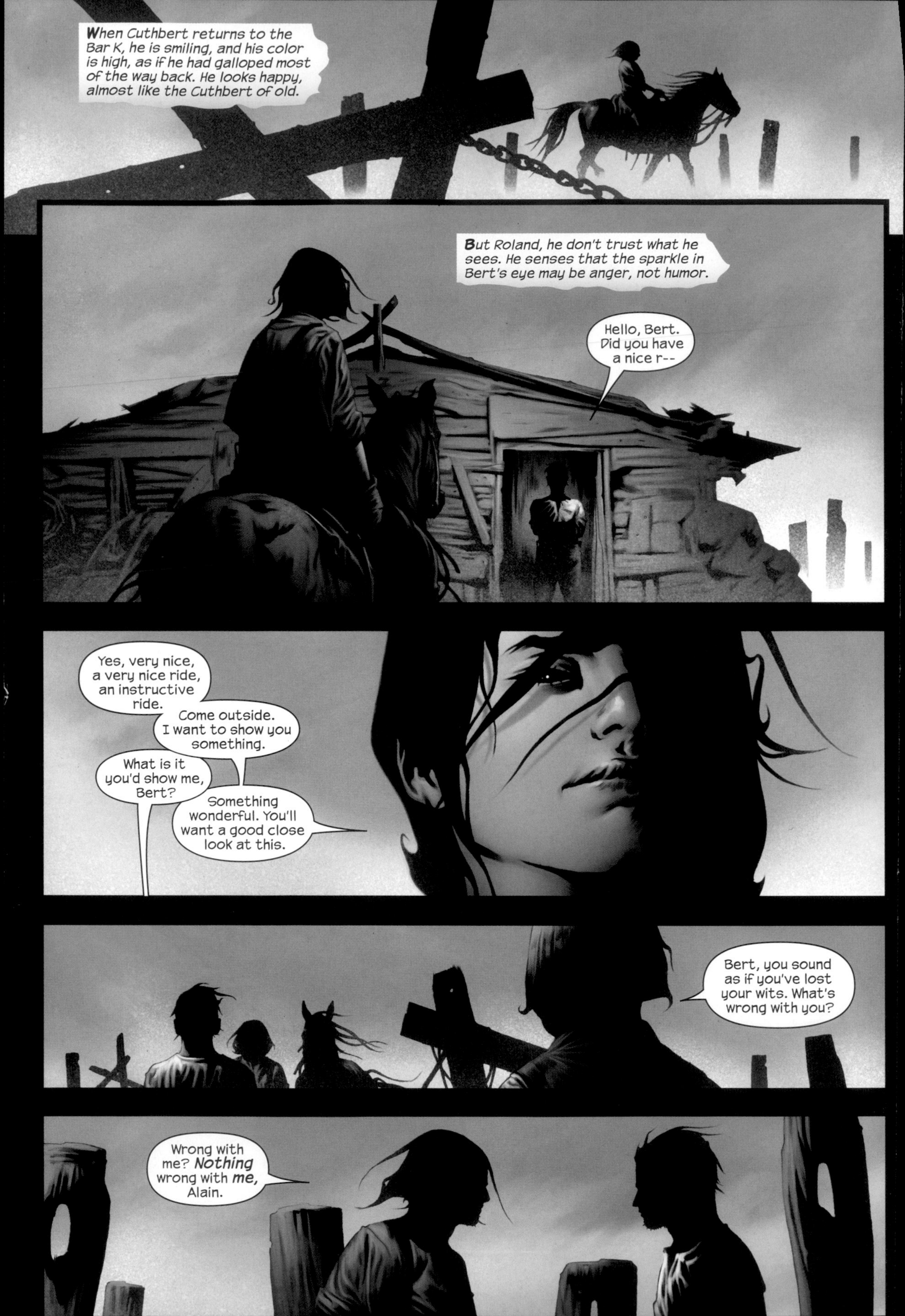
When Cuthbert returns to the Bar K, he is smiling, and his color is high, as if he had galloped most of the way back. He looks happy, almost like the Cuthbert of old.
But Roland, he don't trust what he sees. He senses that the sparkle in Bert's eye may be anger, not humor.
Hello, Bert. Did you have a nice r--
Yes, very nice, a very nice ride, an instructive ride.
Come outside. I want to show you something.
What is it you'd show me, Bert?
Something wonderful. You'll want a good close look at this.
Bert, you sound as if you've lost your wits. What's wrong with you?
Wrong with me? *Nothing* wrong with *me,* Alain.

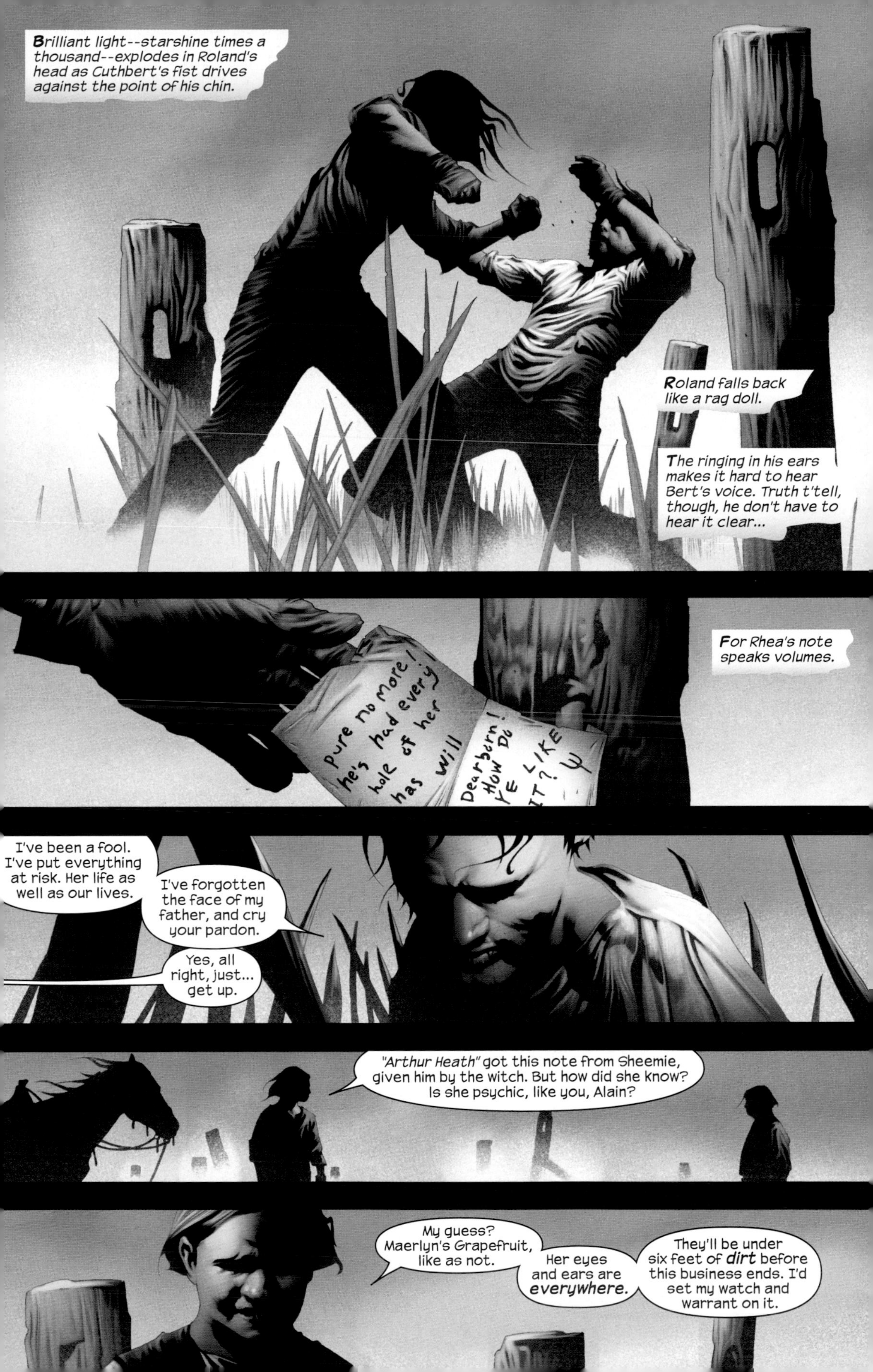
Brilliant light--starshine times a thousand--explodes in Roland's head as Cuthbert's fist drives against the point of his chin.
Roland falls back like a rag doll.
The ringing in his ears makes it hard to hear Bert's voice. Truth t'tell, though, he don't have to hear it clear...
For Rhea's note speaks volumes.
pure no more! he's had every hole of her has will
Dearborn! HOW DO YE LIKE IT?
I've been a fool. I've put everything at risk. Her life as well as our lives.
I've forgotten the face of my father, and cry your pardon.
Yes, all right, just... get up.
"Arthur Heath" got this note from Sheemie, given him by the witch. But how did she know? Is she psychic, like you, Alain?
My guess? Maerlyn's Grapefruit, like as not.
Her eyes and ears are everywhere.
They'll be under six feet of dirt before this business ends. I'd set my watch and warrant on it.

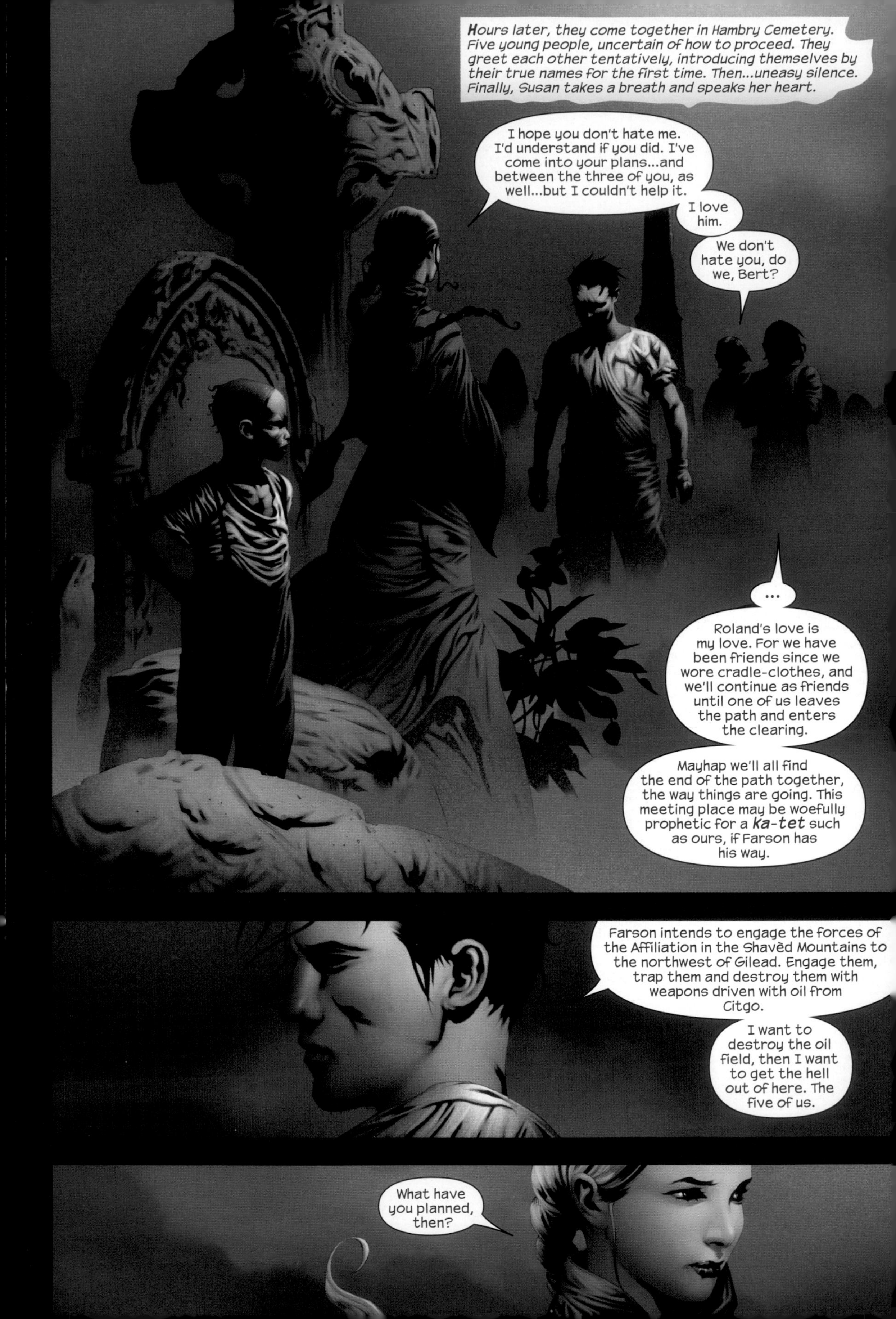
Hours later, they come together in Hambry Cemetery. Five young people, uncertain of how to proceed. They greet each other tentatively, introducing themselves by their true names for the first time. Then...uneasy silence. Finally, Susan takes a breath and speaks her heart.
I hope you don't hate me. I'd understand if you did. I've come into your plans...and between the three of you, as well...but I couldn't help it.
I love him.
We don't hate you, do we, Bert?
...
Roland's love is my love. For we have been friends since we wore cradle-clothes, and we'll continue as friends until one of us leaves the path and enters the clearing.
Mayhap we'll all find the end of the path together, the way things are going. This meeting place may be woefully prophetic for a *ka-tet* such as ours, if Farson has his way.
Farson intends to engage the forces of the Affiliation in the Shavèd Mountains to the northwest of Gilead. Engage them, trap them and destroy them with weapons driven with oil from Citgo.
I want to destroy the oil field, then I want to get the hell out of here. The five of us.
What have you planned, then?

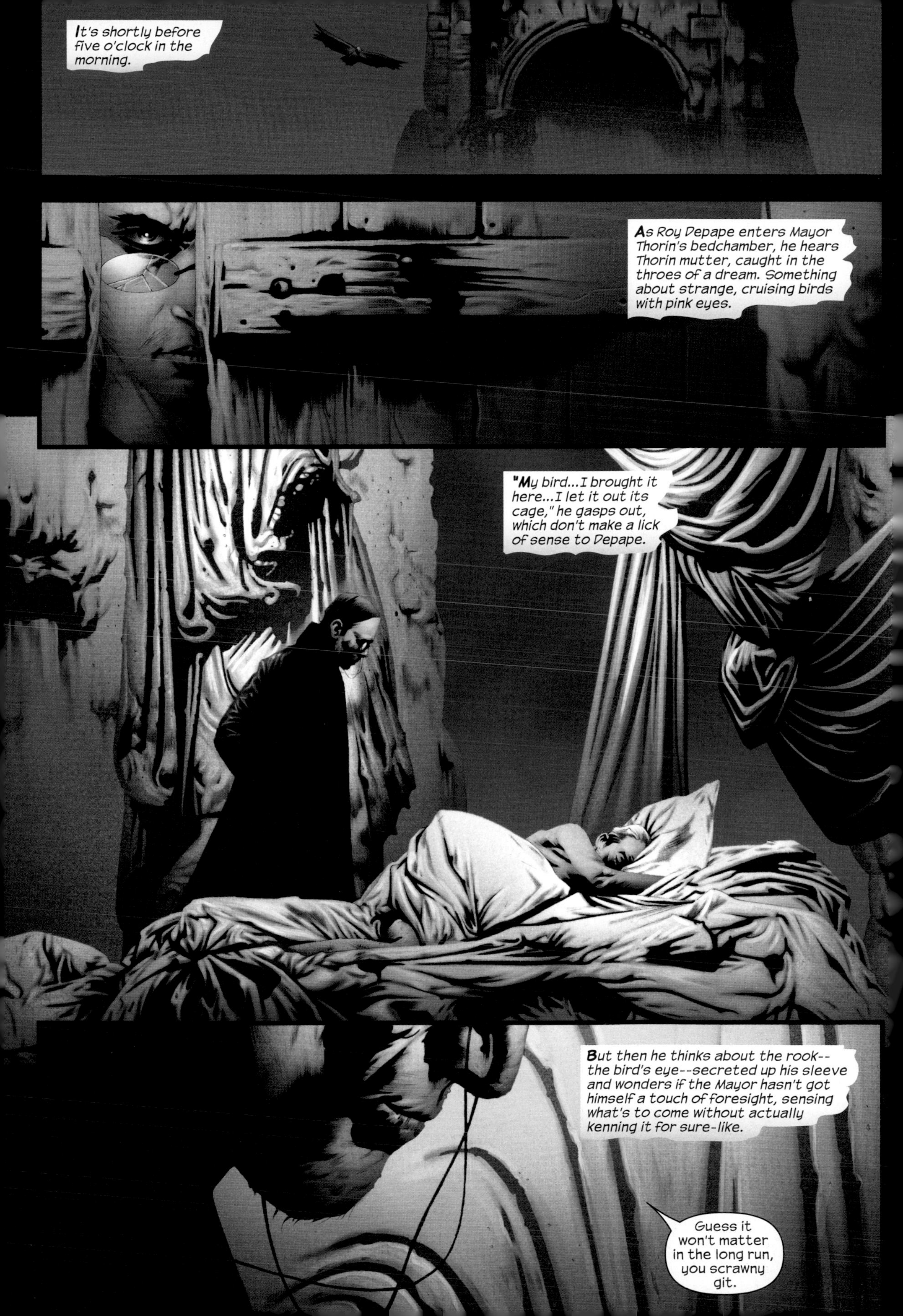
It's shortly before five o'clock in the morning.
As Roy Depape enters Mayor Thorin's bedchamber, he hears Thorin mutter, caught in the throes of a dream. Something about strange, cruising birds with pink eyes.
"My bird...I brought it here...I let it out its cage," he gasps out, which don't make a lick of sense to Depape.
But then he thinks about the rook--the bird's eye--secreted up his sleeve and wonders if the Mayor hasn't got himself a touch of foresight, sensing what's to come without actually kenning it for sure-like.
Guess it won't matter in the long run, you scrawny git.

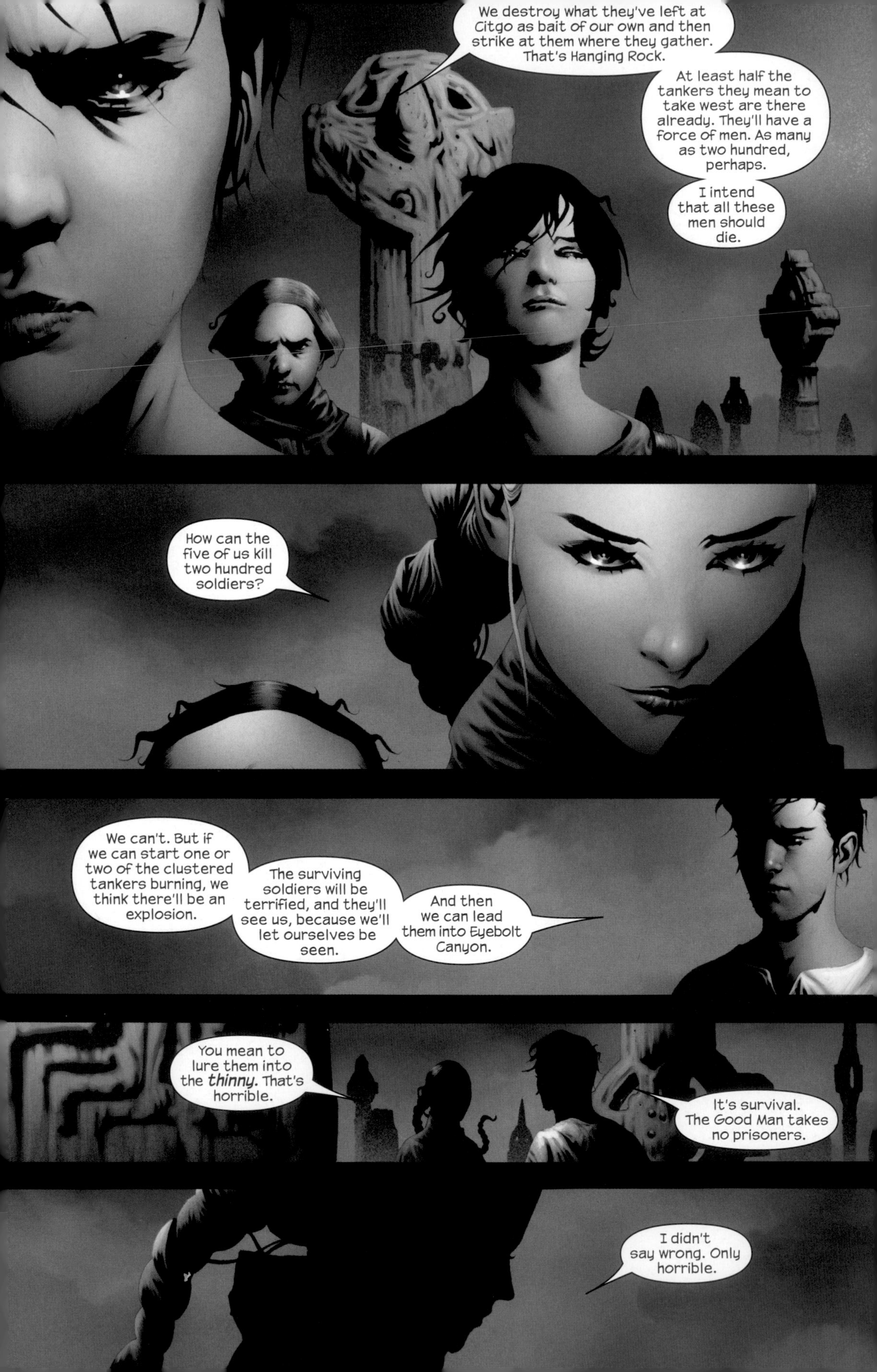
We destroy what they've left at Citgo as bait of our own and then strike at them where they gather. That's Hanging Rock.
At least half the tankers they mean to take west are there already. They'll have a force of men. As many as two hundred, perhaps.
I intend that all these men should die.
How can the five of us kill two hundred soldiers?
We can't. But if we can start one or two of the clustered tankers burning, we think there'll be an explosion.
The surviving soldiers will be terrified, and they'll see us, because we'll let ourselves be seen.
And then we can lead them into Eyebolt Canyon.
You mean to lure them into the *thinny*. That's horrible.
It's survival. The Good Man takes no prisoners.
I didn't say wrong. Only horrible.

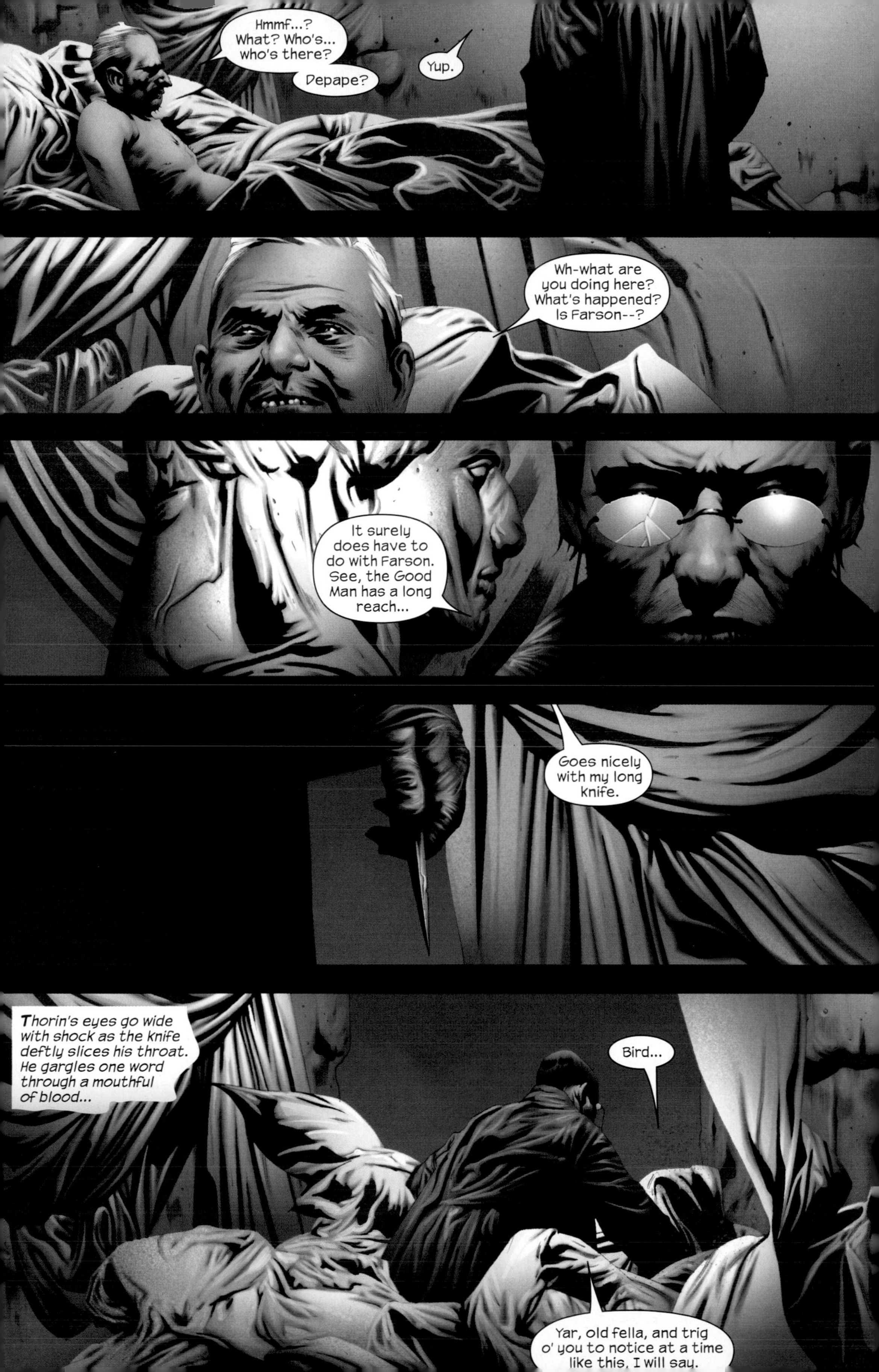
Hmmf...? What? Who's... who's there?
Depape?
Yup.
Wh-what are you doing here? What's happened? Is Farson--?
It surely does have to do with Farson. See, the Good Man has a long reach...
Goes nicely with my long knife.
Thorin's eyes go wide with shock as the knife deftly slices his throat. He gargles one word through a mouthful of blood...
Bird...
Yar, old fella, and trig o' you to notice at a time like this, I will say.

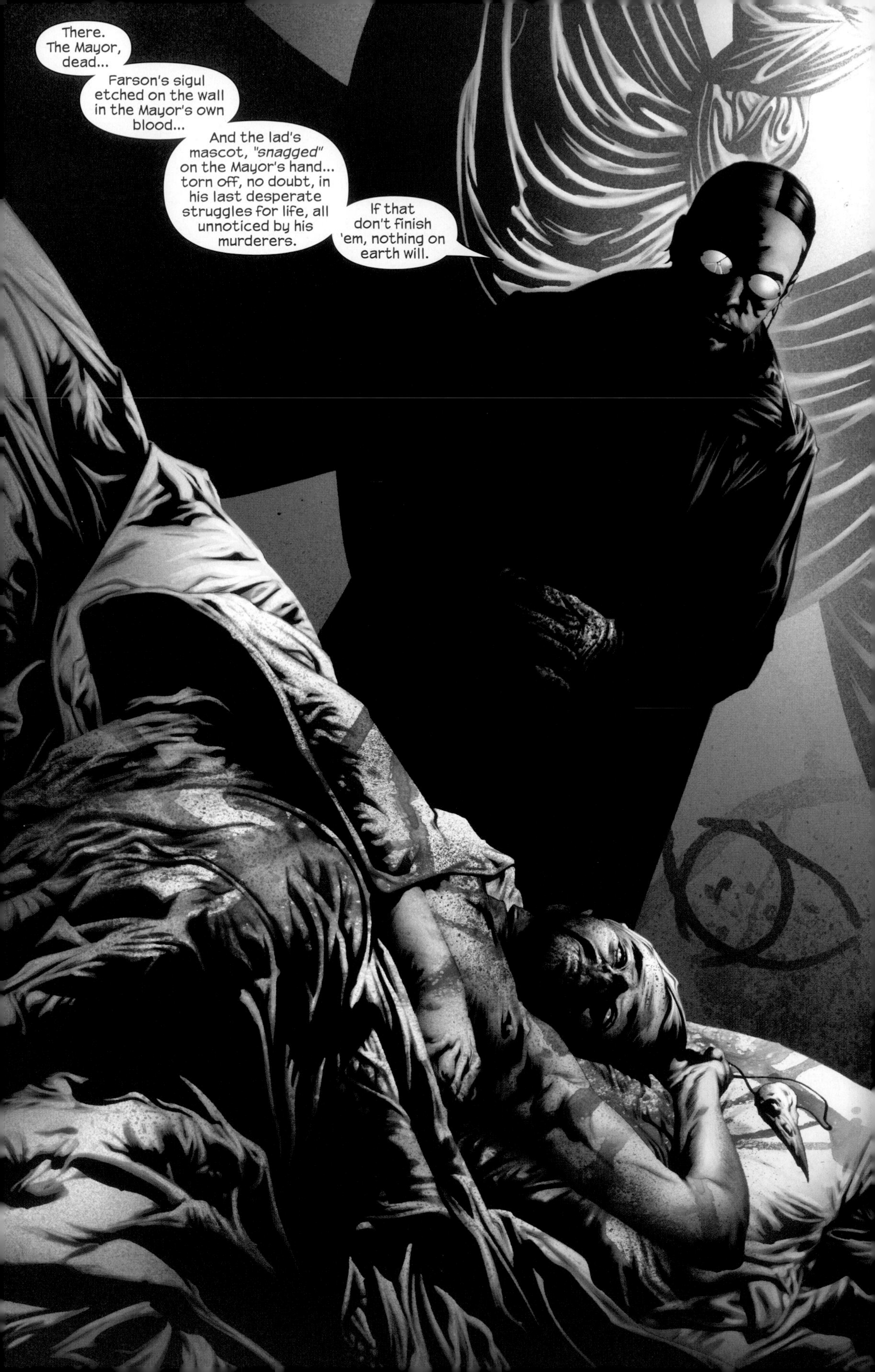
There. The Mayor, dead...
Farson's sigul etched on the wall in the Mayor's own blood...
And the lad's mascot, *"snagged"* on the Mayor's hand... torn off, no doubt, in his last desperate struggles for life, all unnoticed by his murderers.
If that don't finish 'em, nothing on earth will.

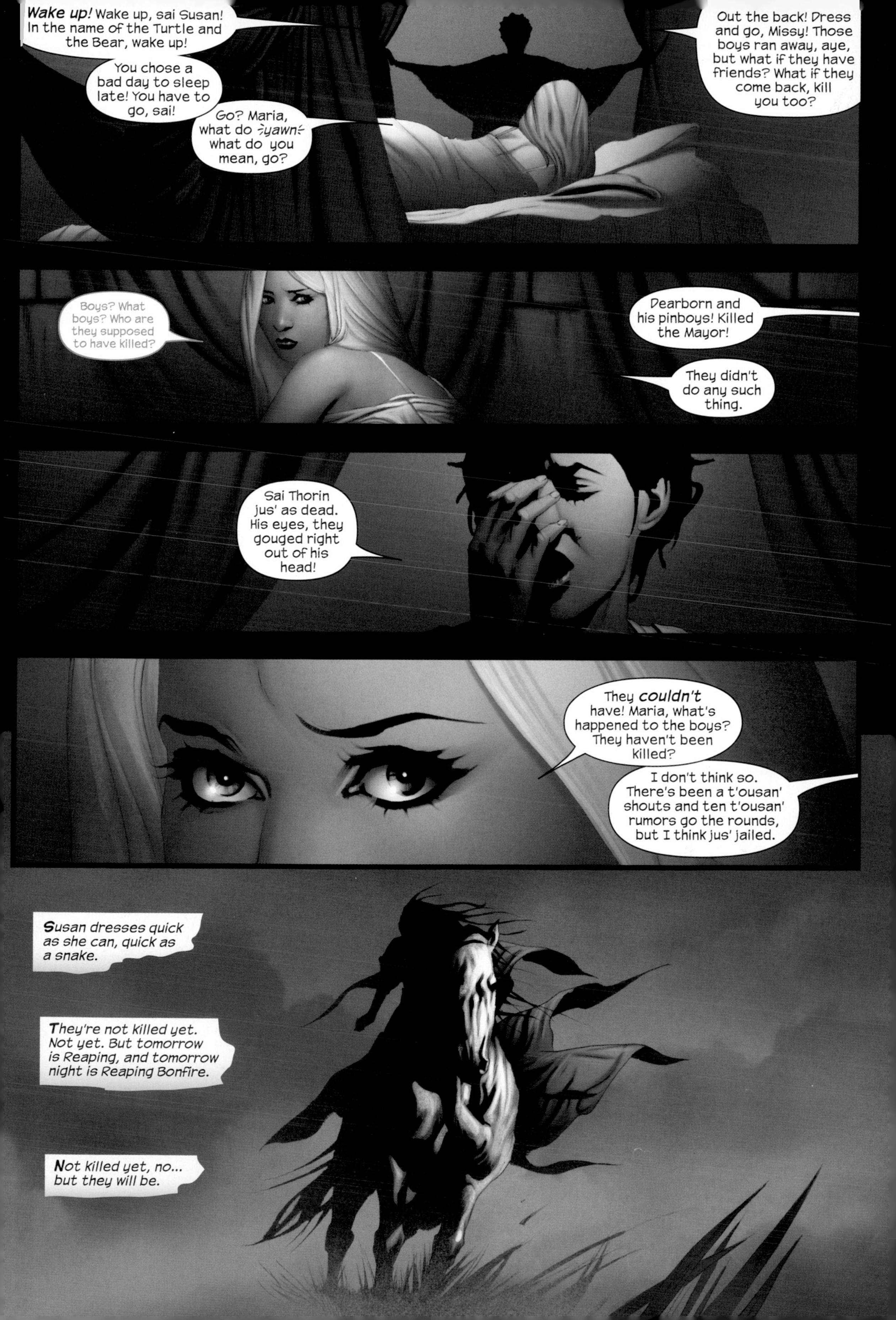

Wake up! Wake up, sai Susan! In the name of the Turtle and the Bear, wake up!
You chose a bad day to sleep late! You have to go, sai!
Go? Maria, what do -yawn- what do you mean, go?
Out the back! Dress and go, Missy! Those boys ran away, aye, but what if they have friends? What if they come back, kill you too?
Boys? What boys? Who are they supposed to have killed?
Dearborn and his pinboys! Killed the Mayor!
They didn't do any such thing.
Sai Thorin jus' as dead. His eyes, they gouged right out of his head!
They couldn't have! Maria, what's happened to the boys? They haven't been killed?
I don't think so. There's been a t'ousan' shouts and ten t'ousan' rumors go the rounds, but I think jus' jailed.
Susan dresses quick as she can, quick as a snake.
They're not killed yet. Not yet. But tomorrow is Reaping, and tomorrow night is Reaping Bonfire.
Not killed yet, no... but they will be.

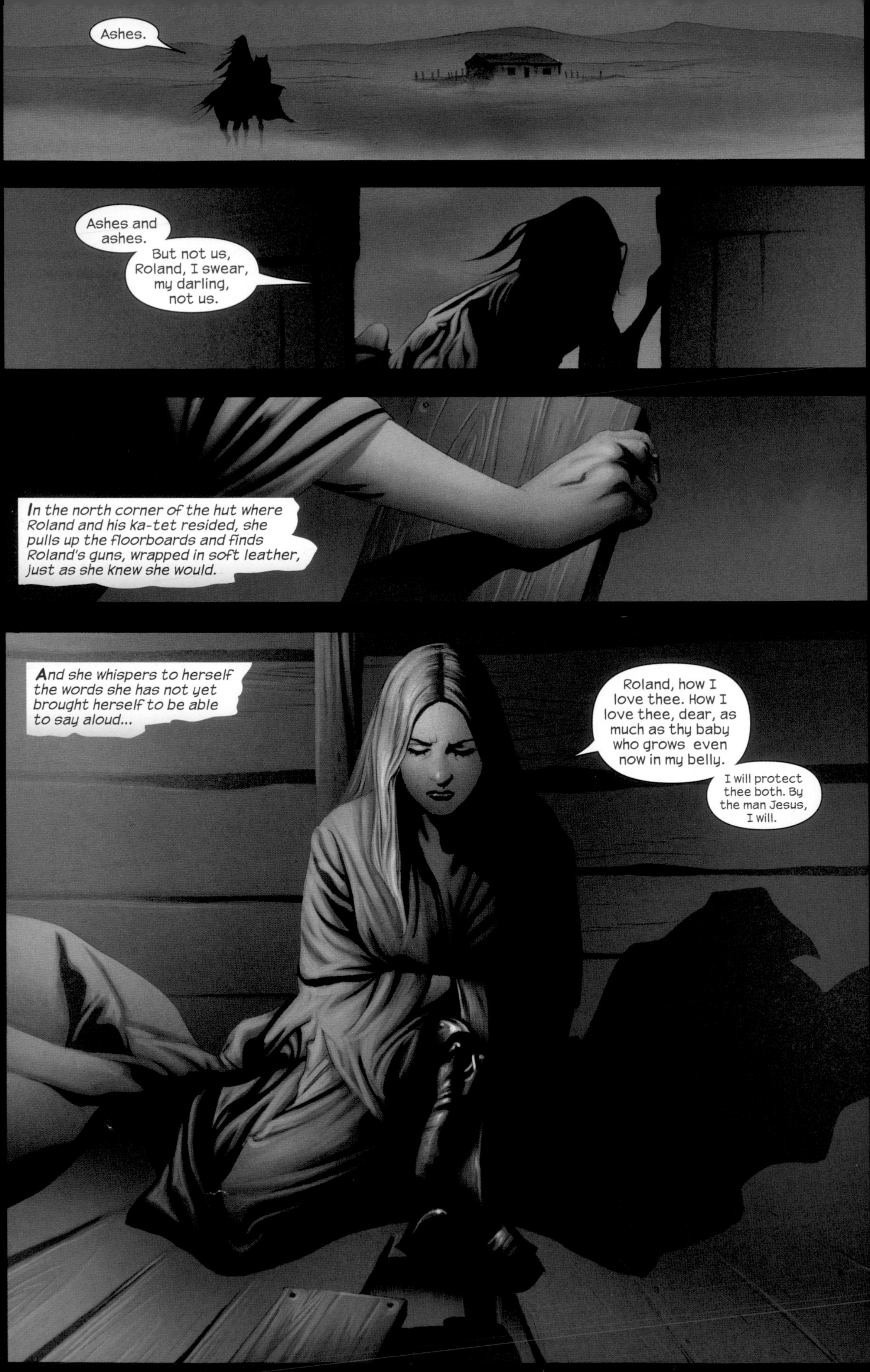
Ashes.
Ashes and ashes.
But not us, Roland, I swear, my darling, not us.
In the north corner of the hut where Roland and his ka-tet resided, she pulls up the floorboards and finds Roland's guns, wrapped in soft leather, just as she knew she would.
And she whispers to herself the words she has not yet brought herself to be able to say aloud...
Roland, how I love thee. How I love thee, dear, as much as thy baby who grows even now in my belly.
I will protect thee both. By the man Jesus, I will.

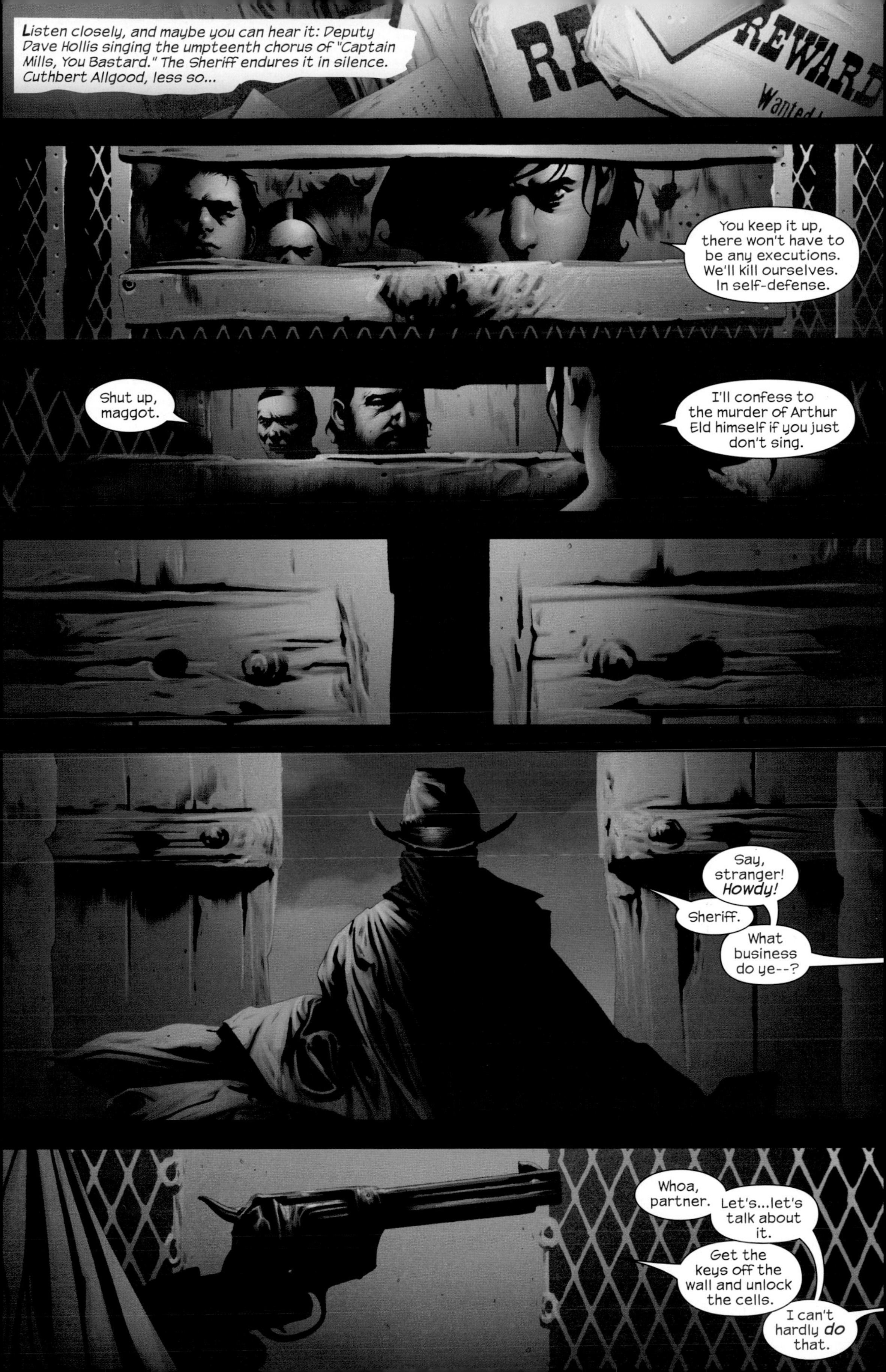
Listen closely, and maybe you can hear it: Deputy Dave Hollis singing the umpteenth chorus of "Captain Mills, You Bastard." The Sheriff endures it in silence. Cuthbert Allgood, less so...
REWARD
Wanted
You keep it up, there won't have to be any executions. We'll kill ourselves. In self-defense.
Shut up, maggot.
I'll confess to the murder of Arthur Eld himself if you just don't sing.
Say, stranger! Howdy!
Sheriff.
What business do ye--?
Whoa, partner.
Let's...let's talk about it.
Get the keys off the wall and unlock the cells.
I can't hardly do that.

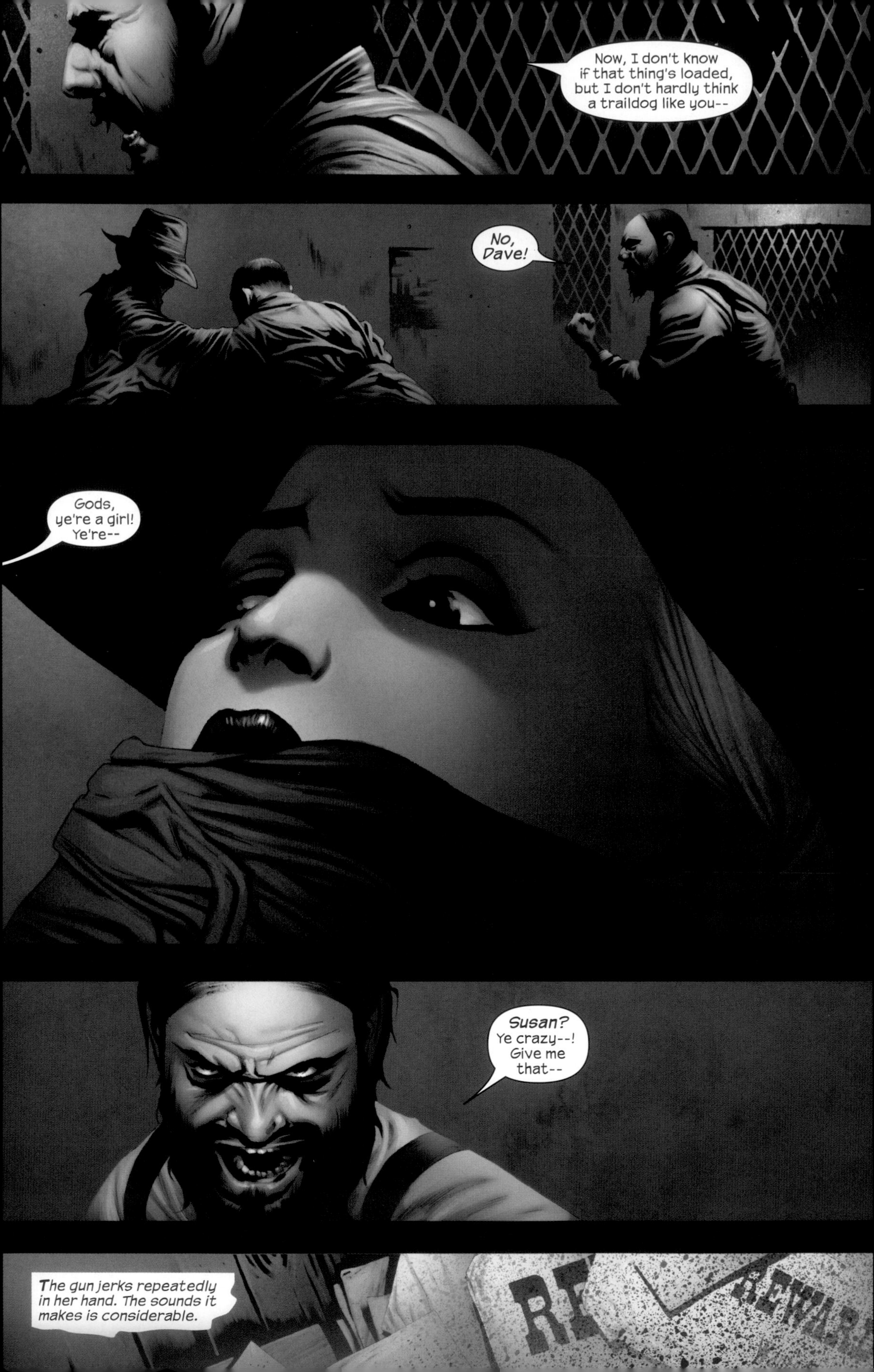
Now, I don't know if that thing's loaded, but I don't hardly think a traildog like you--
No, Dave!
Gods, ye're a girl! Ye're--
Susan? Ye crazy--! Give me that--
The gun jerks repeatedly in her hand. The sounds it makes is considerable.

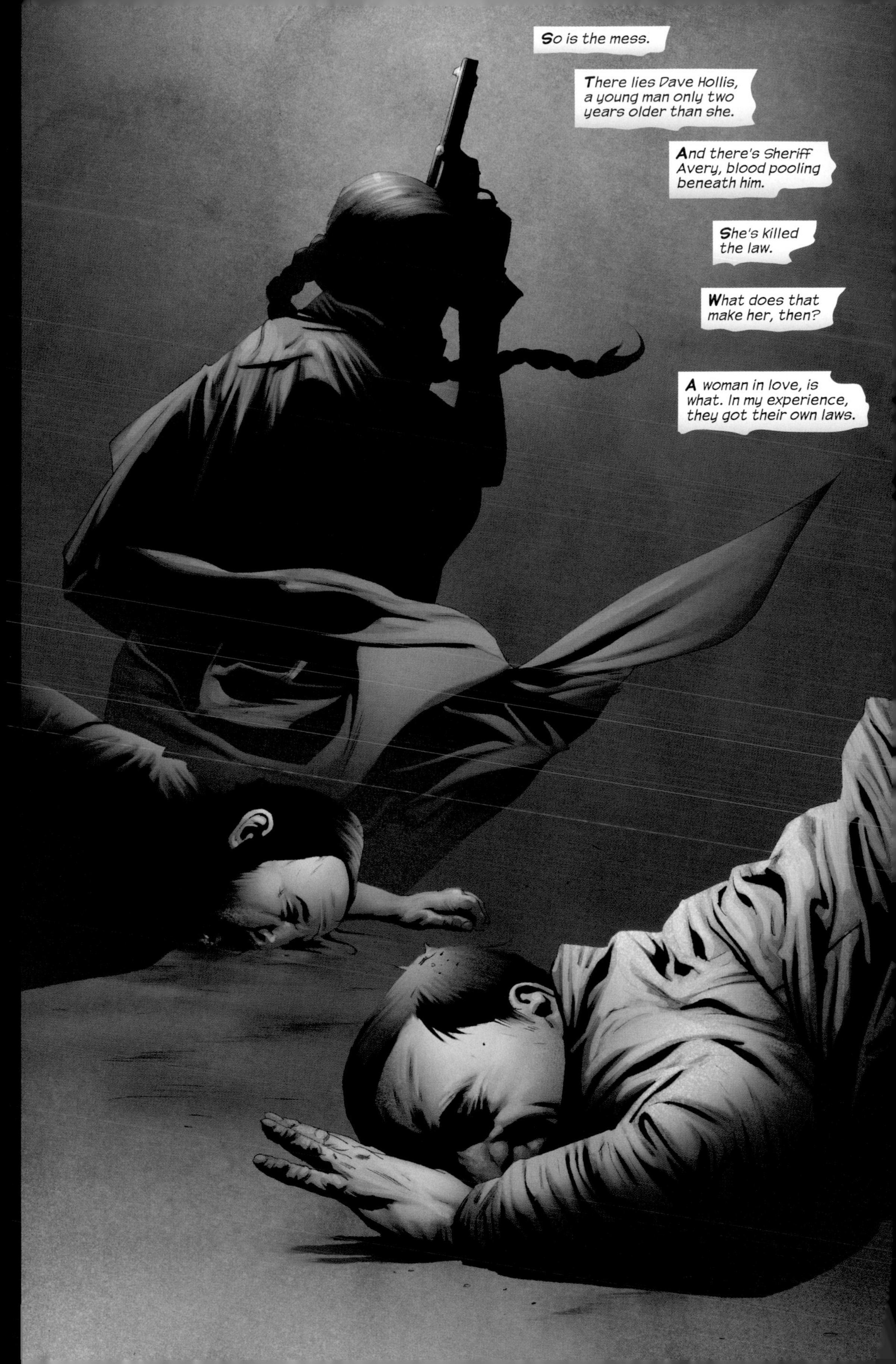
So is the mess.
There lies Dave Hollis, a young man only two years older than she.
And there's Sheriff Avery, blood pooling beneath him.
She's killed the law.
What does that make her, then?
A woman in love, is what. In my experience, they got their own laws.

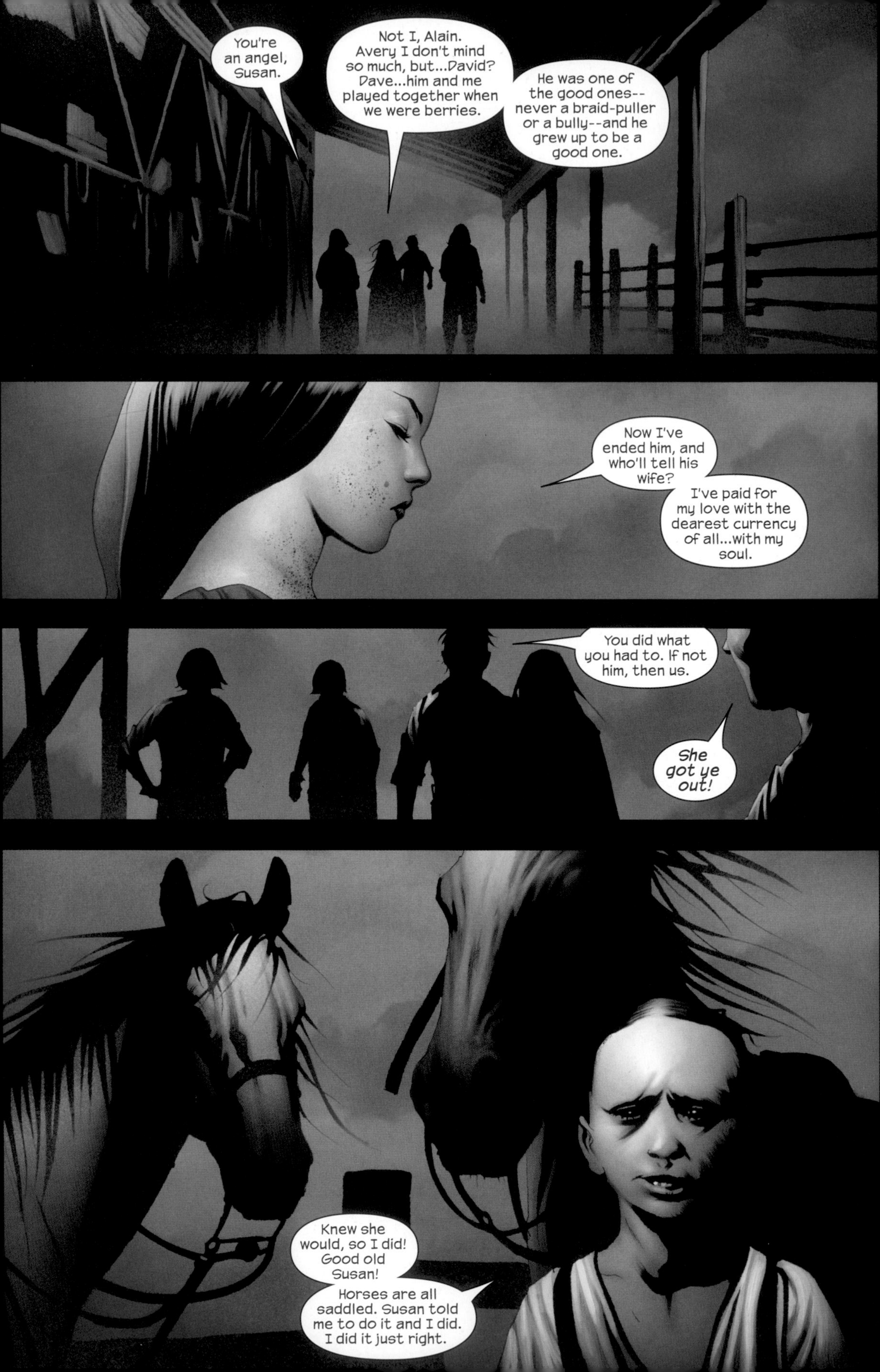
You're an angel, Susan.
Not I, Alain. Avery I don't mind so much, but...David? Dave...him and me played together when we were berries.
He was one of the good ones--never a braid-puller or a bully--and he grew up to be a good one.
Now I've ended him, and who'll tell his wife?
I've paid for my love with the dearest currency of all...with my soul.
You did what you had to. If not him, then us.
She got ye out!
Knew she would, so I did! Good old Susan!
Horses are all saddled. Susan told me to do it and I did. I did it just right.

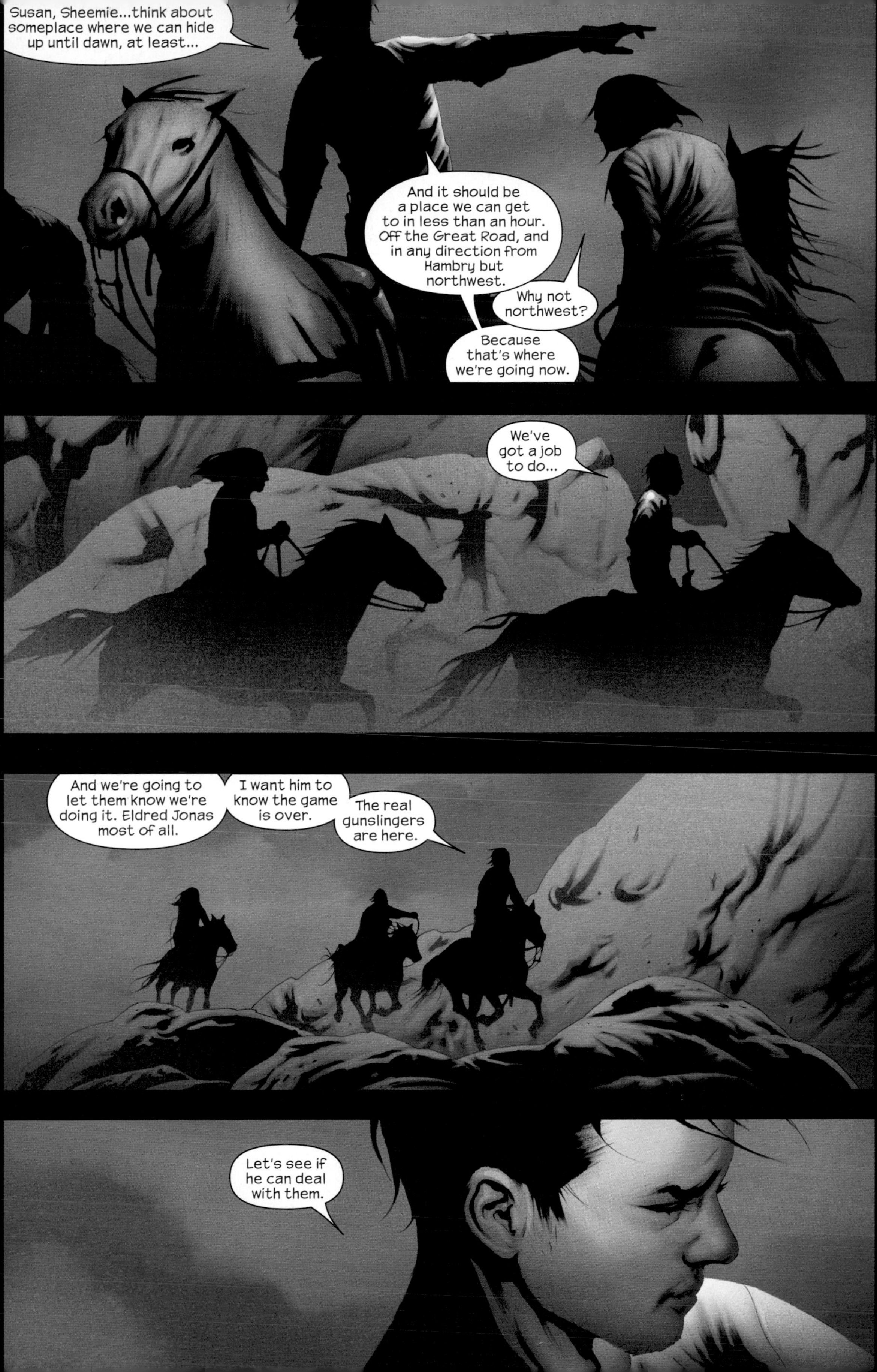
Susan, Sheemie...think about someplace where we can hide up until dawn, at least...
And it should be a place we can get to in less than an hour. Off the Great Road, and in any direction from Hambry but northwest.
Why not northwest?
Because that's where we're going now.
We've got a job to do...
And we're going to let them know we're doing it. Eldred Jonas most of all.
I want him to know the game is over.
The real gunslingers are here.
Let's see if he can deal with them.

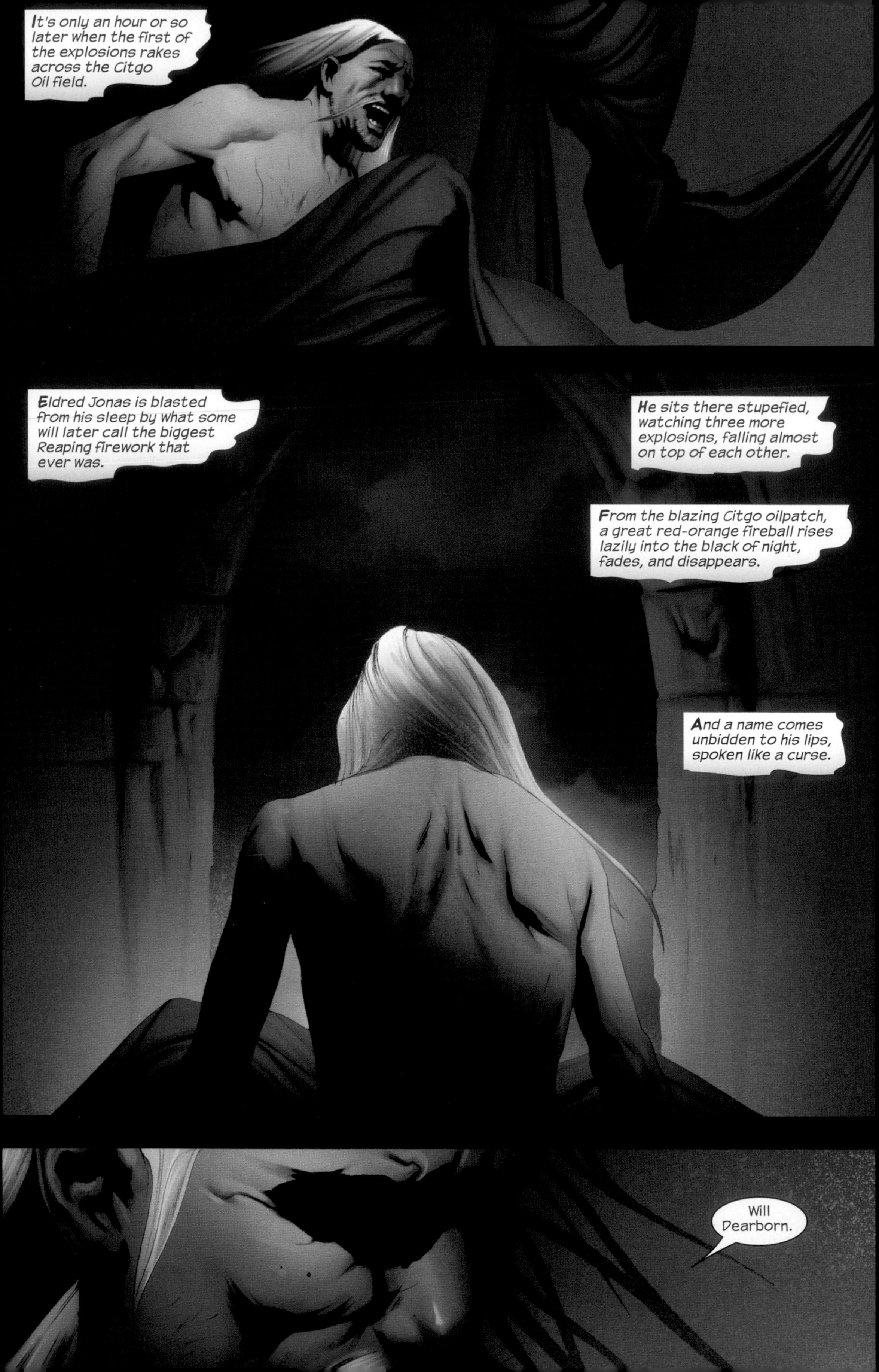
It's only an hour or so later when the first of the explosions rakes across the Citgo Oil field.
Eldred Jonas is blasted from his sleep by what some will later call the biggest Reaping firework that ever was.
He sits there stupefied, watching three more explosions, falling almost on top of each other.
From the blazing Citgo oilpatch, a great red-orange fireball rises lazily into the black of night, fades, and disappears.
And a name comes unbidden to his lips, spoken like a curse.
Will Dearborn.

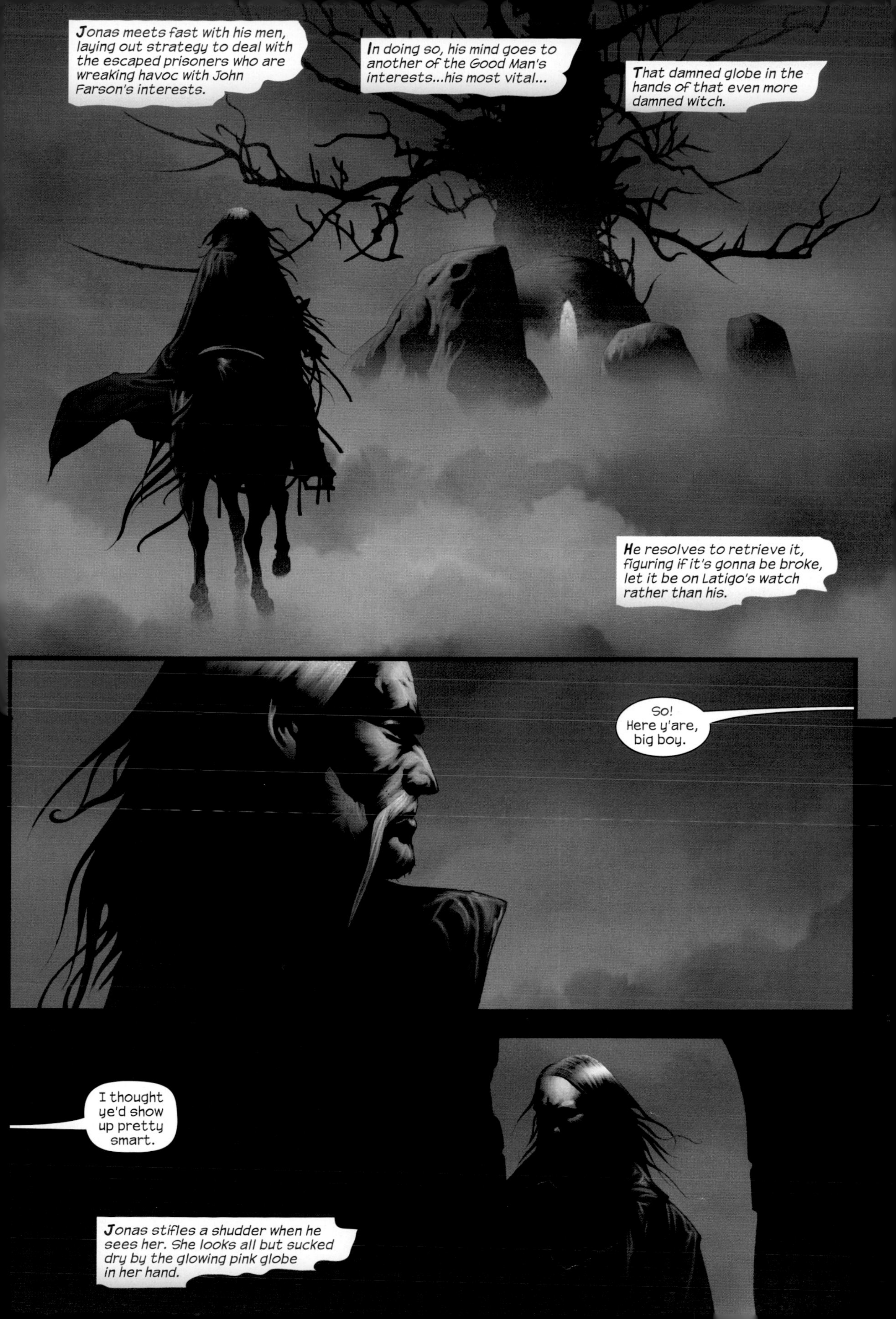
Jonas meets fast with his men, laying out strategy to deal with the escaped prisoners who are wreaking havoc with John Farson's interests.
In doing so, his mind goes to another of the Good Man's interests...his most vital...
That damned globe in the hands of that even more damned witch.
He resolves to retrieve it, figuring if it's gonna be broke, let it be on Latigo's watch rather than his.
So! Here y'are, big boy.
I thought ye'd show up pretty smart.
Jonas stifles a shudder when he sees her. She looks all but sucked dry by the glowing pink globe in her hand.

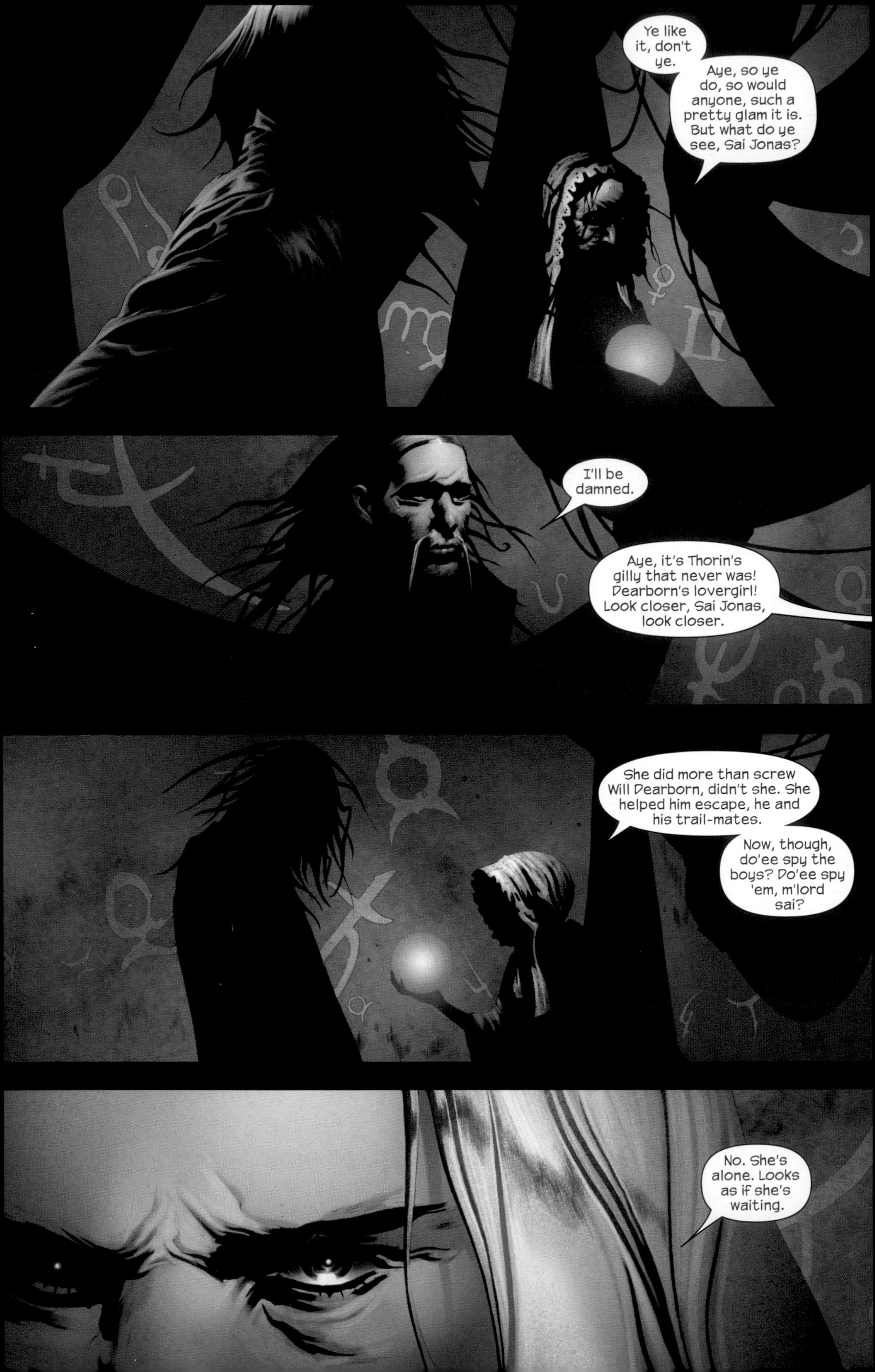
Ye like it, don't ye.
Aye, so ye do, so would anyone, such a pretty glam it is. But what do ye see, Sai Jonas?
I'll be damned.
Aye, it's Thorin's gilly that never was! Dearborn's lovergirl! Look closer, Sai Jonas, look closer.
She did more than screw Will Dearborn, didn't she. She helped him escape, he and his trail-mates.
Now, though, do'ee spy the boys? Do'ee spy 'em, m'lord sai?
No. She's alone. Looks as if she's waiting.

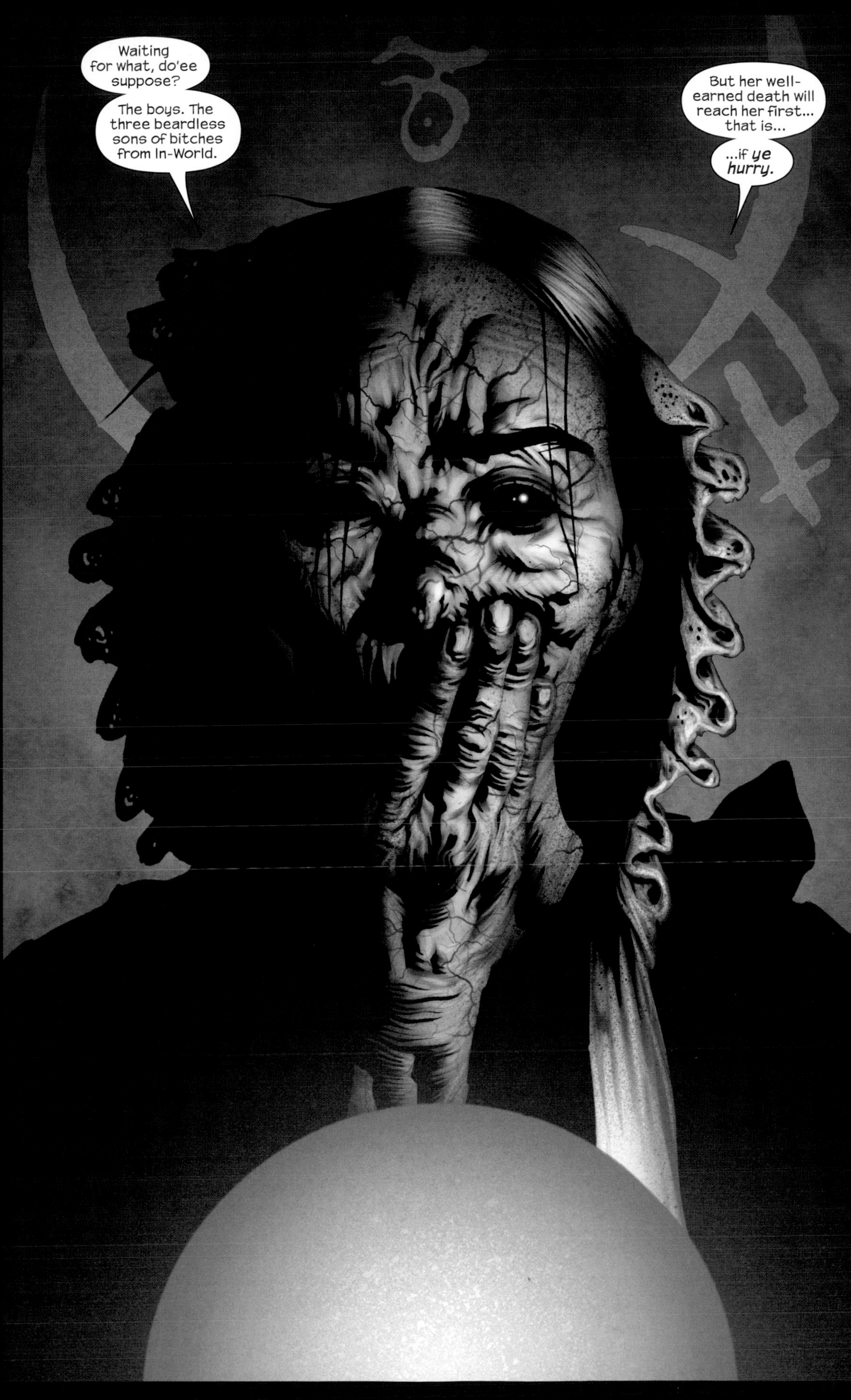
Waiting for what, do'ee suppose?
The boys. The three beardless sons of bitches from In-World.
But her well-earned death will reach her first... that is...
...if *ye hurry.*

STEPHEN KING

THE DARK TOWER

THE GUNSLINGER BORN

CHAPTER SEVEN

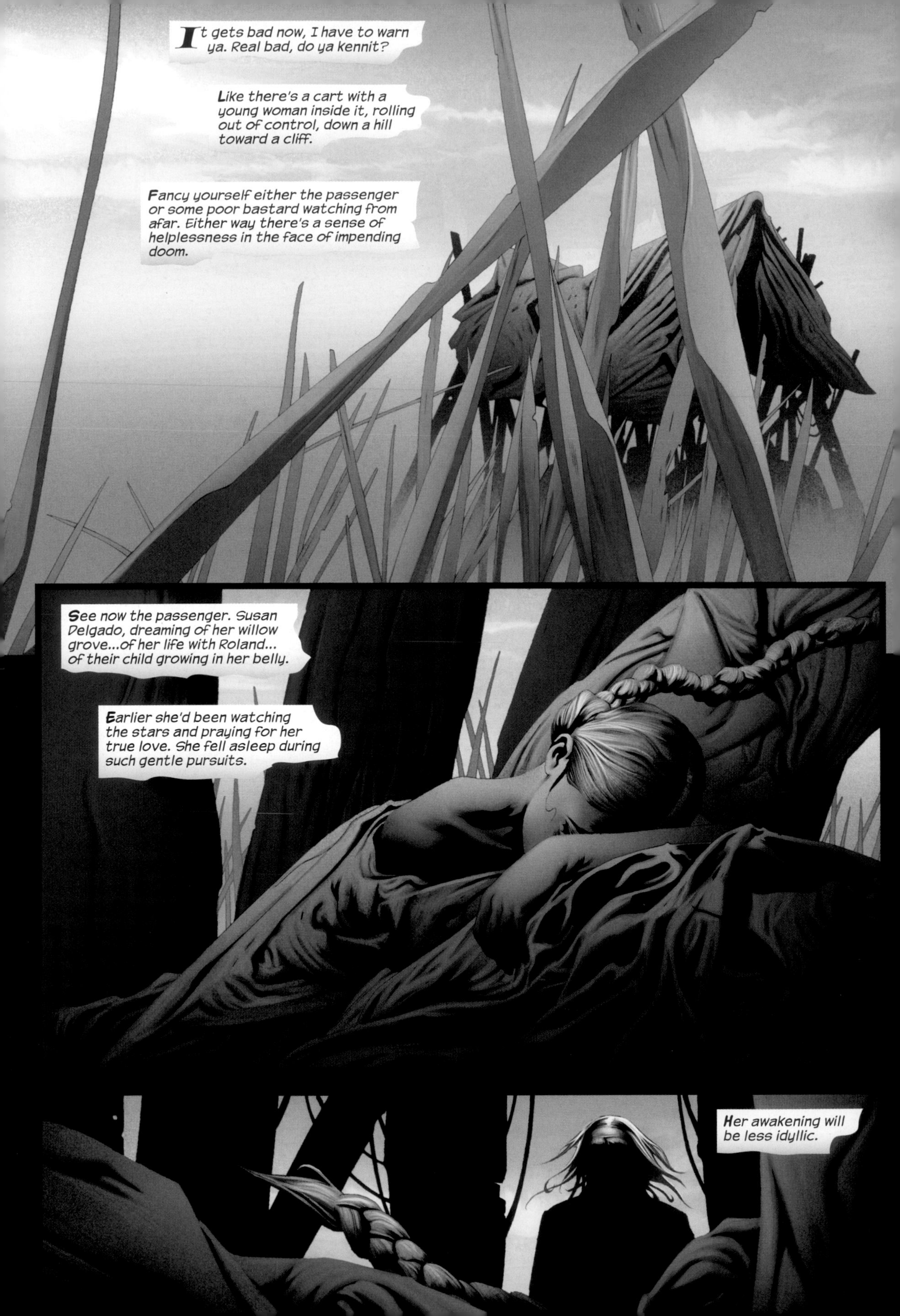
It gets bad now, I have to warn ya. Real bad, do ya kennit?
Like there's a cart with a young woman inside it, rolling out of control, down a hill toward a cliff.
Fancy yourself either the passenger or some poor bastard watching from afar. Either way there's a sense of helplessness in the face of impending doom.
See now the passenger. Susan Delgado, dreaming of her willow grove...of her life with Roland... of their child growing in her belly.
Earlier she'd been watching the stars and praying for her true love. She fell asleep during such gentle pursuits.
Her awakening will be less idyllic.

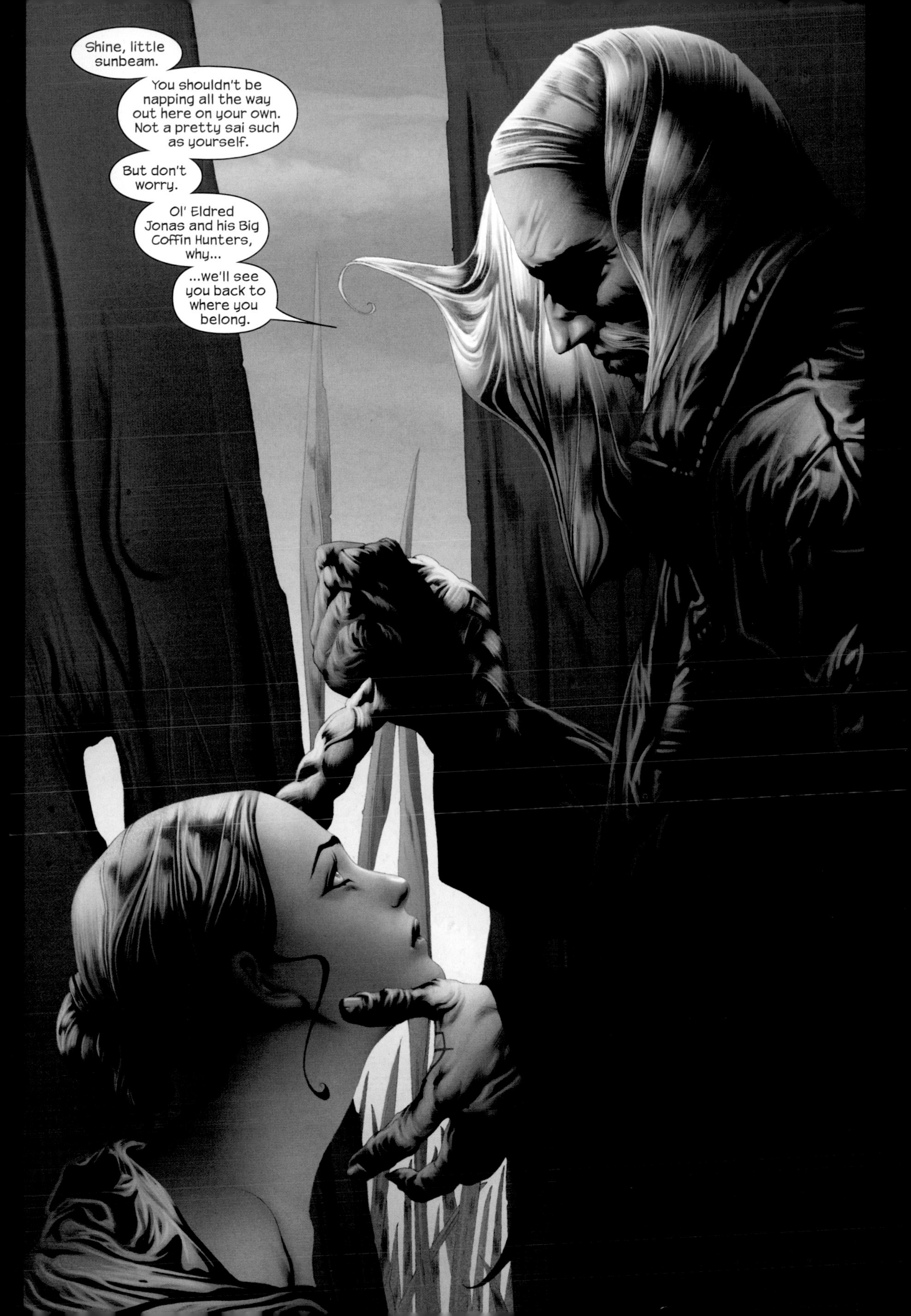
Shine, little sunbeam.
You shouldn't be napping all the way out here on your own. Not a pretty sai such as yourself.
But don't worry.
Ol' Eldred Jonas and his Big Coffin Hunters, why...
...we'll see you back to where you belong.

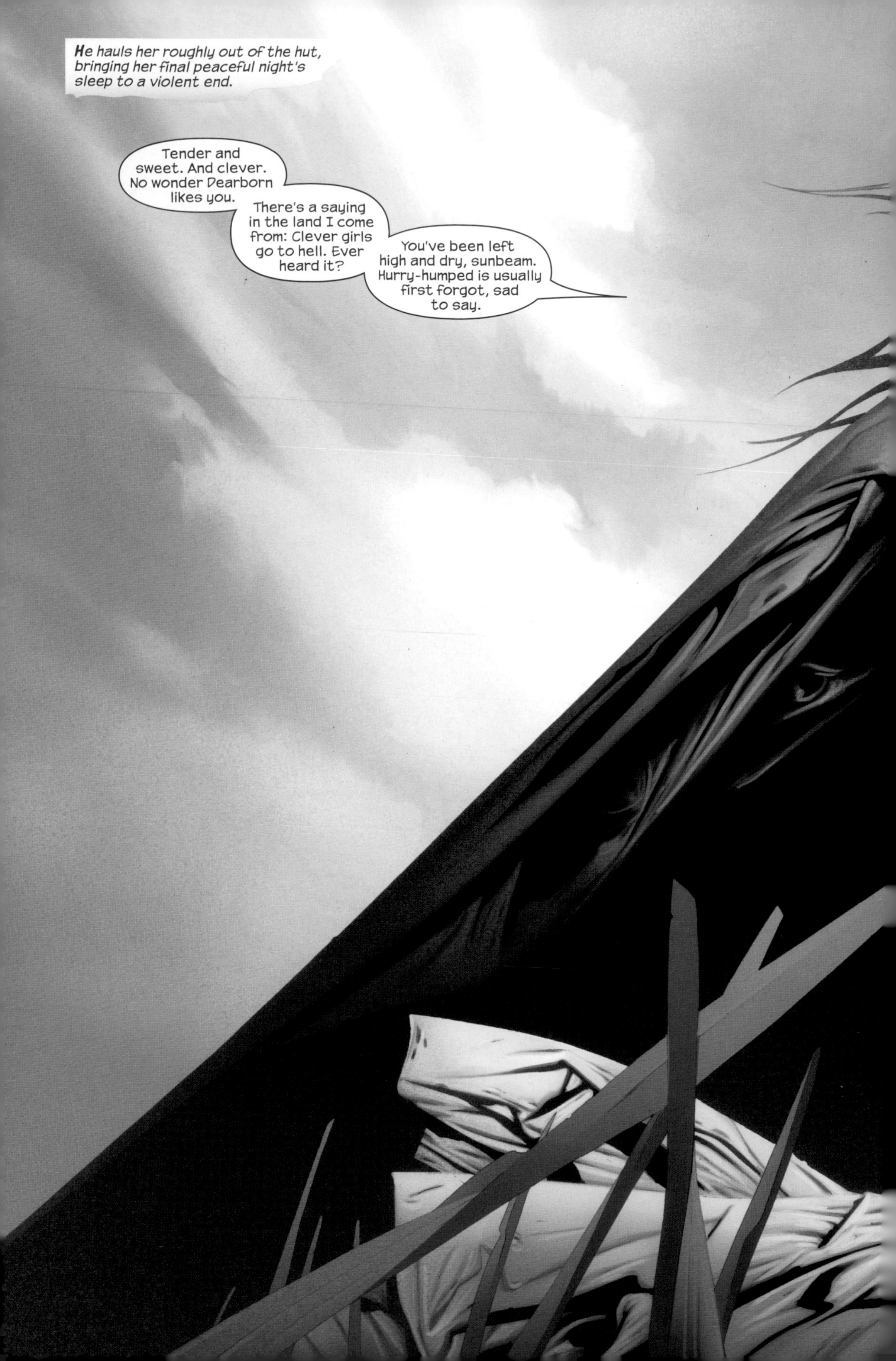
He hauls her roughly out of the hut, bringing her final peaceful night's sleep to a violent end.
Tender and sweet. And clever. No wonder Dearborn likes you.
There's a saying in the land I come from: Clever girls go to hell. Ever heard it?
You've been left high and dry, sunbeam. Hurry-humped is usually first forgot, sad to say.

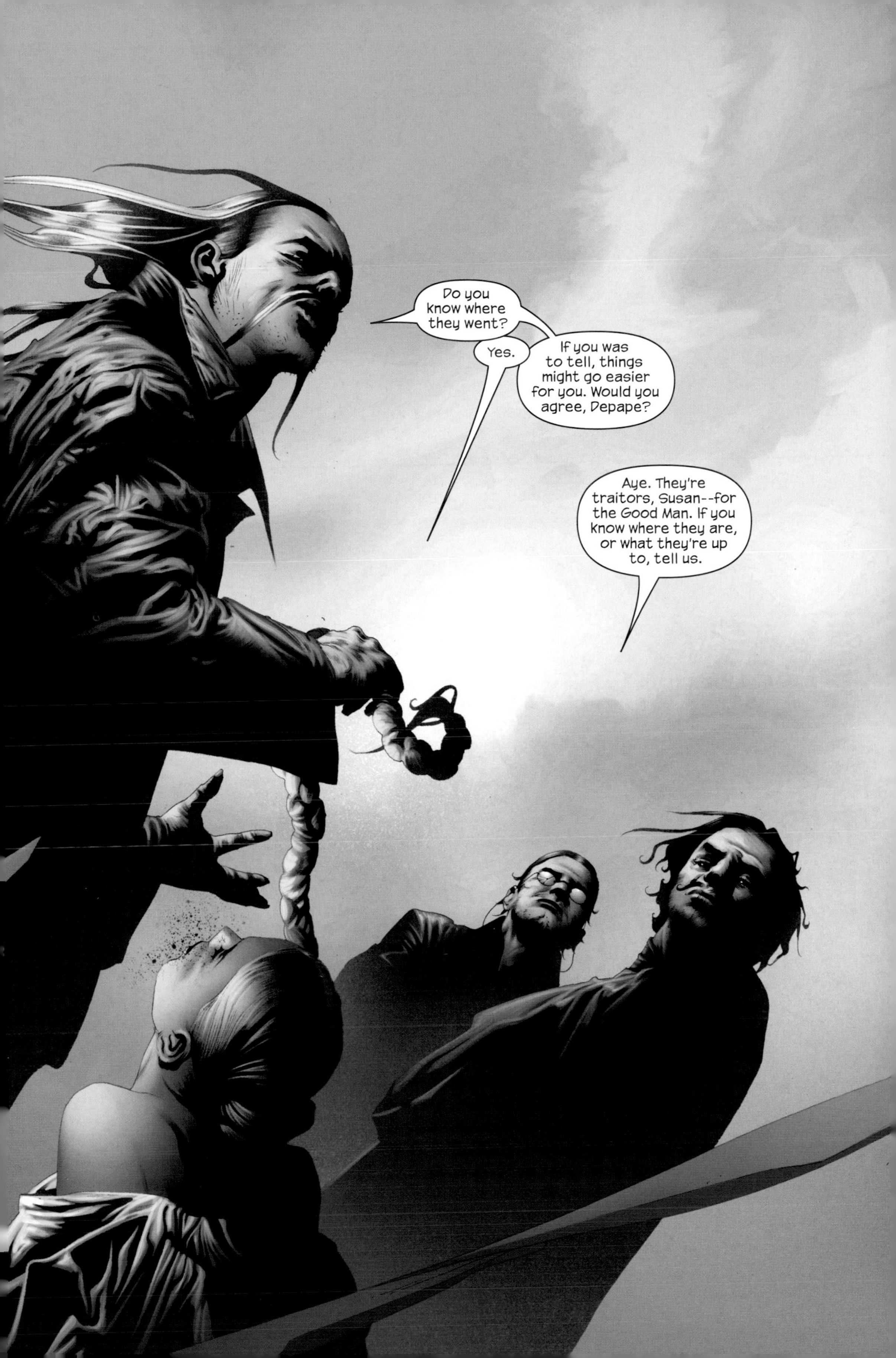
Do you know where they went?
Yes.
If you was to tell, things might go easier for you. Would you agree, Depape?
Aye. They're traitors, Susan--for the Good Man. If you know where they are, or what they're up to, tell us.

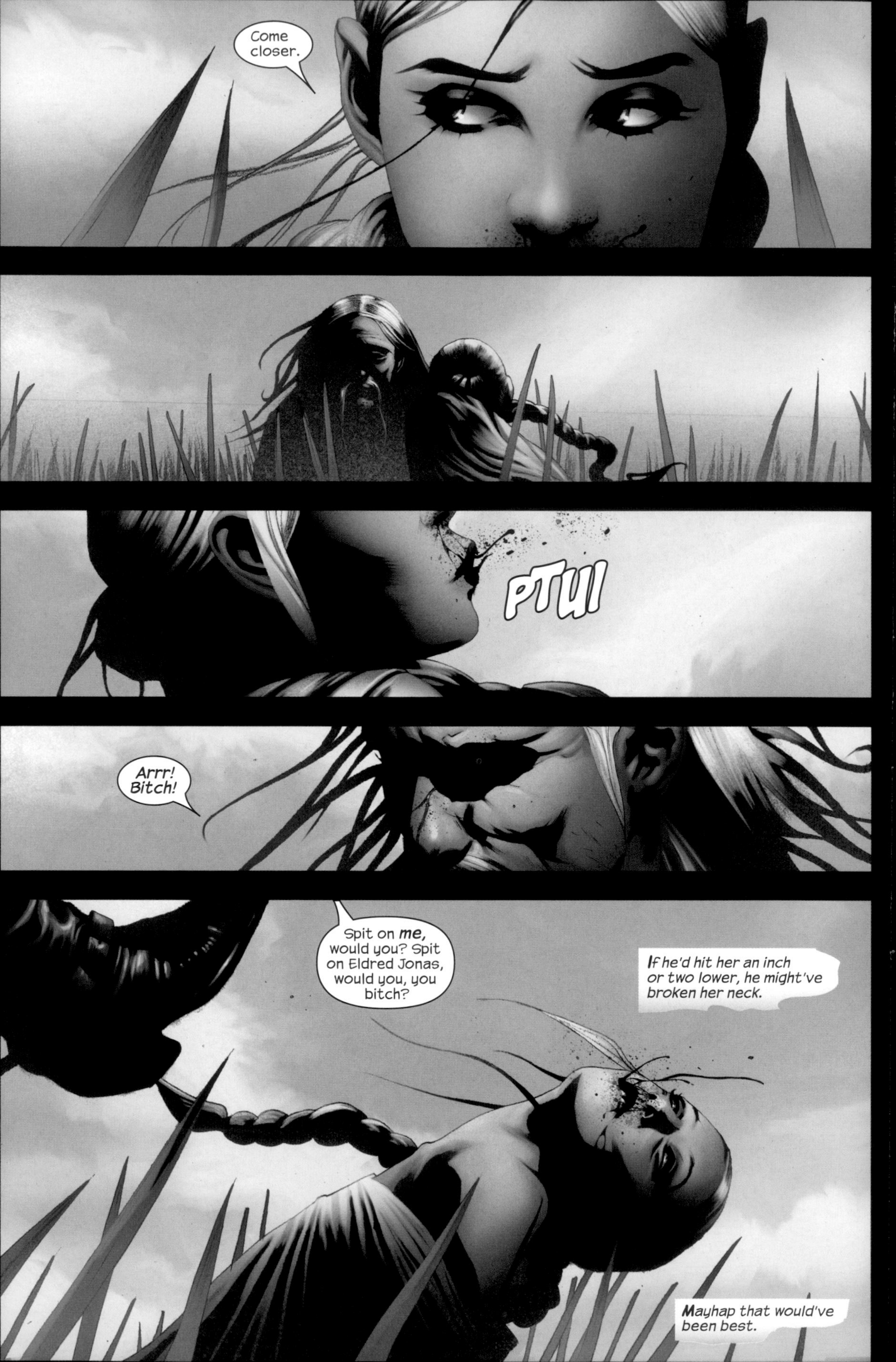

Come closer.
PTUI
Arrr! Bitch!
Spit on *me*, would you? Spit on Eldred Jonas, would you, you bitch?
If he'd hit her an inch or two lower, he might've broken her neck.
Mayhap that would've been best.

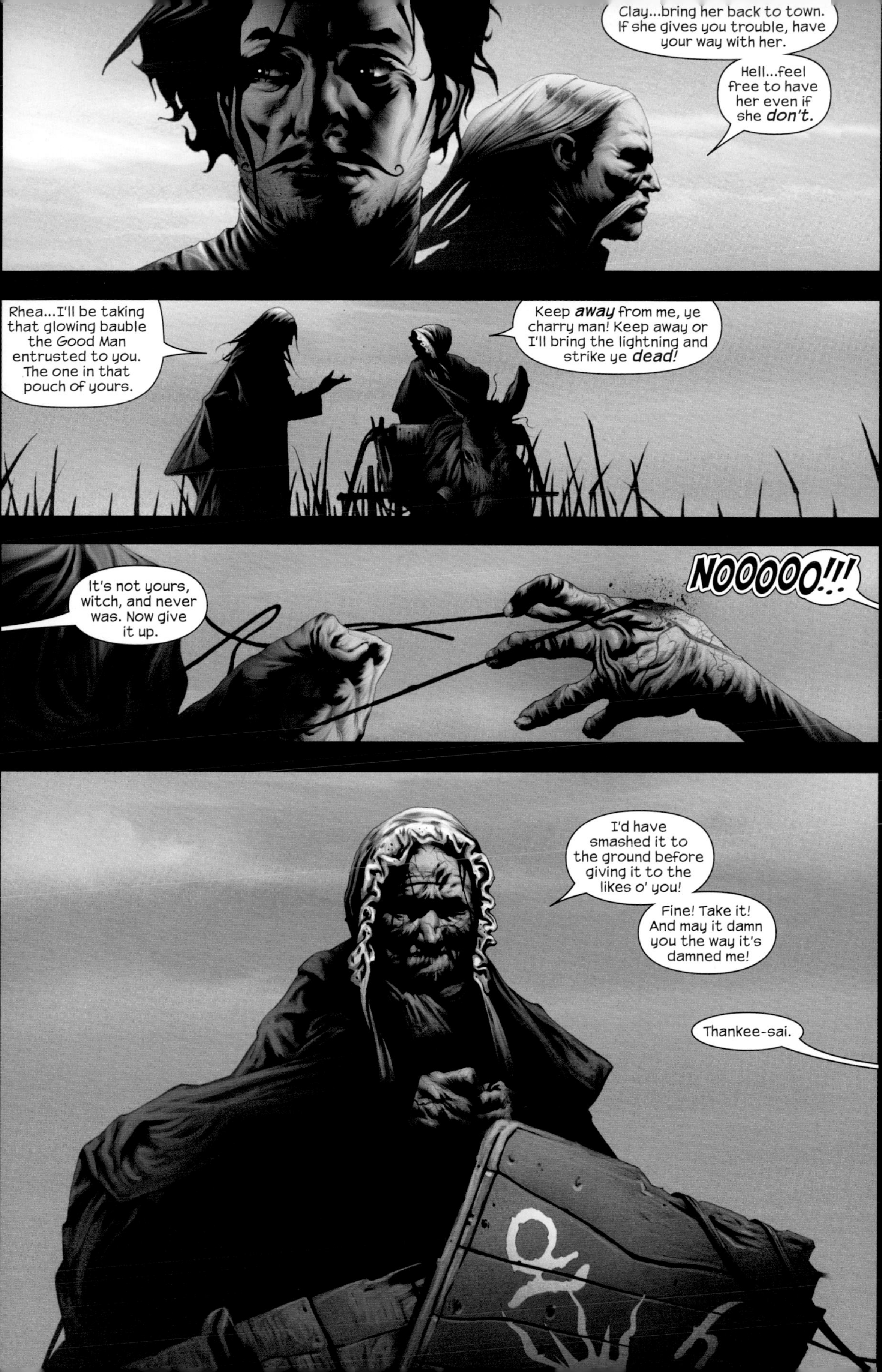
Clay...bring her back to town. If she gives you trouble, have your way with her.
Hell...feel free to have her even if she *don't.*
Rhea...I'll be taking that glowing bauble the Good Man entrusted to you. The one in that pouch of yours.
Keep *away* from me, ye charry man! Keep away or I'll bring the lightning and strike ye *dead!*
It's not yours, witch, and never was. Now give it up.
NOOOOO!!!
I'd have smashed it to the ground before giving it to the likes o' you!
Fine! Take it! And may it damn you the way it's damned me!
Thankee-sai.

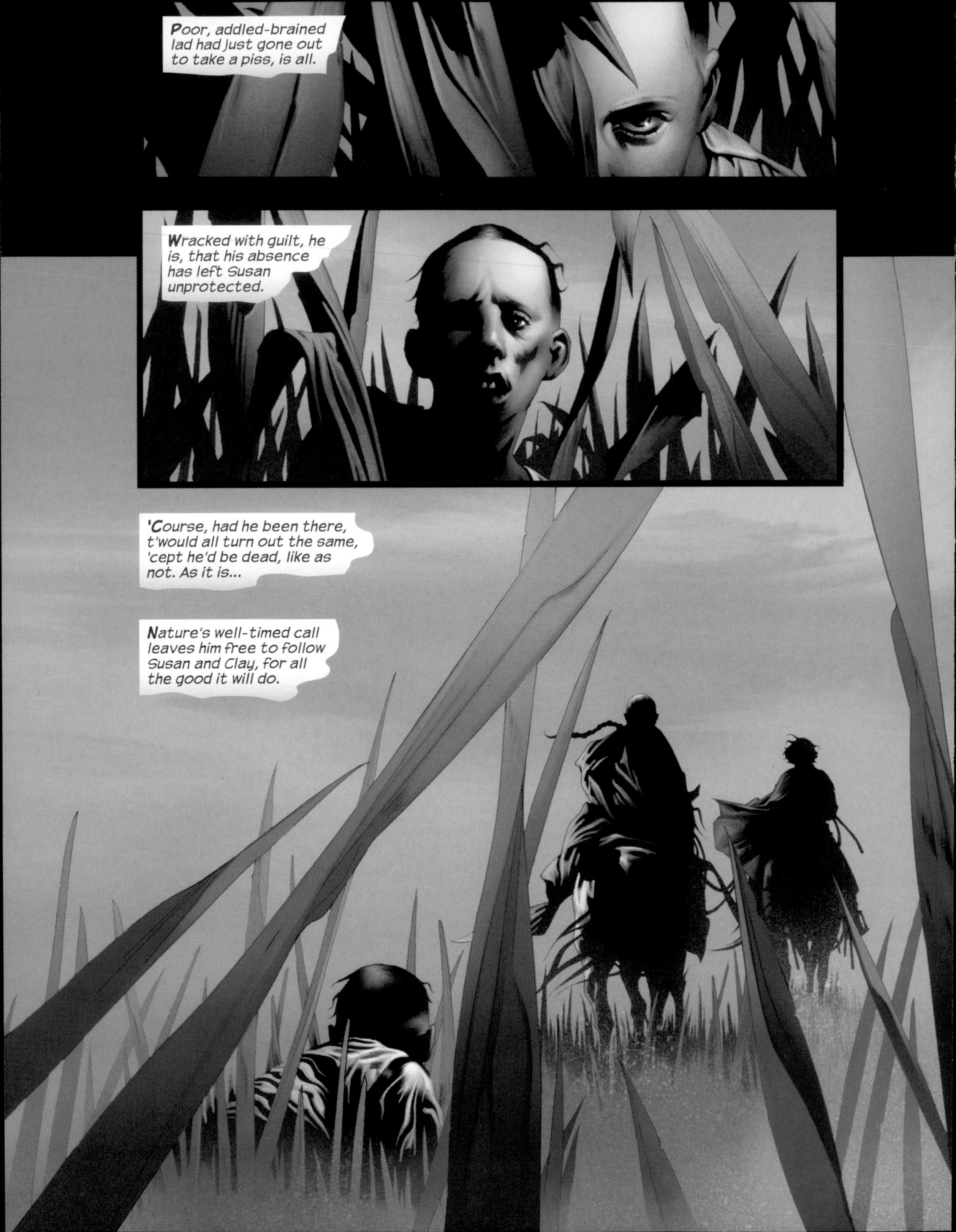
Poor, addled-brained lad had just gone out to take a piss, is all.
Wracked with guilt, he is, that his absence has left Susan unprotected.
'Course, had he been there, t'would all turn out the same, 'cept he'd be dead, like as not. As it is...
Nature's well-timed call leaves him free to follow Susan and Clay, for all the good it will do.

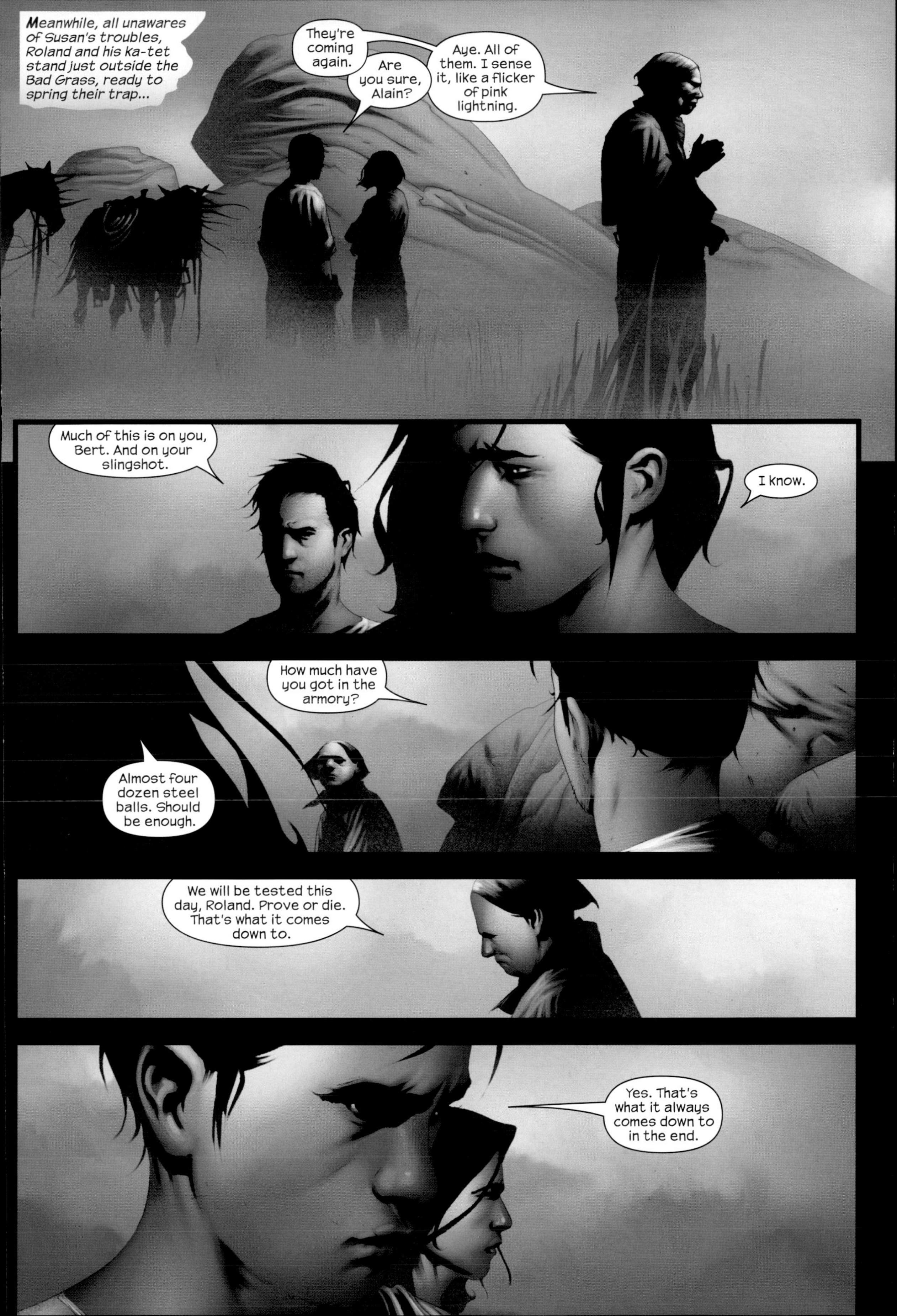
Meanwhile, all unawares of Susan's troubles, Roland and his ka-tet stand just outside the Bad Grass, ready to spring their trap...
They're coming again.
Are you sure, Alain?
Aye. All of them. I sense it, like a flicker of pink lightning.
Much of this is on you, Bert. And on your slingshot.
I know.
How much have you got in the armory?
Almost four dozen steel balls. Should be enough.
We will be tested this day, Roland. Prove or die. That's what it comes down to.
Yes. That's what it always comes down to in the end.

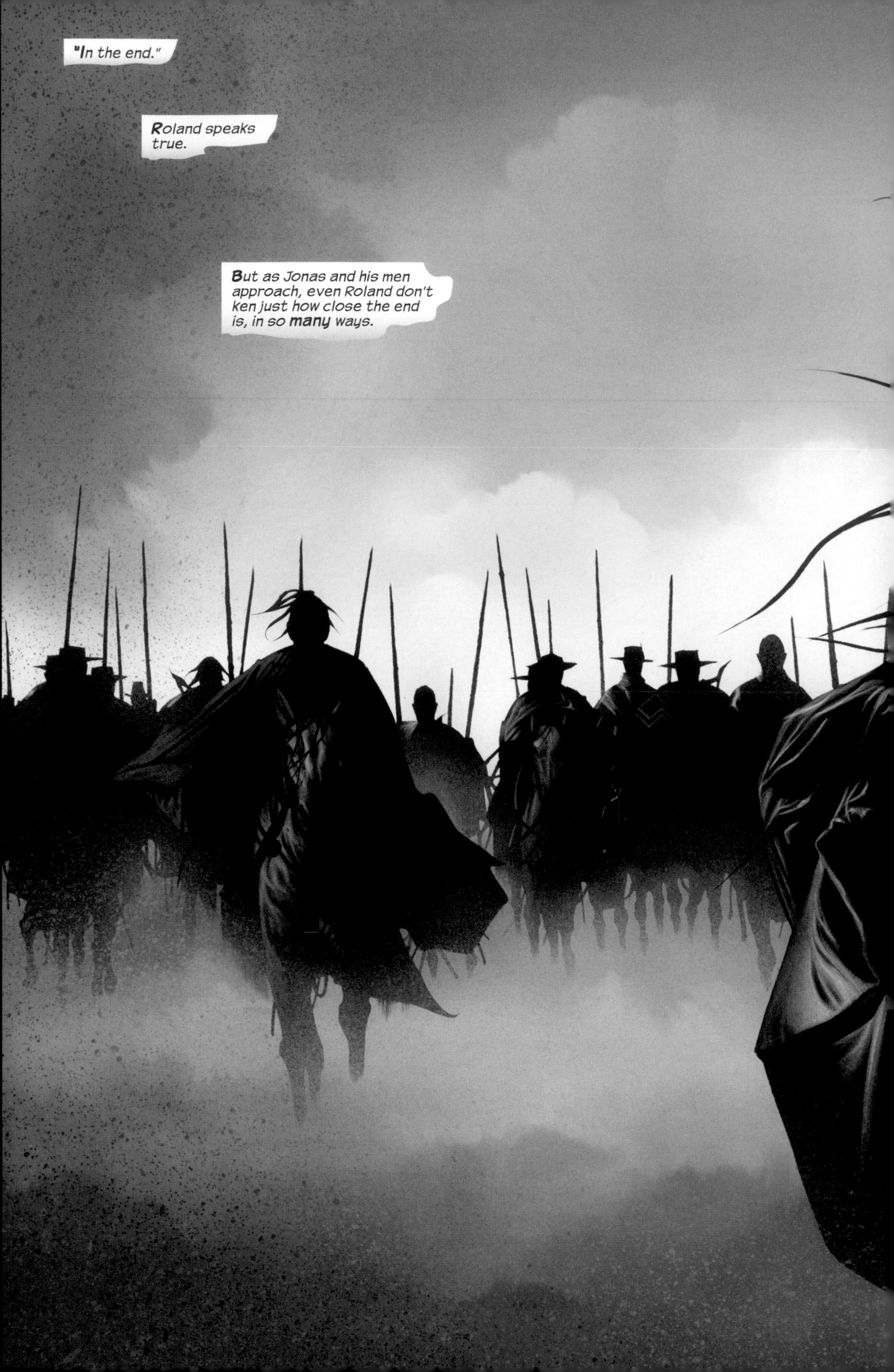
"In the end."
Roland speaks true.
But as Jonas and his men approach, even Roland don't ken just how close the end is, in so many ways.

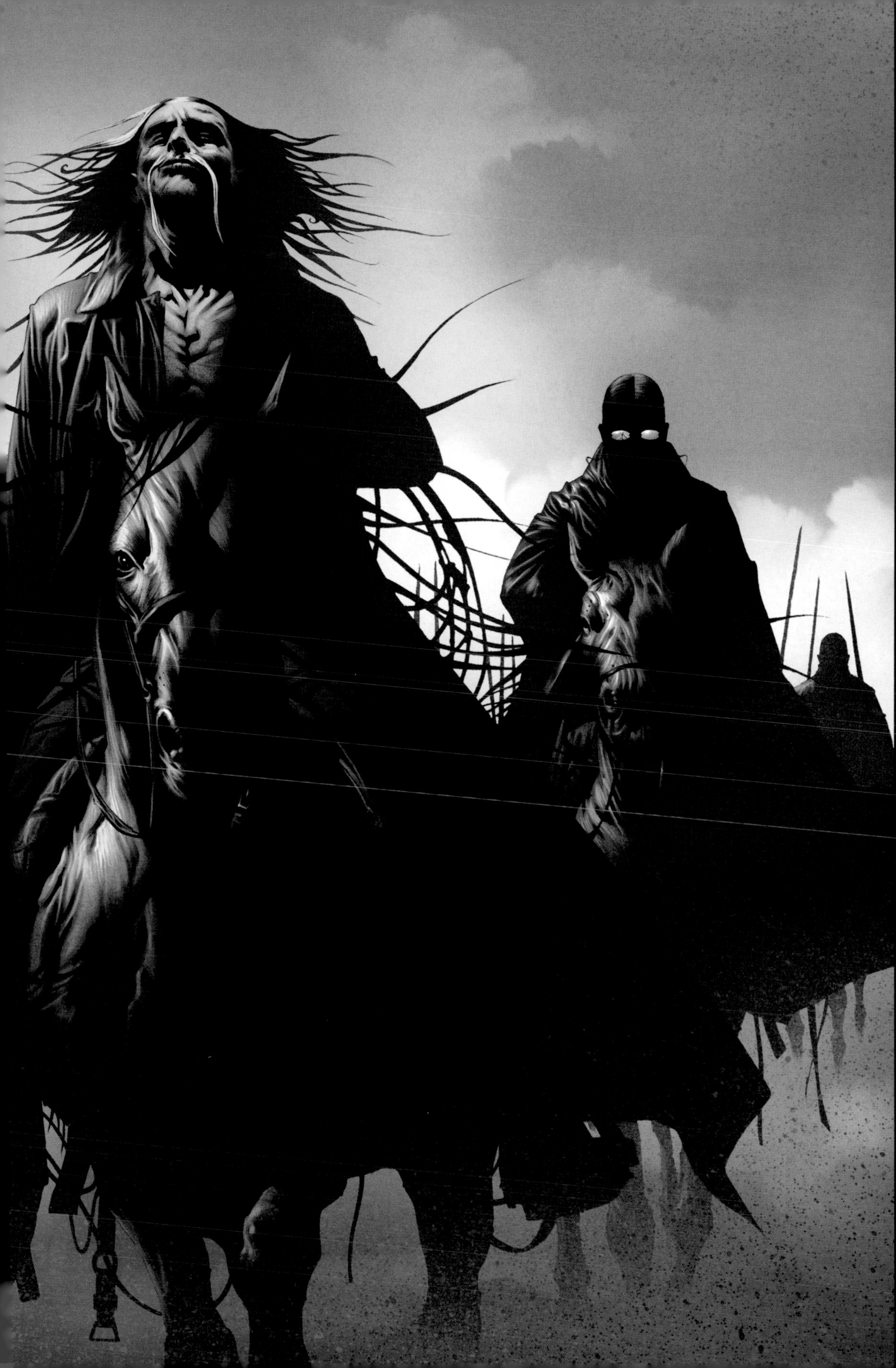

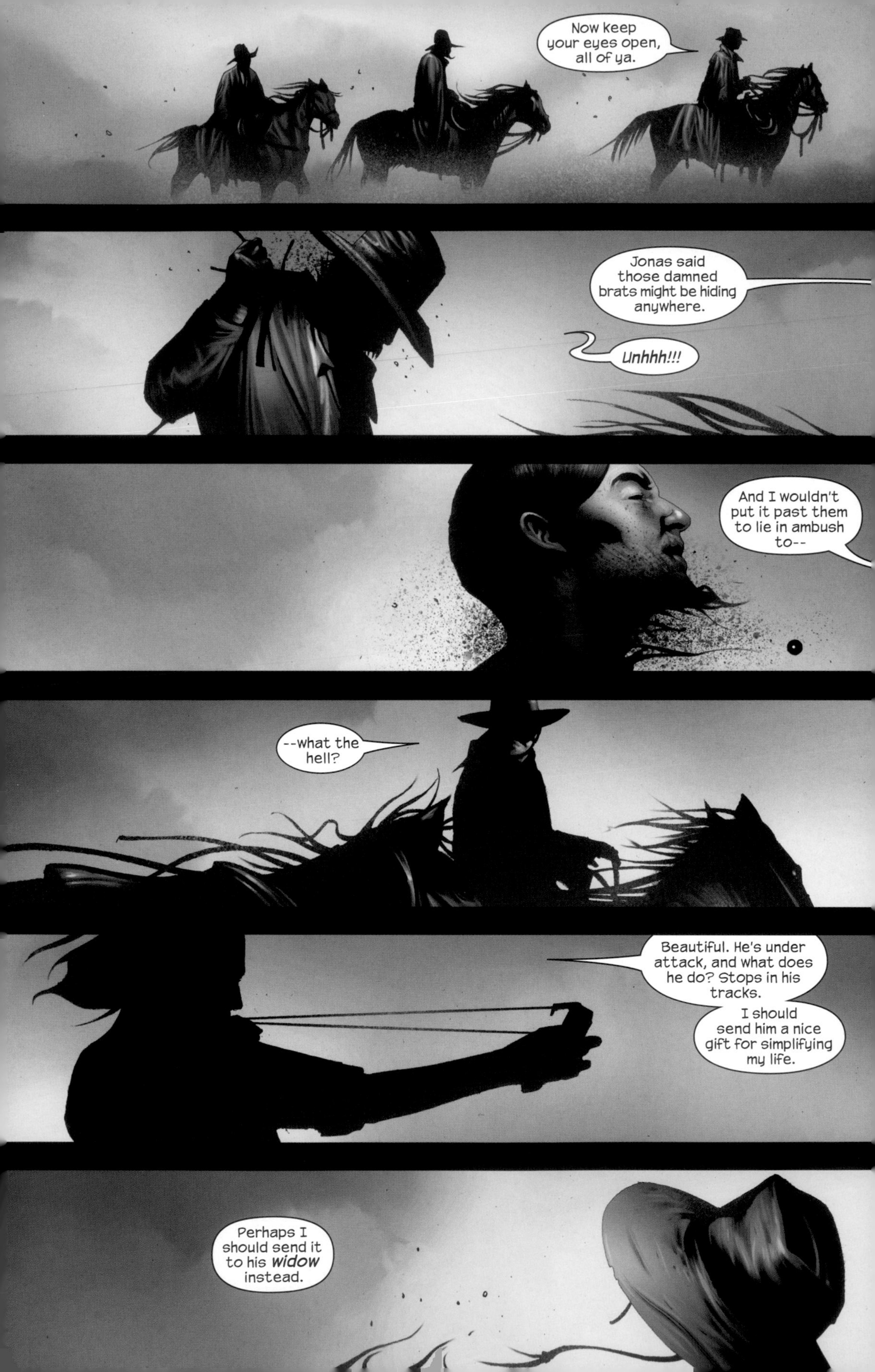
Now keep your eyes open, all of ya.
Jonas said those damned brats might be hiding anywhere.
Unhhh!!!
And I wouldn't put it past them to lie in ambush to--
--what the hell?
Beautiful. He's under attack, and what does he do? Stops in his tracks.
I should send him a nice gift for simplifying my life.
Perhaps I should send it to his *widow* instead.

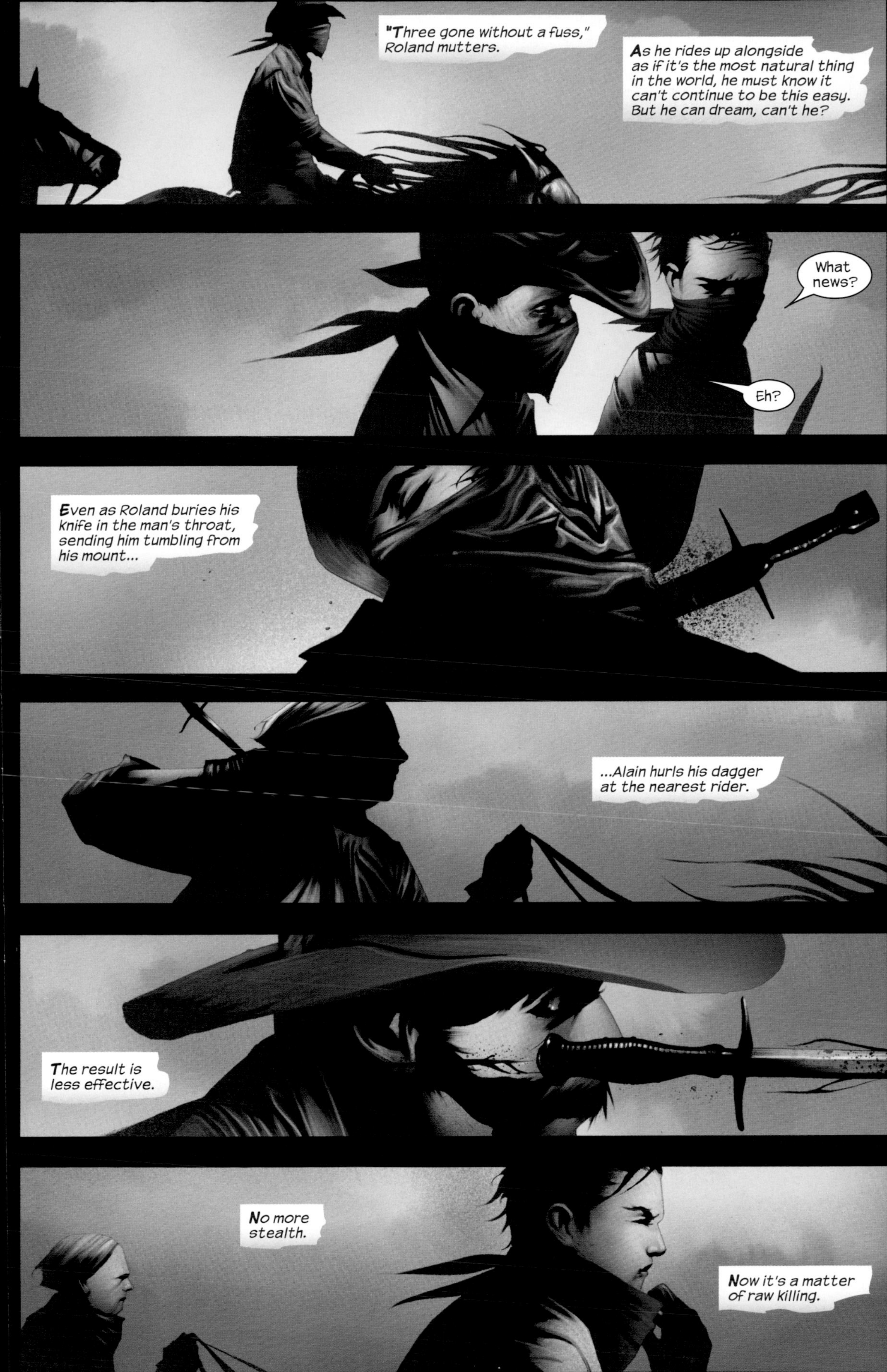
"Three gone without a fuss," Roland mutters.
As he rides up alongside as if it's the most natural thing in the world, he must know it can't continue to be this easy. But he can dream, can't he?
What news?
Eh?
Even as Roland buries his knife in the man's throat, sending him tumbling from his mount...
...Alain hurls his dagger at the nearest rider.
The result is less effective.
No more stealth.
Now it's a matter of raw killing.

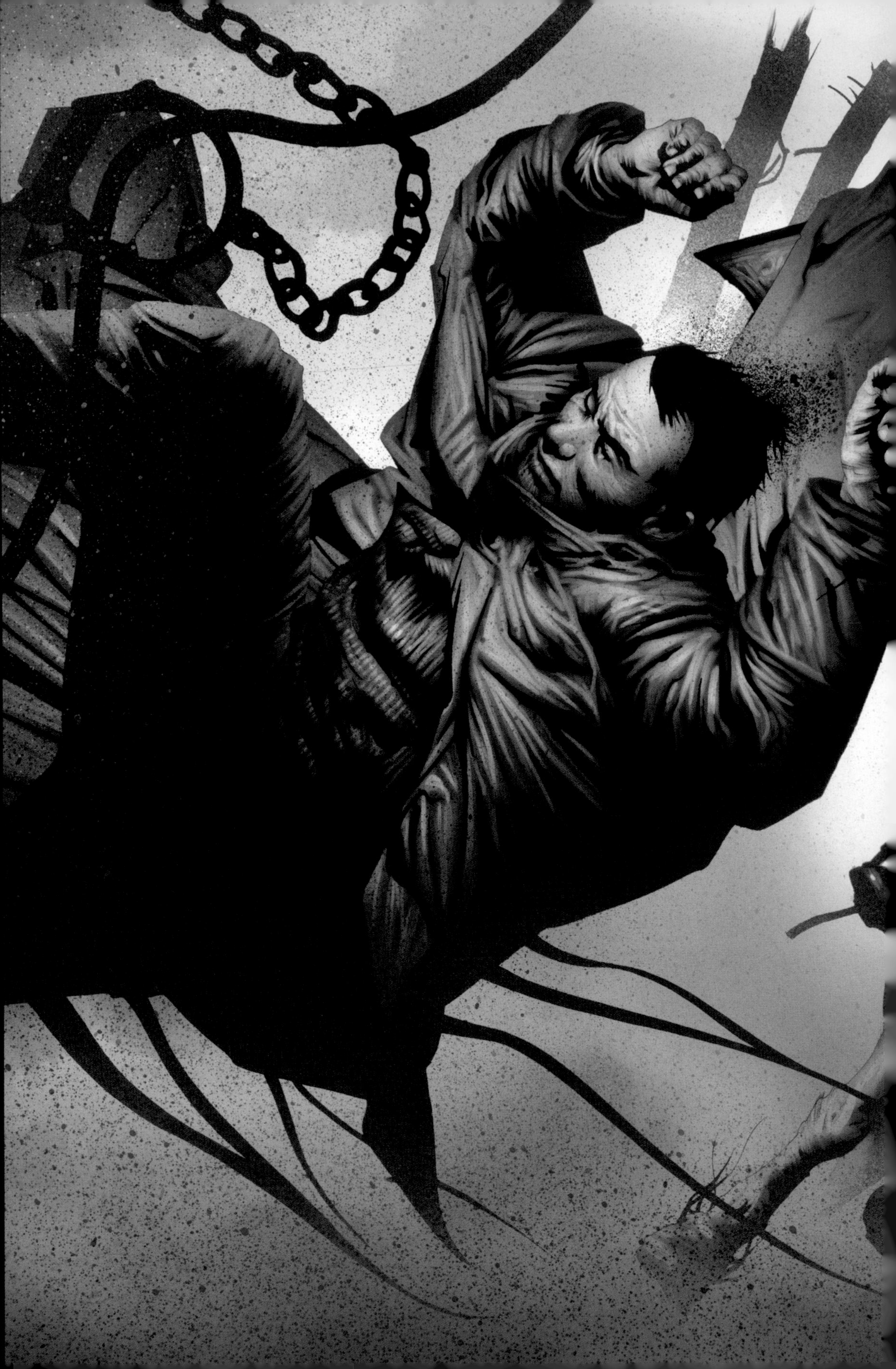

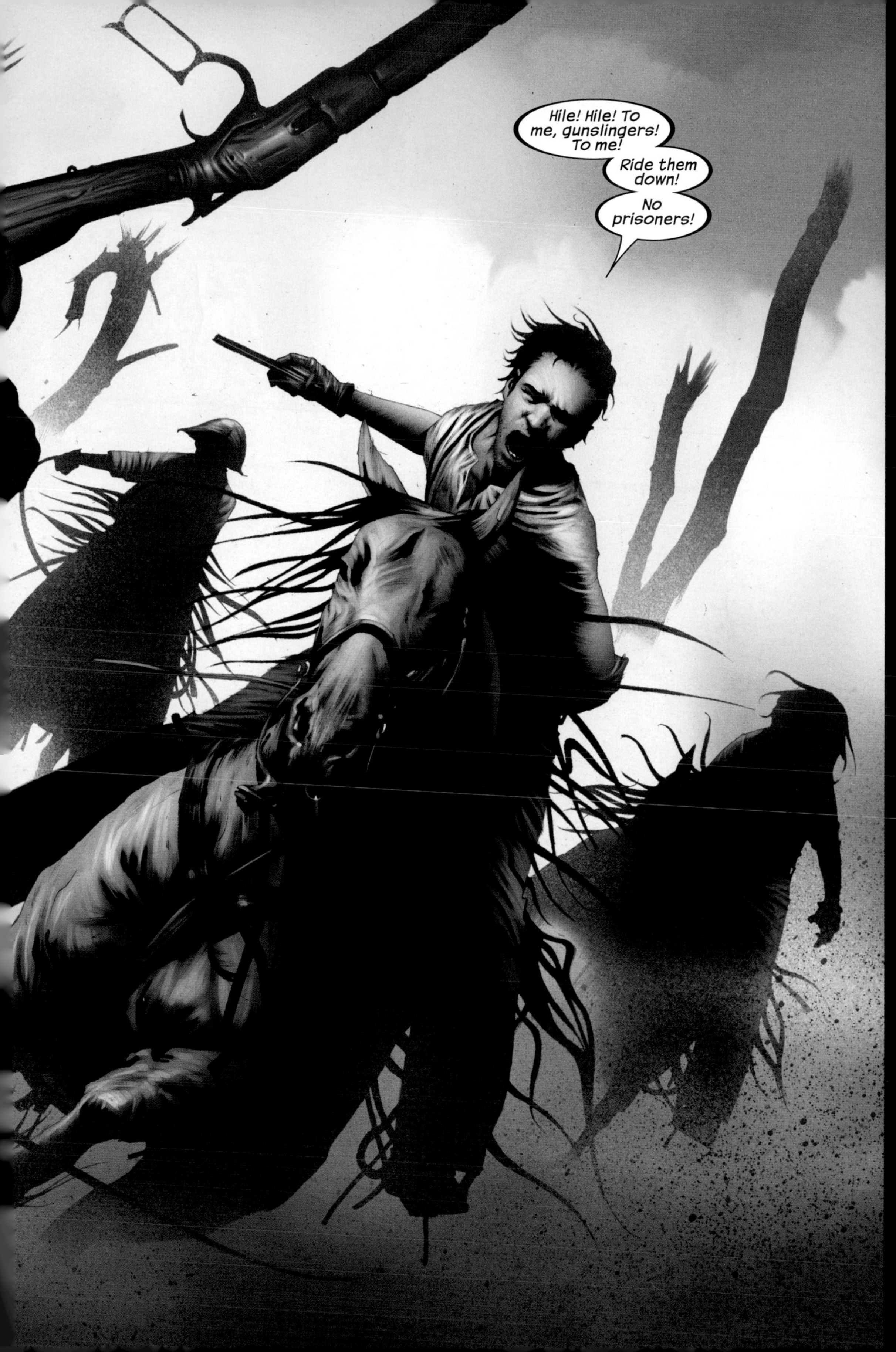
Hile! Hile! To me, gunslingers! To me!
Ride them down!
No prisoners!

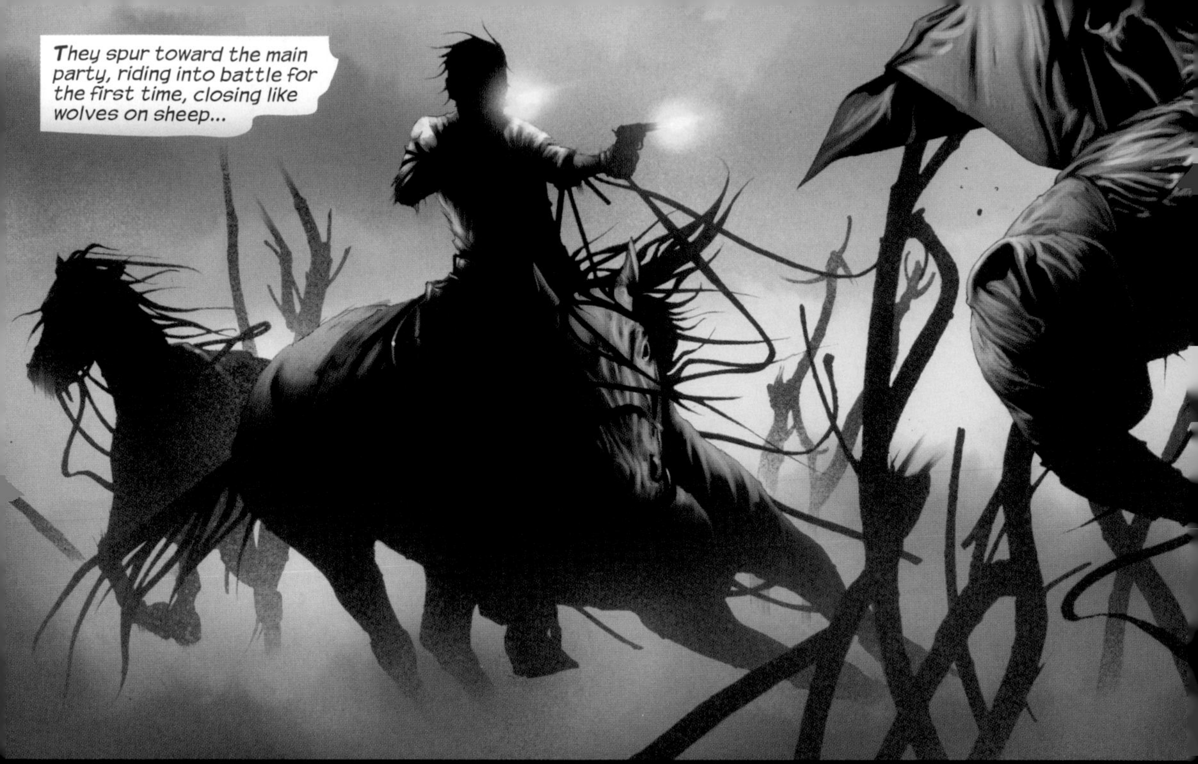
They spur toward the main party, riding into battle for the first time, closing like wolves on sheep...

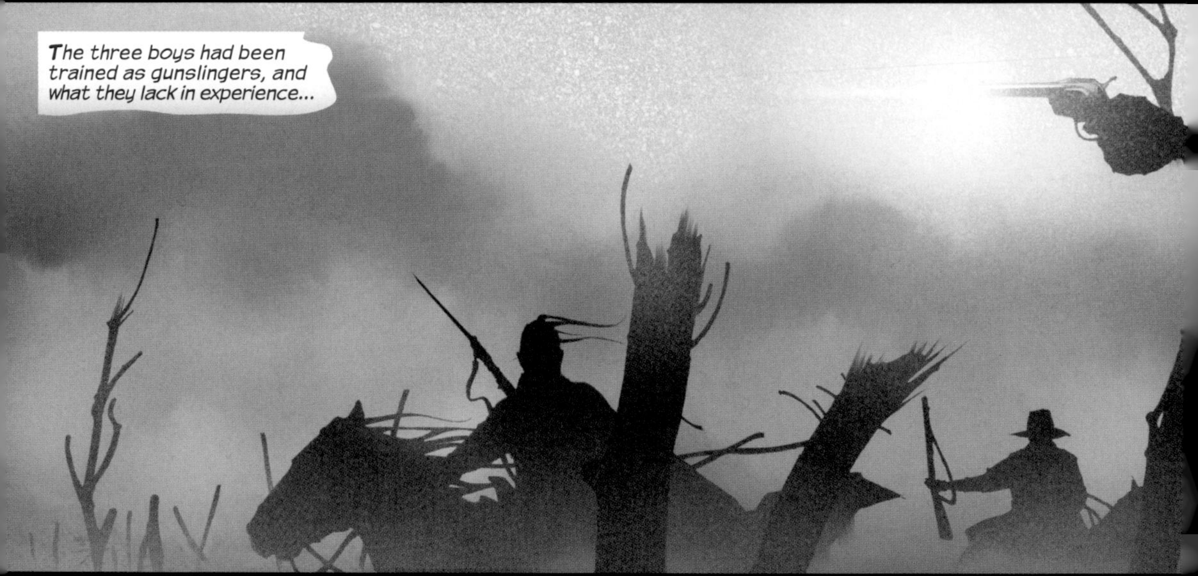
The three boys had been trained as gunslingers, and what they lack in experience...

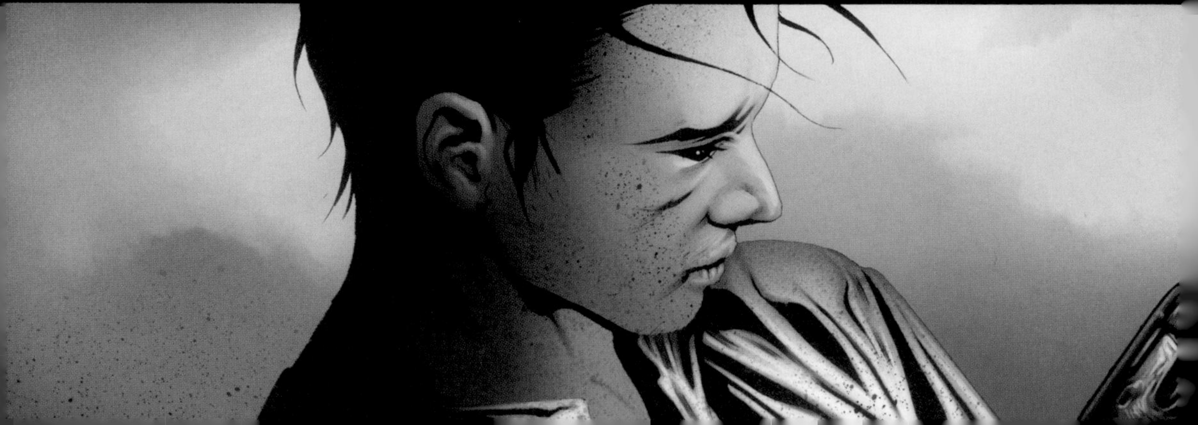

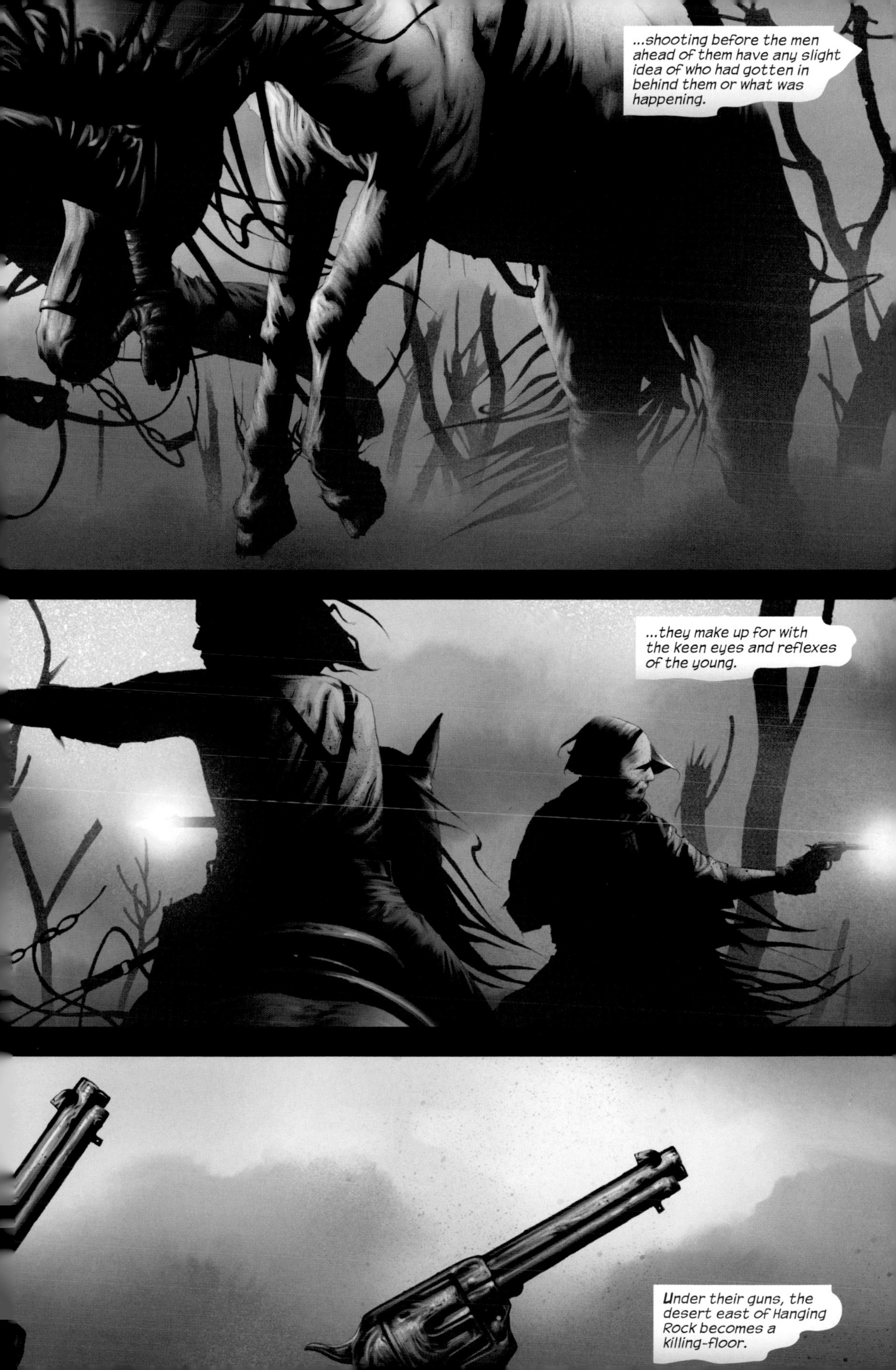
...shooting before the men ahead of them have any slight idea of who had gotten in behind them or what was happening.
...they make up for with the keen eyes and reflexes of the young.
Under their guns, the desert east of Hanging Rock becomes a killing-floor.

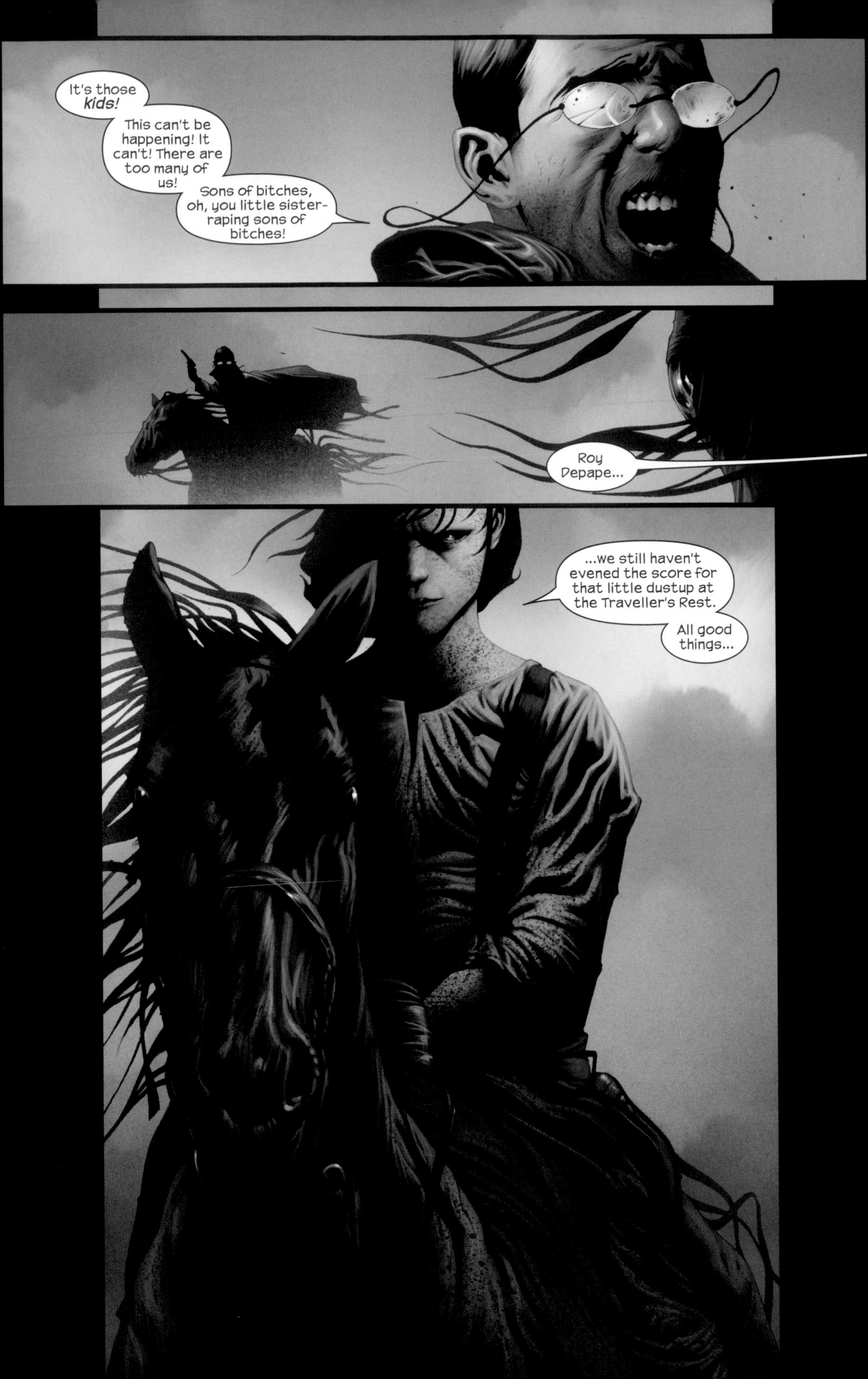
It's those *kids!*
This can't be happening! It can't! There are too many of us!
Sons of bitches, oh, you little sister-raping sons of bitches!
Roy Depape...
...we still haven't evened the score for that little dustup at the Traveller's Rest.
All good things...

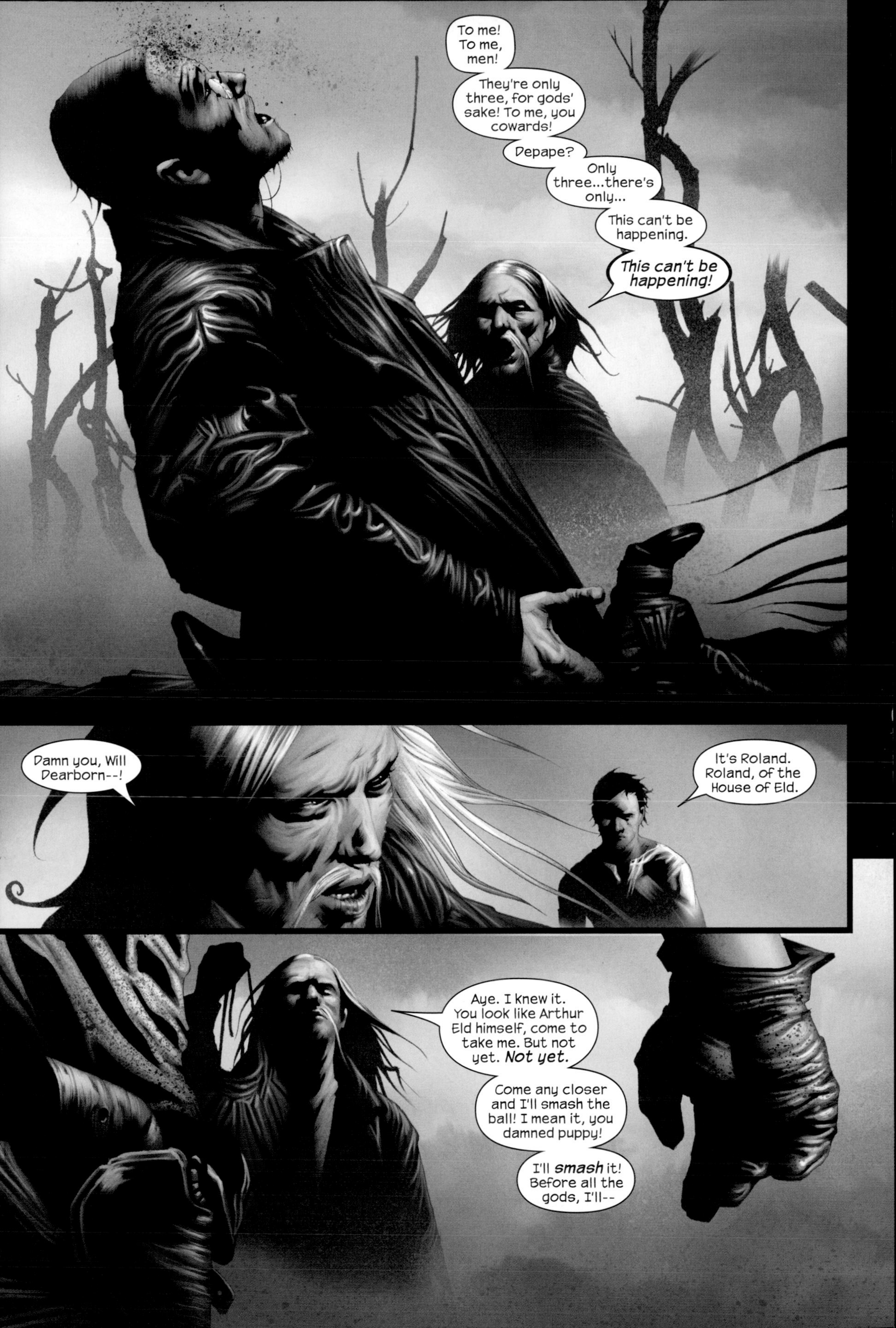
To me! To me, men!
They're only three, for gods' sake! To me, you cowards!
Depape?
Only three...there's only...
This can't be happening.
This can't be happening!
Damn you, Will Dearborn--!
It's Roland. Roland, of the House of Eld.
Aye. I knew it. You look like Arthur Eld himself, come to take me. But not yet. ***Not yet.***
Come any closer and I'll smash the ball! I mean it, you damned puppy!
I'll ***smash*** it! Before all the gods, I'll--

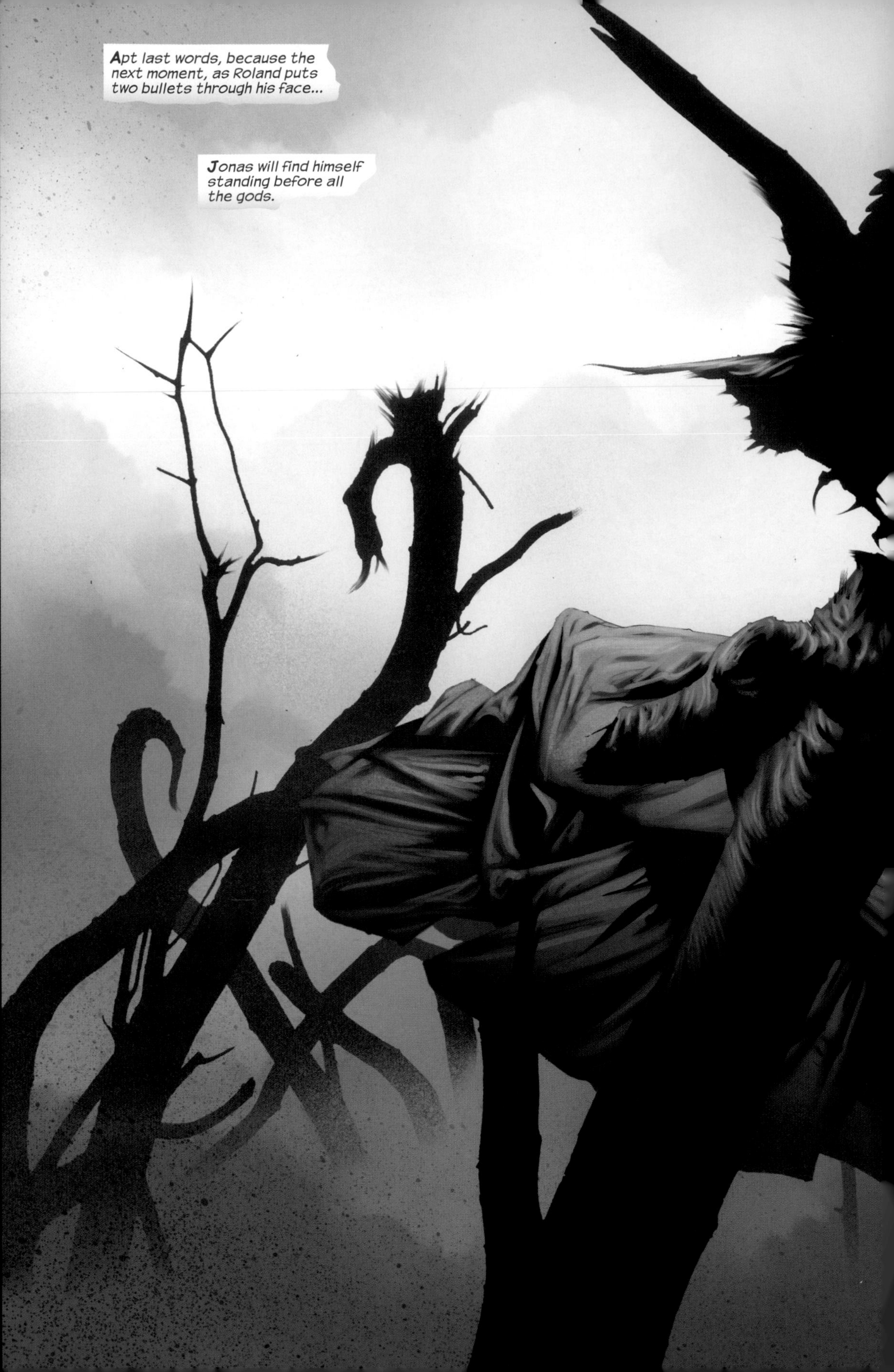
Apt last words, because the next moment, as Roland puts two bullets through his face...
Jonas will find himself standing before all the gods.

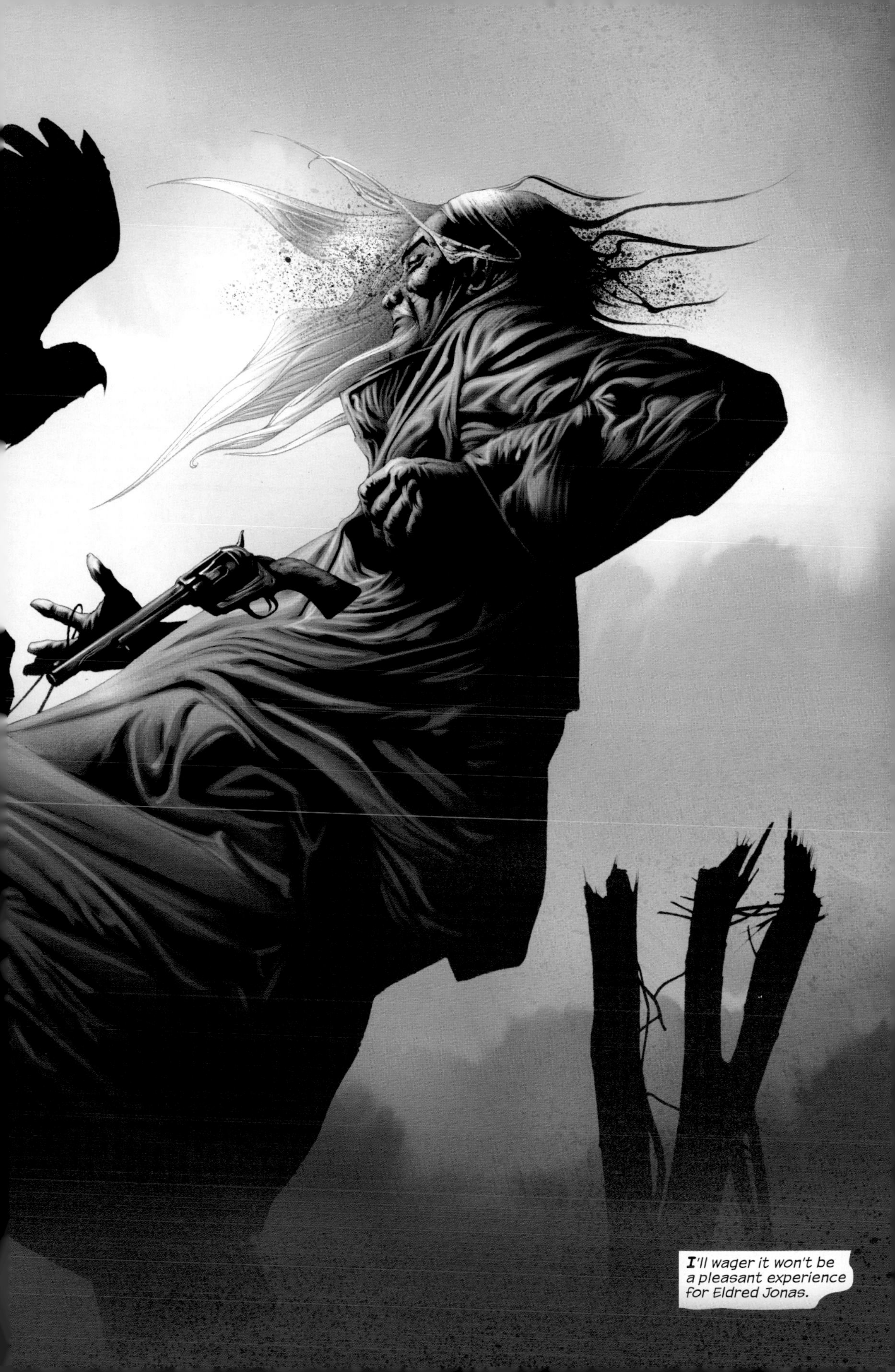
I'll wager it won't be a pleasant experience for Eldred Jonas.

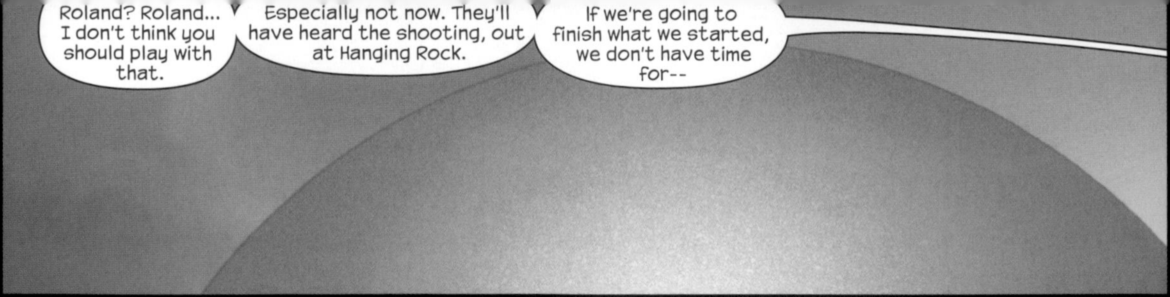
Roland? Roland... I don't think you should play with that.
Especially not now. They'll have heard the shooting, out at Hanging Rock.
If we're going to finish what we started, we don't have time for--

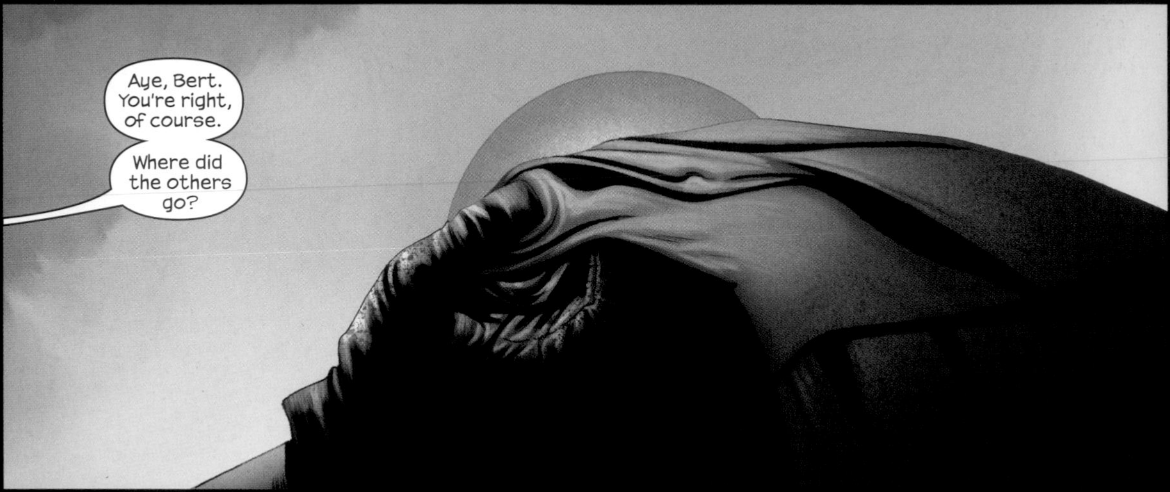
Aye, Bert. You're right, of course.
Where did the others go?

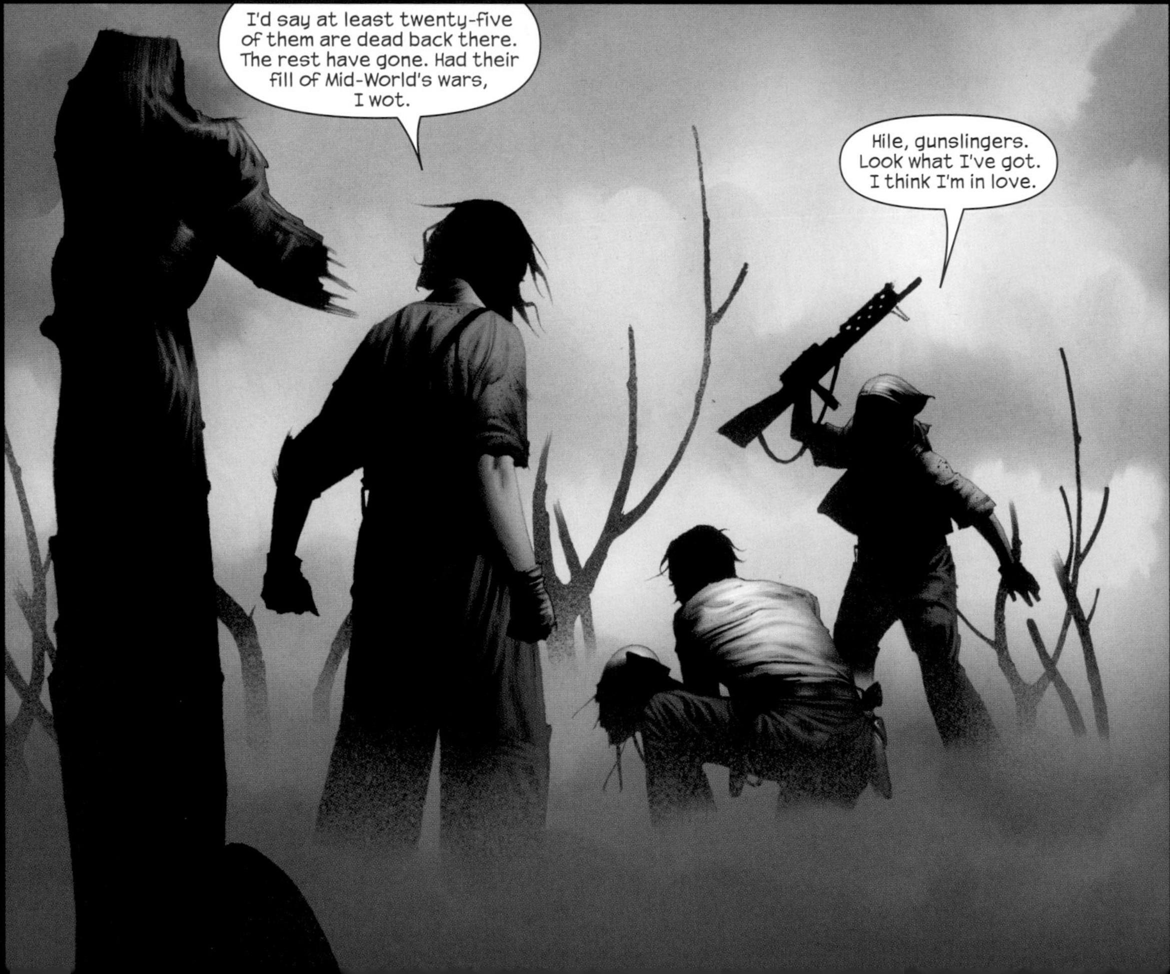
I'd say at least twenty-five of them are dead back there. The rest have gone. Had their fill of Mid-World's wars, I wot.
Hile, gunslingers. Look what I've got. I think I'm in love.

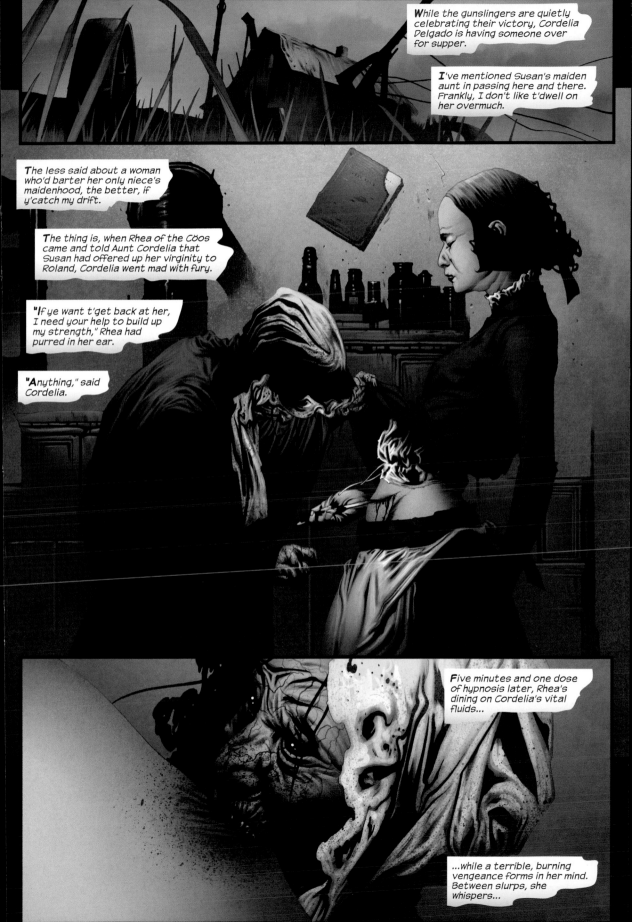

While the gunslingers are quietly celebrating their victory, Cordelia Delgado is having someone over for supper.

I've mentioned Susan's maiden aunt in passing here and there. Frankly, I don't like t'dwell on her overmuch.

The less said about a woman who'd barter her only niece's maidenhood, the better, if y'catch my drift.

The thing is, when Rhea of the Cöos came and told Aunt Cordelia that Susan had offered up her virginity to Roland, Cordelia went mad with fury.

"If ye want t'get back at her, I need your help to build up my strength," Rhea had purred in her ear.

"Anything," said Cordelia.

Five minutes and one dose of hypnosis later, Rhea's dining on Cordelia's vital fluids...

...while a terrible, burning vengeance forms in her mind. Between slurps, she whispers...

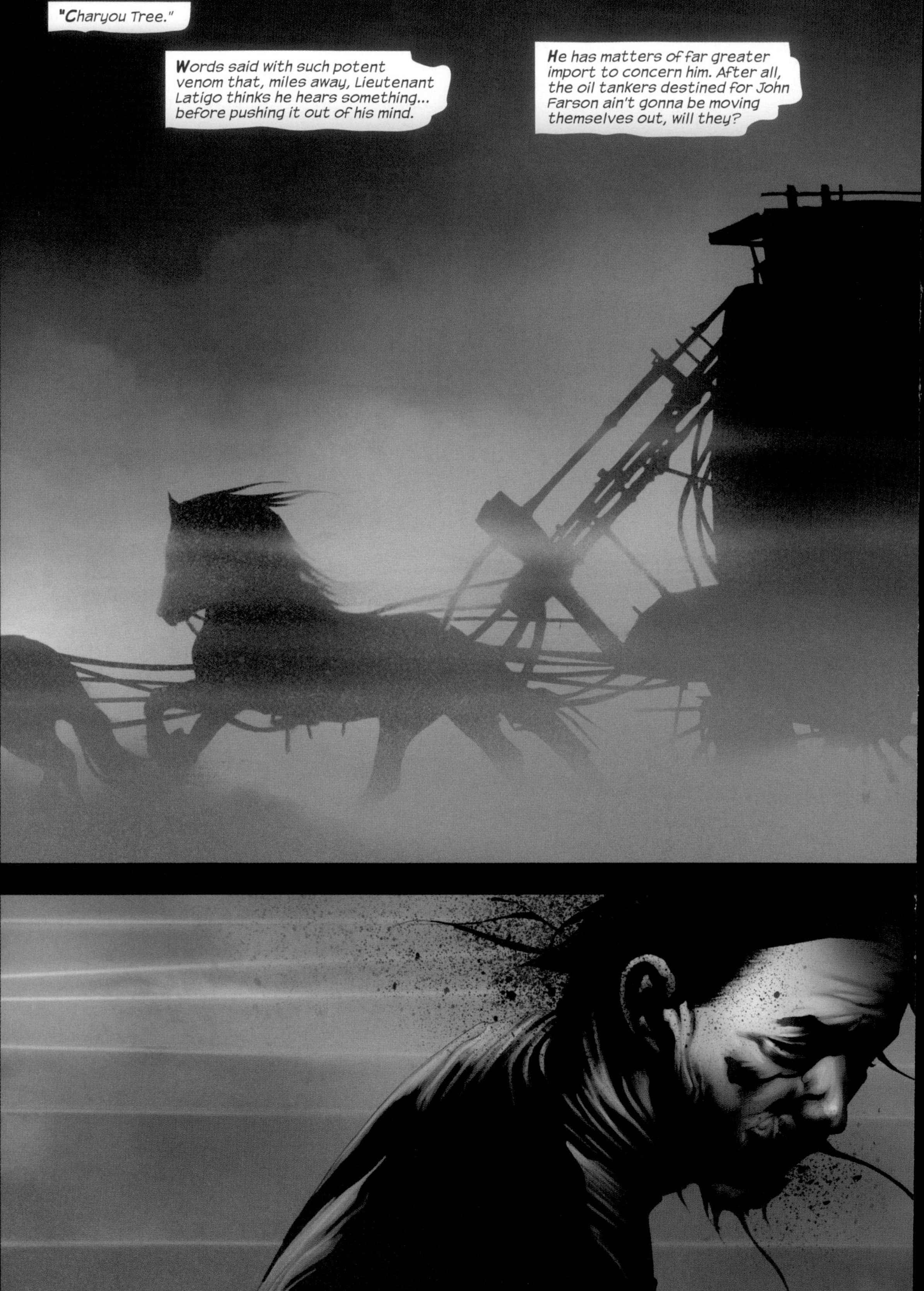
"Charyou Tree."
Words said with such potent venom that, miles away, Lieutenant Latigo thinks he hears something... before pushing it out of his mind.
He has matters of far greater import to concern him. After all, the oil tankers destined for John Farson ain't gonna be moving themselves out, will they?

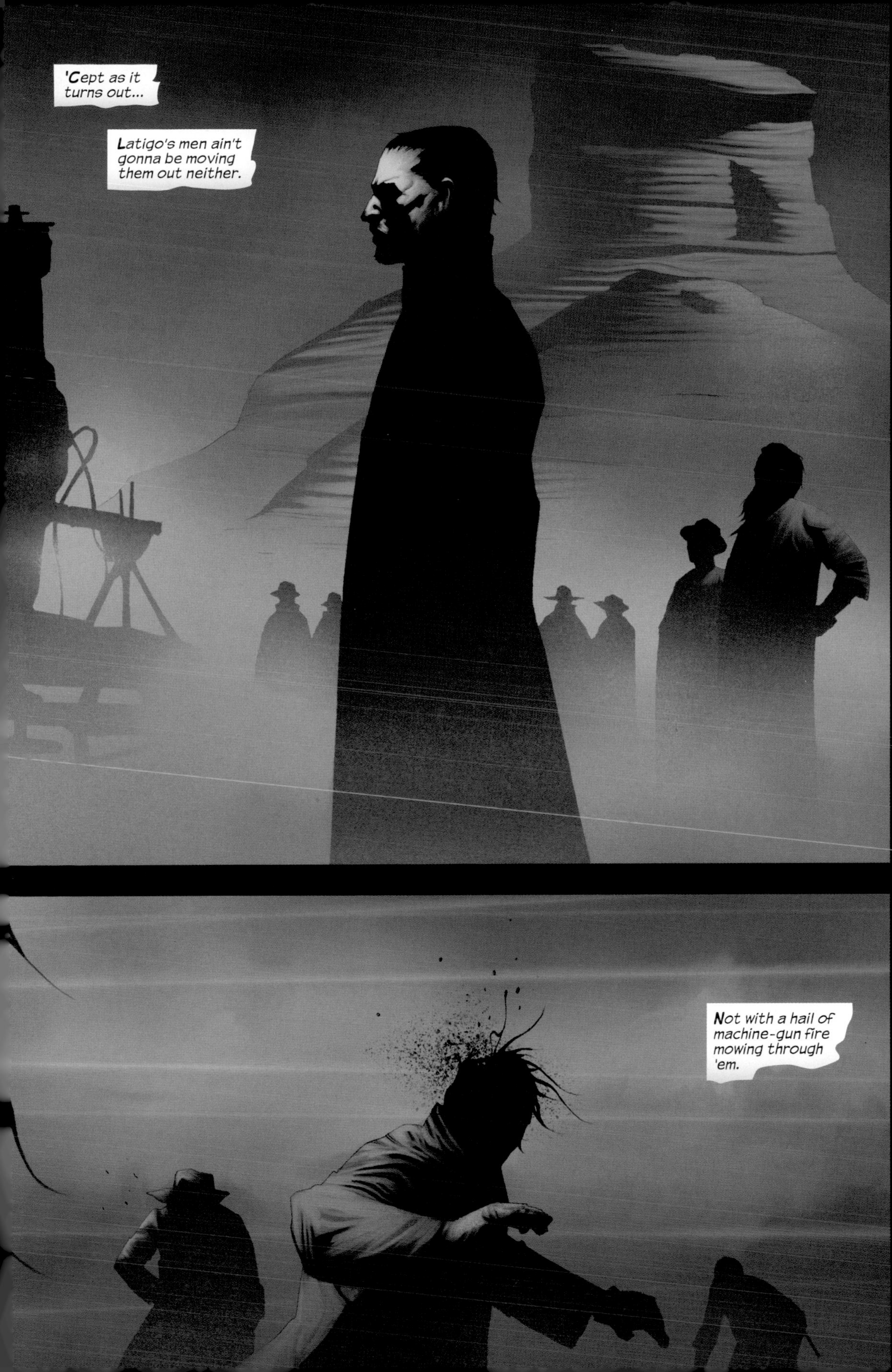
'Cept as it turns out...
Latigo's men ain't gonna be moving them out neither.
Not with a hail of machine-gun fire mowing through 'em.

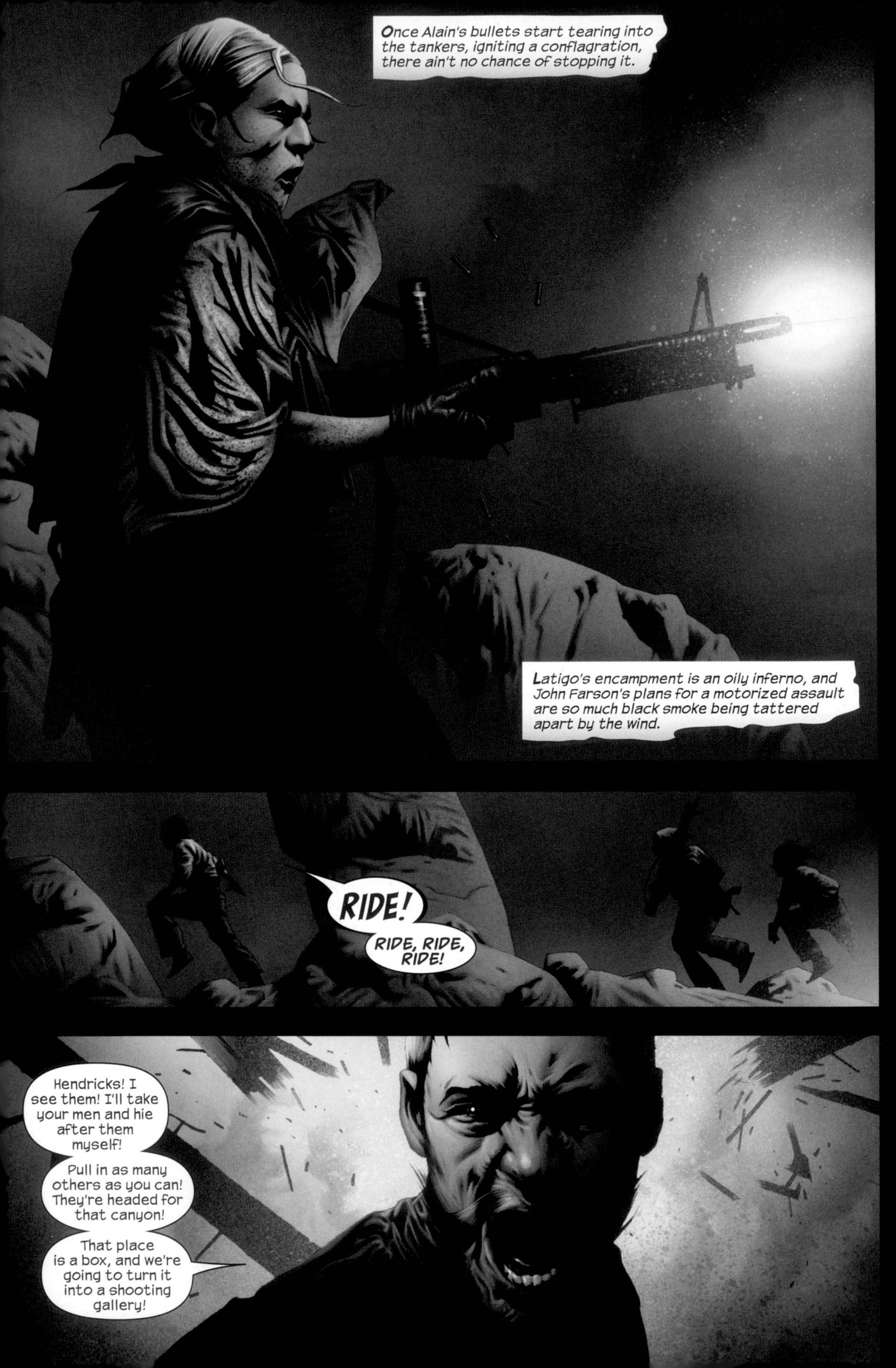
Once Alain's bullets start tearing into the tankers, igniting a conflagration, there ain't no chance of stopping it.
Latigo's encampment is an oily inferno, and John Farson's plans for a motorized assault are so much black smoke being tattered apart by the wind.
RIDE!
RIDE, RIDE, RIDE!
Hendricks! I see them! I'll take your men and hie after them myself!
Pull in as many others as you can! They're headed for that canyon!
That place is a box, and we're going to turn it into a shooting gallery!

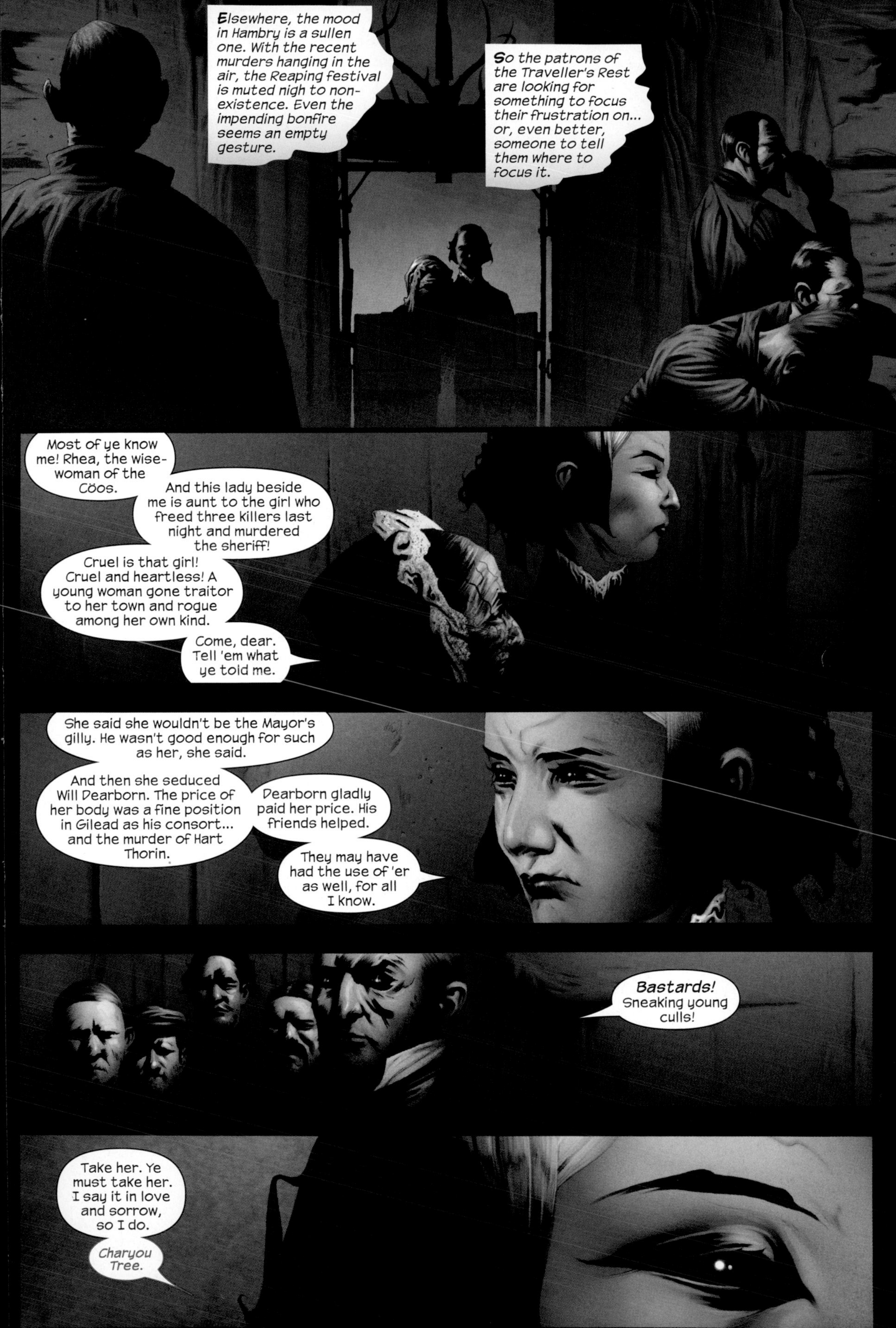
Elsewhere, the mood in Hambry is a sullen one. With the recent murders hanging in the air, the Reaping festival is muted nigh to non-existence. Even the impending bonfire seems an empty gesture.
So the patrons of the Traveller's Rest are looking for something to focus their frustration on... or, even better, someone to tell them where to focus it.
Most of ye know me! Rhea, the wise-woman of the Cöos.
And this lady beside me is aunt to the girl who freed three killers last night and murdered the sheriff!
Cruel is that girl! Cruel and heartless! A young woman gone traitor to her town and rogue among her own kind.
Come, dear. Tell 'em what ye toid me.
She said she wouldn't be the Mayor's gilly. He wasn't good enough for such as her, she said.
And then she seduced Will Dearborn. The price of her body was a fine position in Gilead as his consort... and the murder of Hart Thorin.
Dearborn gladly paid her price. His friends helped.
They may have had the use of 'er as well, for all I know.
Bastards! Sneaking young culls!
Take her. Ye must take her. I say it in love and sorrow, so I do.
Charyou Tree.

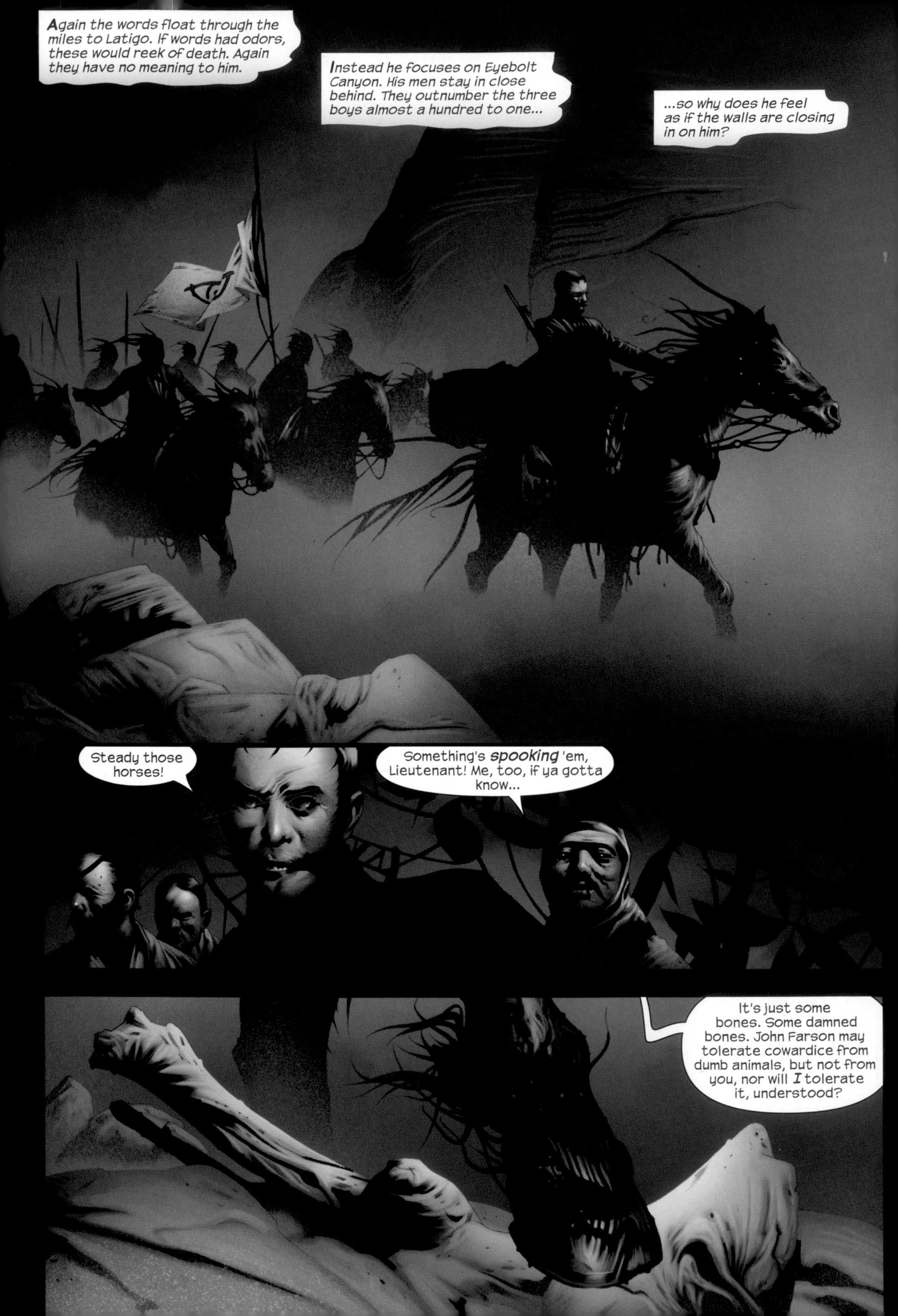
Again the words float through the miles to Latigo. If words had odors, these would reek of death. Again they have no meaning to him.
Instead he focuses on Eyebolt Canyon. His men stay in close behind. They outnumber the three boys almost a hundred to one...
...so why does he feel as if the walls are closing in on him?
Steady those horses!
Something's spooking 'em, Lieutenant! Me, too, if ya gotta know...
It's just some bones. Some damned bones. John Farson may tolerate cowardice from dumb animals, but not from you, nor will I tolerate it, understood?

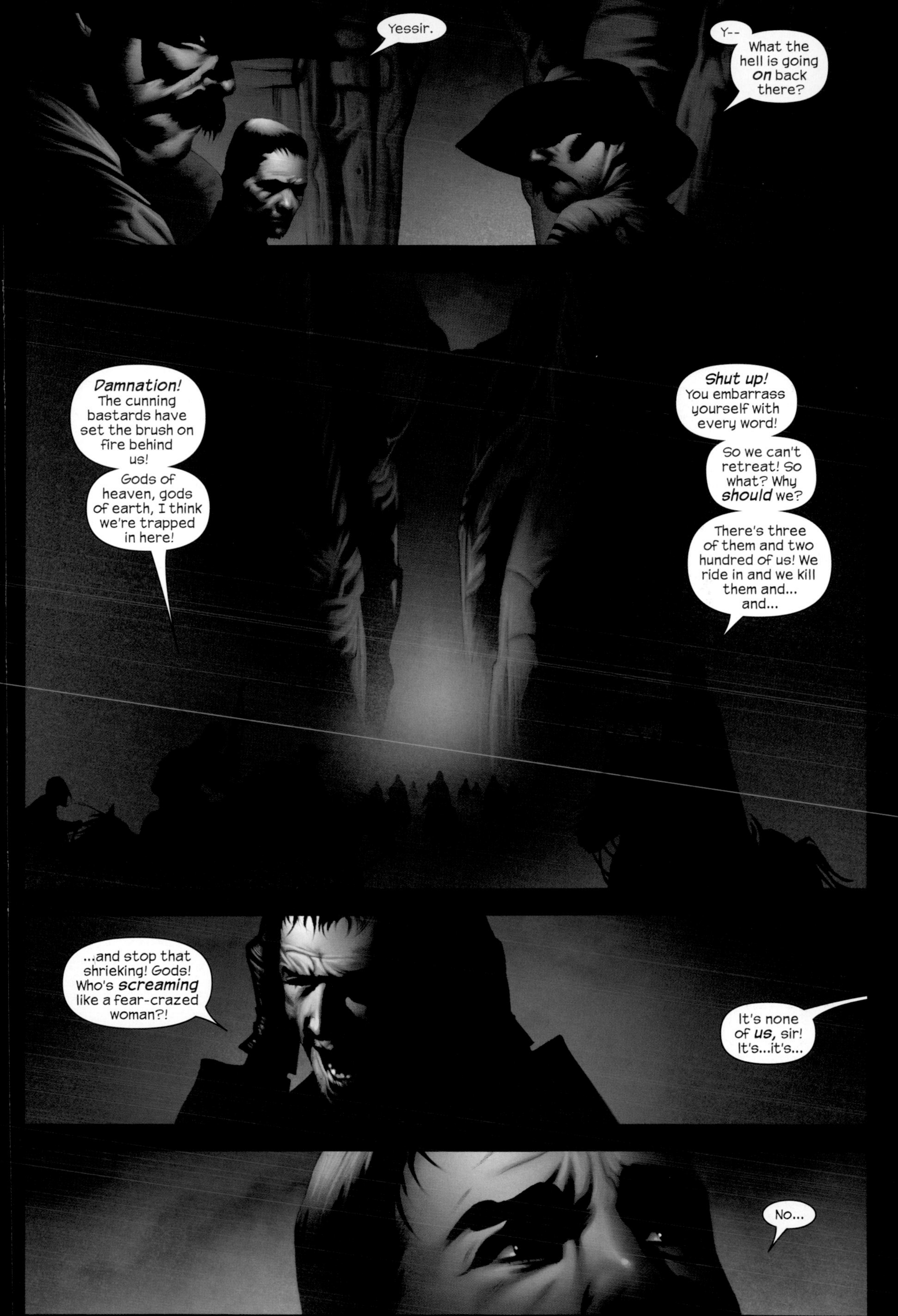
Yessir.
Y--
What the hell is going on back there?
Damnation! The cunning bastards have set the brush on fire behind us!
Gods of heaven, gods of earth, I think we're trapped in here!
Shut up! You embarrass yourself with every word!
So we can't retreat! So what? Why should we?
There's three of them and two hundred of us! We ride in and we kill them and... and...
...and stop that shrieking! Gods! Who's screaming like a fear-crazed woman?!
It's none of us, sir! It's...it's...
No...

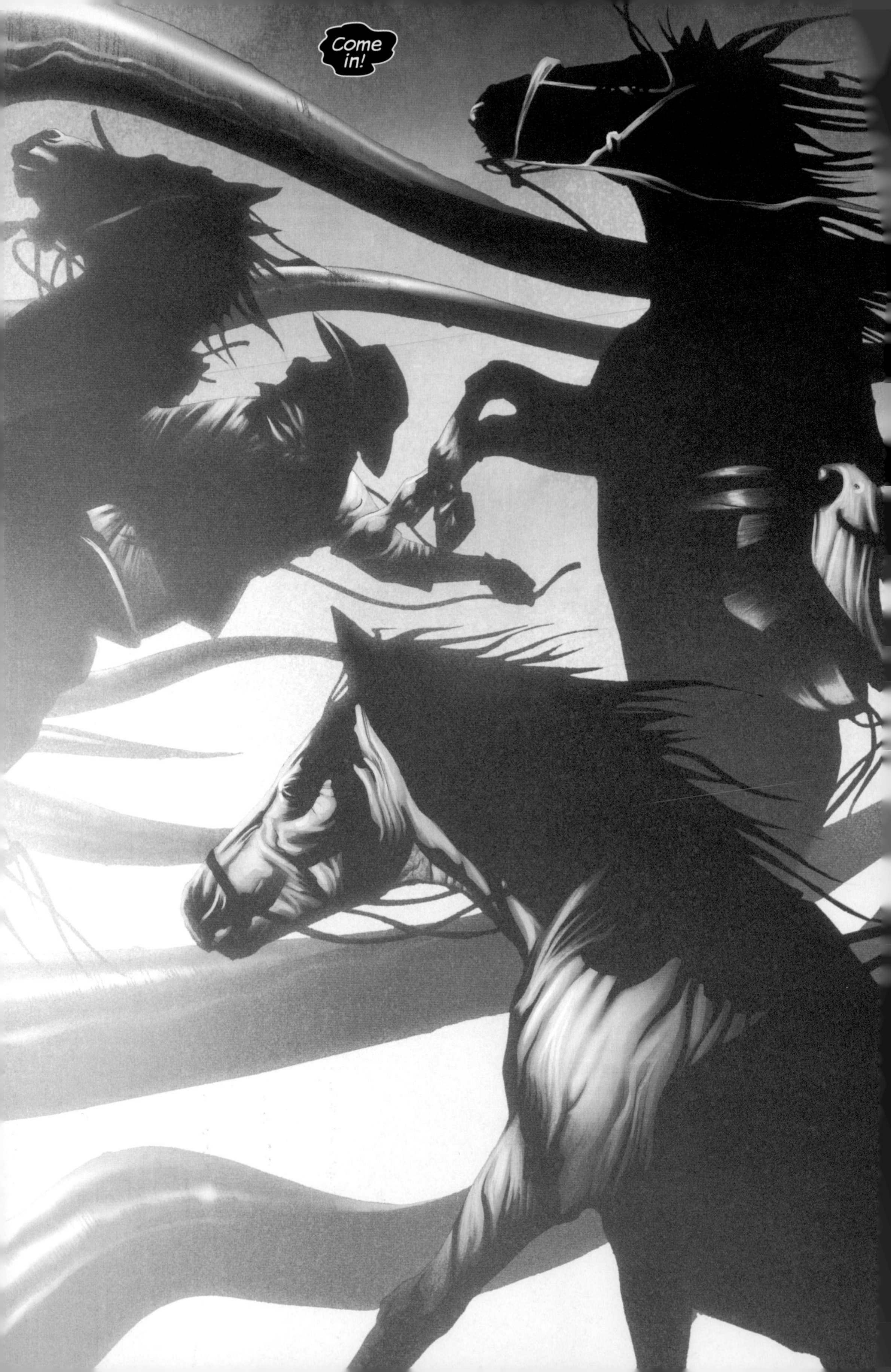
Come in!

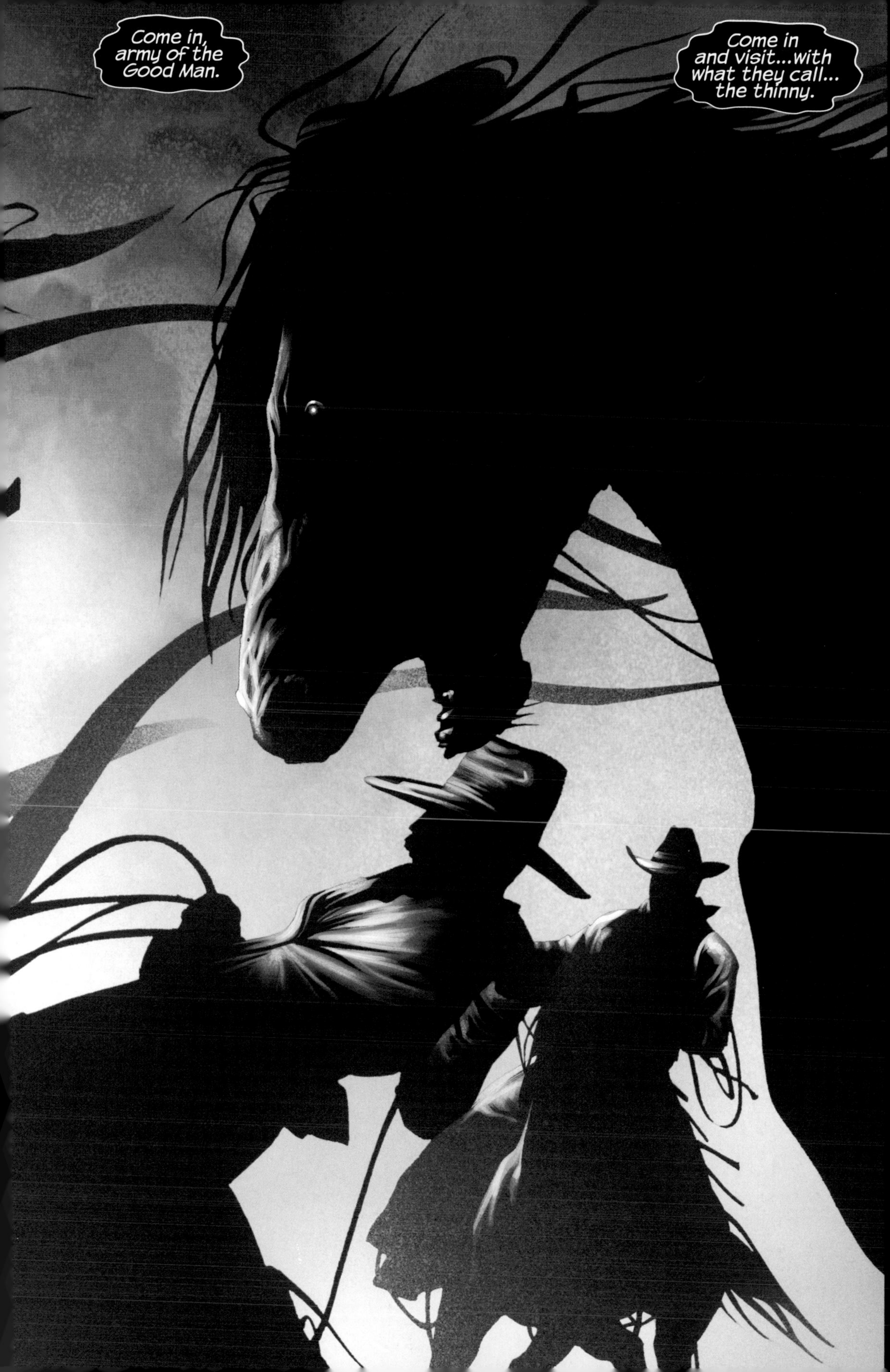
Come in, army of the Good Man.
Come in and visit...with what they call... the thinny.

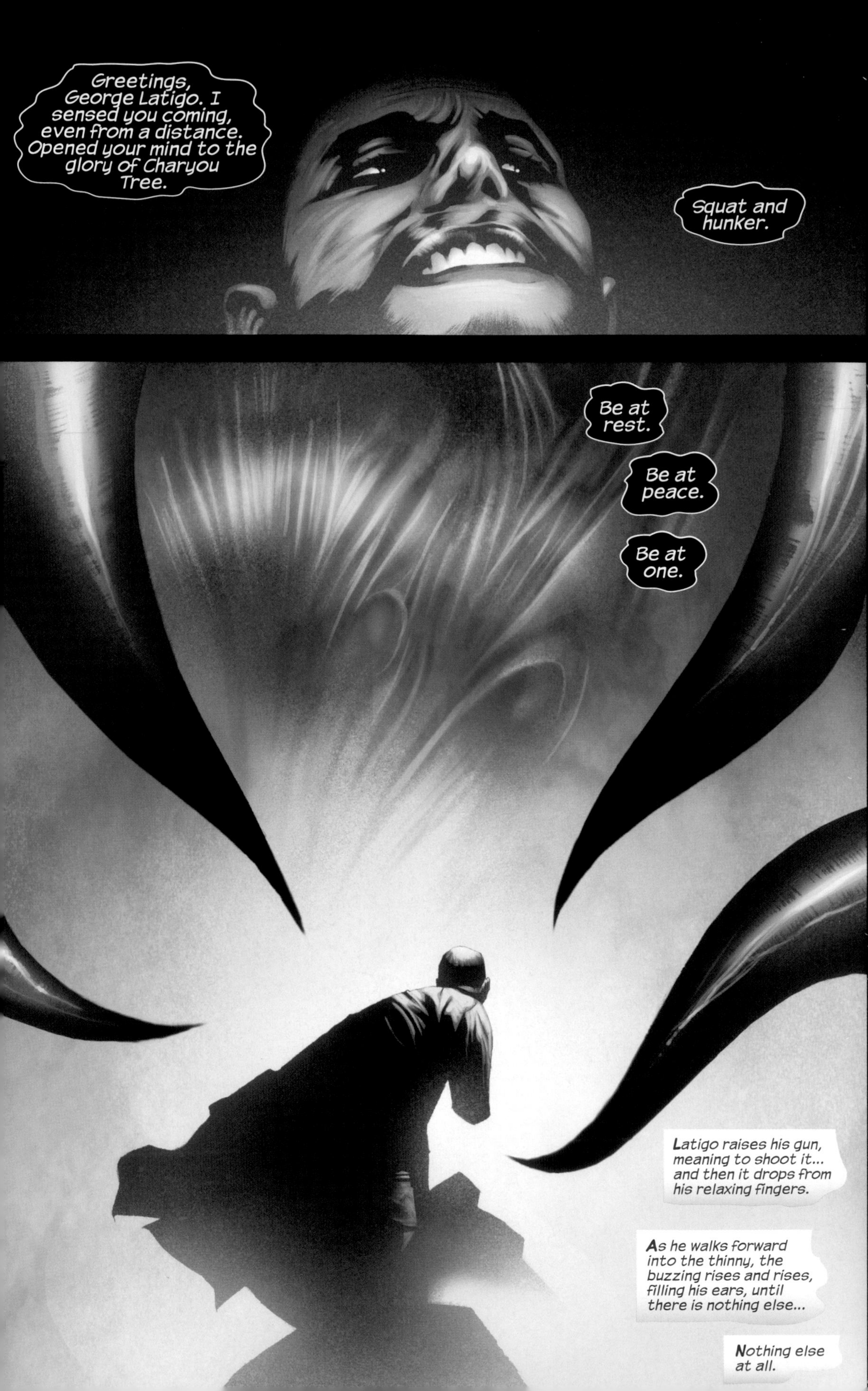
Greetings, George Latigo. I sensed you coming, even from a distance. Opened your mind to the glory of Charyou Tree.
Squat and hunker.
Be at rest.
Be at peace.
Be at one.
Latigo raises his gun, meaning to shoot it... and then it drops from his relaxing fingers.
As he walks forward into the thinny, the buzzing rises and rises, filling his ears, until there is nothing else...
Nothing else at all.

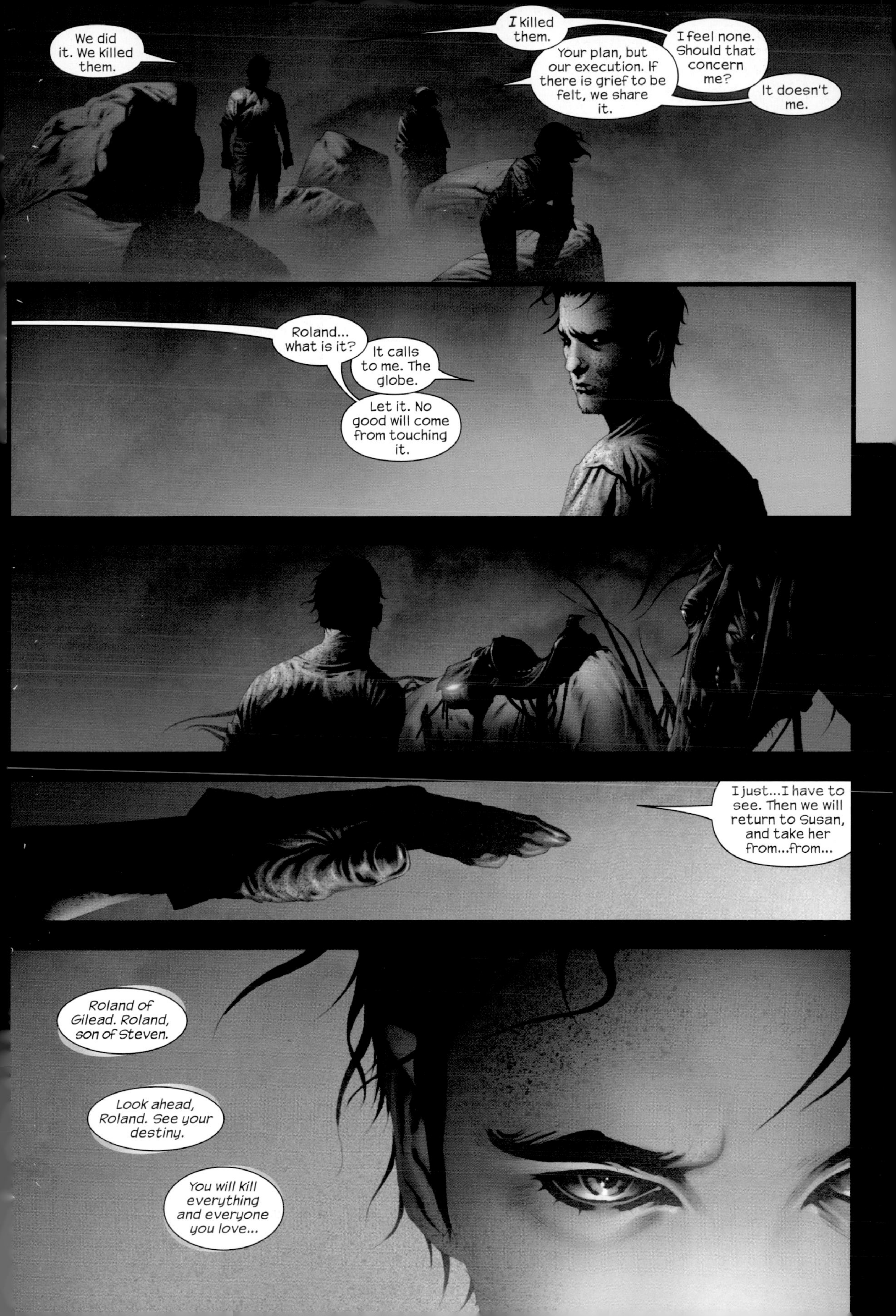
We did it. We killed them.
I killed them.
I feel none. Should that concern me?
Your plan, but our execution. If there is grief to be felt, we share it.
It doesn't me.
Roland... what is it?
It calls to me. The globe.
Let it. No good will come from touching it.
I just...I have to see. Then we will return to Susan, and take her from...from...
Roland of Gilead. Roland, son of Steven.
Look ahead, Roland. See your destiny.
You will kill everything and everyone you love...

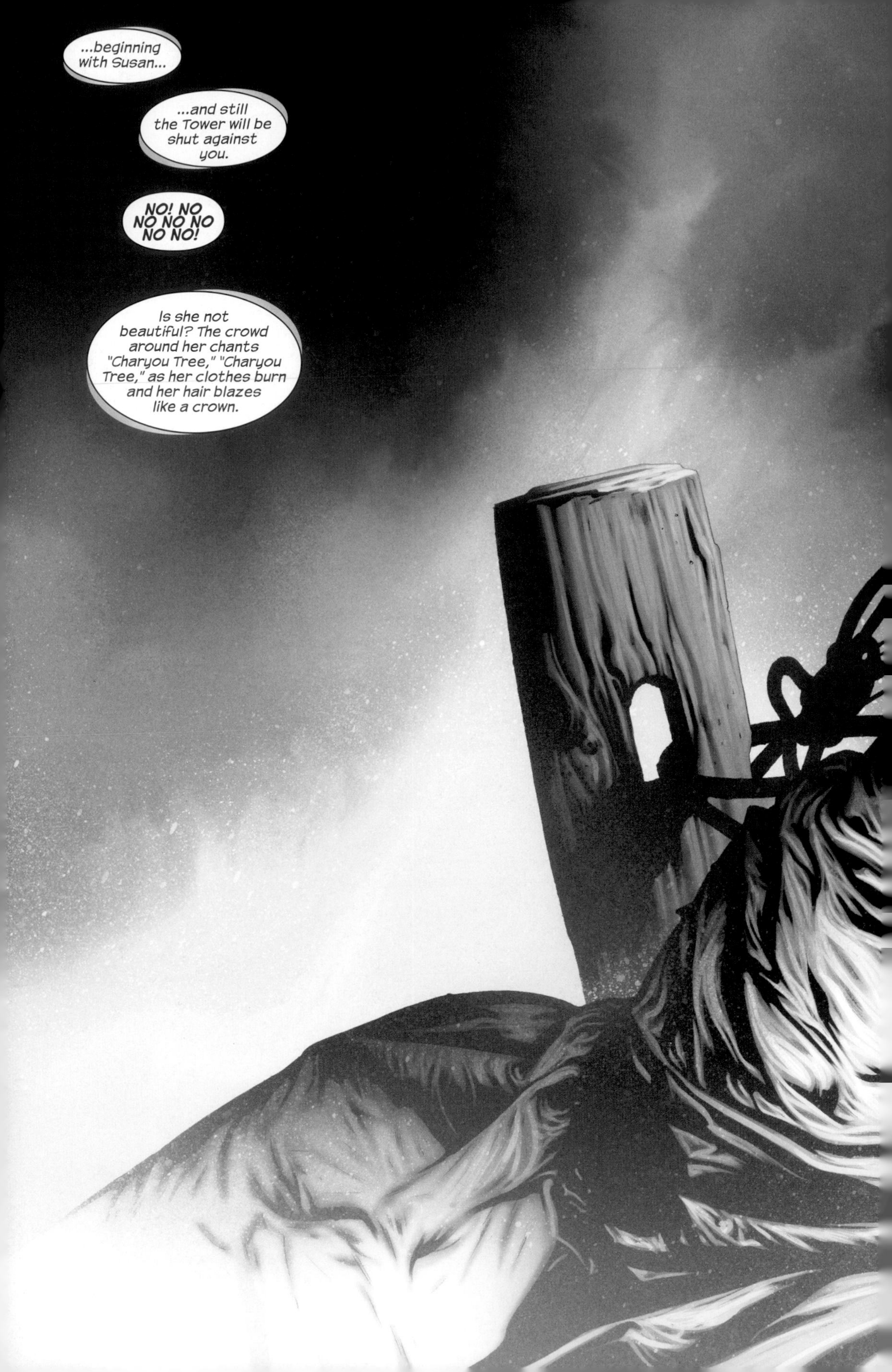
...beginning with Susan...
...and still the Tower will be shut against you.
NO! NO NO NO NO NO NO!
Is she not beautiful? The crowd around her chants "Charyou Tree," "Charyou Tree," as her clothes burn and her hair blazes like a crown.

At the end of her life she is aware of heat but not pain, and she thinks of you laughing with an ease and freedom you will never find again in your long life...
And it is your laughter she takes with her as she cries out her last words...
ROLAND, I LOVE THEE!

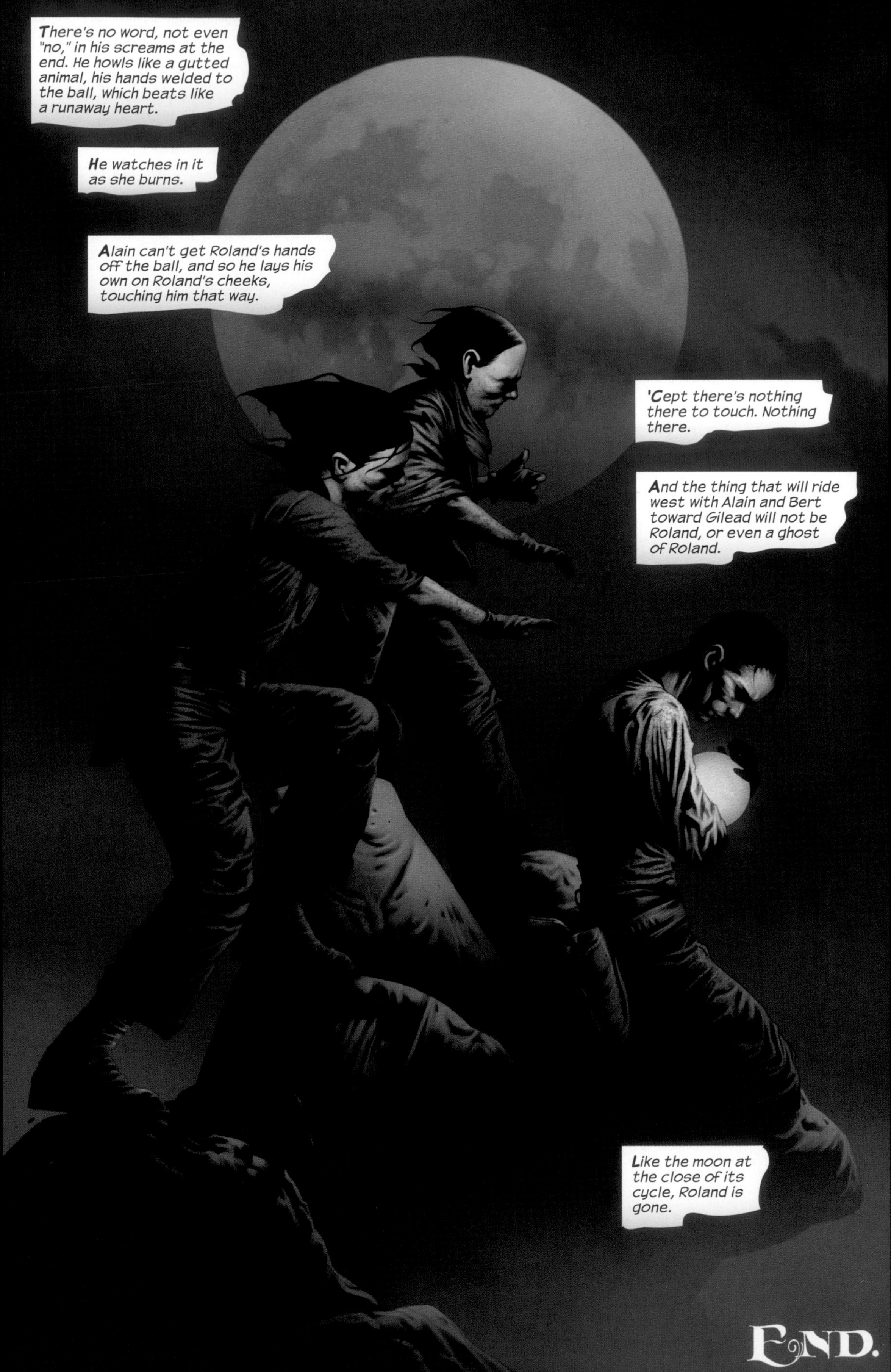
There's no word, not even "no," in his screams at the end. He howls like a gutted animal, his hands welded to the ball, which beats like a runaway heart.
He watches in it as she burns.
Alain can't get Roland's hands off the ball, and so he lays his own on Roland's cheeks, touching him that way.
'Cept there's nothing there to touch. Nothing there.
And the thing that will ride west with Alain and Bert toward Gilead will not be Roland, or even a ghost of Roland.
Like the moon at the close of its cycle, Roland is gone.
END.

An open letter from
STEPHEN KING

I actually thought of doing this as a comic script — you and me kicking this thing around in a dusty desert barroom, perhaps in the town of Tull, with ole Sheb pounding out "Hey Jude" on the tinklebox, but then I started to see strange creatures in the corners…and a dust storm blowing up outside…and a Mutant Posse somewhere close at hand. Because that's how my mind works. Pretty soon it'd be a story, and then I'd be here all night. So a letter will have to do. A rambling one.

But a script would have been amusing, *n'est-ce pas?* Oh well.

I asked Chuck Verrill (agent) if he remembered how I wound up in bed with Marvel (with me it's always love, never business), and he says that at some point, when responding to a question about who he'd like to work with — maybe even in *Marvel Spotlight!* — Joe Quesada said, "Stephen King." This got back to me and I said to someone — maybe Chuck or Marsha DeFilippo (assistant) — that working with Marvel sounded like it would be the cat's meow. I mean, I grew up, but so did the comics, and I never really left them behind.

I don't know who suggested the *Dark Tower* books, but I latched on at once. Having read *Watchmen* and *Preacher* and *V for Vendetta*, I thought a graphic version of the Tower stories — or stories about Roland the gunslinger that had never been told — could work like a really cool movie, or a great TV miniseries.

Also, I'm curious. I'm always curious, and open to seeing what new formats can do for old works. And the books are unimpeachable, beyond change (as long as the censors are kept at bay). So there's really no risk, is there? It's why I tend to say "yes" to a lot of movie offers, and why I okayed a kind of camp version of Carrie off-Broadway (not to mention an operatic version of *Dolores Claiborne* that someone's currently screwing around with in London). I mean, some of these things will probably suck, but who really cares? Readers can always go back to the books, which don't suck (some critics would beg to differ).

Plus! You always judge the talent involved. Right now there's a huge amount of talent in the graphic/comix world, and a lot of it's at Marvel. I talked with them about it, but I didn't really have to be persuaded; I know the market, after all. I've been reading Marvel since around the time Stan Lee started to shave. Nah…but I've been there since Jack Kirby was drawing *Fantastic Four*, and can remember when Spidey supplanted the gone-but-not-forgotten *Plastic Man* (and the immortal Woozy Winks) in my affections and regard.

Other novels I might consider (for future comic adaptations)? *Firestarter* would be a natural, but I don't know what the rights situation is. Original projects? You bet. I'd like to do a kickbutt, zombies-overrun-the-world story told from the viewpoint of several girls who start out as Valley Drones and become tough take-no-prisoners survivors. I'd like to tell a time-travel story where this guy finds a diner that connects to 1958…you always go back to the same day. So one day he goes back and just stays. Leaves his 2007 life behind. His goal? To get up to November 22, 1963, and stop Lee Harvey Oswald. He does, and he's convinced he's just FIXED THE WORLD. But when he goes back to '07, the world's a nuclear slag-heap. Not good to fool with Father Time. So then he has to go back again and stop himself…only he's taken on a fatal dose of radiation, so it's a race against time.

Or how about a suburban neighborhood where all the women are witches and the battle of good vs. evil is going on just below the surface of soccer games, car washes, and Tuesday night poker games (the guys are downstairs in the rec room, playing seven-card; the gals are in the backyard, calling up Nyarlahotep the Blind Fiddler from Beyond Space).

There are so many ideas, I can't even begin to tell you. When the Grim Reaper comes for me, I'll probably say, "Wait! Wait! I gotta tell you the one about…" And so on. Yadda-yadda-yadda.

Would I actually write any of these comics? Heck, yes. I like the process, which I've had a chance to watch close up during the creation of the *Dark Tower/Gunslinger* books. And it's close enough to screenwriting to make me believe I'd be comfortable with that process. Too many books to do, though, I guess, although the quality of the current *DT* series is totally gratifying. I've rarely felt so good about a project that was still in the process of creation. Jae Lee is amazing, and the quality of the writing — a team effort, and what a team — is high. I think the fans are going to be blown away.

And if I could write any Marvel comic, about any character? Spider-Man, of course. Peter Parker, the original Sufferin' Superhero. I'm not sure what I'd do with him…except I see a nervous breakdown…and a growing tangle of OCD behavior that can't be fixed with medication (screws up the powers, of course), and some tropical island rehab…an earthquake, of course…or maybe a volcano…a growing belief that if he doesn't touch the door exactly twenty-three times before leaving his condo, the world will end… oh, and a sense that the costume is getting tighter… making it hard to breathe…

Stuff like that. Lots more. But I gotta go before this gets serious. Long days and pleasant nights, and may ya do well.

Stephen King

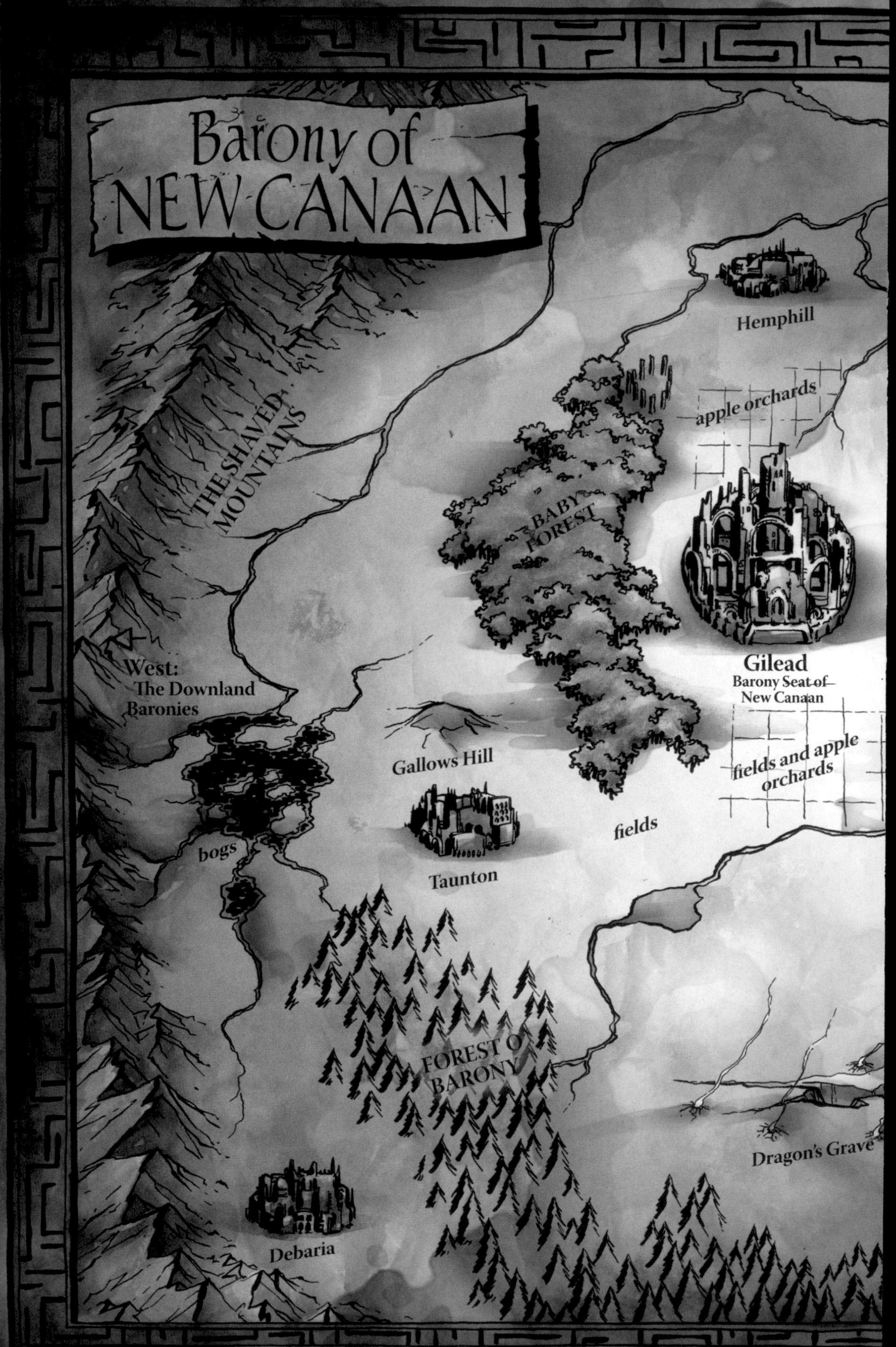
Barony of
NEW CANAAN
Hemphill
apple orchards
THE SHAVED MOUNTAINS
BABY FOREST
Gilead
Barony Seat of New Canaan
West:
The Downland Baronies
Gallows Hill
fields and apple orchards
fields
bogs
Taunton
FOREST O' BARONY
Dragon's Grave
Debaria

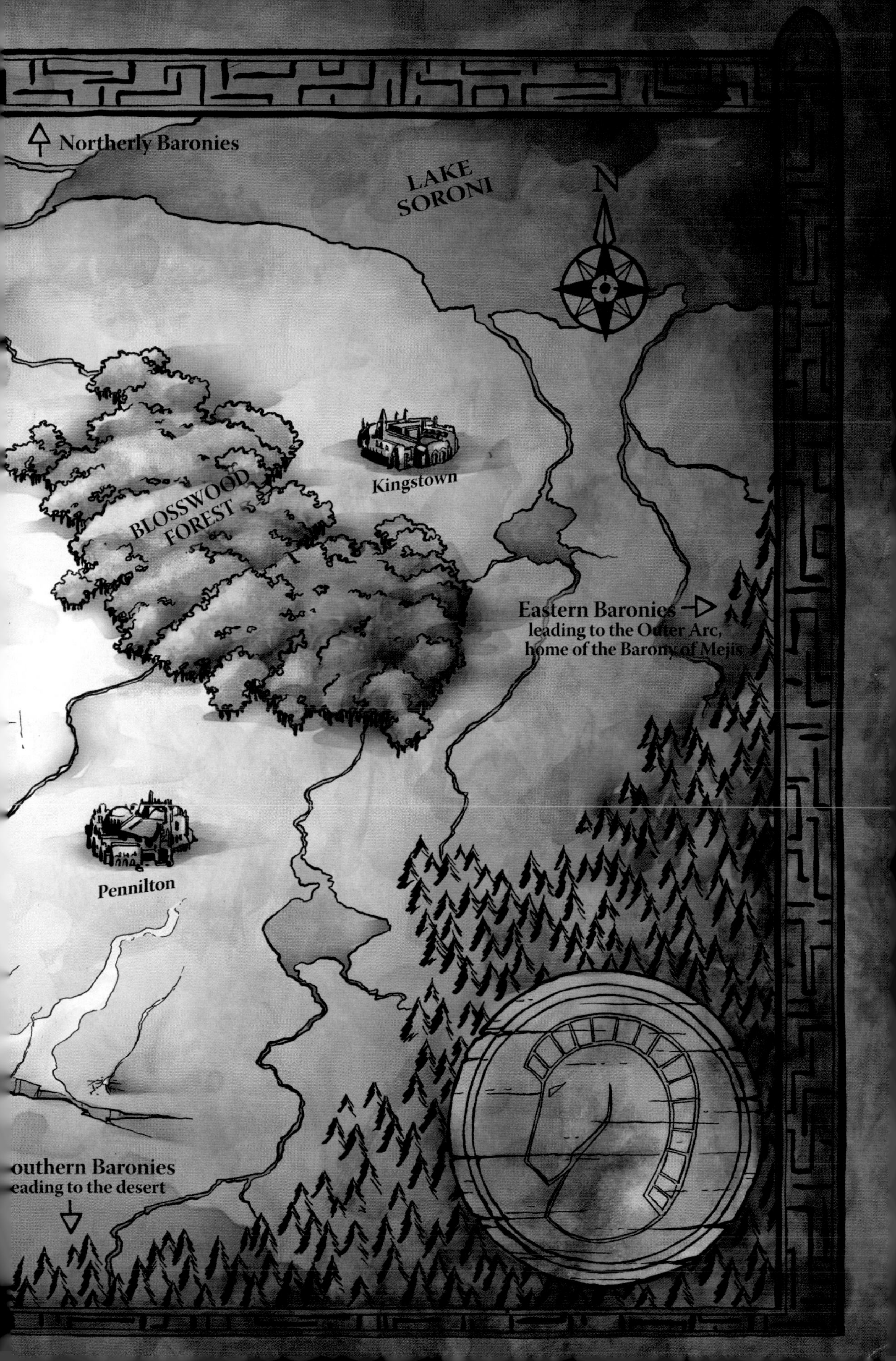
Northerly Baronies
LAKE SORONI
N
BLOSSWOOD FOREST
Kingstown
Eastern Baronies
leading to the Outer Arc,
home of the Barony of Mejis
Pennilton
outhern Baronies
eading to the desert

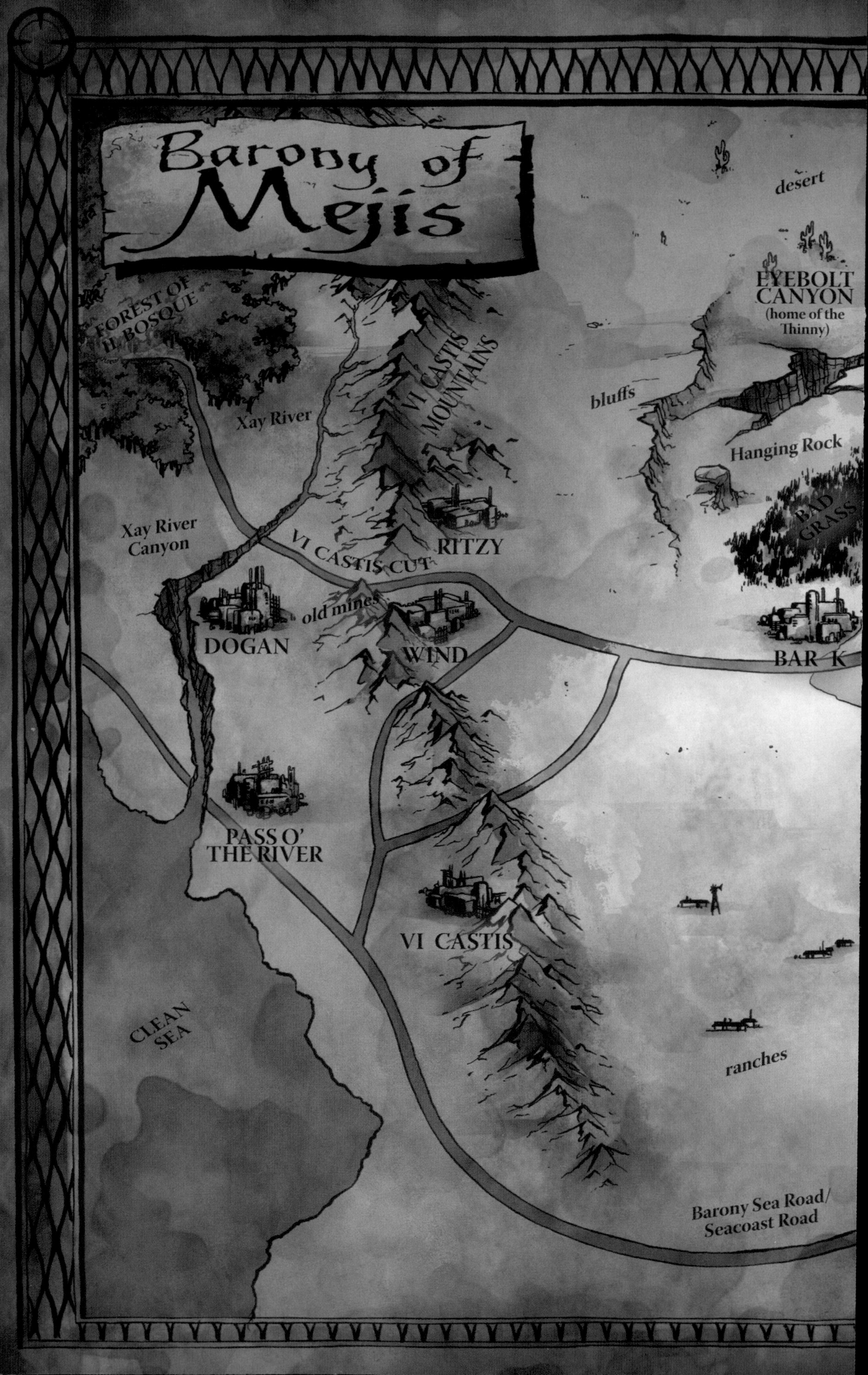
Barony of Mejis
desert
EYEBOLT CANYON
(home of the Thinny)
FOREST OF IL BOSQUE
VI CASTIS MOUNTAINS
bluffs
Xay River
Hanging Rock
BAD GRASS
Xay River Canyon
RITZY
VI CASTIS CUT
old mines
DOGAN
WIND
BAR K
PASS O' THE RIVER
VI CASTIS
CLEAN SEA
ranches
Barony Sea Road/
Seacoast Road

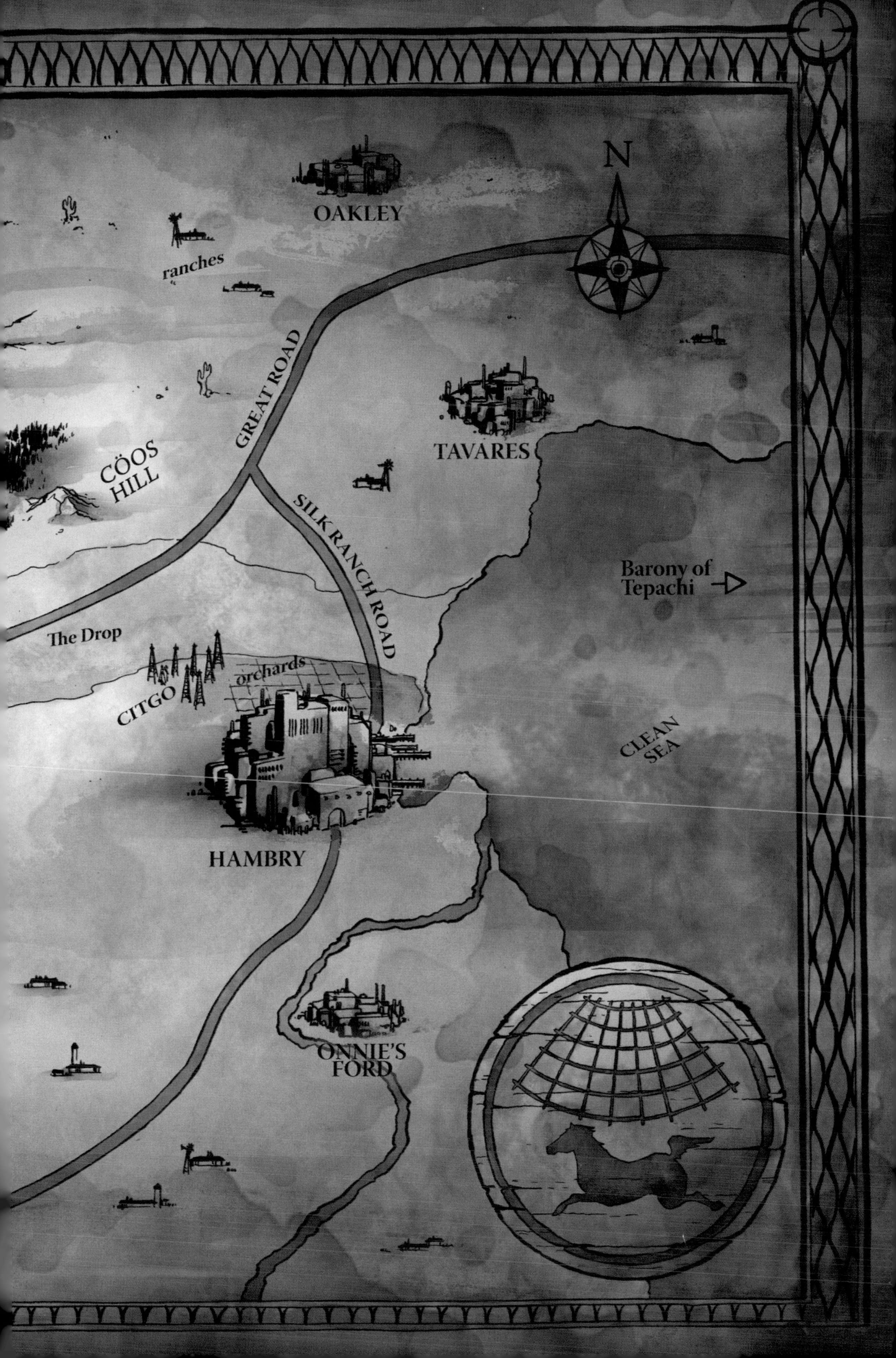

N
OAKLEY
ranches
GREAT ROAD
CÖOS HILL
TAVARES
SILK RANCH ROAD
Barony of Tepachi
The Drop
orchards
CITGO
CLEAN SEA
HAMBRY
ONNIE'S FORD

Cover to *Gunslinger Born* #1 by **Jae Lee** & **Richard Isanove**

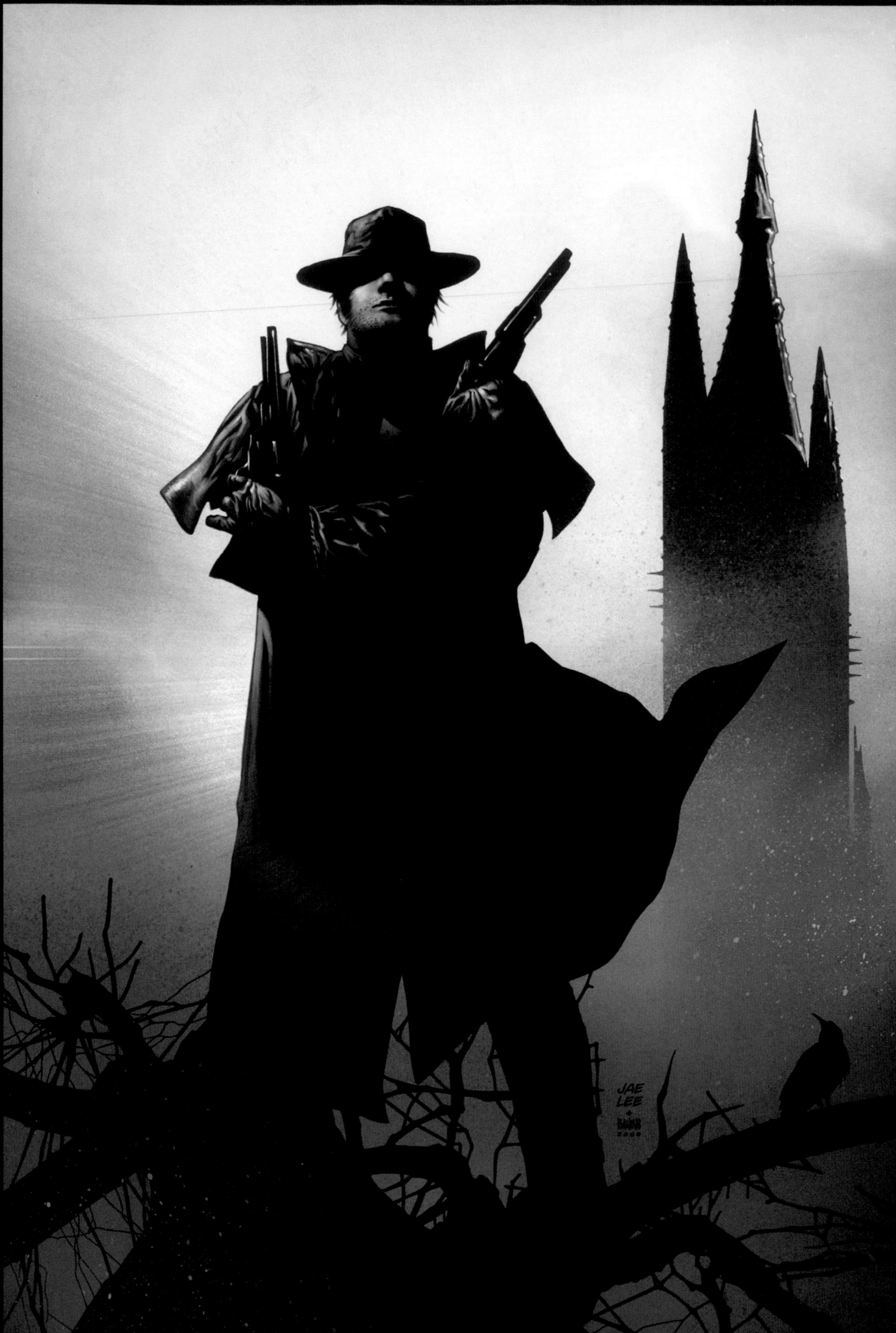
JAE
LEE

Sketch Variant Cover to *Gunslinger Born* #1 by **Jae Lee**

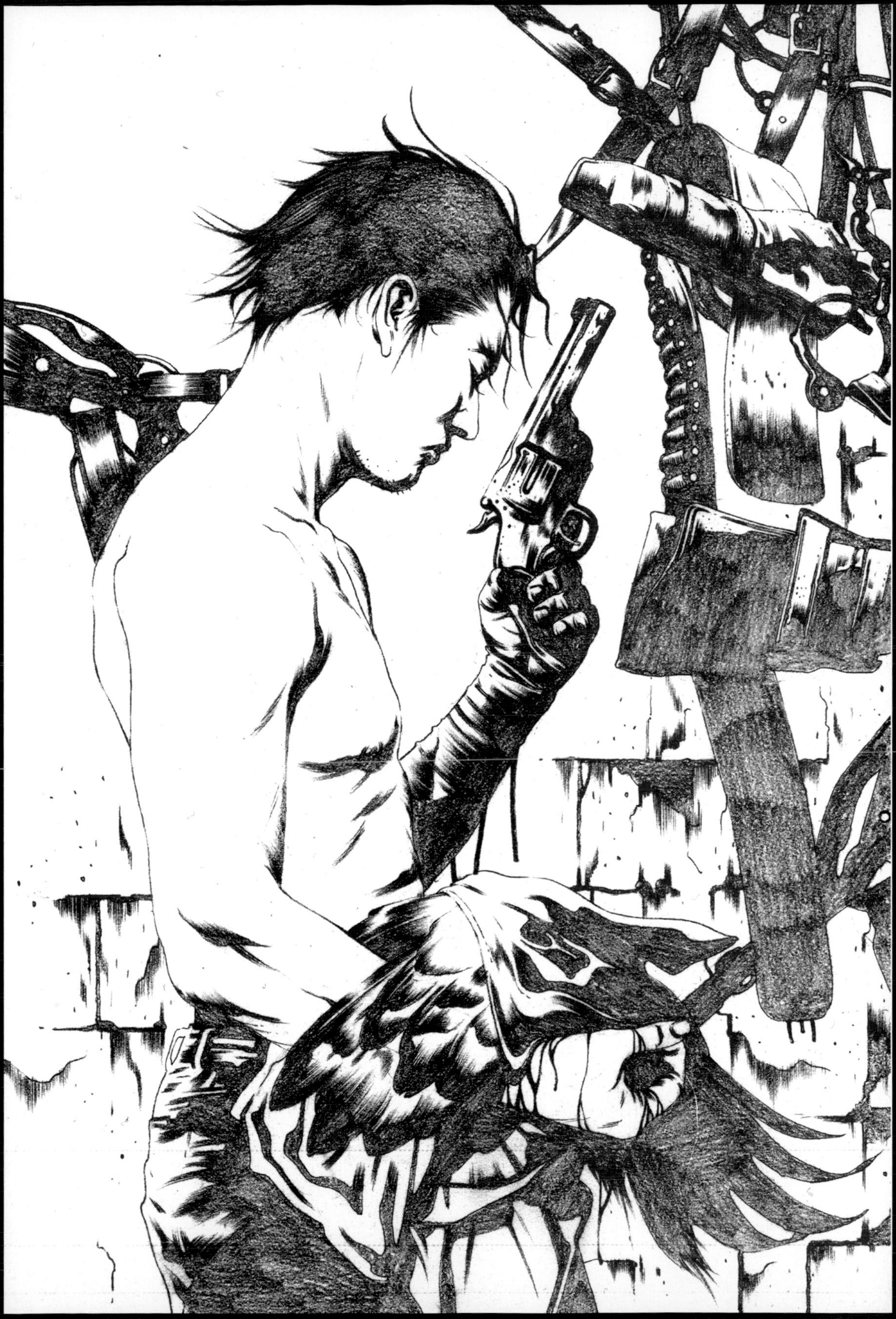

Variant Cover to *Gunslinger Born #1* by **Joe Quesada** & **Richard Isanove**

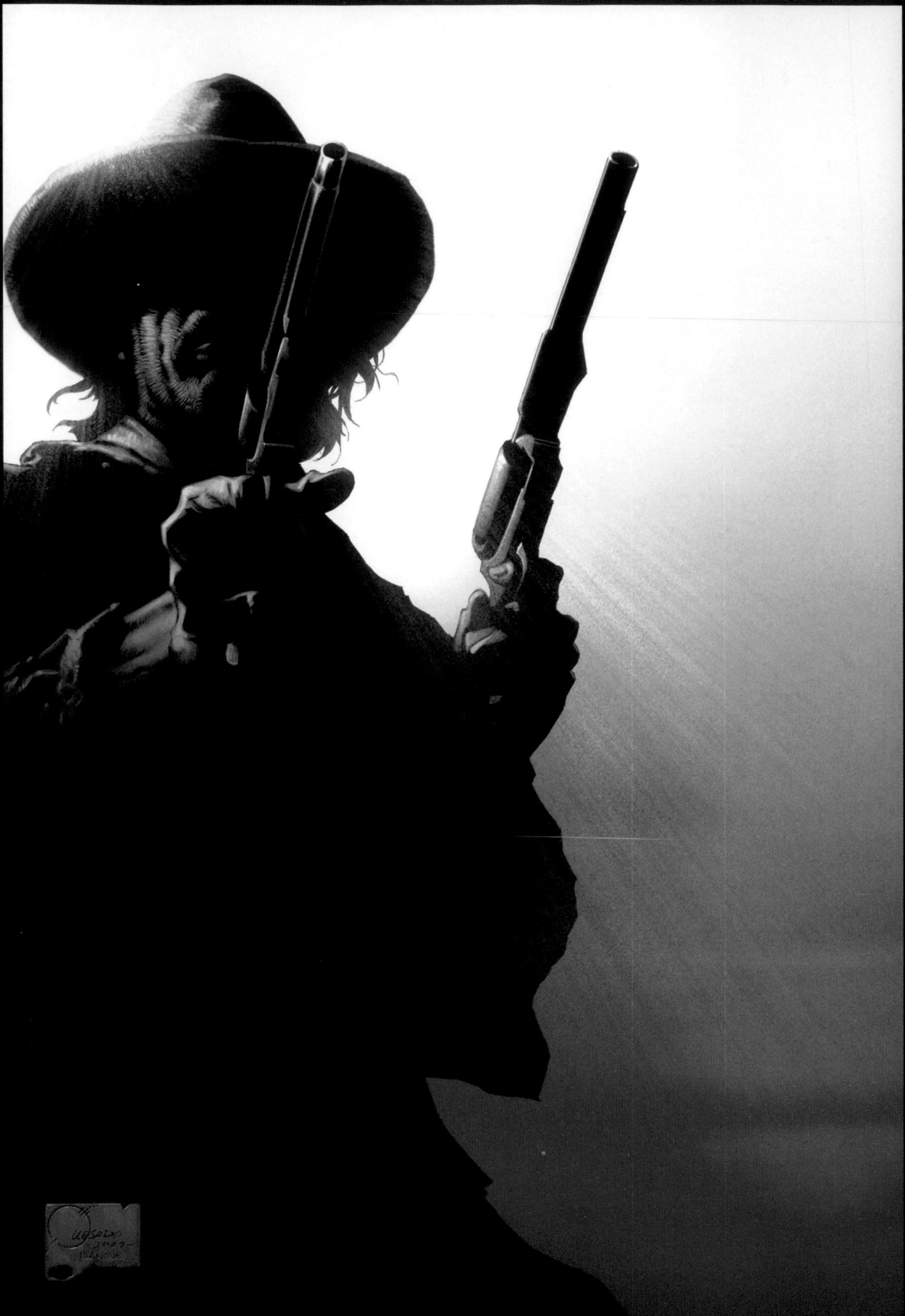

Cover to *Gunslinger Born #1 (2nd Printing)* by **Joe Quesada** & **Richard Isanove**

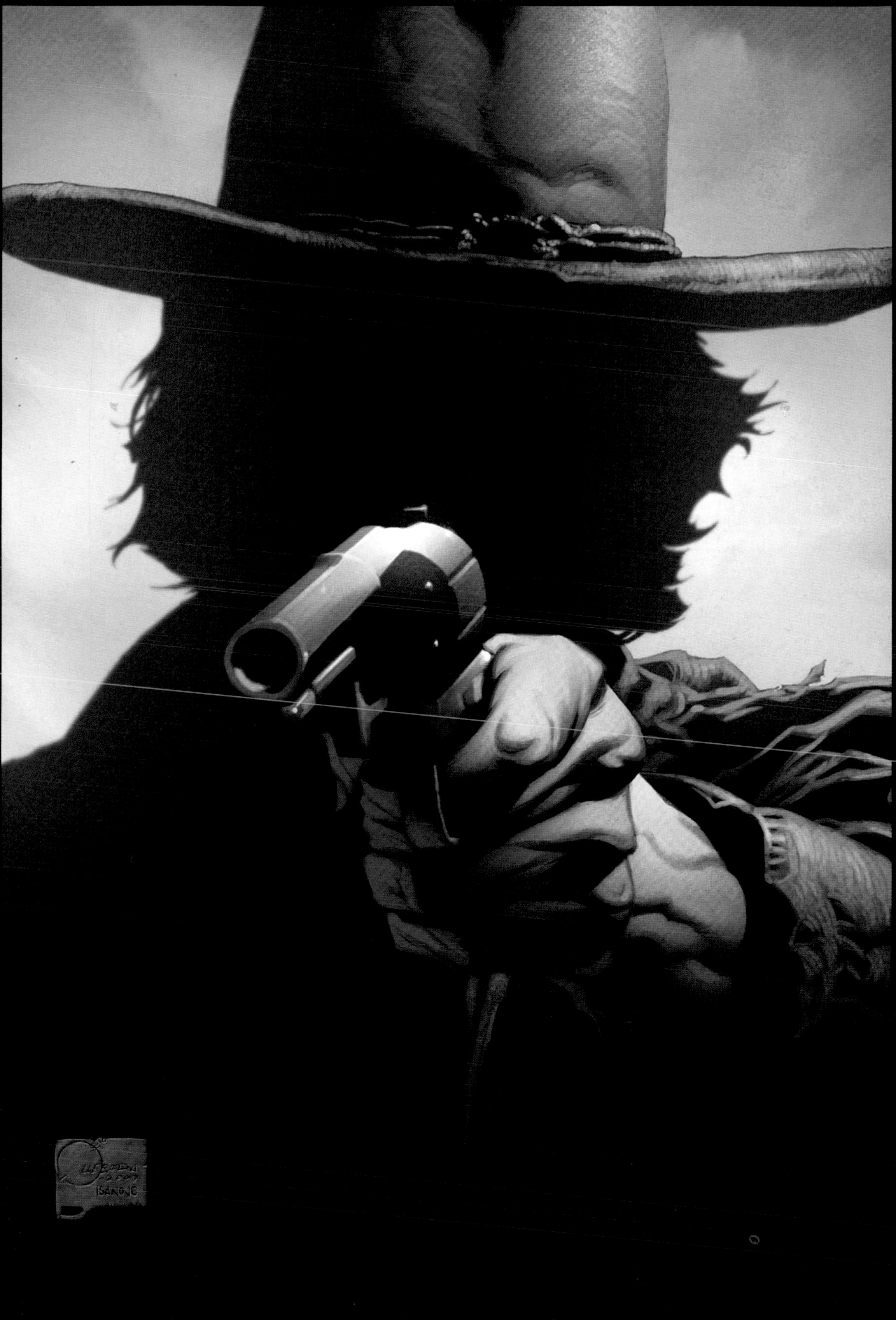

Cover to *Gunslinger Born* #2 by **Jae Lee** & **Richard Isanove**

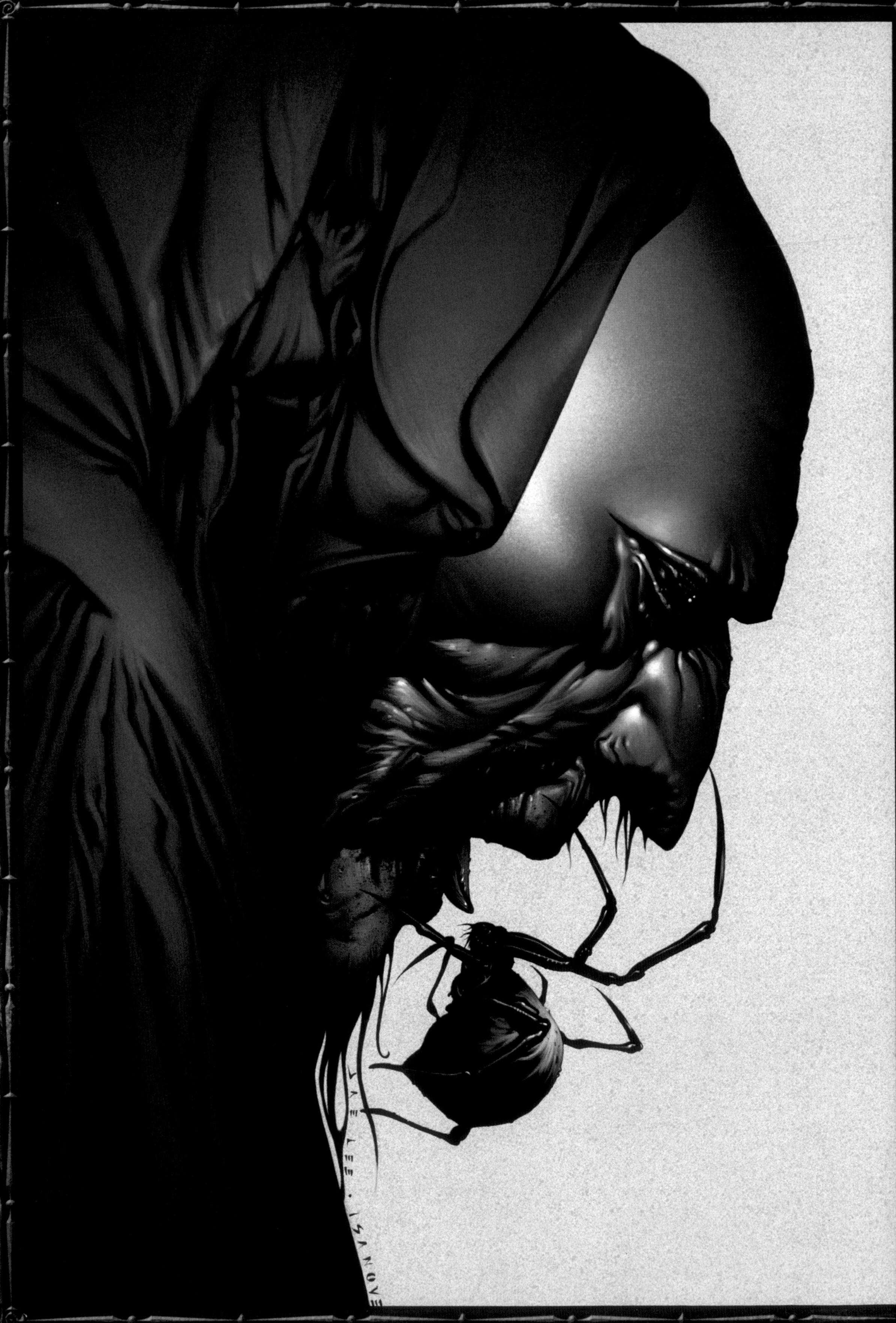
JAE LEE · ISANOVE

Sketch Variant Cover to *Gunslinger Born* #2 by **Jae Lee**

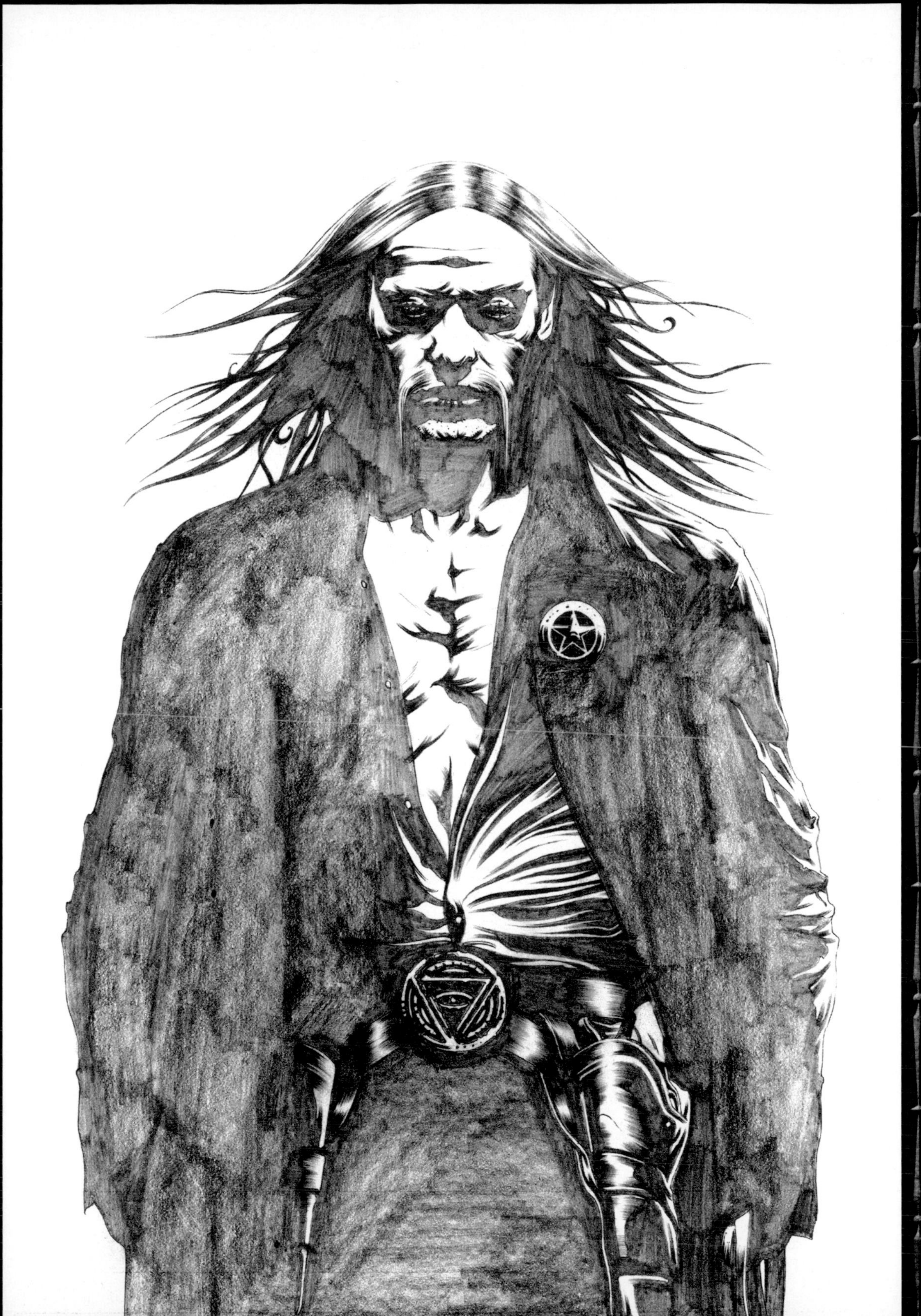

Variant Cover to *Gunslinger Born* #2 by **David Finch**, **Danny Miki** & **Paul Mounts**

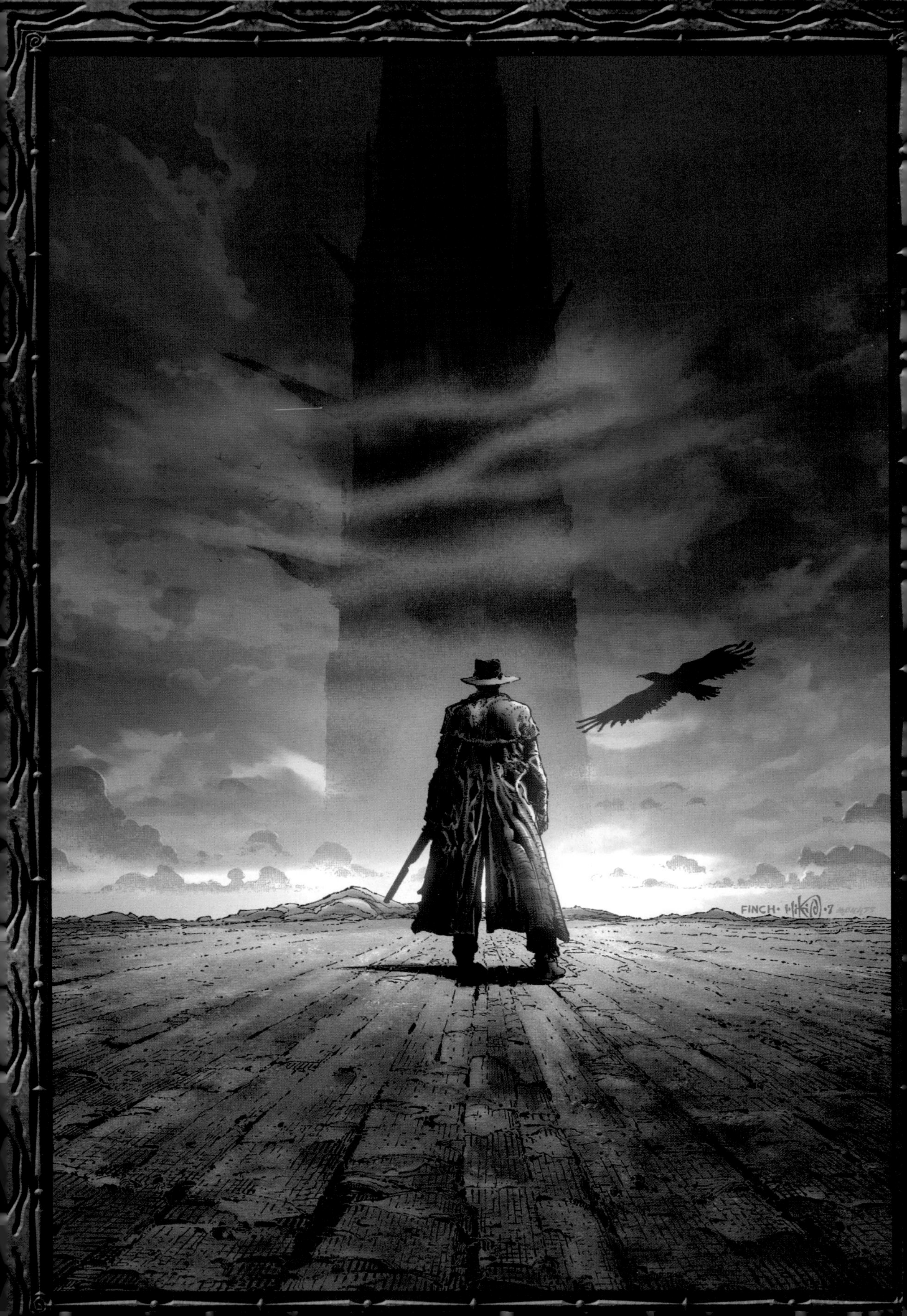
FINCH

Cover to *Gunslinger Born #2 (2nd Printing)* by **Stuart Immonen**

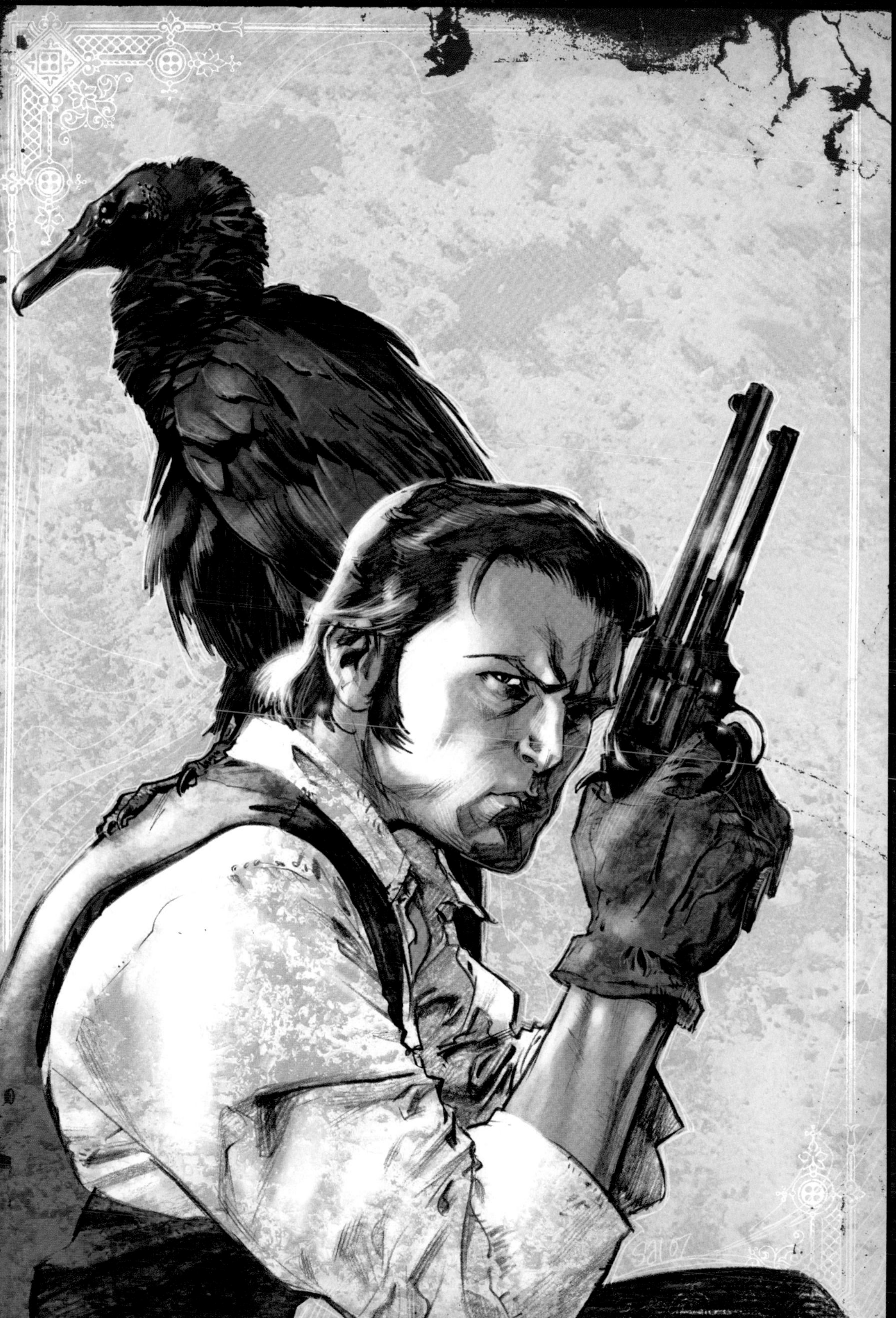

SGI 07

Cover to *Gunslinger Born* #3 by **Jae Lee** & **Richard Isanove**

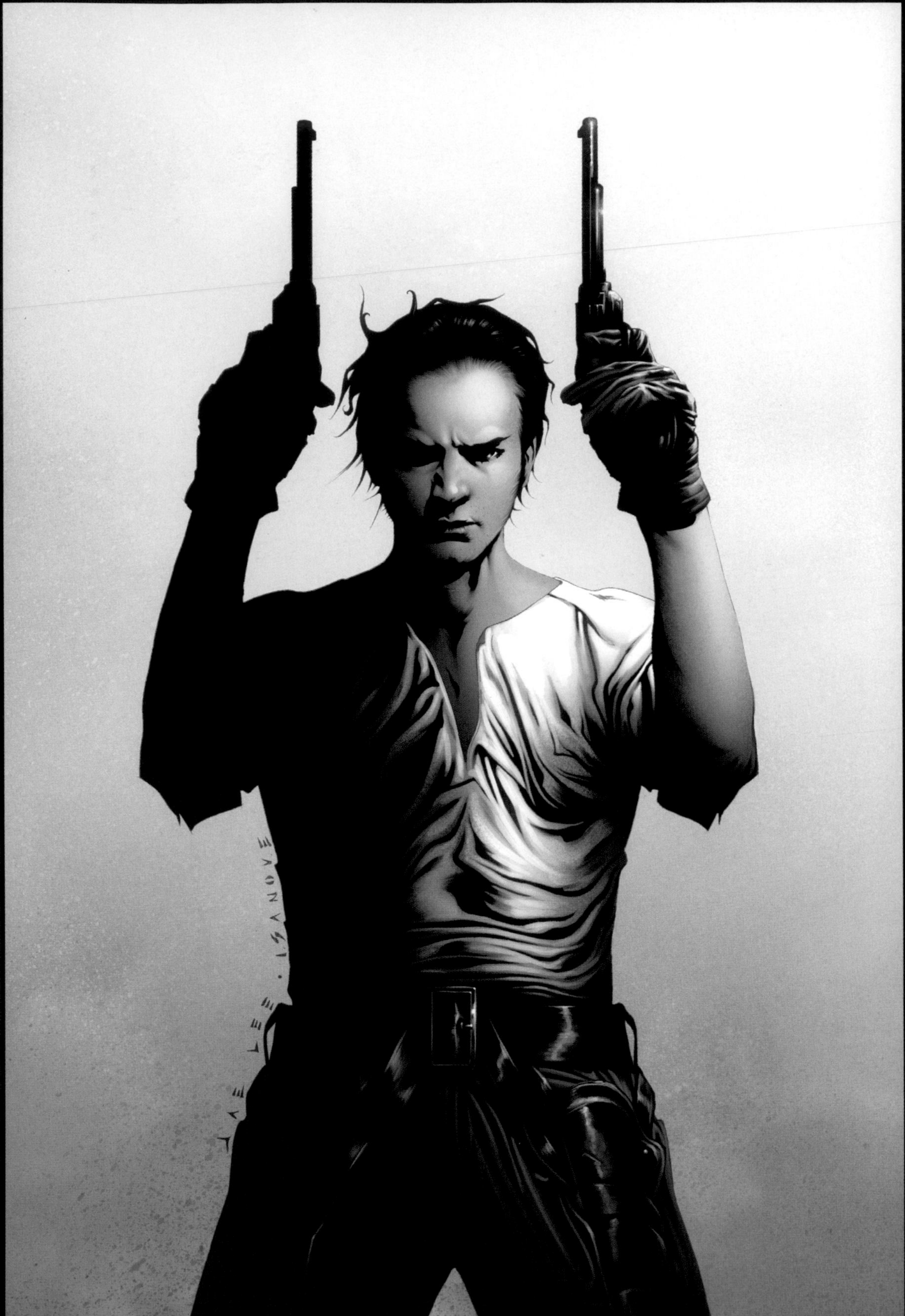
JAE LEE · ISANOVE

Sketch Variant Cover to *Gunslinger Born* #3 by **Jae Lee**

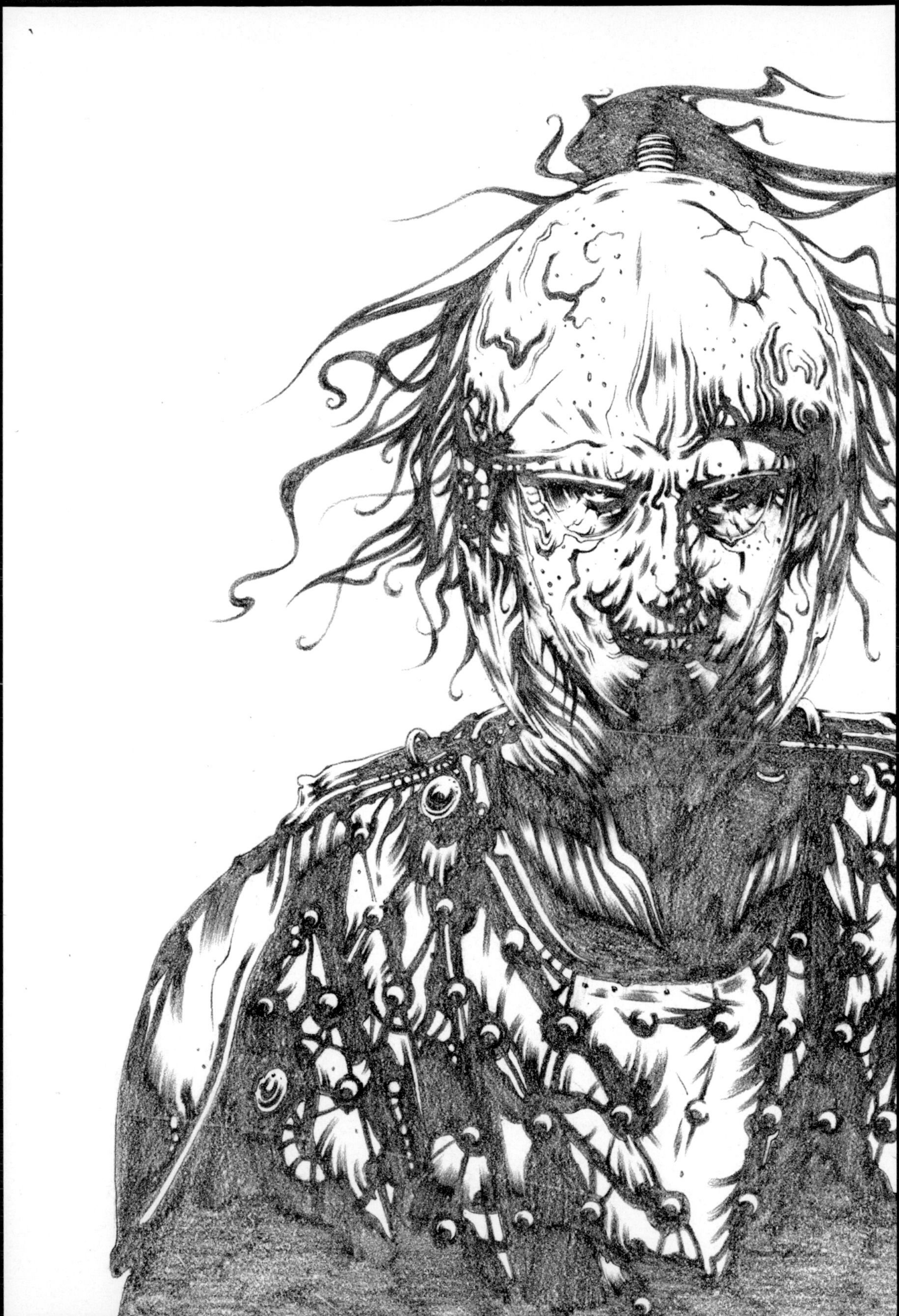

Variant Cover to *Gunslinger Born* #3 by **Leinil Francis Yu** & **Dave McCaig**

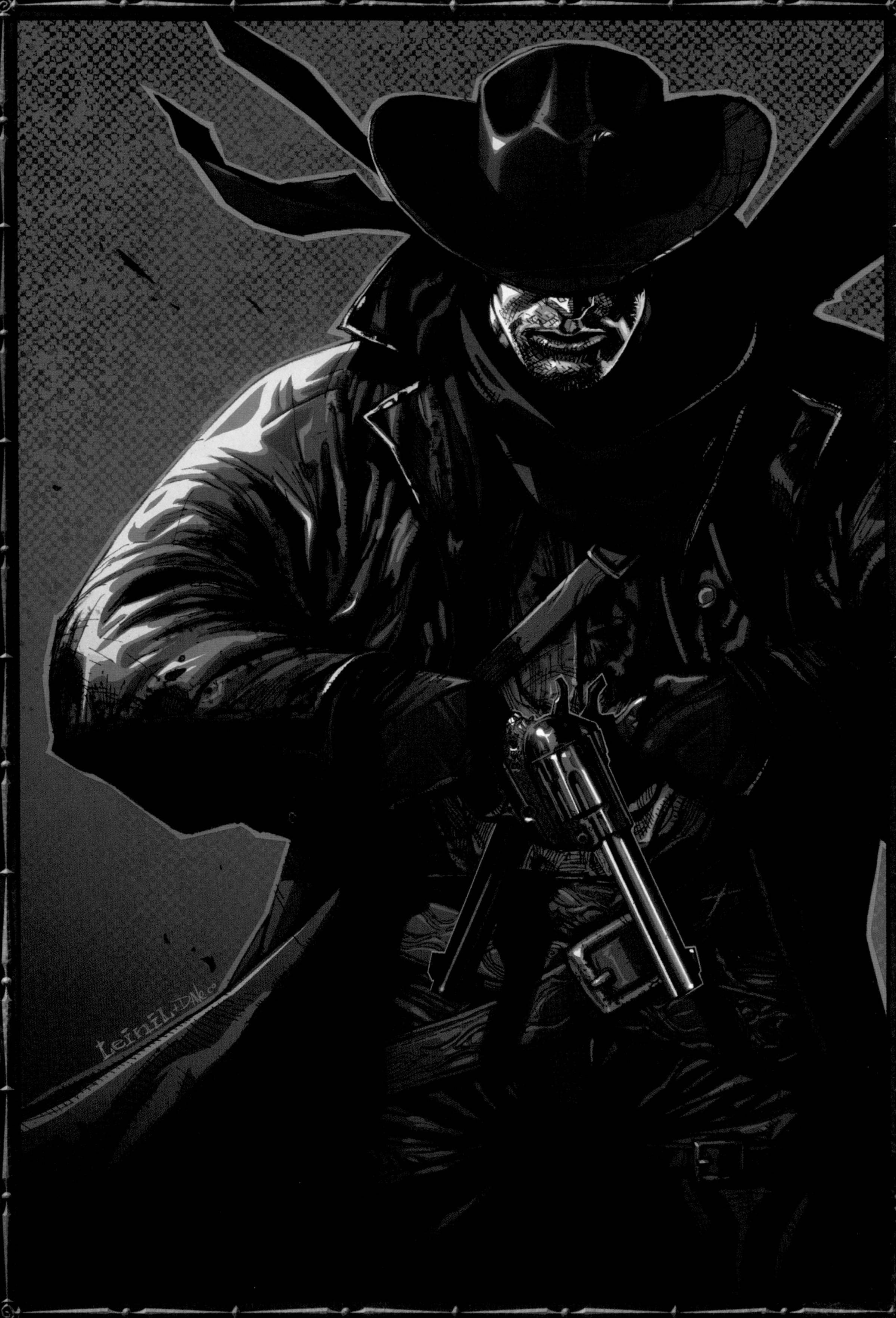

Cover to *Gunslinger Born #3 (2nd Printing)* by **John Romita Jr.**, **Klaus Janson** & **Jason Keith**

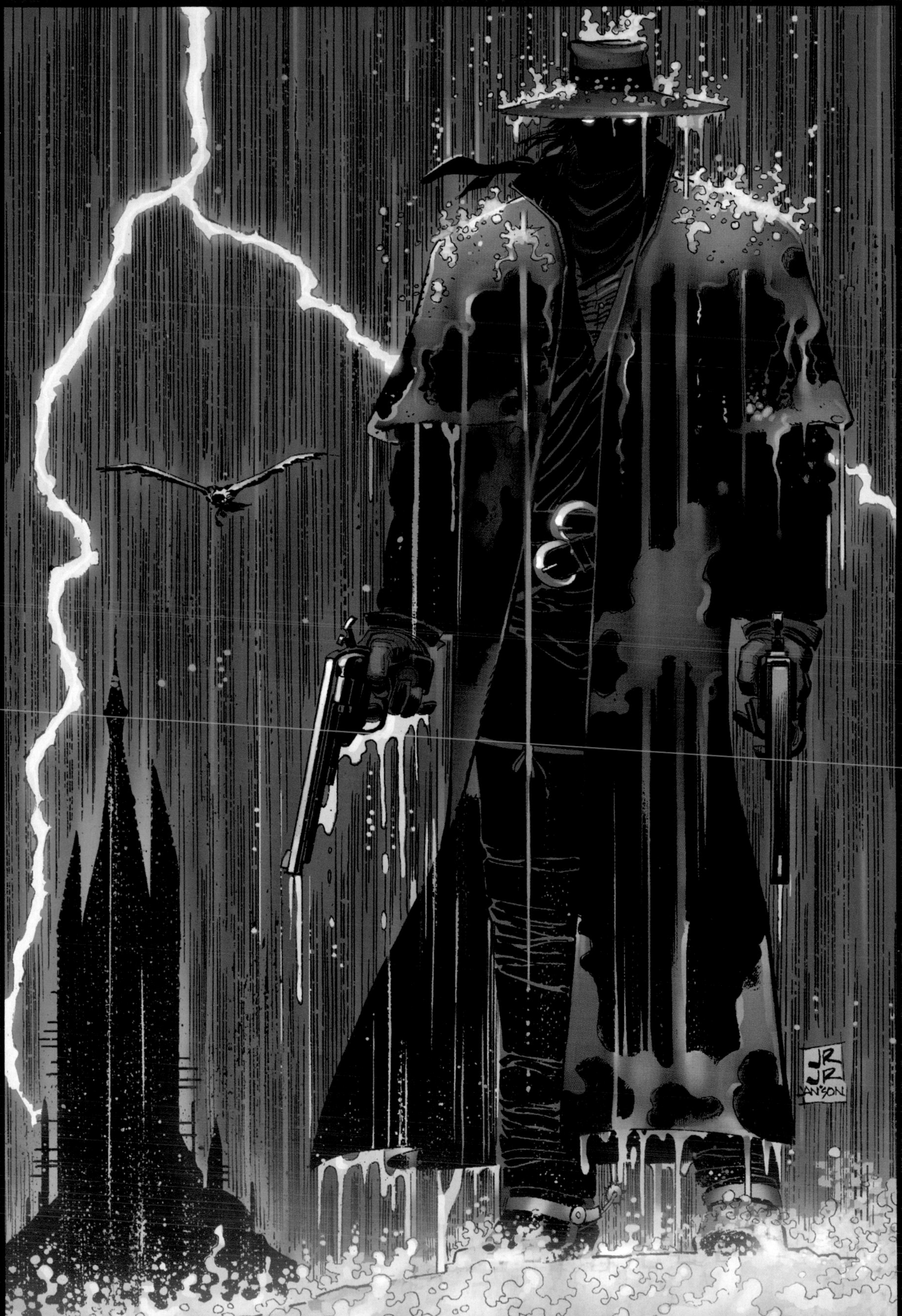
JR JR
JANSON

Cover to ***Gunslinger Born* #4** by **Jae Lee** & **Richard Isanove**

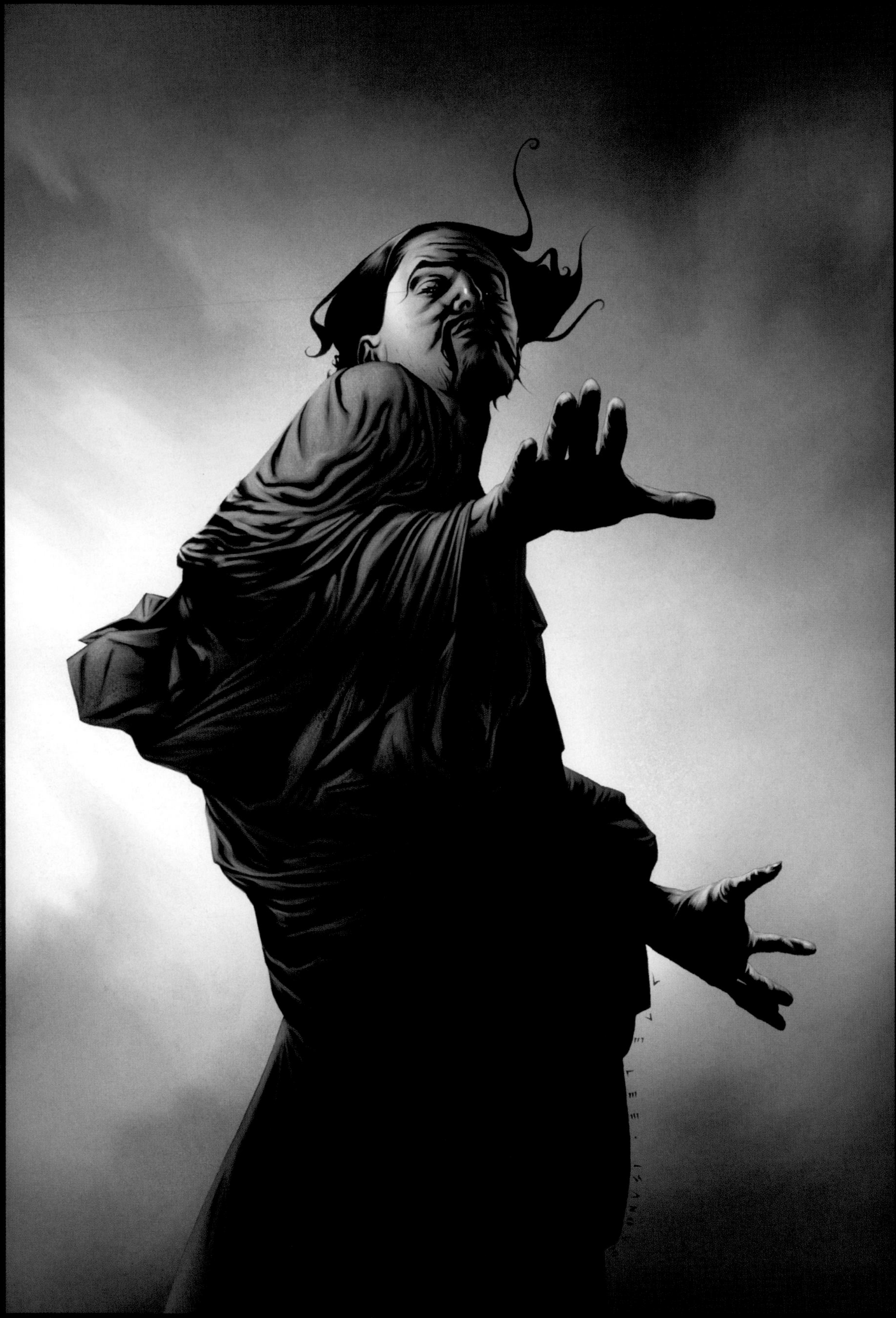

Sketch Variant Cover to *Gunslinger Born* #4 by **Jae Lee**

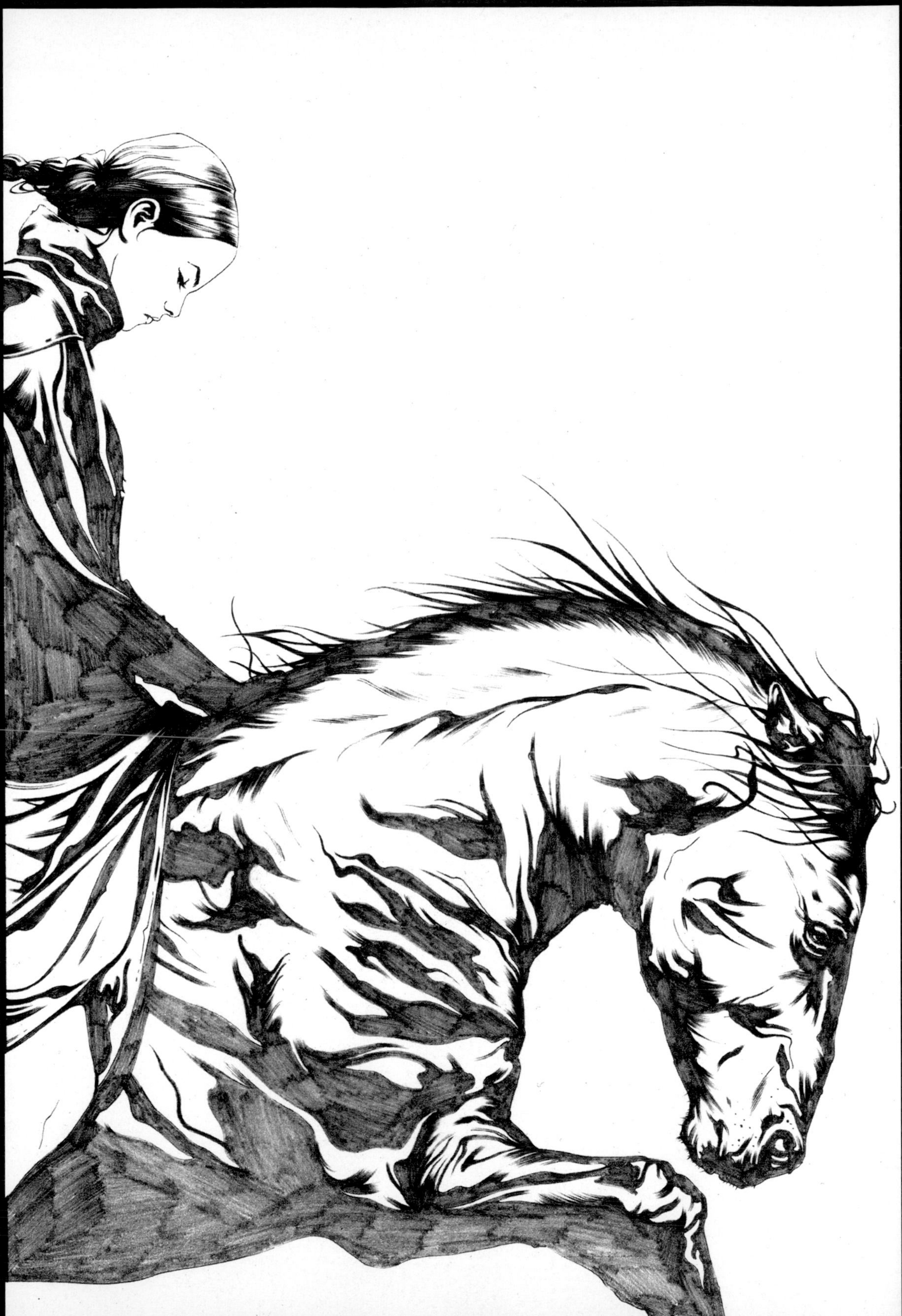

Variant Cover to *Gunslinger Born* #4 by **Steve McNiven** & **Morry Hollowell**

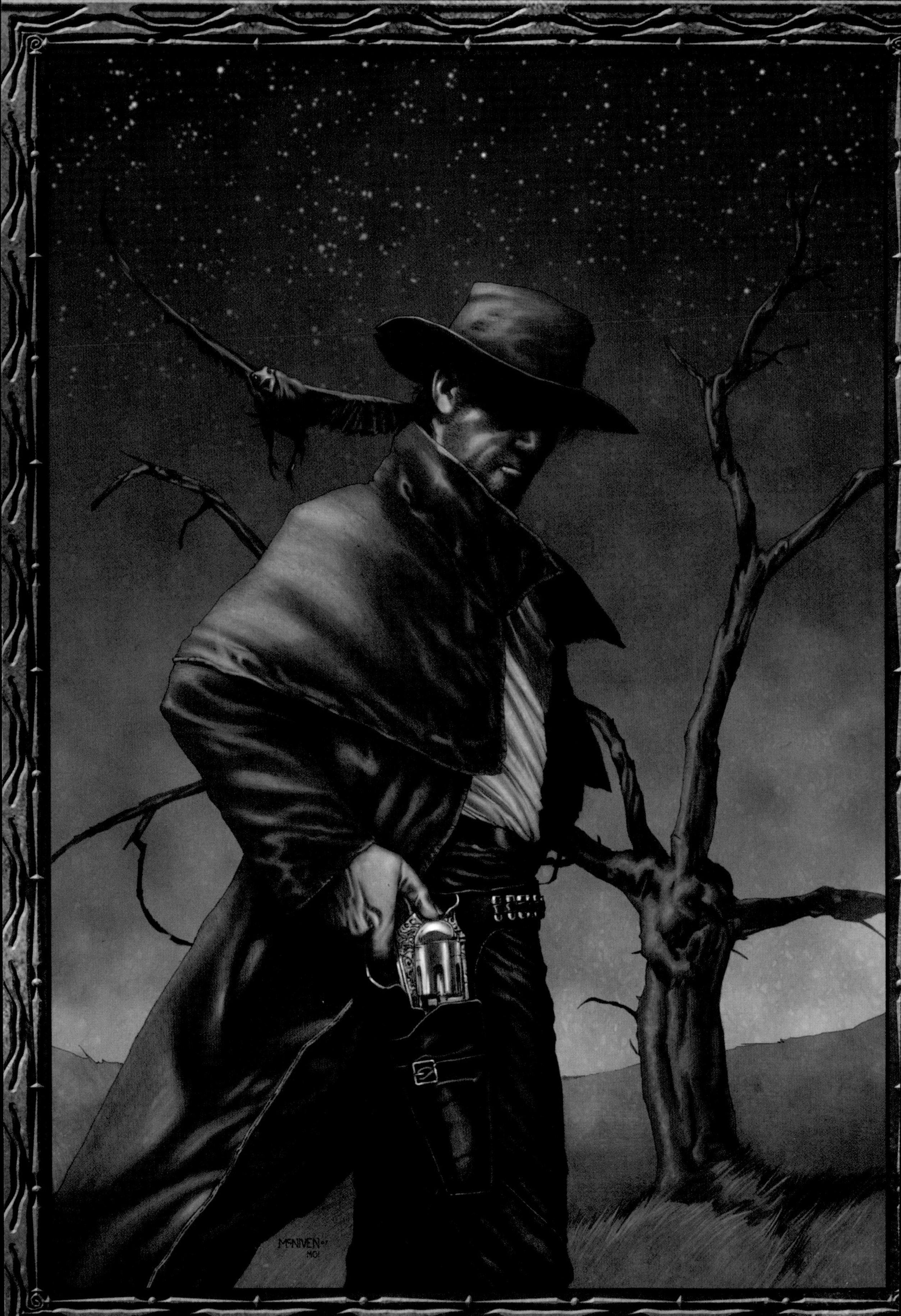

Cover to *Gunslinger Born #4 (2nd Printing)* by **Billy Tan** & **Dean White**

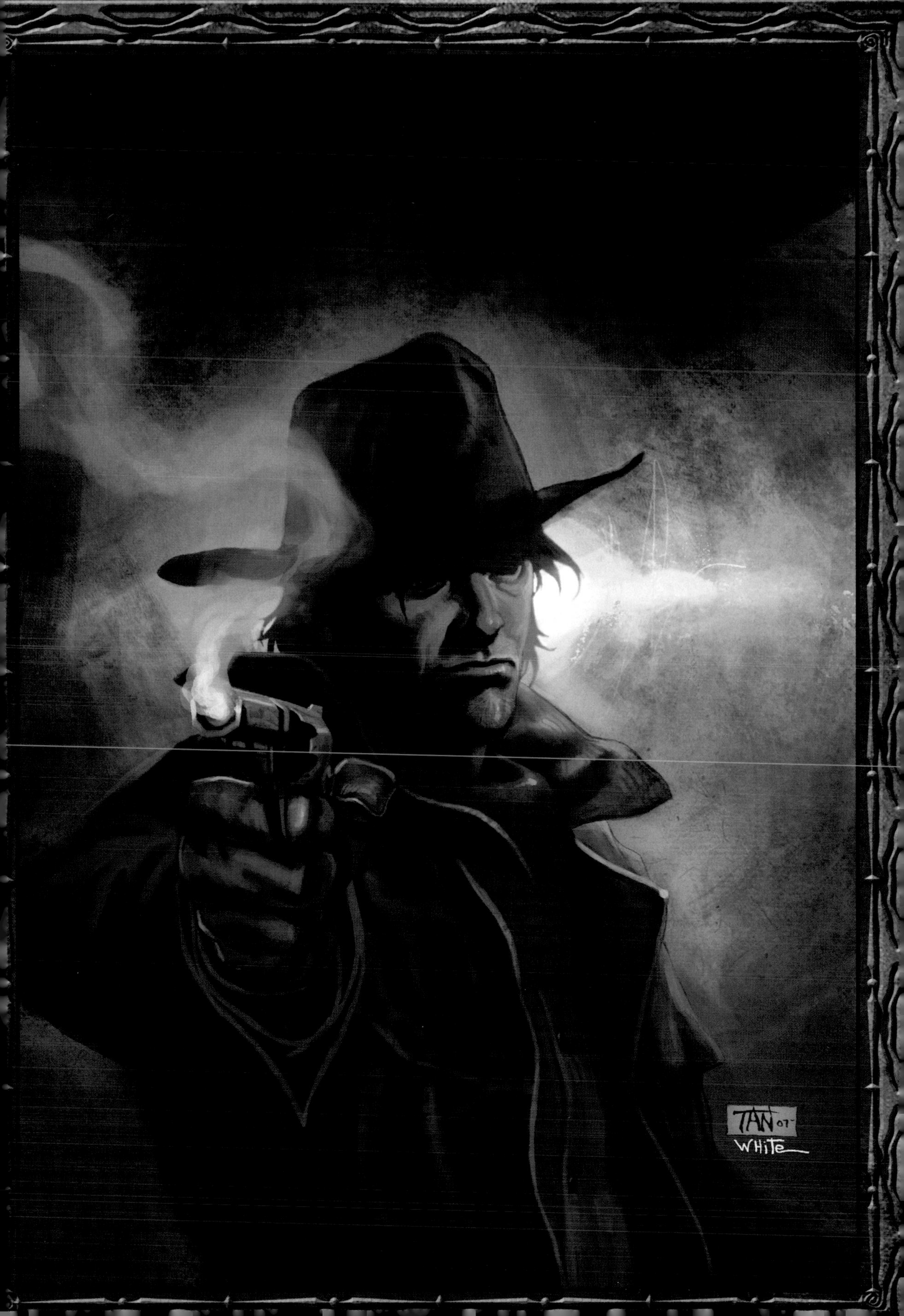
TAN 07
WHITE

Cover to *Gunslinger Born #5* by **Jae Lee** & **Richard Isanove**

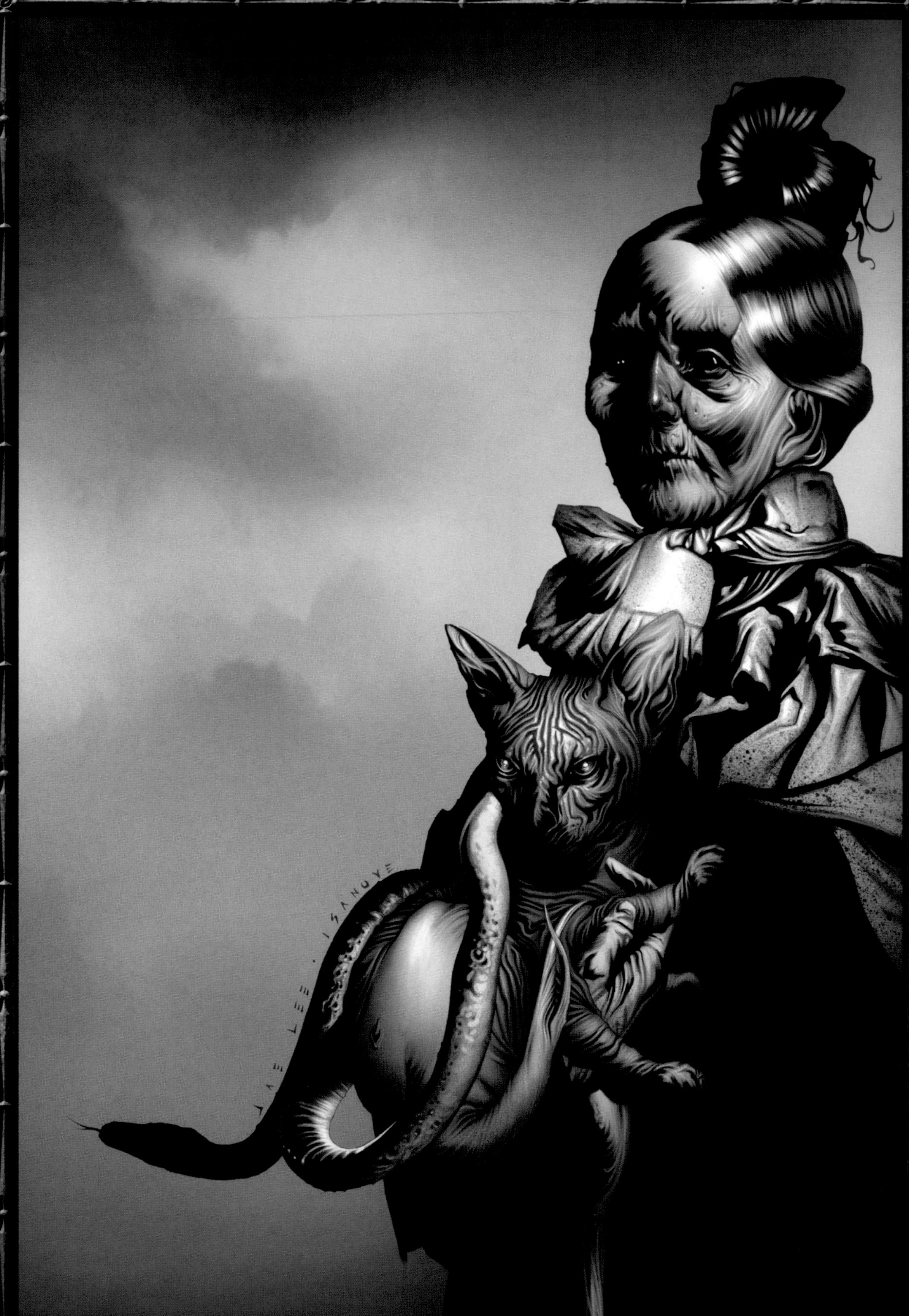
JAE LEE · ISANOVE

Sketch Variant Cover to *Gunslinger Born* #5 by **Jae Lee**

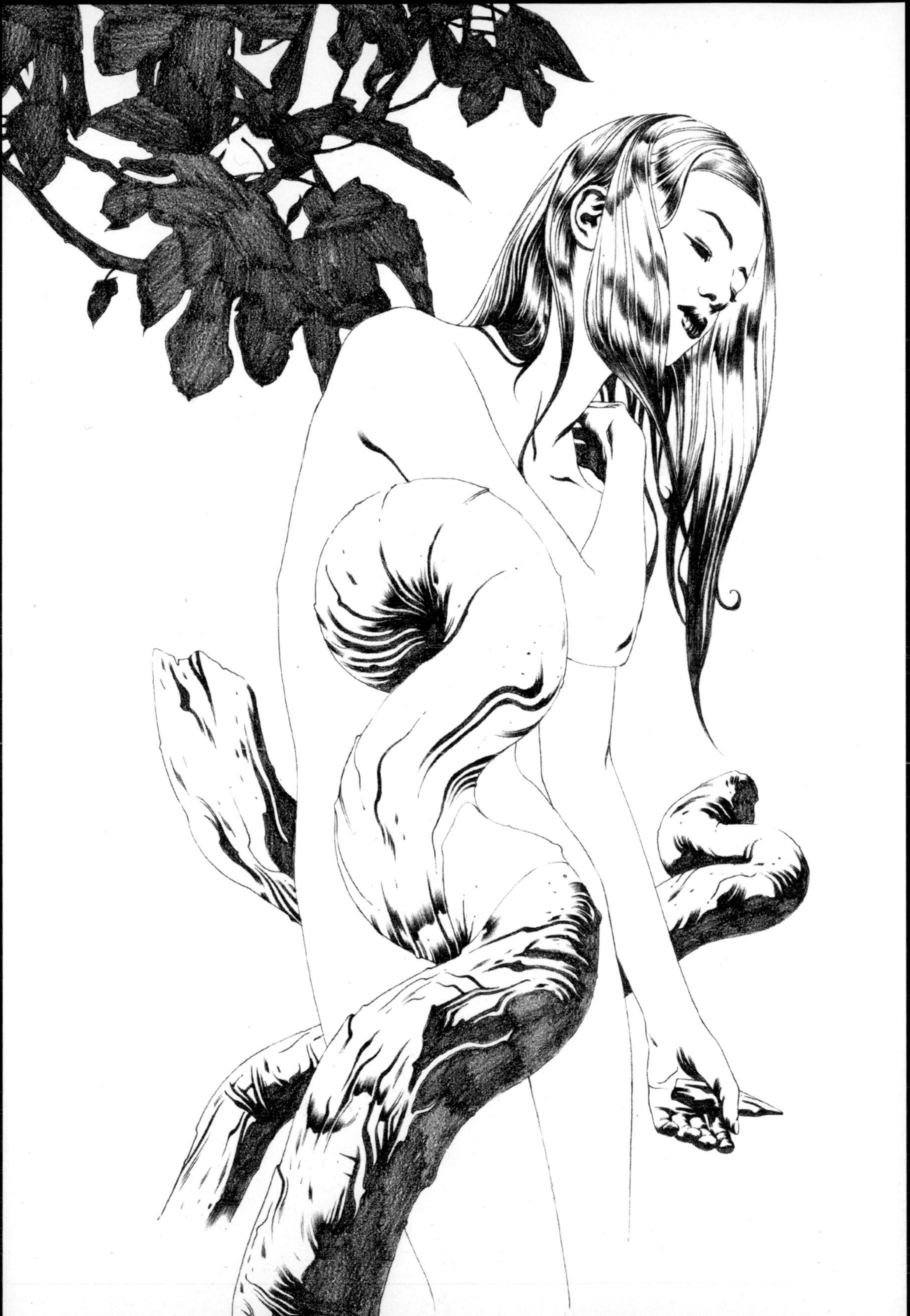

Variant Cover to *Gunslinger Born* #5 by **Greg Land**, **Jay Leisten** & **Justin Ponsor**

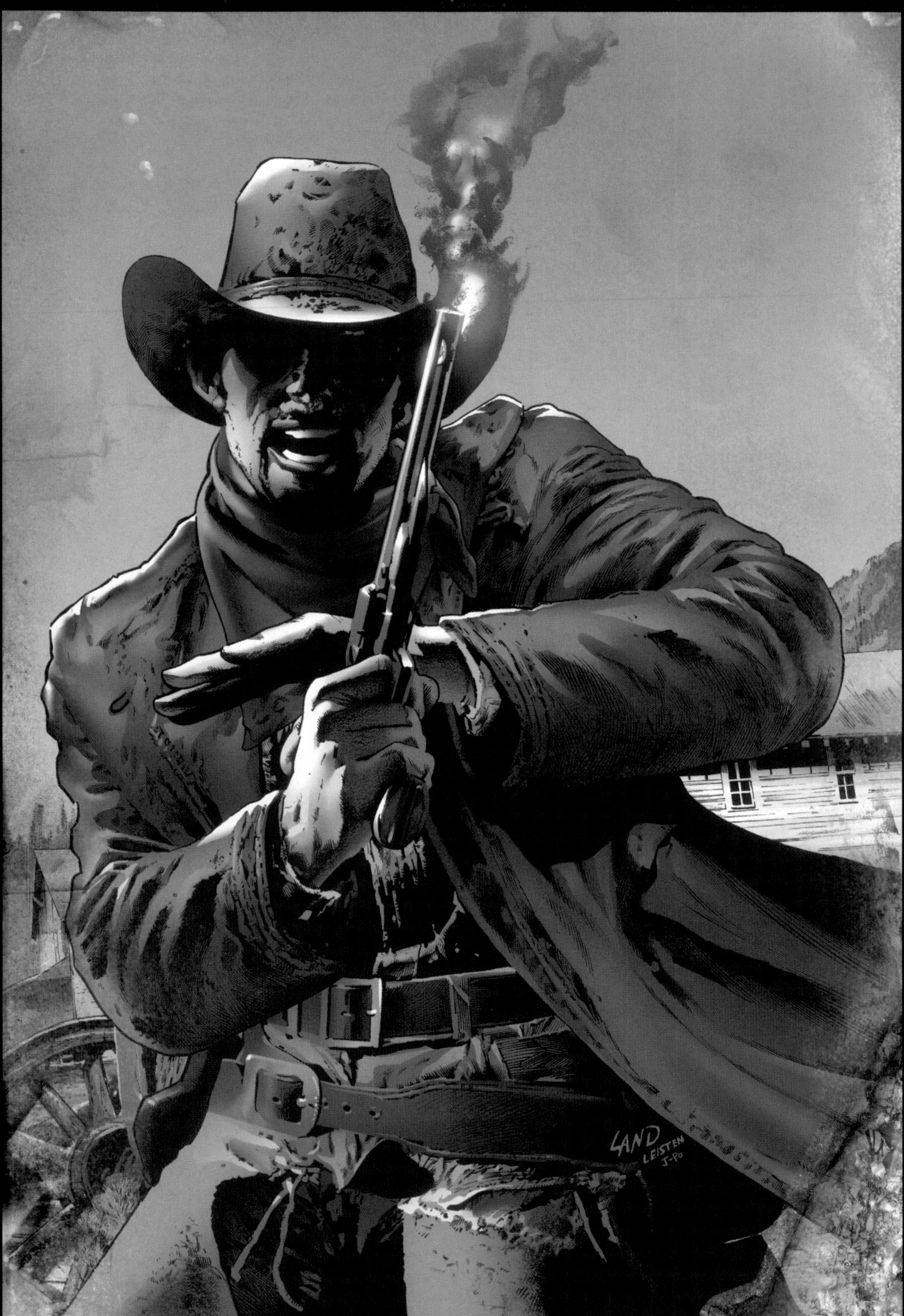
LAND
LEISTEN
J-Po

Variant Cover to *Gunslinger Born #6* by **J. Scott Campbell** & **Edgar Delgado**

Cover to *Gunslinger Born #6* by **Jae Lee** & **Richard Isanove**

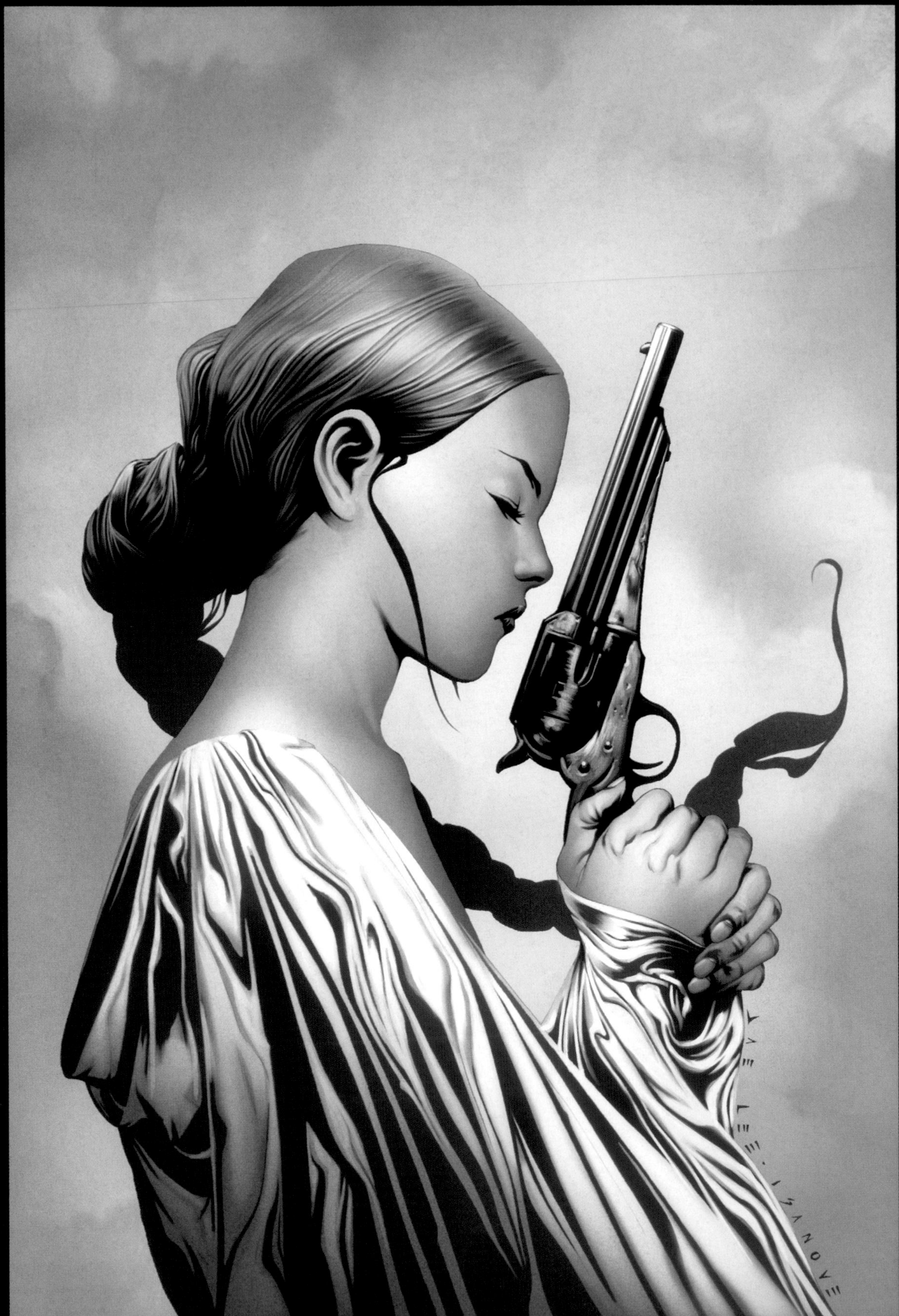
JAE LEE · ISANOVE

Sketch Variant Cover to *Gunslinger Born #6* by **Jae Lee**

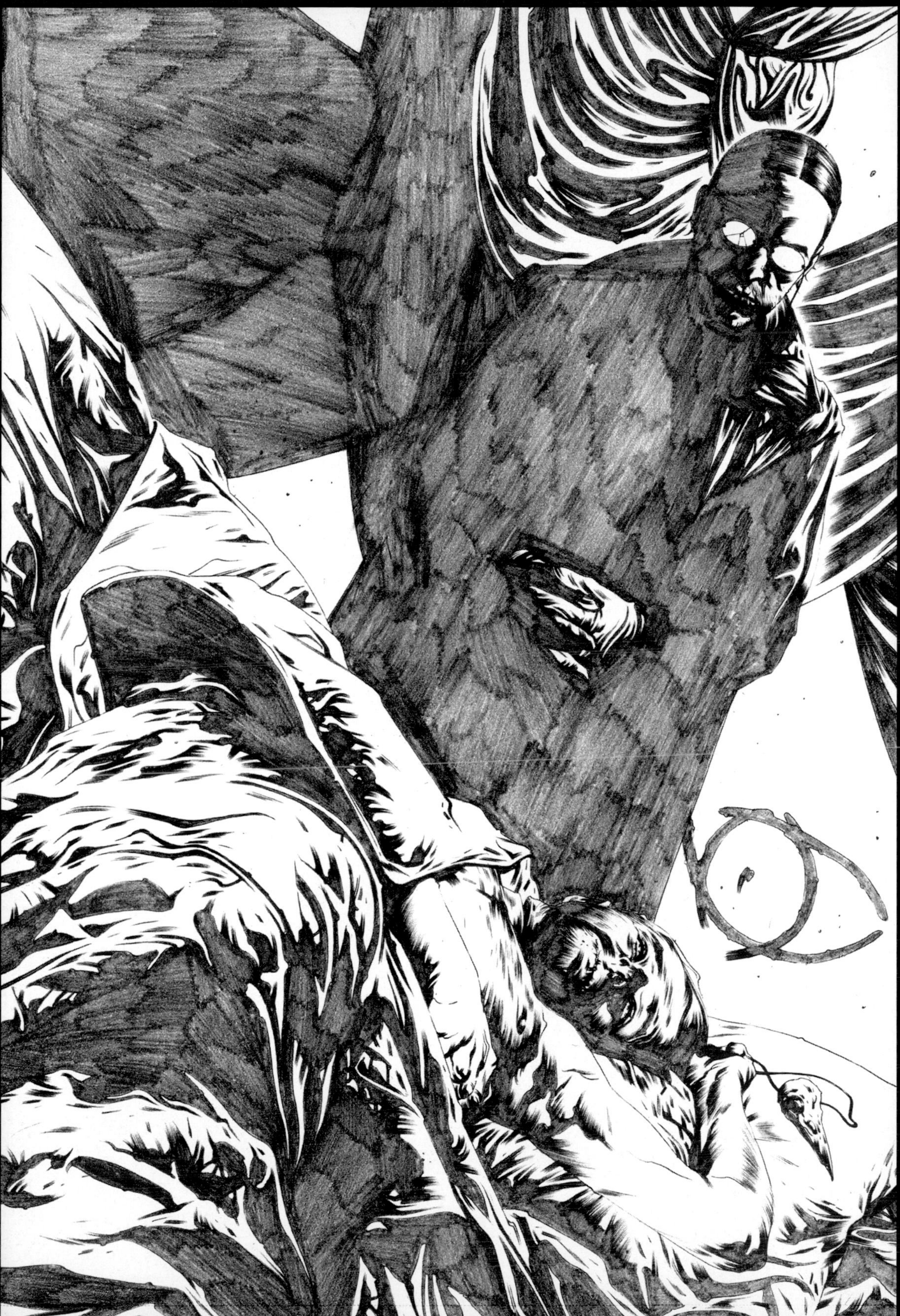

Cover to *Gunslinger Born* #7 by **Jae Lee** & **Richard Isanove**

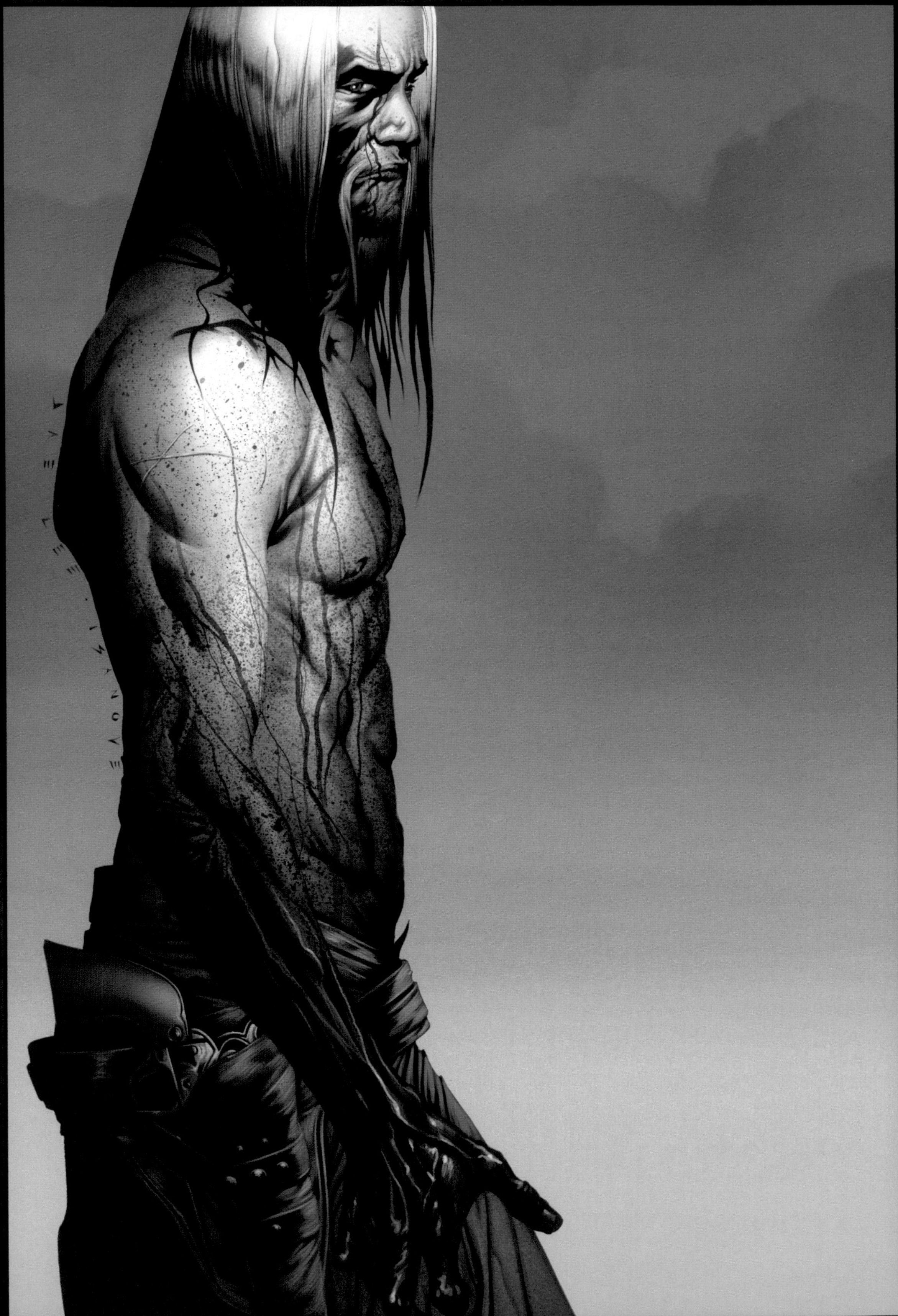

Sketch Variant Cover to *Gunslinger Born* #7 by **Jae Lee**

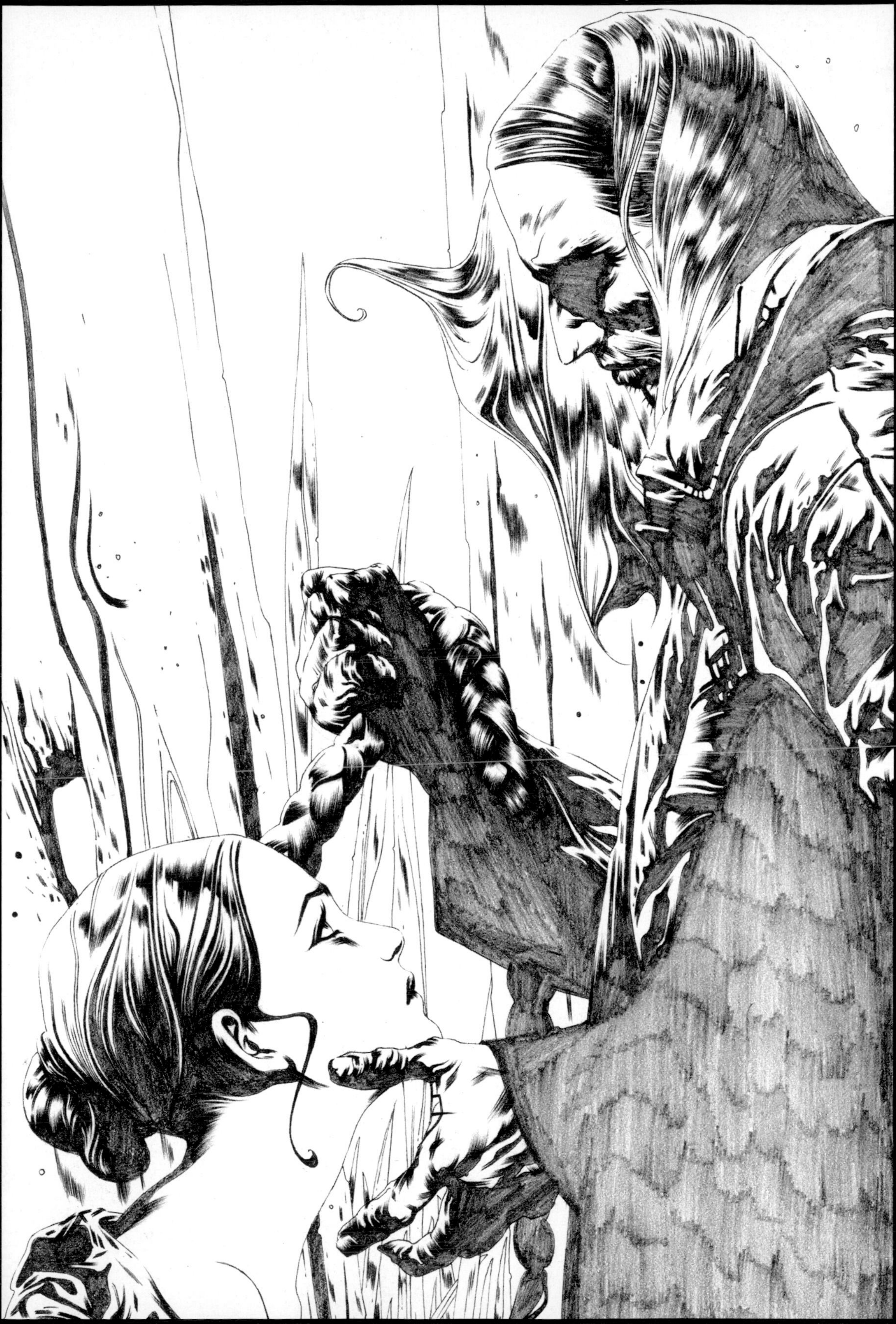

Variant Cover to *Gunslinger Born* #7 by **Olivier Coipel** & **Justin Ponsor**

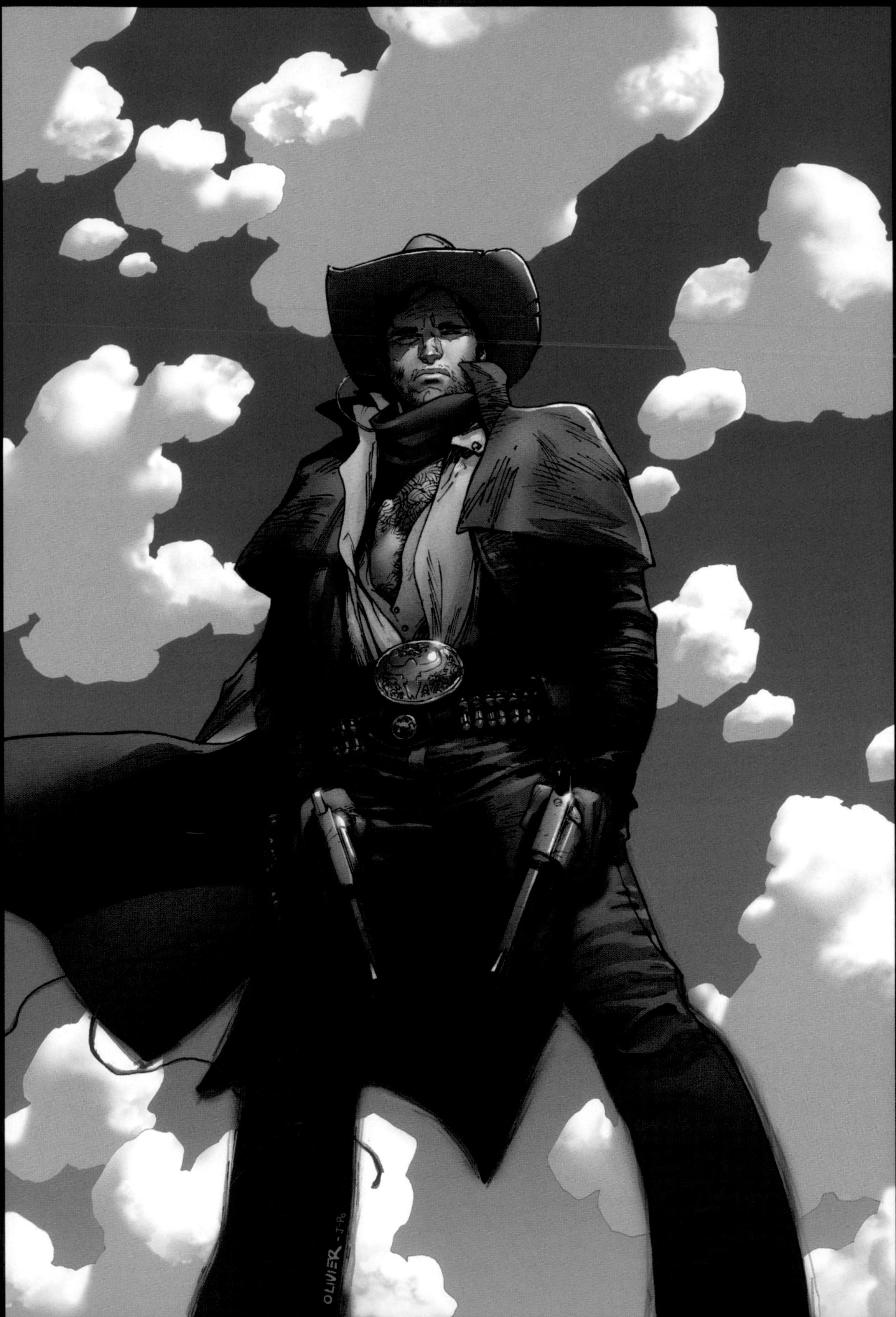

Character Sketches by **Jae Lee**

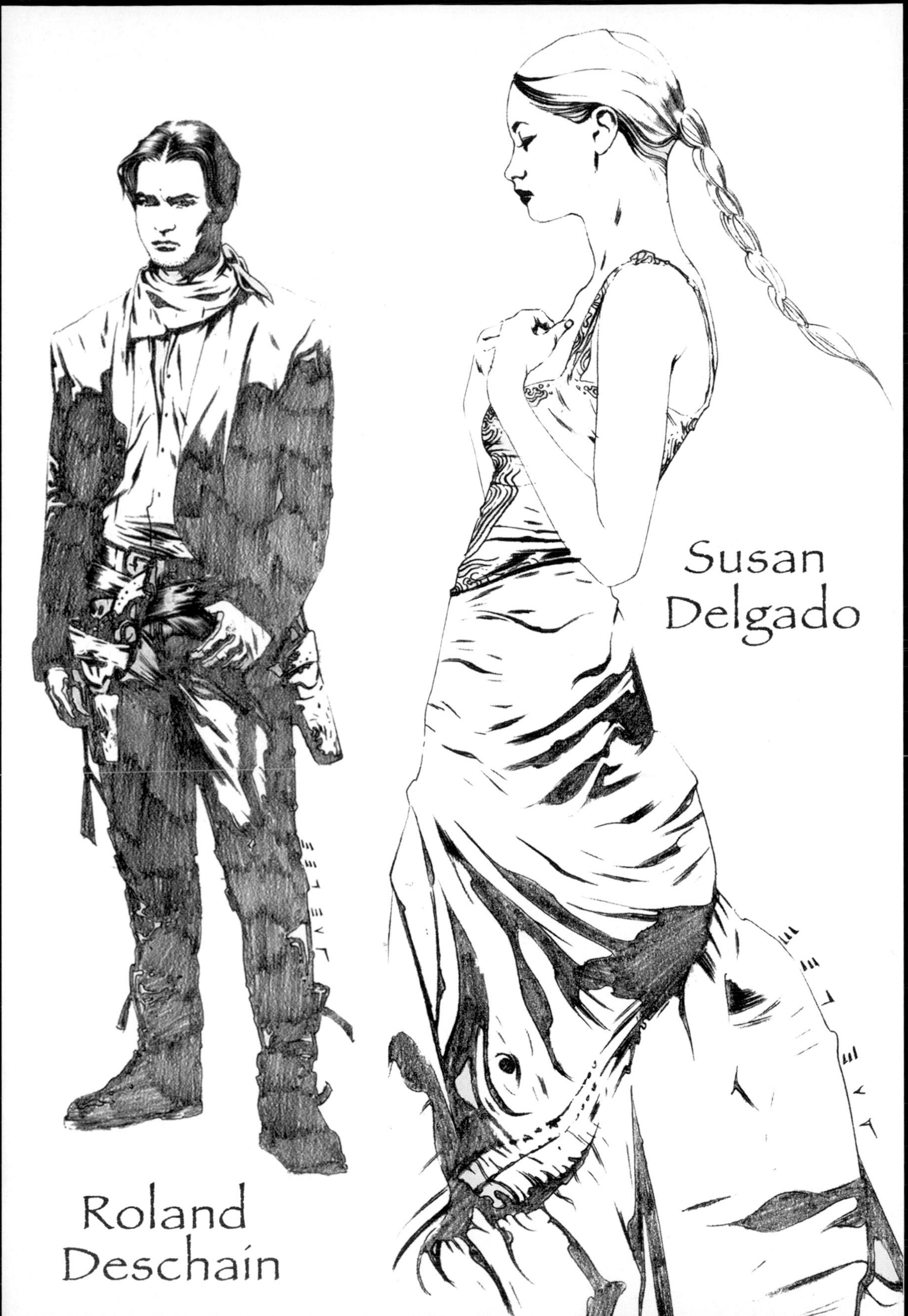
Susan
Delgado
Roland
Deschain

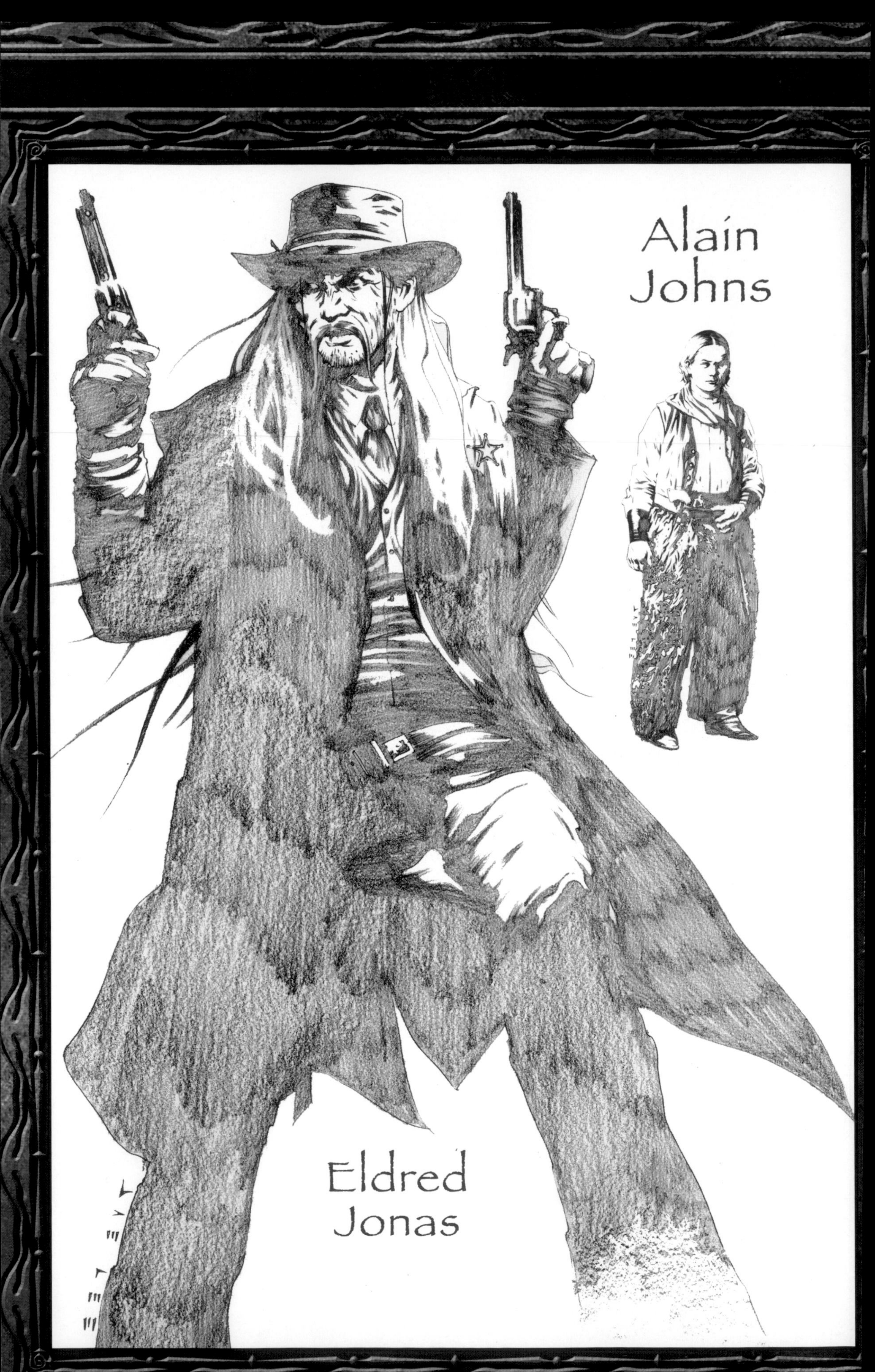
Alain
Johns
Eldred
Jonas

Gunslinger Born **#1**, Page 24 Pencils by **Jae Lee**

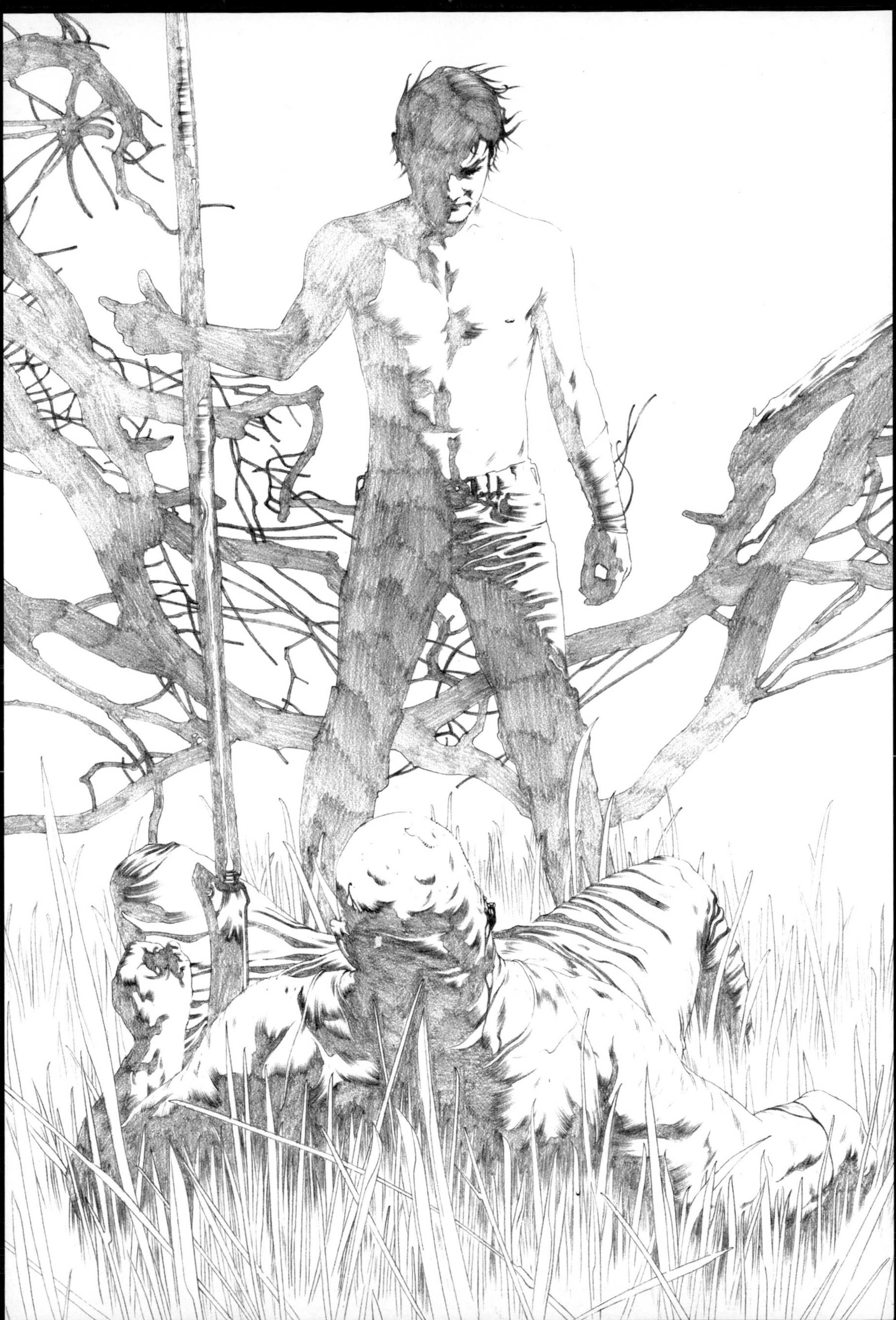

Gunslinger Born #2, Page 6 Pencils by **Jae Lee**

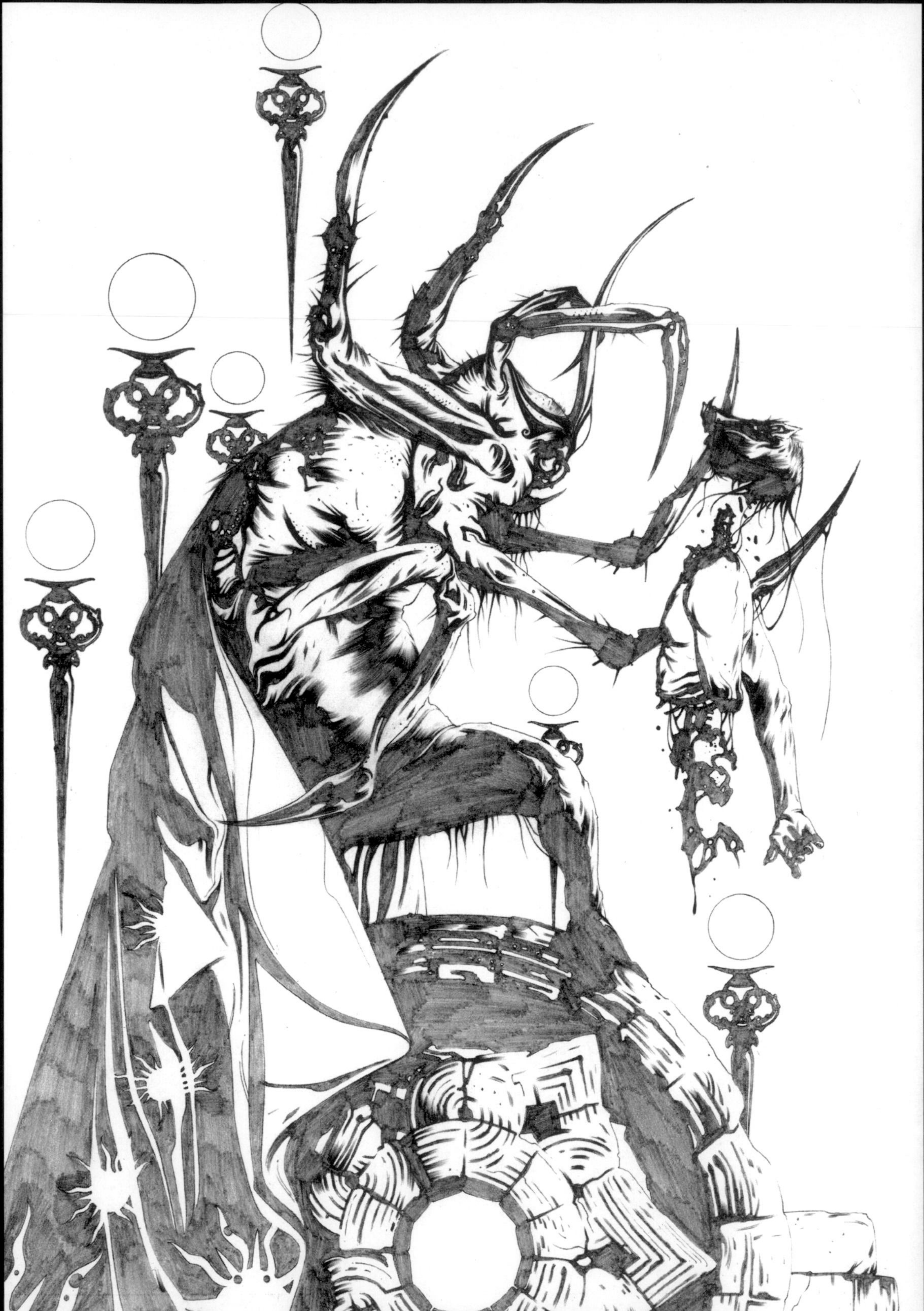

Gunslinger Born #2, Page 24 Pencils by **Jae Lee**

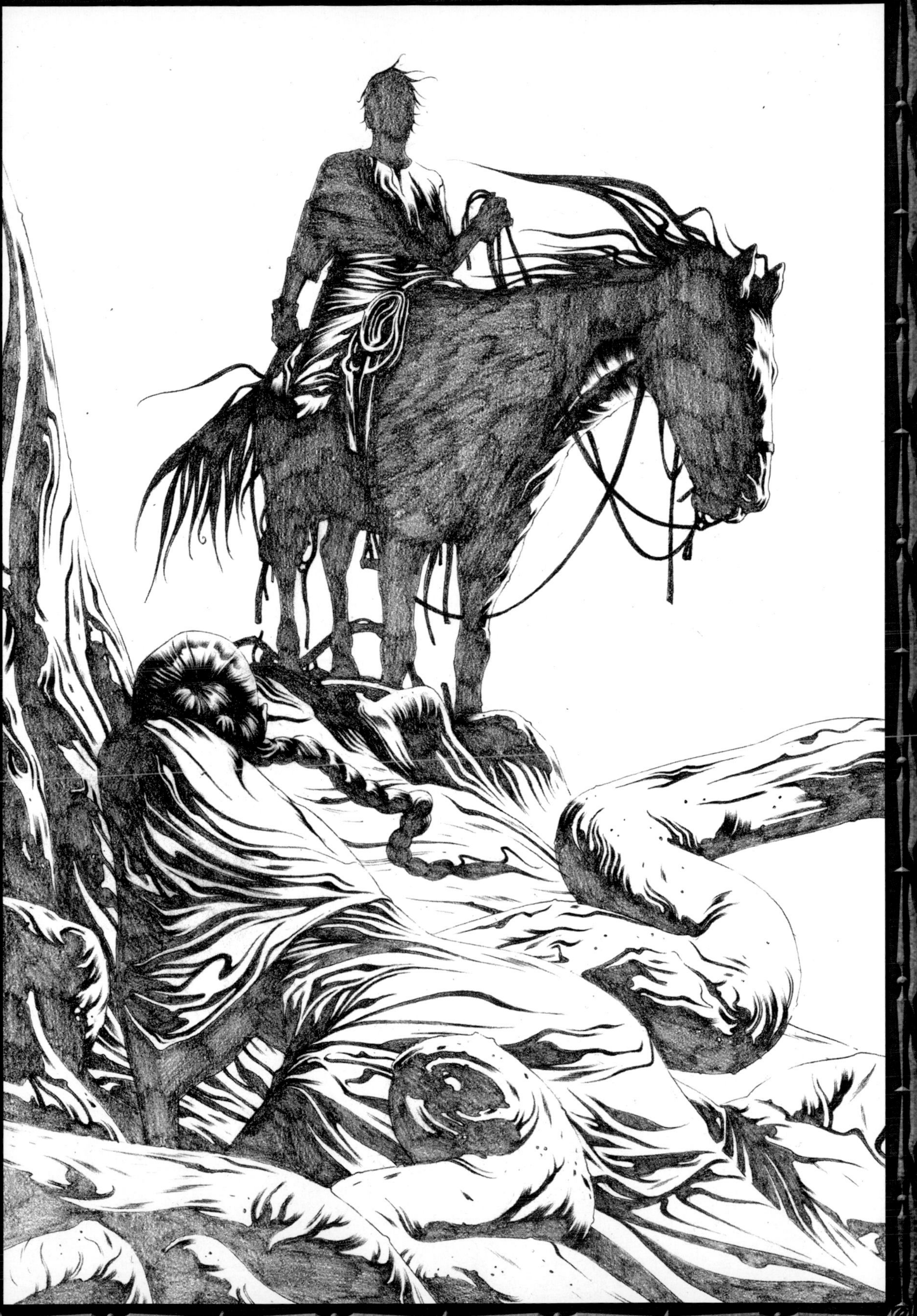

Unused Pencils to *Gunslinger Born* #3, Page 6 by **Jae Lee** with Initial John Farson Design

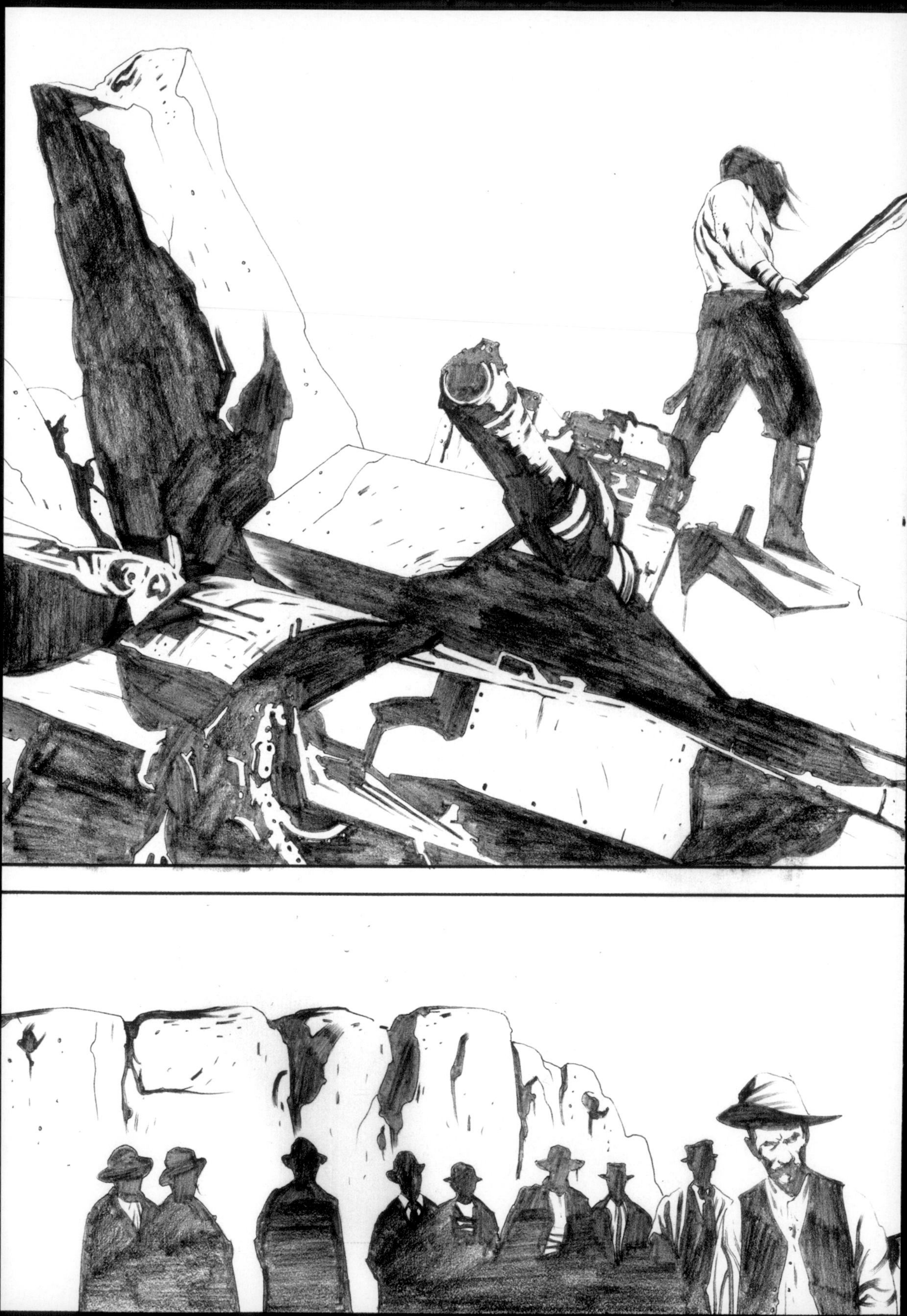

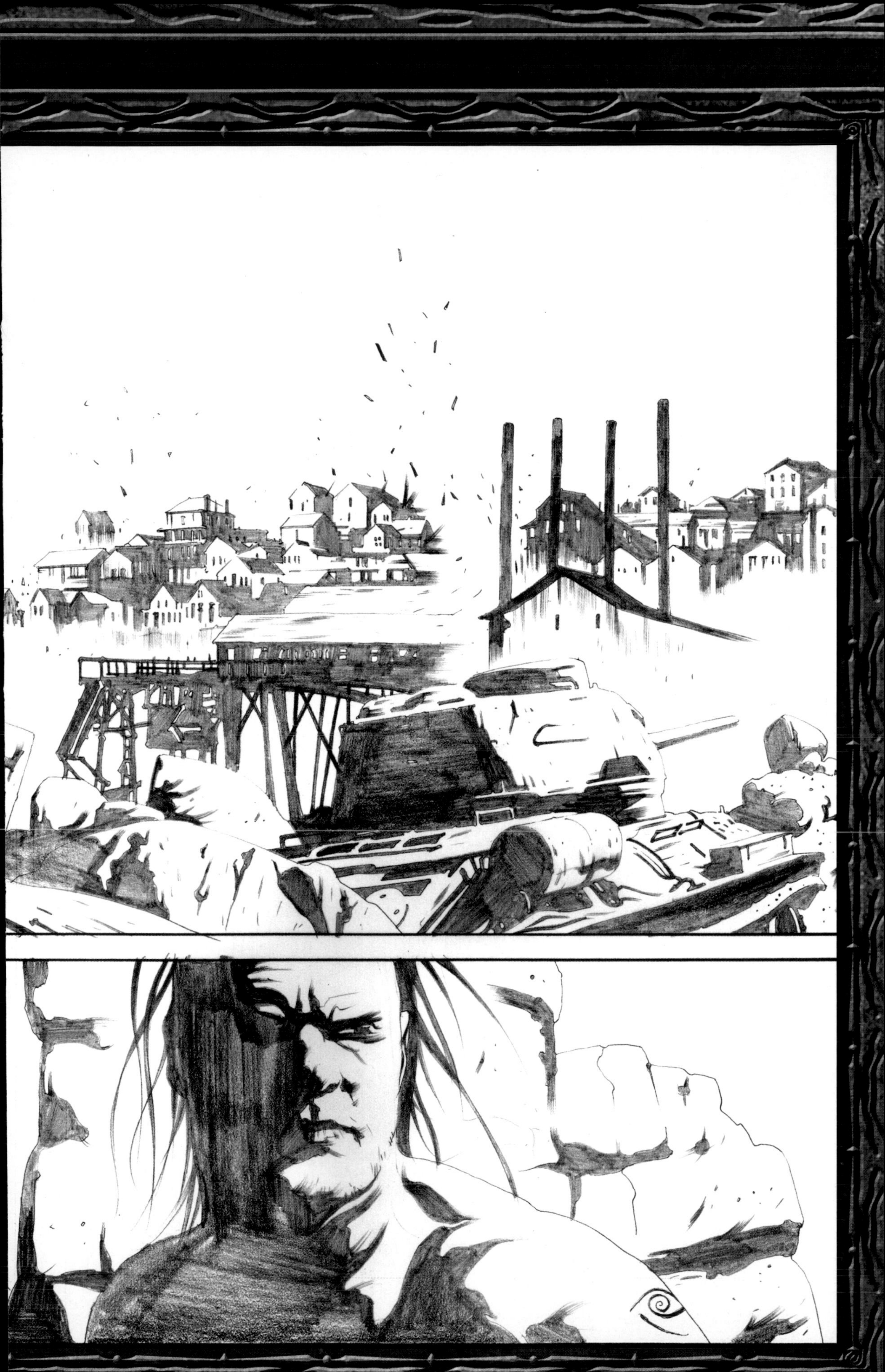

Gunslinger Born #3, Page 6 Pencils by **Jae Lee** with Final John Farson Design

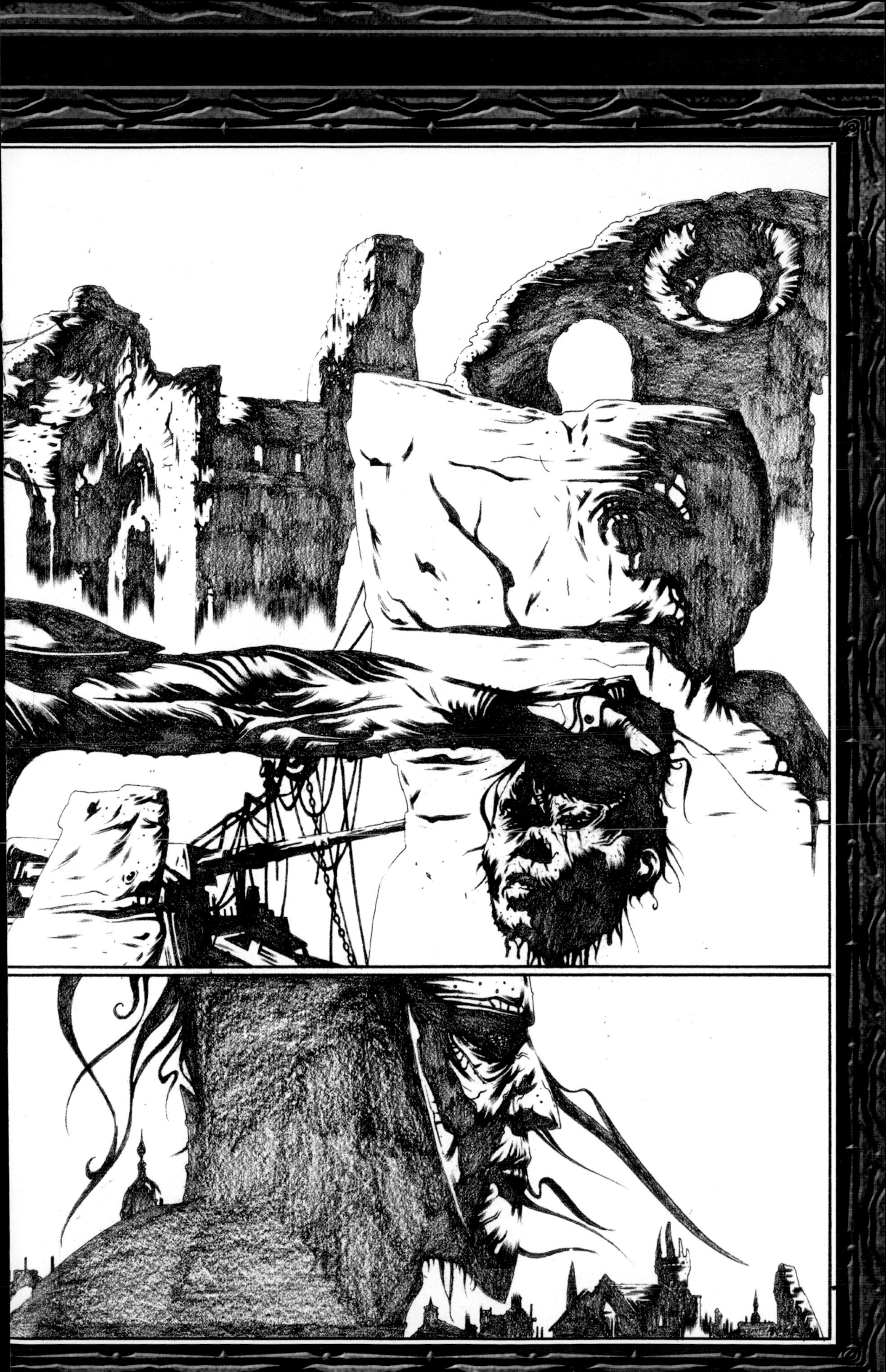

Gunslinger Born #7, Page 34 Pencils by **Jae Lee**

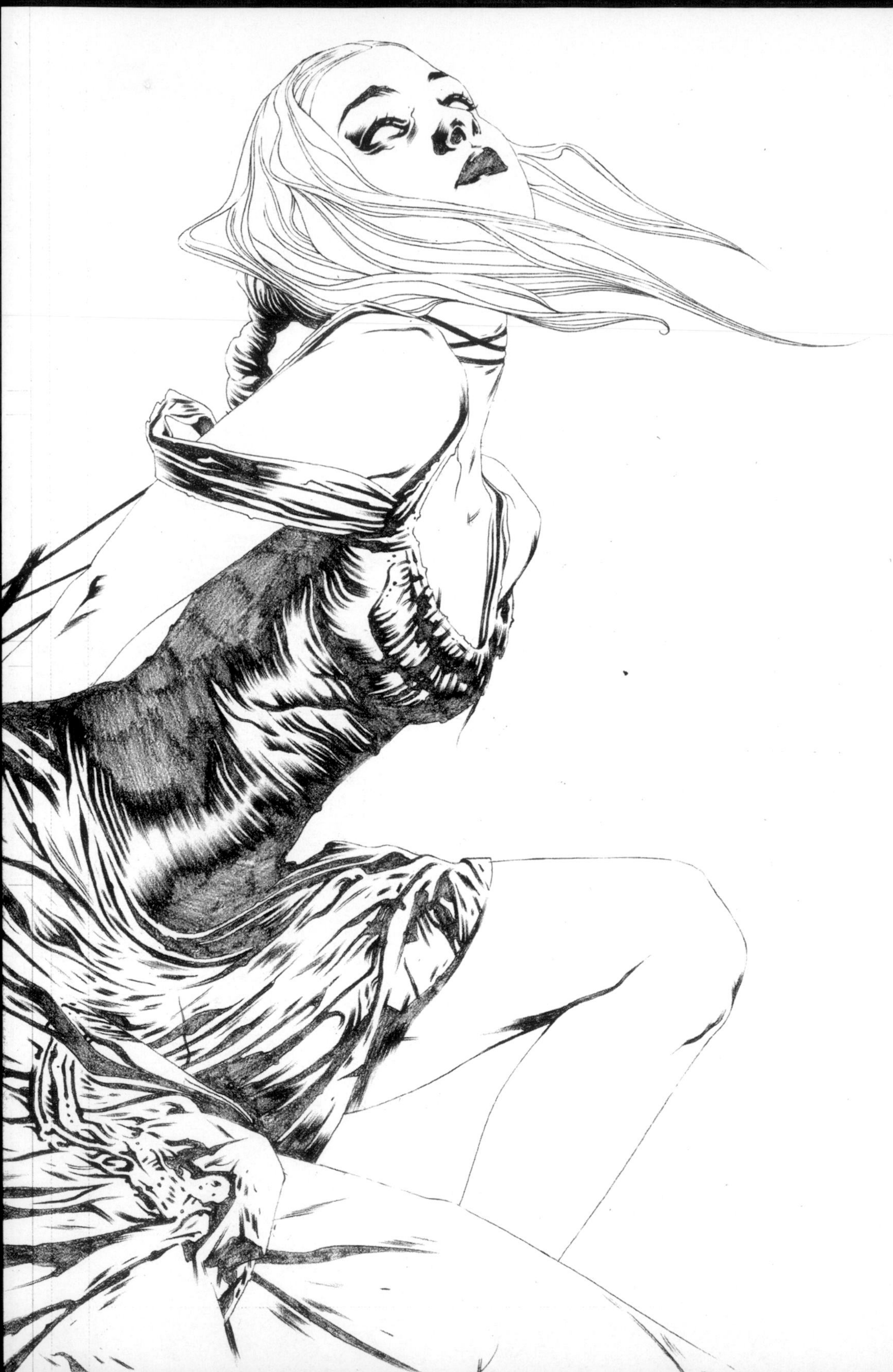

THE PAINTED PROCESS by Richard Isanove

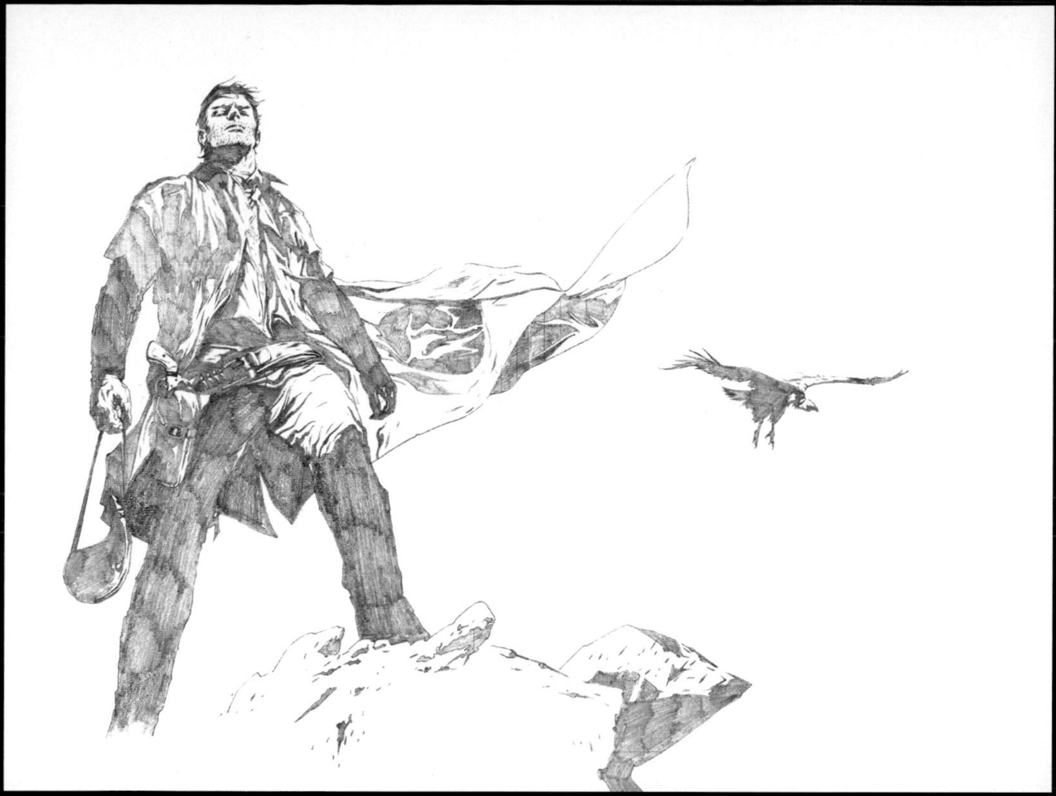

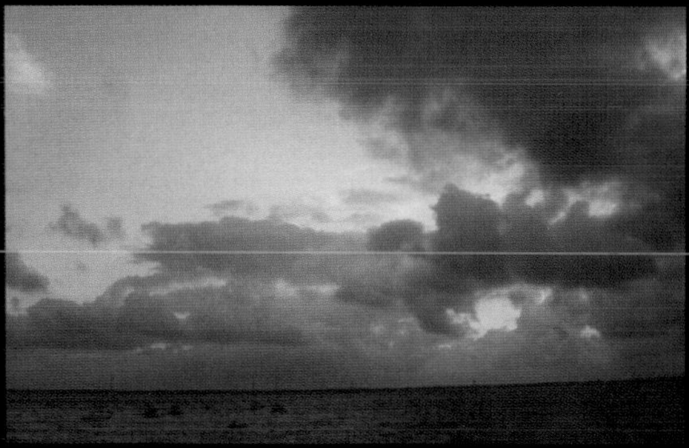

1. I CHOSE THIS PICTURE I HAD TAKEN A FEW YEARS AGO IN THE SOUTHWEST OF FRANCE,

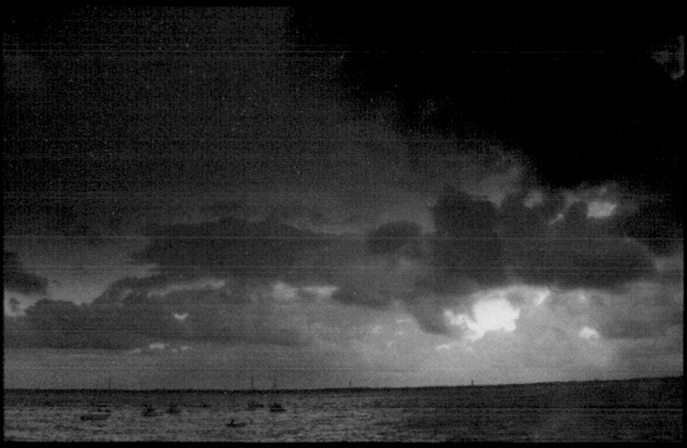

2. AND TWEAKED IT UNTIL I OBTAINED THE DESIRED COLOR SCHEMES.

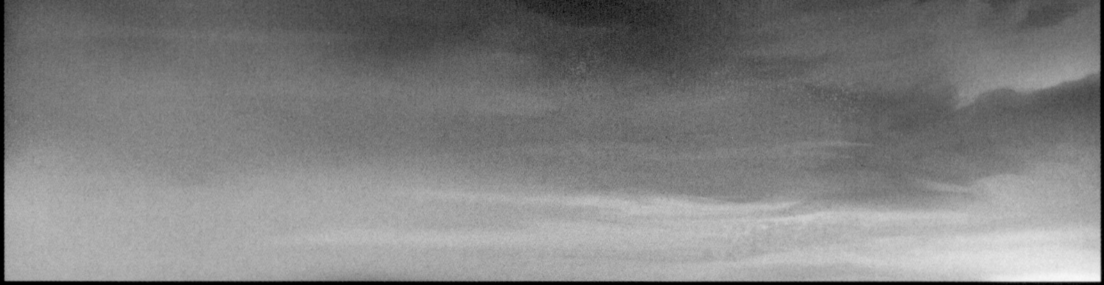

3. USING IT AS A TEMPLATE, I PAINTED OVER THE PHOTO, COVERING IT UP WITH BRUSHSTROKES, SMUDGES AND SPLATTERS.

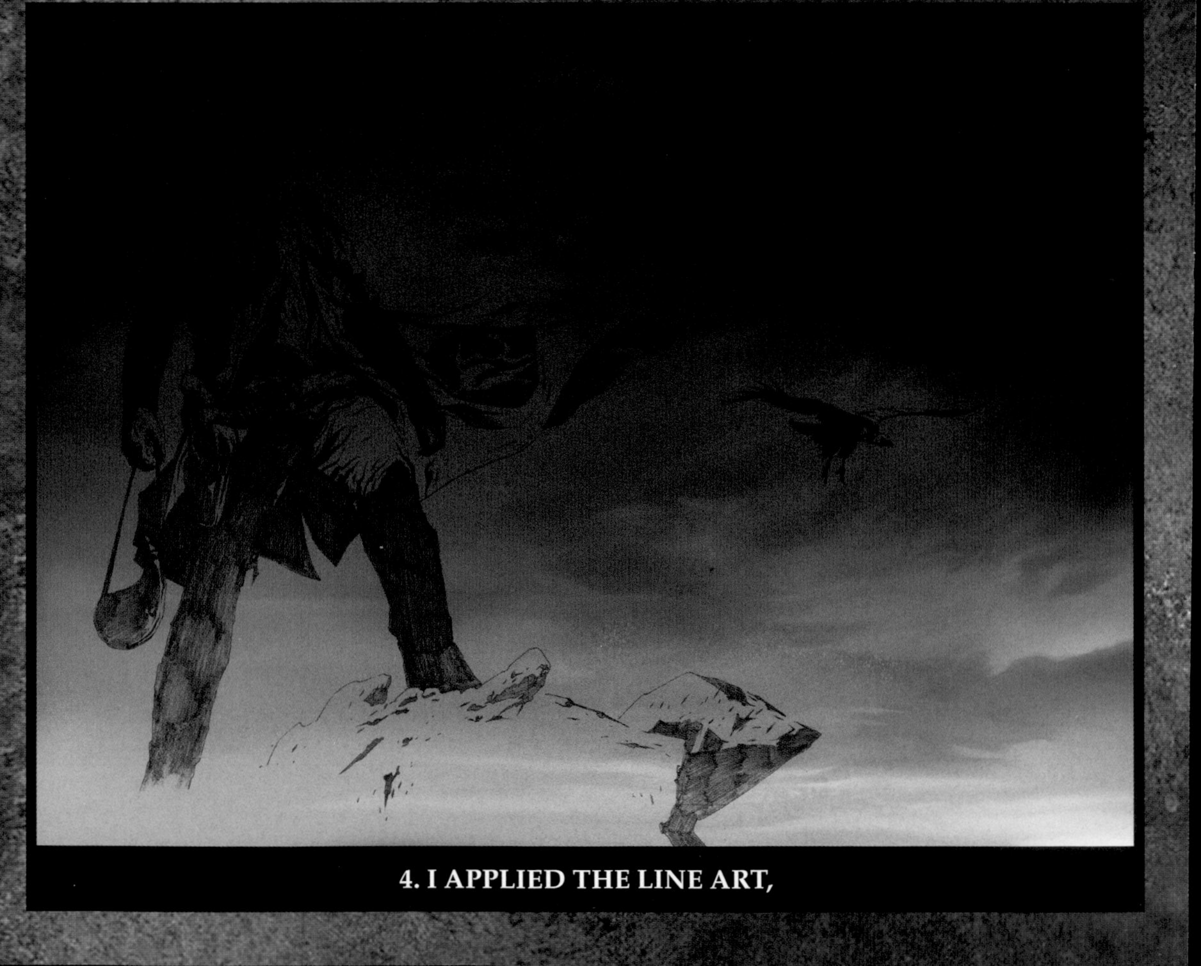

4. I APPLIED THE LINE ART,

5. BLACKED OUT ALL THE SHADOW AREAS,

6. FILLED THE LIGHT AREAS WITH THE DARKEST COLOR I COULD PICK FROM THE BACKGROUND,

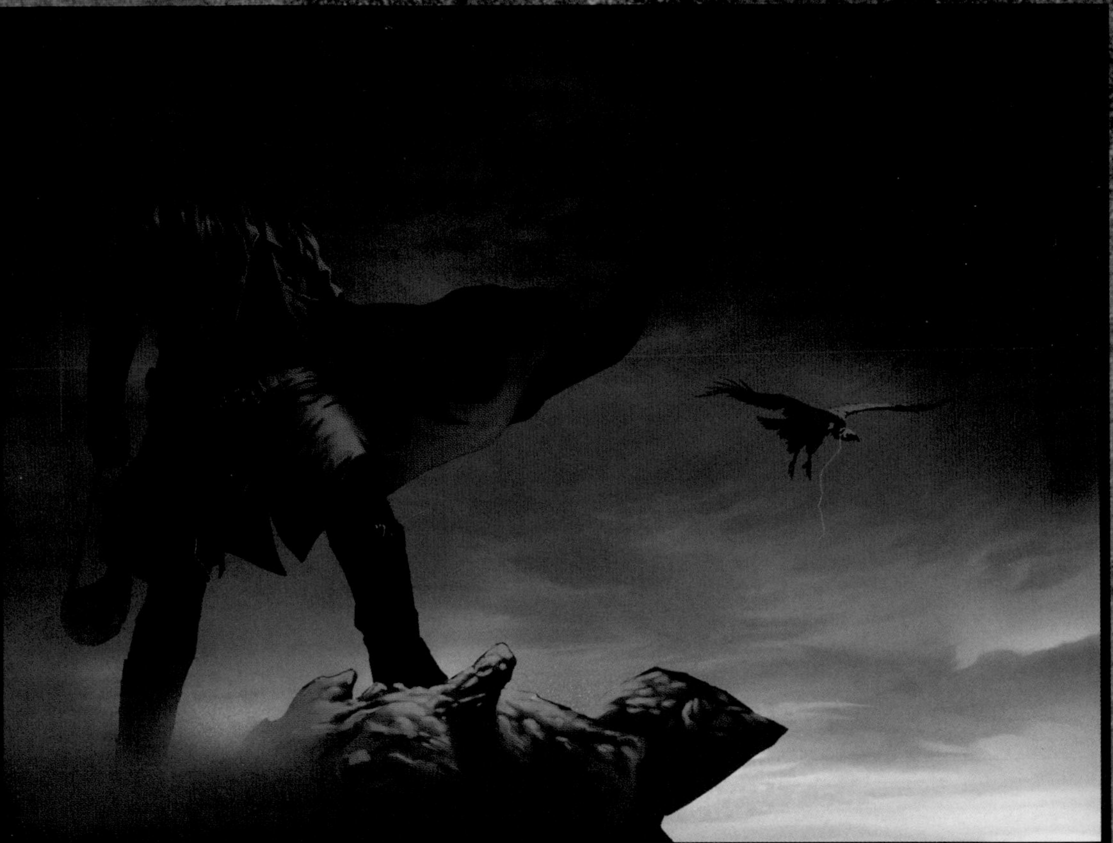

7. THEN STARTED MODELING WITH MID-TONES.

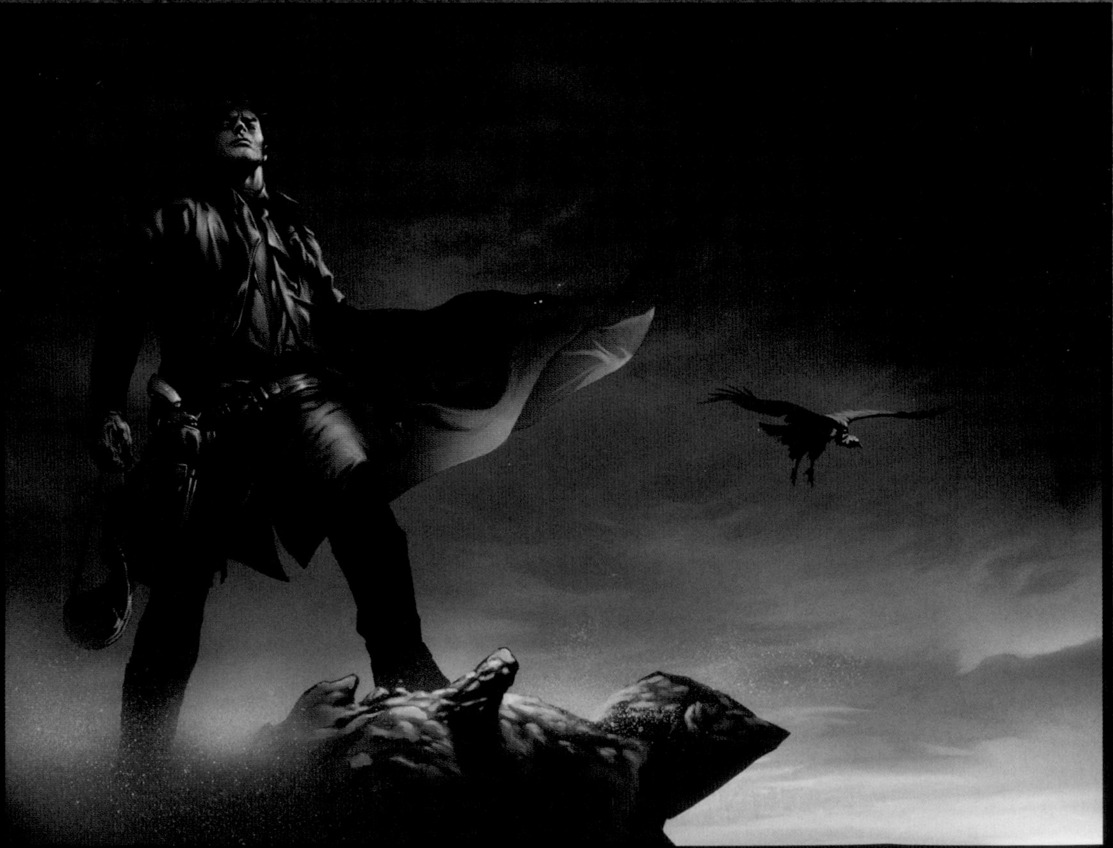

8. A FEW HIGHLIGHTS, SOME TOUCH-UPS TO BLEND LINE ART AND BACKGROUND, AND VOILA.